German Football

History, Culture, Society

Edited by
**Alan Tomlinson and
Christopher Young**

Routledge
Taylor & Francis Group

LONDON AND NEW YORK

First published 2006
by Routledge
2 Park Square, Milton Park, Abingdon, Oxon OX14 4RN

Simultaneously published in the USA and Canada
by Routledge
270 Madison Ave, New York, NY 10016

Routledge is an imprint of the Taylor & Francis Group

© 2006 Alan Tomlinson and Christopher Young

Typeset in Goudy by
Florence Production Ltd, Stoodleigh, Devon
Printed and bound in Great Britain by
TJ International Ltd, Padstow, Cornwall

British Library Cataloguing in Publication Data
A catalogue record for this book is available from the British Library

Library of Congress Cataloging in Publication Data
A catalog record for this book has been requested

ISBN10 0–415–35195–2 (hbk)
ISBN10 0–415–35196–0 (pbk)

ISBN13 978–0–415–35195–9 (hbk)
ISBN13 978–0–415–35196–6 (pbk)

Contents

Contributors

The editors

Alan Tomlinson is Professor of Leisure Studies at the Chelsea School, University of Brighton. He has researched and written extensively on World Cup history, Olympic ideology and related themes of consumption and spectacle. He has authored/edited over twenty volumes and was until recently Editor of the *International Review for the Sociology of Sport*.

Christopher Young is Senior Lecturer at the University of Cambridge. He has authored/edited five books on German language, literature and culture, and is currently engaged on a monograph on the Munich Olympics 1972. He has been a Fellow of the Alexander von Humboldt Foundation (in Cologne).

Together, they co-edited a special issue of the *American Behavioral Scientist* (with Andrei Markovits, University of Michigan) on sport and cultural space (2003), and a research monograph on sport and spectacle (2006) for SUNY (State University of New York Press).

The contributors

Alexander Brand is Lecturer and doctoral researcher at Dresden University. His current research focuses on theories of international relations and politics of development. He is co-editor of a book on new trends in development research, published in 2004.

Paul Cooke taught in Cologne and Aberystwyth before moving to the University of Leeds where he is Senior Lecturer. He is an expert in contemporary German literature and has authored and co-edited four volumes on various comparative aspects of East and West German culture and literature. He has just completed a monograph on the phenomenon of *Ostalgie*.

Mike Dennis is Professor of Modern German History at Wolverhampton University and former editor-in-chief of the journal *East Central Europe*.

He has authored four books on the history of the GDR, its socio-economic transformation since 1990 and the Ministry of State Security, including, most recently, *The Stasi: Myth and Reality* (2003). His current research focuses on ethnic, sexual, youth and other minorities in the GDR during the 1970s and 1980s.

Erik Eggers is a freelance journalist who lives in Cologne. As well as articles for the national press, including *Financial Times German Edition*, *Frankfurte Rundshau* and *Die Zeit*, he has authored several books on German sport, including, most recently, a biography of Herbert Zimmermann, the legendary radio 'voice' of Germany's first World Cup triumph in 1954.

Gunter Gebauer is Professor of Philosophy and the Sociology of Sport at the Free University in Berlin. He has authored many books and articles on both topics, including *Sport – Eros – Tod* (1986) and *Olympische Spiele, die andere Utopie der Moderne. Olympia zwischen Kult und Droge* (1996).

Dirk Halm is a Research Fellow in Migration Studies at the Foundation Centre for Studies on Turkey at the University of Duisburg-Essen. His main fields of research are cultural change in the Turkish community in Germany and the interconnection between integration, ethnicity and sports. He is a member of numerous governmental and non-governmental commissions on integration policy. His publications include the yearly *Migration Report* of the Centre for Studies on Turkey (since 2002).

Markus Hesselmann is Editor-in-Chief of the Sports section of the German national daily *Der Tagesspiegel*. He has co-authored two books on football, one on Hansa Rostock, the other on soccer in Africa. He is currently working with Christopher Young on a book about German football culture.

Roman Horak is Associate Professor at the Department of Aesthetics, Cultural Studies/Art Pedagogy, University of Applied Arts, Vienna. From October 1988 to March 1989 he was Honorary Visiting Fellow at the Department of Sociology, University of Leicester. He is Associate Member of Staff at the International Centre for Sports History and Culture, De Montfort University, Leicester, and member of the Editorial Board of the journal *Cultural Studies*. His latest publications include *Die Praxis der Cultural Studies* (Vienna: Loecker 2002).

Robert Ide was brought up in East Berlin and is the 'East German' expert for *Der Tagesspiegel* where he is assistant sports editor. He has been acclaimed for his recent work on the anniversary of the 17 June uprising and Leipzig's faltering bid for the 2012 Olympics.

Sanna Inthorn recently completed her Ph.D. at the University of Cardiff on the representation of national identity in the German media, and is Lecturer in media studies at the University of Portsmouth. Her work has been published in the *European Journal of Cultural Studies* and she has co-authored a book for the Open University Press.

Lothar Mikos is Professor of Television Studies at the Academy of Film and Television 'Konrad Wolf' in Potsdam. Among many general works on the media, he has authored studies on the 1954 World Cup, and Sport and the Media in the GDR.

Arne Niemann is Lecturer and post-doctoral researcher at Dresden University. His main research interests focus on empirical and theoretical dimensions of European integration. His publications include a monograph on explaining EU decision outcomes (Cambridge University Press, 2006), an edited book on German foreign policy (2005) and two articles in the *Journal of European Public Policy* (1998, 2004).

Gertrud Pfister has held teaching posts at the University of Regensburg, the Ruhr-University in Bochum and the Free University of Berlin. She is currently Professor at the University of Copenhagen. She is President of the International Sociology of Sport Association, and Vice-President of the German Gymnastics Federation. She has authored countless articles on women, gender and sport, seven monographs, and eleven edited volumes, including, most recently, the three-volume *International Encyclopedia of Women and Sport* (with Karen Christensen and Allen Guttmann, 2001) and *Sport and Women. Social Issues in International Perspective* (with Ilse Hartmann, 2003).

Wolfram Pyta taught at the universities of Cologne, Bonn and Tübingen, and was a Fellow of the Centre for Historical Studies in Munich before becoming Professor of Modern History at the University of Stuttgart, where he is also Director of the Ludwigsburg Research Centre for the History of National Socialism. He has authored four books on nineteenth- and twentieth-century history and is the editor of *Der lange Weg zur Bundesliga: Zum Siegeszug des Fussballs in Deutschland* (2004).

Jürgen Schwier is Professor at the Department of Sport Science and Centre for Media and Interactivity at the University of Giessen, and has researched and written on MediaSport, the development of alternatives to formal sports, the sociology of football and related themes. He has authored/edited fourteen books. His recent publications include: *Sport as Popular Culture, Football, Fans and the Internet* and *MediaSport – An Introduction* (ed.).

Preface

Alan Tomlinson and Christopher Young

The most dramatic and high-profile of world spectacles have been the modern Olympic Games and the men's football World Cup, events owned by the International Olympic Committee (IOC) and FIFA (the governing body of world football). Such sporting encounters and contests have provided a source of and focus for the staging of spectacle and, in an era of international mass communications, the media event. The growth of FIFA and the IOC, and of their major events, has provided a platform for the articulation and expression of national pride and prestige. Greece saw the symbolic potential of staging an international event such as the first modern Olympics in 1896 to both assert its incipient modernity and deflect domestic tensions. Uruguay, having cultivated double Olympic football champions in the 1920s, helped FIFA's aspirations take off by hosting the first football World Cup in 1930 in the year of the country's centenary. From modest beginnings, each event grew in stature and significance as more nations came to recognise the potential benefits of participation in such events and the international status that might accrue from hosting and staging them.

In the age of modernity, sporting spectacle has been hugely important to Germany. The 1936 Olympic Games is an obvious case in point. In the post-war era, all major sporting spectacles in Germany have stood in its shadow. The ill-fated 1972 Olympic Games in Munich and the World Cup finals two years later, which culminated in the same stadium, were intended as a show-case for Germany's complete rejection of its complex historical legacy. The Miracle of Berne in 1954, when Germany beat the magisterial Hungarian side in the final, exemplified the power of sport to contribute to the remaking of national identity: as one commentator has recently observed, the Federal Republic was founded not in 1949 but in 1954.

The World Cup finals return to Germany in 2006 at an uncertain time for the country. Post-unification euphoria has firmly given way to a wave of nostalgia for the former East, the Berlin Republic has made controversial strategic alliances (with France and 'Old Europe' against the United States), and the SPD government has had to live through denied recession and to promote major yet difficult social change. As this book goes to press, the result of the German election in September 2005 only seems to have cast a deeper question mark over the country's future direction. In the context of global football politics, Germany outflanked South Africa to win the bidding wars to stage these finals, and generated widespread resentment across the sporting world. The leadership of world football will be under a media spotlight, and perhaps contested in the period leading up to and following on from the 2006 event — and German football politicians will be prominent in the power brokering underlying this process. Whatever happens, Franz Beckenbauer, the first man to have both captained and coached a World Cup winning side, will be centre stage. For these reasons — football's importance to Germany's sense of identity and Germany's closeness to the operations of FIFA, the foremost INGO (International Non-Governmental Organisation) in world sport — it is the ideal time to subject German football history, culture and society to a critical analysis and review.

The primary themes that emerge in this analysis are:

- Myths, cultural symbols and historical resonances
- Region and community as sources of the expression of identity
- Representation and imaginings of national character
- Everyday and institutional politics of football
- Mega-event management
- Fandom and agency
- Commercialism and consumer culture in the new Europe
- Literary and media refractions.

Reinterpretations of Germany's first World Cup are central to any cultural history of German football history. The German national team's victory in Berne, nine years after capitulation in the war, is a more pivotal point for German football than 1966 was for the English national game. If the English victory — to date still the only triumph in any major international championship — was a reassertion of assumed strength and status in the world game, it has turned out in retrospect to be an apogee in the footballing fortunes of the nation. It is now a matrix both of longing and of self-doubt. In Germany, the 'Miracle of Berne' was not simply a much-needed boost to the national psyche. It was also the formative moment in the transformation of the game from its base in regional, local culture towards an institutionalised national phenomenon, which found its culmination in the inaugural season of the *Bundesliga* in the 1963–64 season.

The strong local roots of football in Germany are dramatically embodied in the widespread idealization of a club such as Schalke 04. Based in an industrial suburb of Gelsenkirchen in the heart of the Ruhr, the club has sustained its position among the elite of German football despite the 'metropolitanization' of the national game. Schalke's biggest rival for the status of Germany's most popular club is Bayern Munich – triple European

Champions in successive years in the mid-1970s and heirs to Ajax's crown – a club synonymous with glamour and city chic. Bayern is also Germany's most hated club. In this dynamic between the city and the regions, Schalke continues to provide an important source of expression of traditional forms of football loyalty and identity. This traditionalism is felt to be under threat from the forces of modernization and commercialization within the game. Fans are caught up in a complex web of incorporation into, and resistance to, the consumer model. The combination of the economic and the cultural in the game is now so interwoven that the limits of a romanticized agency among fans becomes obvious. Even on the national level, in a globally organised media market such as European club and international competitions, traditional notions of the national give way to the brand of the sponsor and the celebration of the transnational celebrity. This is more complex still when one's country has disappeared and one's team is forced to survive on players imported from cheaper markets – as is the case in the club sides of the former East Germany.

Perhaps more than in any other European country, football in Germany has provided a revealing focus for debates concerning national identity and the way in which conceptions and stereotypes of national character have been constructed and represented. Behind the stalwart trench-man Fritz Walter, the 1954 side marched as a comradely unit over the individual skills of the sublime Hungarian invincibles. In 1974, Germany's second World Cup success show-cased the swaggering post-1960s style and affluence of Kaiser Franz Beckenbauer *et al.* In Italia '90, the year of German reunification, at the most glamorously packaged World Cup finals ever staged, the finely tuned, ruthlessly efficient German squad steamrollered its way to victory. All these, of course, are stereotypes, which are constantly ebbing and flowing in and out of the media-generated popular consciousness. In 1974, for instance, 1954 was unexcavated cultural territory. By its fiftieth anniversary, however, the Miracle of Berne was a central pillar in the archaeology of German football history. In post-unification Germany, it filled the void of expectation opened up by the overbearing presence of the actors of 1974. The year 1990 is still caked in dust awaiting its rediscovery. Such cultural reappropriations are generated by a variety of media forms – from the broadcast to the print media, from the literary to the cinematic. In these latter categories, the discursive freedom of the genres facilitates an expansion of the interpretive agenda.

It is a truism that football culture has more significance than the mere drama and activities unfolding on the field of play. There is a cultural politics at work in the sport. Much of the history of the game has concentrated upon the world of masculinity, yet beyond this sphere, Germany has produced some of the most outstanding individuals and internationally successful competitive teams. Many accounts stress the core Northern European origins and traditions of football within Germany. Yet, since the upheavals of the Second World War and the increase in the immigrant population, there is an expanding multicultural dimension to the 'national game'. If Turkey and Germany reach a World Cup final in 2006 – an achievement which at one point in Japan/Korea 2002 looked far from impossible – it will put to the test the rhetoric and policy intent of the multicultural theme prominent in the run-up to the tournament. Less prominent in the national football culture is the impact of the great achievements of German women footballers, and at the heart of this book we have sought to remind readers and scholars of the story of the struggles leading to those achievements.

Staging international sporting events has long been a means of making wider political and economic points. Germany is no exception. The Berlin Olympics in 1936, the Munich Olympics in 1972 and the 1974 World Cup each asserted the new role of a peaceful Germany in the world order – the former after 1914–1918, the latter two after 1939–1945. The 2006 World Cup will be yet another opportunity to present yet another new Germany. This Germany is acutely aware of its increasing ethnic diversity, its European connectedness and commitments, and its own internal post-unification obligations. It is also moving into a cautious yet fascinating period of re-evaluating its past. As Minister of the Interior Otto Schily publicly reasserted in 2004, Germany should show itself to be an 'open, lively and hospitable country'. This chimes in perfect and co-ordinated harmony with the event's official slogan – 'Time to make friends'. As our volume shows, this 'making' of friends is a complex process of media representation, event management, lived experience of the football festival, and aspirational politics. In all of this, sport's contribution to the remaking of the past – through its own and interconnected histories and discourses – is paramount.

1 German football

A cultural history

Wolfram Pyta

Culture and football

This contribution is based on the belief that football is a major cultural phenomenon (Tomlinson, Markorits and Young 2003). Football's triumphal march towards becoming Germany's most popular sport by far is due mainly to the fact that it contains a cultural creative power that can blossom under certain historical conditions. Before this can be demonstrated via a brief survey of the history of German football over the past 100 years, some preliminary issues have to be assessed. As a result of the renaissance of the term of 'culture' in the humanities, the concept has lost its preciseness and has become an indefinable factor which has come to represent a conceptual cipher for very disparate facts. Hence a precise definition of the concept of 'culture' that underlies this contribution is essential.

The following analysis is guided by reflections indigenous to a hermeneutics-orientated cultural sociology and philosophy (see in particular Andreas Reckwitz's brilliant studies of 1999 and 2000). According to this, culture is about collective forms of meaningful adoptions of the world. Culture results from hermeneutic processes during which subjects start a process of understanding and provide the world with a meaning. But this cognitive adopting cannot be achieved by an autonomous individual who, in doing so, creates to a certain extent the world of ideas out of his subjectivity. The subject's capacity for understanding can only be fully reached against the background of a collective inventory of knowledge and shared rules of interpretation. These webs of meaning structure the process of interpreting, and they define the conditions under which things can then have a certain meaning. But how are individual interpretation and the embedding in collective systems of meaning combined? Interpretive cultural theory refers in this case to the central significance of actions. It is always in actions that the adoption and translation of cognitive knowledge of order by the actor takes place. Understanding the world always has references to action – regular and routine actions indicating underlying systems of meaning. For this reason we have a concept of 'culture' that includes practical expressions of collective systems of meaning: thus culture is 'action-orientated configuration of meaning' (Luckmann 1988).

In order to identify these cultural contents it is not sufficient to look to the inexhaustible pool of classical texts, in which man has formed the world according to his imagination. A cultural historian has to be especially attentive to those fields of action that show strong structures of meaning.

This brings us to football. Football as an ordered and constant mode of behaviour may be understood as one of these practices that has collective patterns of meaning embedded in it. During its recent history, football has extended its fields of action: initially a sport purely for enthusiasts of *das runde Leder* ('round leather'), it advanced to a spectator sport that fascinated tens of thousands who had never played it themselves under competitive conditions. Eventually, in the 1950s, it managed to become a mass-media phenomenon in Germany and was even used for political purposes. The reasons for 'King Football's' rapid territorial expansion can in essence only be understood from a cultural historical perspective. To do so, one has to ask the central question: why could football be used as a space of projection and place of expression for schemes of interpretation embedded in German history?

We can approach this core question by looking at the processes of cultural change with respect to the intrinsic power of social shaping. By understanding collective cognitive contents – i.e. culture – a high degree of integrating effects that are essential for constructing communities are released. The power of such collective interpretations of meaning for constructing communities has been impressively demonstrated by historically-orientated cultural sociology (Giesen 1999). These findings suggest that football can carry and transmit non-sporting webs of meaning and become the focal point of processes of socialization. Football is a cultural phenomenon which is open to interpretation and in which diverse patterns of meaning have been recognized (Knoch 2002: 119–20). With football as the raw material, socializations of varying denseness and durability could be formed that were subject to cultural change.

Finally, German football has a very special attribute that has helped its development into a major cultural phenomenon: the capacity to have symbolic meanings. Symbols play a decisive role in constructing communities. They enrich the interpretation of behaviour patterns with a degree of aesthetic condensation that facilitates the communication of shared cultural contents. Symbols act as perceivable expressions of those cultural dispositions that circulate in communities. The development of a long-lasting collective identity is not possible without the use of symbols, which form shared meanings and values and provide it with vital visibility (Giesen 1999: 17–18).[1]

Germany is probably the only country in Europe where football has managed to gain symbolic qualities in such great measure. The reason for this is the exceptional situation after the Second World War that left Germany in a situation of such symbolic devastation that football could fill the gap.

Origins and cultural meanings

At the beginning, it did not seem as though football in Germany could ever achieve such importance. Initially it was an import from England, played by young sportsmen who experienced enthusiasm for a dynamic and physical team sport as opposed to 'German gymnastics' which they felt to be stereotyped and boring. Until 1914, football in Germany was a minority sport in a society that, to a considerable extent, regarded sport with contempt (Eisenberg 1999: 209–14). However, football had an enormous inherent potential for development. It was mainly discovered by the expanding new middle classes: by the growing number of young employees who had enough leisure and money to play football on Sundays (ibid.: 180–9). The breakthrough from a marginal to a mass sport came with the First World War. For the first time, millions of German soldiers came into contact with this sport when matches were arranged, mainly on (the more peaceful sections of) the Western Front to relieve the monotony of military life (ibid.: 319–21; Pyta 2004a: 13–15). In November 1918 they brought these experiences back home with them in their rucksacks. Therefore it is not surprising that the war was followed by a wave of the formation of football clubs, with football played in an organized way even in provincial backwaters.

The meteoric rise of football was only possible because football qualified as an expression for configurations of meaning which were mainly formed by the experience of the First World War. It is important to note that the war established a new attitude towards physicality. Without doubt the ubiquity of death lowered respect for physical integrity and led to a greater willingness for violence that manifested itself in excesses of unprecedented political violence (Ziemann 2003).

Sport was also an outlet for a new mode of bodily behaviour. The social association with the human body manifested in sports was not characterized solely by exhibitions of brute force and masculinity. A man's pure physical strength did not count for much – in comparison to abilities such as the dynamic use of the body or virtuoso interaction of body and military technique required to survive the war. Playful control of a football by a dexterous body that could be adapted to the speed of the game may therefore be seen as a social practice that expressed this new body culture.[2]

Football's ability to adapt to the mass cultural tendencies that were on the increase after 1918 was equally important. Rapidly growing industrialization and urbanization laid the foundations in Imperial Germany for the propagation of popular culture. Around 1900, popular arts and amusements characterized the everyday life of many Germans in large cities (Maase 2001: 9–28). After the end of the empire this trend also applied to the growing affection for sports. The increasing number of people interested in sports were recruited not only from active participants but also from those who did not actively take part in sports themselves but enjoyed matches as spectators (Saldern 1992, 1999). Football in particular profited from this development. During the Weimar Republic, it left all its rivals in the shade and became the people's most popular sport by far (Eggers 2001: 70–1).

In this respect football was class-independent. It was no longer the property of the middle classes. Rather, it was particularly popular with the working classes. The socialist labour movement went to great efforts to arrange football-playing workers into a socialist Workers' Gymnastics and Sports Organization (*Arbeiter- Turn- und Sportbund*) to attract them away from the bourgeois *Deutscher Fußballbund* (DFB). In the end all efforts to act against the class-independent maelstrom, driven by the cultural phenomenon football, were in vain. Most workers practised their sport in associations that were affiliated with the apolitical DFB. They did not wish to articulate their class-consciousness in a football match, wanting instead to play football in front of an increasing number of spectators. Financial aspects did, of course, play an important role for them. As a result of the growing number of spectators, football in the 1920s became a financially lucrative activity, in which considerable sums could be earned by prominent players. Although most of the DFB officials cherished the amateur ideal, they were not able to prevent covert payments to prominent players (Oswald 2004). Famously, the officials of the *Westdeutscher Spielverband* made an example of the workers' club, FC Schalke 04 from Gelsenkirchen in the Ruhr area, by suspending nearly the whole team due to violations of the amateur regulations. There was much hypocrisy in this decision, because other teams quietly paid their best players. However, the example of Schalke 04 shows that even miners – which most of the players were – were not immune to the temptations of the commercialization of football, which was nowhere more despised than in the socialist sports movement (Gehrmann 2004).

Football even conquered the religious boundaries which are so characteristic of German history. Although political Catholicism tried to integrate the expanding game of football into its differentiated organization of clubs and societies by founding a Catholic sports association, it was difficult to persuade football-loving Catholics to practise their sports exclusively within a Catholic microcosmos (Preißler 2004). In the end, football withstood all attempts to make it a compliant part of a socialist or Catholic organizational culture.

Yet why did tens of thousands of spectators throng into the stadiums in the 1920s to watch a match? Their need for spectacle is not in itself enough to explain why enthusiasm for this kind of sport created such a stir. The cultural power of football derived from the fact that spectators could interpret it in a non-sporting way. This inscription of a certain cultural signification propelled football in Germany towards a cultural mass phenomenon. Let us now go back to some thoughts that were articulated earlier and the question of how football could complement the processes of socialization in the 1920s and 1930s.

The secret of football's success was that it could amalgamate with extraordinarily strong local and regional cultural traditions. The German Empire had only been recently founded in 1871 as a national state – but this did not mean that the single states which existed until then ceased to exist. The structural principle of the Empire was characterized by a distinct federalism. Under the *Bundesstaaten,* which gained their territorial shape mostly in the early nineteenth century, older regional traditions remained intact and were diligently cultivated.

German 'regions' are normally not geographically clear-cut entities but exist on the basis of cultural construction (Mergel 2000). 'Region' as a cultural space needs a set of meaning carriers which act as regional trademarks and show affiliation to a region.

Football was predestined to adapt to regional traditions, because it heightened the impact of large cities in their metropolitan area. Such large cities provided services for a region; from the 1920s, sports in general and especially the flourishing sport of football formed a part of this. Football played an important role insofar as certain cities could be established as central locations.[3]

Football clubs were especially suited to acting as the figurehead and focal point of a large city and its metropolitan area because the teams usually consisted of players born in that city or region who spoke in local dialect and therefore achieved a high degree of identification. The most famous players of the dominant German football team in the 1930s, FC Schalke 04, were Fritz Szepan and Ernst Kuzorra, both born in Gelsenkirchen. And in the dominant team of the 1920s, 1. FC Nürnberg, the legendary keeper Heiner Stuhlfauth and centre-half Hans Kalb, both from Nürnberg, set the pace (Gömmel 2004). Enticed by under-the-table salary pay-outs, some leading players changed their clubs, but most remained faithful to their home teams. Compared to England, football was under-professionalized, but that acted only to strengthen club bonds and, consequently, the regional embedding of popular football clubs.

Big-city football clubs also connected with their regions because they had stadiums that could hold large crowds. In Stuttgart, Düsseldorf and Cologne, but also elsewhere, top clubs profited from the fact that in the 1920s the communal authorities spent enormous amounts of money (Eggers 2004c: 97–8; Nielsen 2002: 601–8) on building multifunctional sporting arenas that offered space for 50,000 to 70,000 spectators. It was not only the local football clubs that profited from these communal services, because in these stadiums other major sporting events such as gymnastics and athletics could also take place. But as the finals (at the very least) of the German championship took place in these large arenas, successful clubs could play in front of huge audiences that could not be achieved in the course of ordinary league business.

Such stadiums were not only purpose-built, they also offered a unique experience in which communication between the masses and the players took place in an atmosphere that allowed the audience to share the players' enthusiasm. Famous stadiums such as the legendary Zerzabelshof in Nürnberg formed a space[4] in which dynamic processes of understanding between spectators and players could evolve. These processes enfold, of course, due to a shared commitment to a city and its region. As a result, football stadiums became important centres of regional identity.

Furthermore, the organizational structures of German football favoured regional ties. As opposed to England and other great footballing nations, there was no national league in Germany until 1963. The ordinary competition took place in seven regional associations, all of which were members of the DFB. The best teams of each regional association qualified at the end of a season for the final round of the German championship, which was carried out in a knock-out system ending in a final. This extreme federal structure mirrored the regional alignment of German football.

Little changed in the regional roots of German football until the 1950s. Football remained in its local and regional environment – and that is where the force of its socialization was. At a national level football did not initiate a process of socialization. This was due, on the one hand, to the fact that the concept of a German nation was strongly rooted in military values. The idea of Germany as an armed and well-fortified nation left no room for football as a national figurehead. Overzealous DFB functionaries occasionally stressed that football complemented military training.[5] But this ingratiation often had perspicuous reasons, because in nationalistic circles football, being English, was treated with suspicion.[6] Therefore it tried to defend itself from these attacks by stressing its supposed military usefulness (Pyta 2004a:10–12). But those webs of meaning manifested in football eluded any short-sighted military functionalization – attending a football match was not a continuation of war by other means.

On the other hand, German football lacked notable success at international level; since the proof of German superiority was missing there was no exploitation of football, especially during the period of National Socialism. At the World Cup in Italy in 1934 the German team surprisingly reached fourth place, but at the 1936 Olympic Games in Berlin, where German sportsmen won the most gold medals of all nations, the footballers failed and were defeated in the preliminary round 2–0 by the 'football dwarf' Norway. In 1938, the post-Anschluss 'Great German' national football team disgraced itself, failing to get past the first round, being eliminated after losing to Switzerland. Even if Germany did have deficits with respect to national symbols, football was completely unsuitable in demonstrating feelings of national superiority. Nevertheless, football continued to flourish during the period of National Socialism. The boom in spectators continued and reached new peaks. The reasons for this development are still unclear since a cultural history of football during the Third Reich has not yet been written. Still, some patterns of explanation may be discerned.

When, on 7 June 1936, the two dominant clubs of their time, FC Schalke 04 and 1. FC Nürnberg, competed in the semi-finals of the German championship in neutral Stuttgart, the capital of Württemberg, at least 75,000 people watched the game. This was the highest number of spectators ever to attend a football match in Germany.[7] Approximately 35,000 spectators travelled from other regions to Stuttgart, but most of the spectators came from Stuttgart and its environment.[8] But why did people from Württemberg rush to a game, in which none of the players were from Württemberg? And why did most of them support Schalke 04 of all teams,[9] a club from the distant Ruhr, rather than the team from Nürnberg, which was at least – like Stuttgart – part of southern Germany?

Schalke 04 is a phenomenon which needs to be explained, since its fan community reaches far beyond the usual regional borders. There was no regional centre behind Schalke 04, such as Nürnberg (the centre for Franken), the Hamburger SV (for northern Germany) or Fortuna Düsseldorf (for the Rhineland). This club did not even take its name from the city of Gelsenkirchen, but from a district in which the club was rooted. Even Gelsenkirchen was not, by any measure, a metropolis of the Ruhr territory. This was the most densely populated area in Europe at that time, containing, over a length of 80 km and a width of 40 km, ten major cities like beads on a string along the rivers Ruhr and Emscher. The steel city of Gelsenkirchen remained economically and culturally far behind Dortmund, Essen and Duisburg.

This club from a suburb of Gelsenkirchen managed to garner support from beyond the borders of its home town throughout the Ruhr territory, becoming a part of the Ruhr area's identity (Gehrmann 2004). But its attraction reached far beyond the Ruhr region. This could be easily observed in the finals of the championships that were played in Berlin from 1936 onwards. Here Schalke 04 was supported by a huge majority of the neutral spectators from Berlin, giving Schalke practically home advantage. Of course, most football experts were enthused by Schalke's inimitable style, which was known as the *Schalker Kreisel*, an outstanding example of perfect link-up play. Moreover, in Ernst Kuzorra and Fritz Szepan the club from the Ruhr area possessed two exceptional footballers who were highly popular throughout Germany. Kuzorra and Szepan could be called the first German football stars; they were even the object of a star cult (Berns and Wiersch 1936). The main reason for this response to Schalke in Germany may have been that it served as a substitute for a national team that failed to be a focus of identity due to its lack of success.

However, there are also indications that Schalke 04 served as a projection surface for non-sporting patterns of meaning. The National Socialist regime had destroyed socialist and Christian labour movements, and consequently both of these important social forces lacked an organizational centre.

Therefore one can suppose that in those circles a demonstration of sympathy for FC Schalke 04 meant a demonstration of sympathy for the no longer existing labour movement, since Schalke 04 – as a workers' club – could be regarded as a part of it. Conversely, the National Socialist regime did not dislike the sporting successes of the labour club, since this could be regarded as an appreciation of the working classes in Hitler's Germany (Fischer and Lindner 1999: 156–63). As a symbol for the progressing integration of the workers into the Nazi state, the triumph of FC Schalke had a significance that reached far beyond sports.[10]

Filling the symbolic void

Overall, football remained, until the end of the German Reich, a cultural phenomenon, whose community-creating power was restricted mainly to the regions. After the fall of Hitler this would change – football achieving a unique triumph as a cultural asset in the 1950s due to its rise to a symbol of political-cultural orientation for the West German people. In no other European country has football established such a symbolic character in the post-war period. Why was this the case in West Germany?

Until 1945 the highest community-creating power in Germany emanated from nationalism. The profound desire to overcome all social, confessional and political rifts, which were particularly evident in German society, was expressed in the 'spirit of 1914'. The drive towards political unity, unbroken after the end of the First World War, underwent its symbolic incarnation in the persons of Hindenburg and Hitler. Hindenburg, the Commander in the First World War, was regarded as the personification of this national will for unity (Pyta 2004b). Adolf Hitler could connect with this via his core message of *Volksgemeinschaft*, which evolved an enormous internal integrative impact while threatening so-called *Gemeinschaftsfremde* with physical extermination (see, at great length, Wehler 2003). Hitler drove nationalism so far that in 1945 Germany was in ruins, with German nationalism in all its forms and varieties also disqualified as a community-building force for the foreseeable future. Thus all the normative dispositions that had served as cultural suppliers for nationalism were contaminated. Military ideals were especially ostracized to such an extent that West Germans, in their tentative search for a new collective identity, could find no support in the fund of traditional German nationalism with its martial emphasis.

In a symbolic respect the 'zero hour' in West Germany struck in 1945. The Federal Republic of Germany, established in 1949, took care to avoid anything in its profile that could offer even the slightest nationalistic echo. This symbolic reorientation was the prerequisite for football to slip into the symbolic gap. For this purpose, however, a decisive event was needed, namely the triumph of the West German team in the World Cup final on 4 July 1954. The German outsiders beat the Hungarian dream team and great favourites 3–2. Previously the Hungarians had been considered invincible, having humiliated England on the 'hallowed turf' of Wembley 6–3. This unexpected German success gave football a significant symbolic leverage.

Until the legendary 4 July 1954, football in Germany had continued on an upward trend – although it still only created identity at a regional level. Regional consciousness survived relatively undamaged during the period of National Socialism and was also available as a *Vergemeinschaftungsofferte* after 1945 because it had not been infiltrated by hyper-nationalism. The federal German culture of the 1950s was therefore affected by the retreat into home and region (Applegate 1990; Holtmann 1998), from which football, with its close connection to regional culture, also benefited. But football's popularity was also enhanced by economic development in the 1950s. The 'economic miracle' that began in the 1950s led to the lower classes' participation for the first time in economic prosperity, and 1950s' Germany transformed itself increasingly into a consumer society (Prinz 2003; Siegrist *et al.* 1997).

On the one hand, this development meant that the consumption of football in the form of attendance at football matches was open to more and more classes (Eisenberg 2003). On the other hand, it enhanced the cultural constructive force of football, since, in the 'levelled-out middle-class society' of the 1950s and 1960s, conventional social stratifications lost their binding power (Goch 2003). The social cohesion of the working class declined visibly as the slogan 'wealth to everyone' became honoured in the daily life of the German industrial working class. The dogmatic Catholic milieu shrunk proportionately as the spread of consumer society advanced the secularization of the Catholic environment. Furthermore, considerable population shifts – the influx of millions of refugees and displaced persons, and, (since the 1960s) of foreign guest-workers – fundamentally changed the structure of the population after 1945.

In this period of eroding traditional social relations, the commitment to a region as a focal point of identity gained new significance – and in this way football clubs became more and more important as figureheads of regions which were subjected to rapid social change. This development may be demonstrated by the examples of 1. FC Kaiserslautern and VfB Stuttgart. 1. FC Kaiserslautern eked out its marginal existence as a mere local figure in the Palatinate until the end of the 1940s. But its sporting success, which is associated inseparably with the name Fritz Walter, captain of the German World Cup-winning team, turned this football club in the Palatinate, which ran through a fundamental structural change due to the deployment of tens of thousands of US soldiers after 1950, into a trade mark of Palatine identity. Since some five players of the victorious World Cup team belonged to 1. FC Kaiserslautern, the Palatines could proudly proclaim that it was actually the Palatinate that had become World Champion on 4 July 1954 (Herzog 2004). In contrast to the less well-developed infrastructure of the

Palatinate, the middle Neckar Valley around Stuttgart, Baden-Württemberg's capital, underwent a veritable economic boom in the 1950s. The population in Greater Stuttgart increased rapidly – and with it also the long-established Swabian need to emphasize their own identity in the face of social change. As the population of the old Württemberg had to undergo the creation of the Federal State of Baden-Württemberg in 1952, which involved very heterogeneous cultural landscapes, VfB Stuttgart provided a perfect projection surface for the quest for and articulation of regional identity during a difficult time. VfB Stuttgart was extremely successful in the 1950s (both German Champions and German Cup winners twice) – and its teams consisted, almost without exception, of Swabians born and bred (Pyta 2004a).

In the early 1950s the spectators' reception of football reached record dimensions. It had long become German sports enthusiasts' favourite sport. Yet still there was a huge number of Germans who were neither interested in sports in general nor in football in particular. Until the World Cup in 1954, football in West Germany remained a cultural niche product – but this would change fundamentally with the unexpected victory. Until the semi-final against Austria, which was won 6–1 on 30 June 1954, the German public had not taken much notice of the national team's performance during the World Cup (Brüggemeier 2004: 174–81). Most intellectuals gave football the cold shoulder and sneered at the trend towards stereotyping which the sport supposedly aided and abetted. Extremely significant in this respect is the fact that the *Frankfurter Allgemeine Zeitung* (FAZ), the journalistic flagship of the liberal middle classes, did not find the team's first game of the tournament, the first meeting with Hungary on 21 June 1954 – won by the imperious Hungarians – worthy of mention on the front page. Instead the FAZ dedicated an article to the opening of the sailing regatta in Kiel, thus reporting on an exclusive sport which was much closer to FAZ readers' hearts than football: the sport of the masses (Brüggemeier 2004: 174). However, when a wave of football enthusiasm erupted in Germany after they won the semi-final, not even middle-class intellectuals could entirely ignore this phenomenon anymore – although they continued to treat it with incomprehension until the 1960s (Brüggemeier 2004: 144–54, 324, 331).

The football euphoria that erupted after the final is not due solely to the fact that the final offered all the elements of a perfect drama: after only nine minutes the German team were 2–0 down against the overwhelming favourites Hungary, then managed to equalize after eighteen minutes, overcame a period in the second half in which the Hungarians surged continually towards the goal, only to seal victory with a powerful left-foot shot by forward Helmut Rahn from just inside the penalty box six minutes before the final whistle. It was decisive that not only the approximately 20,000 Germans among the 65,000 spectators in the Wankdorf-Stadium in Berne watched these dramatic events on the spot: via radio broadcasts to millions, the whole of Germany was there live. The World Cup final of 1954 was the first sports event in Germany to become a gigantic media event. This is why they could captivate millions of Germans who until then had viewed football with scepticism, but were infected with the football virus due to the World Cup final and its presence in the media.

Until then, reporting on football had played only a marginal role in the press and radio. There had already been an expanding sports press since the 1920s, with the daily newspapers also giving a certain amount of space to sports. But these reports catered, without exception, for expert readers who actively played football themselves. The coverage of sports on the radio was also aimed primarily at well-informed people (Eggers 2004c: 99–100). But the commentaries from the World Cup final on 4 July 1954 opened the hearts of those who had not been particularly interested in football and who were following a football match on the radio for the first time in their lives. The German commentator Herbert Zimmermann, a mere 37 years old, delivered an unforgettable moment of sporting journalism. For he did not resort to jargon which was familiar only to football insiders but translated this match with his voice into German living rooms so that even absolute beginners were infected by the drama of this event.[11] Without Zimmermann's warming commentary the effect of the World Cup victory would not have been as long-lasting, and this event, which had been, first of all, purely sporting in nature, would not have become a symbol of the cultural orientation in West Germany.

Therefore, since half of the nation were sitting by their radios that day, Zimmermann's commentary made a deep impression on the collective imagination of millions of Germans. The towns were virtually deserted that Sunday afternoon (Brüggemeier 2004: 210–12), since every household possessed a radio. Television had a considerably lower scope, although the victories of the German team bestowed a sales boom to this young medium in June and July of 1954. But in all, probably only around 40,000 TV sets were available on the day of the final – making them rare and precious goods. On 4 July there was therefore an enormous run on those public houses that possessed one of these precious sets; seats at the bar even had to be reserved by paying a small fee (Brüggemeier 2004: 210; Fest 2004; Goch 2003: 432). On balance, the final leveraged football in Germany into the media. From then on, football became an evergreen in the media and entered into a close alliance with the breathtaking rise of the entertainment industry. Thus football's rise as a part of everyday culture took place in parallel with the expansion of the entertainment industry in the telemedia age (Knoch 2002: 132–5).

Community and comradeship – Berne 1954 and after

However, the decisive question – why did the enthusiasm for the World Cup title become more than just a passing fancy going out as quickly as it had flared up? – still requires an answer. Why could 4 July 1954 achieve a symbolic quality and make football a heavily symbolic cultural possession? What meaning, outside of sport, could millions of Germans, who had hitherto paid only scant attention to football, put into football?

Decisive in this respect was the fact that the victory produced a connection with a form of collective community which was still well known from the Second World War: namely that of comradeship. The way in which sporting success was publicly commentated on in Germany makes it clear that the discourse used to explain the victory borrowed directly from the world of imagination still well known from the war. Reporting on football of the 1920s and 1930s still used a language which was purely inherent to football: accordingly, a match was won due to superior skill, because a team was technically more well versed, because it had better individual players or sometimes even because the referee had favoured it. In 1954, however, the biggest newspaper of the Ruhr Valley, the *Westdeutsche Allgemeine Zeitung* which was published in Essen, explained to its readers the following recipe for success behind the winning of the World Cup: 'A team of eleven comrades fighting unquestioningly did it.'[12] This chimed with Bundestrainer Herberger, who repeatedly pointed out in news conferences during the tournament the central importance of comradeship for sporting success (Brüggemeier 2004: 177). This was taken up by the leader of the Federal German State of Bavaria, Hans Ehard, in his speech at the reception for the world champions in Munich on 6 July 1954: 'a game in which comradeship and mutual understanding often mean more than the artistic art of ball control.'[13]

As a result, the public, politicians and sports writers and functionaries identified the community of fighting comrades – a community that millions of Germans had experienced as members of the German *Wehrmacht* – as a key to success on the pitch. The 'politically united people', in the form of an excessive nationalism, had had its day as a cultural system of reference after 1945 – but with the end of the war the form of camaraderie experienced more or less intensively by almost twenty million soldiers (Kühne 1998) had not lost its effect in creating a community.

'Comradeship' – which the soldiers of the Second World War, like those of the First World War before them, brought home with them in their rucksacks – was something that gave everything meaning, and it survived defeat undamaged. Moreover, emphasizing comradeship also allowed typically male ideals to live on in a time which was otherwise less receptive to the mythical transfiguration of great military feats and especially shied away from the public celebration of war heroes (Moeller 2001). The picture of the soldier in the early Federal Republic of Germany was not one of an upright warrior undefeated on the field as it was after 1918, it was not the emphasis of supposedly glorious deeds of the German generals, but a retreat to the popular perception of the ordinary 'Landser' (Knoch 2001) who had always remained loyal to the ideal of camaraderie while the political and military leadership had been gambling away the victory which was within reach. Via the popular value of 'camaraderie', ideas of male bonding seeped into the federal German culture, which otherwise had no great demand for military heroes. Thus a constellation was created that gave a completely new meaning to a sporting success, stylizing the 'Miracle of Berne' as a triumph of comradeship (Knoch 2002). Thus, the symbolic resonance of the victory of Berne derives from the fact that it could be interpreted within the discursive formations of comradeship and could therefore take on collective patterns of meaning which had survived the war defeat undamaged.

The symbolic potential attributed to this sporting event also derives from another factor: the Federal Republic of Germany. Unable to focus on individuals to exemplify abstract meaning the republic suffered from an obvious lack of symbols in the early 1950s. Normally, individuals offer particular symbolic potential because they are especially suitable for the visualization of the collective imagination. However, the symbolic market for individuals in West Germany was void at the beginning of the 1950s. A survey of a representative cross-section of West Germans from November 1953 (Allensbach 1956: 132) – answering the question which great German had achieved the most for Germany – made this obvious. Otto von Bismarck came first by a considerable margin. However, Bismarck was not suitable as a symbolic advertisement for a Federal Republic of Germany in the process of integration into the West. Well behind in second place, alongside the incumbent Chancellor, Konrad Adenauer, came the one person who had brought disaster upon Germany and the world: Adolf Hitler. Admittedly, Adenauer was later to rise to *the* symbol of a liberal and European-minded Germany which orientated itself towards the West. This, however, did not happen until the 1960s after his controversial domestic policy of integration into the West and of the domestic social market economy had been adopted by the political opposition (Schwarz 1986, 1991).

In the early 1950s there was, however, an obvious lack of a symbolic figure who could illustrate the cultural roots of the new Bonn republic. This constellation allowed, for the first time, a large-scale sporting event to become the imaginative focal point of the cultural condition of the West Germans. The symbolic accession of 'King Football' is therefore also an expression of the civilization of collective identity formation in West Germany from the 1950s on.[14] No less a person than the then Minister of the Interior Gerhard Schröder, articulated this connection when he welcomed the football world champions in the name of the Federal government during their visit to Bonn, proclaiming:

> There is great enthusiasm for football in Germany and therefore your victory in Berne has made such a strong impression on us. We are not as rich as other nations in terms of national events and symbols which provide a strong collective experience. Therefore we are all the more grateful for every event which mediates such a real sense of community to us.[15]

The swinging 70s and the German football brand

Thus the symbolic adaptation of the World Cup victory in 1954 paved the way for football to become a cultural phenomenon which was able to create collective identity at a national level. The cultural ranking of football in Germany may be seen from the history of the interpretation of 4 July 1954. It is a fact that the 'Victory of Berne', as a cultural asset open to interpretation, has experienced various new interpretations which mirror the changes in cultural development in West Germany over the course of the past fifty years. It is therefore necessary to focus, in a cultural-historical journey through the history of German football since 1945, on the significance of the winning of the World Cup, the manifestation of which is closely connected to the revival of German football on a national and international level in the early 1970s.

The foundation of a German league in 1963 – the *Bundesliga* – brought professional football to Germany for the first time, when football clubs from the north, west and south played in one league to determine the German champion. The introduction of the *Bundesliga* was also a success story because the cards were shuffled afresh and new clubs became the focus of attention as a result of their extraordinary performances. In 1969 a ten-year dominance by two football clubs that left their mark on the young Bundesliga began: Borussia Mönchengladbach and Bayern Munich. Until 1968 a different club had won the championship every year, but in the following nine years from 1969 to 1977 only these two clubs were champions: Borussia Mönchengladbach – a hitherto unknown club from the Lower Rhine province – triumphed five times; FC Bayern – a club that, like its great rival, was not considered worthy of belonging to the founding members of the *Bundesliga* in 1963 – won four times.

The domination of these two clubs opened up new cultural ground for football in Germany. Admittedly, the *Bundesliga* clubs of the 1960s and 1970s could still fall back on the fact that they had strong regional roots and that they could rely on loyal regular supporters from the close surroundings. In addition, the outstanding players of the two top teams, Borussia Mönchengladbach and Bayern Munich, came from the Lower Rhine and Upper Bavaria respectively so that the supporters could easily identify with the players (Pyta 2004a: 27). However, as illustrated by their exceptional player personalities – Günter Netzer and Franz Beckenbauer – it may be shown that top German players started to emancipate themselves from the so far dominating regional-cultural monopolization of football until that point and were destined to become a personal projection space for the cultural upheavals of the 1960s and 1970s (Böttiger 1994: 20).

Günter Netzer and Franz Beckenbauer were both footballers who left their mark on German football in its heyday from 1970 to 1974. Both interpreted their respective role on the pitch in an inimitable way: Günter Netzer, the long-haired blond midfielder, embodied the perfect midfield player who passed the ball brilliantly, demonstrated perfect ball control and, to top it all, scored goals from free kicks. His Bavarian adversary Franz Beckenbauer was an equally brilliant player but who had withdrawn from his original position in midfield to the deeper role of 'free man' in front of and sometimes behind the defence. Beckenbauer gave the role of the 'libero', which was tailor-made for his skills, a new interpretation: he was not just a sweeper-up but a player who got involved in the attack and brought his centre forward into an ideal shooting position via perfect one-twos.

It was, however, not only Netzer's and Beckenbauer's virtuosity that raised German football to a new cultural level. Decisively, both players also represented those upheavals in the value system that rapidly became evident in West Germany, especially from 1968 onward. Traditional emphasis on values and corresponding ways of life such as the bourgeois family lost their validity to such a degree that an increase in cultural autonomy led to a pluralism of lifestyles (Rödder 2004: 28–30). Netzer and Beckenbauer, in this respect, were very much children of their time and exponents of the 1970s' cultural experimentation. Both were born in simple homes, in 1944 and 1945 respectively, in the city where their football career started. Yet both set off for new shores in football and in their private lives. Netzer left the football idyll on the Lower Rhine to progress to new levels at world-famous Real Madrid. Beckenbauer remained loyal to his FC Bayern until 1977, before moving to America to open up new perspectives for himself in New York.

Moreover, both led private lives that fitted very well with the cultural upheavals of the 1970s. Netzer cultivated the image of the 'the rebel with the ball' with great success. He was an articulate lover of fast sports cars, was very fashion-conscious and stood out away from the pitch by running a fashionable disco. He became the darling of left-wing German intellectuals who saw in him someone who broke with conservative traditions on and off the pitch: on the pitch because Netzer celebrated a way of playing that represented a radical break from the supposed German 'football virtues' of competitive strength and eagerness; in private because he was regarded as a nonconformist (Böttiger 1994: 104–10). Although Netzer's rebellious image was rather artificial, having been created by intellectuals, it is, however, in no small way thanks to him that German football was now also accepted culturally by these intellectuals (Seitz 1987: 89–93). This sector finally dropped its reservations about football because the new German football style of the 1970s, in conjunction with cultural emancipation tendencies, permitted Günter Netzer and his team mates to become legitimate objects of literary reflection. Symptomatic of this is the expression: 'Netzer kam aus der Tiefe des Raums' ('Netzer came out of the depth of space'). It put the power of fascination and the aesthetic quality of football as a culturally legitimated object into words and became a familiar quotation in intellectual circles (Harig and Kühn 1974; Pyta 2004a: 2; Wolf 1980).

Franz Beckenbauer, on the other hand, was viewed rather critically by the intellectuals of the 1970s, although, at the time, he led a far more turbulent family life than the reliable Netzer. But politically Beckenbauer had declared himself to be a supporter of the conservative CSU with its leading politician Franz Josef Strauß (Wiedermann 2002: 57), something that the Left considered a deadly political sin for a long time. However, in a cultural-historical perspective, Beckenbauer is an even truer reflection of the cultural development of his time than is Netzer (Beckenbauer 1992). Beckenbauer the footballer, however, could become a culturally provocative figure on whom opinions were divided because until 1977 he remained in a symbiotic relationship with FC Bayern Munich. Beckenbauer symbolized the rise of this former Bavarian provincial club to a football superpower in Germany. FC Bayern Munich was the second German football club after Schalke 04 whose support could no longer be regionally localized. No football club has experienced such support outside of its home region since the 1970s. At the same time, no club has encountered such sheer hatred (Schulze-Marmeling 1997). The rise of FC Bayern Munich to an all-German football brand testifies to the fact that football started to shed its regional-cultural embodiment at the time of cultural upheaval in the 1970s. Now the steadily growing numbers of people interested in football projected cultural patterns of interpretation into football of quite different origin: FC Bayern Munich mobilized not only a dislike which was rooted in regional-cultural views of Bavarians outside of Bavaria, it also upset the 'man in the street' who sensed in this economically successful club a classic example of sporting high finance, a club whose victories were made possible only by the power of money. In contrast to this perception of FC Bayern as a reflection of an arrogant economic football enterprise was the equally strong positive connotation of the enormous economic and cultural rise of Bavaria and its capital Munich. The former agrarian federal state of Bavaria had mutated into the most dynamic economic growth region in Germany, attracting forward-looking industries thanks to a farsighted industrial policy in the 1960s. Parallel to this development was Munich's advancement to the 'secret cultural capital' of Germany. This was perhaps only natural in a country without a proper capital and which had, in Bonn, a seat of government that was, at first, only provisional. This development finally found its cultural expression in the field of sport: with the 1972 Olympic Games, Munich carried off an image coup as the cultural show-case of a modern Germany (Young 2003: 1478–86). In the realm of football this corresponded to the rise in popularity of FC Bayern, which was the only club that could count on a loyal supporter community from all over Germany.

With Franz Beckenbauer and Günter Netzer, the 1970s gave German football two shining lights who put the 'heroes' of the victorious World Cup team of 1954 in the shade. With the exception of the captain, Fritz Walter, nobody in this team received any special public attention twenty years later, when Beckenbauer led Germany to World Cup victory on home territory (Eggers 2004b; Raithel 2004: 126–9). Moreover, the sporting success of the German national team in the period from 1970 to 1976 obscured the perception of the World Cup victory of 1954, because in these six years German football achieved a chain of sporting triumphs on a two-year rhythm which is unmatched to this day: 1970, third place at the World Cup in Mexico; 1972, European Champions; 1974, World Champions; 1976, European runners-up. During that period the German team displayed skills of utmost perfection. The breakthrough was marked by the first leg of the quarter-finals of the European Championships against England on 29 April 1972, when a German team not only triumphed (3–1) for the first time on the 'hallowed turf' of Wembley, but also achieved this victory in such a manner that even the English press expressed the highest praise for its rather 'un-German' style of play (Downing 2000: 141–4). The German team not only played technically superior, attacking football, but possessed, above all, personalities on the pitch who were perfectly able to express a rare sense of ease.

With German football experiencing such an enormous leap in standards, the success of Berne was bathed in a new light. Once great individualists who could decide a game with a stroke of genius were in demand on the pitch in the 1970s, the memories of 4 July 1954 faded. The secret of the success of 1954 – the group of eleven friends who stuck together – seemed drab in a time of football revolution when outstanding individual players rather than a well-oiled football collective achieved victories by playing cultivated football and not just demonstrating pure spirit (Seitz 2004: 6). Such a point of view admittedly disparaged the playing performance of the 1954 team, which set high standards and played what was – for the time – modern football (Brüggemeier 2004: 182–91, 274–6). However, at the apex of German footballing achievement, not only did the memory of the creative play of Herberger's team fade, but also the cultural coding of the victory of Berne as a triumph of male comradeship seemed antiquated.

It was not until the course of the 1990s that the victory of Berne was rediscovered, reaching its temporary climax on the occasion of the sixteenth anniversary in 2004. The victory on 4 July 1954 now also meant something to literary figures and film-makers, and they used the day of the winning of the World Cup as a dramatic focal point and illustration for their messages. In the wake of the mythical transfiguration, the 'victory of Berne' was reinterpreted as the 'Miracle of Berne' (Raithel 2004: 133–45). In a cultural-historical perspective the reception history of 4 July 1954 shows in a particularly succinct manner the transition of a symbol to the status of a myth. Admittedly, myth and symbol equally fulfil the function of integration in large-scale communities via agreement on cognitive contents. The myth, moreover, distinguishes itself by a special narrative structure which is in a position to release emotions and emotionally strengthen a collective identity (Behrenbeck 1996: 40–4; Dörner 1996: 26–45).

The dramatic final on 4 July 1954, when the German team was seemingly hopelessly 2–0 down, then equalized within ten minutes and scored the winning goal just before the final whistle, did indeed provide a perfect topic around which myths could grow (Breitmeier 2004; Eggers 2004b: 175–7). However, the decisive question is: why did this mythic charge to the 'Miracle of Berne' only come about forty years after the actual event? In the 1990s the Federal Republic finally arrived culturally in the West (Schildt 1999). Germany, which had grown after reunification in 1990, was also politically and culturally clearly orientated towards the West. The avowal to the Western community of values, the result of Adenauer's policy which was controversial in the 1950s, now united all the relevant social movements in the country. It was exactly then that the mature second German democracy was able to start its search for the cultural roots of its success story. Modern state politics also need a founding myth – and it is characteristic of the symbolic capacity of football in Germany that the event which in the meantime had become idealized as the 'Miracle of Berne' was transfigured into such a founding myth. The infinite number of versions of the story about 4 July 1954 boiled down to the fact that for the first time since the end of the war the Germans had carried out a change for the better through typical 'German virtues' such as discipline, competitive strength and a never-slackening will, and in doing so had again gained a leading position on the international stage. This story which was told a million times and which found an impressive cinematic expression in the movie about *The Miracle of Berne* by the director Sönke Wortmann pushed the football action on to the sidelines. The victory on 4 July 1954 seemed in this way to be the most impressive example of how a depressed people can manage to find their feet again through hard work (Breitmeier 2004; Eggers 2004b: 172–7).

After the millennium, political protagonists participated increasingly in the construction of a cultural founding myth of the Federal Republic of Germany. The handing over of a piece of the pitch's grass on which the supposed 'Miracle of Berne' had taken place on 4 July 1954 was stage-managed with great media effort. After the demolition of the Berne Wankdorf Stadium in August 2001, the Swiss Embassy in Berlin presented a sod to the German Chancellor Gerhard Schröder on 12 December 2001. Schröder offered a special place for it in the garden of the Chancellery (Breitmeier 2004: 148–9). The historical-political dimension also came to fruition with the fact that in October 2003 Chancellor Schröder saw the film *The Miracle of Berne* in a private screeening shortly before its public release and, according to press reports, shed tears of emotion.

In July 1954, the then Minister of the Interior, Gerhard Schröder, had honoured the world championship victory in a quiet, restrained manner in the name of the Federal government – almost fifty years later his namesake used the forum of the public celebration of the memory of this event mystically to transfigure 4 July 1954. This occurrence illustrates in an impressive manner the openness of interpretation of football as a cultural phenomenon. In this respect – not only in Germany – football history is always a seismograph for changes in cultural tectonics.

Notes

1 See also the cultural philosopher Cassirer (1927), and on Cassirer, Paetzold (1994).
2 Here I refer to Henning Eichberg's approach of 'body culture', which he evolved for the sociology of sport (1998: 117, 143, 161–3).
3 This is emphasized by the human geographer Walter Christaller taking up the theory of 'zentrale Orte'; see Nielsen (2002: 589–90).
4 This was demonstrated impressively for the Munich Olympic Stadium by Young (2003).
5 Such voices are overestimated by Eisenberg (1999: 323–34).
6 The nationalistic Right in Germany did not clearly face the sports which were defined as 'German' as well as it did the Olympic movement; on this see a piece by Otto Bleck, editor of the national-conservative newspaper *Neue Preußische Zeitung*, to the chairman of the nationalistic DNVP, Graf Westarp, 5 July 1928, in the family archive of Freiherr Hiller von Gaertringen, estate Westarp, file 'Kreuzzeitung'.
7 'Das vorweggenommene Endspiel', *Rheinfront*, 6 June 1936.
8 'Schalke – Nürnberg vor 75 000' *Stuttgarter Neues Tagblatt*, 6 June 1936; 'Ra-ra-ra – der Club ist wieder da!', *Stuttgarter NS – Kurier*, 8 June 1936.
9 'Alte Klasse behauptet sich', *Rheinfront*, 8 June 1936.
10 Parts of the labour movement did integrate into the Hitler state – more deeply than former research has suggested. This is emphasized by Herbert (1989) and Schneider (1999: 480–92).
11 A primary source is the monograph by E. Eggers (2004a: 170–7); see also Brüggemeier (2004: 226–7).
12 Report of 5 July 1954, reprinted in Knüpfer and Potthoff (2004: 96).
13 Ehard's speech is documented in Raithel (2004: 153).
14 Suggested, too, in Mergel (2002).
15 The text of Schröder's speech is documented in Raithel (2004: 162).

References

Allensbach (1956) *Jahrbuch der öffentlichen Meinung 1947–1955*, Allensbach: Verlag für Demoskopie.
Applegate, C. (1990) *A Nation of Provincials: The German Idea of Heimat*, Berkeley: University of California Press.
Beckenbauer, F. (1992) *Ich: Wie es war*, Munich: Bertelsmann.
Behrenbeck, S. (1996) *Der Kult um die toten Helden*, Vierow: SH-Verlag.
Berns, H. and Wiersch, H. (1936) *Das Buch vom deutschen Fußballmeister: Fritz Szepan und Ernst Kuzorra*, Wattenscheid: Busch.
Böttiger, H. (1994) *Günter Netzer – Manager und Rebell*, Frankfurt/Main: Georg Simader.
Breitemeier, F. (2004) 'Ein Wunder, wie es im Drehbuch steht: Die WM 1945 – ein deutscher Erinnerungsfilm', in W. Pyta (ed.) *Der lange Weg zur Bundesliga*, Münster: Lit.

Brüggemeier, F.J. (2004) *Zurück auf dem Platz: Deutschland und die Fußball – Weltmeisterschaft 1954*, Munich: DVA.

Cassirer, E. (1927) 'Das Symbolproblem und seine Stellung im System der Philosophie', *Zeitschrift für Ästhetik und allgemeine Kunstwissenschaft*, 21: 295–312.

Dörner, A. (1996) *Politischer Mythos und symbolische Politik*, Reinbek: Rowohlt.

Downing, D. (2000) The *Best of Enemies – England v. Germany: A Century of Football Rivalry*, London: Bloomsbury.

Eggers, E. (2001) *Fußball in der Weimarer Republik*, Kassel: Agon-Sportverlag.

—— (2004a) *Die Stimme von Bern: Das Leben von Herbert Zimmermann, Reporterlegende bei der WM 1954*, Augsburg: Wißner.

—— (2004b) 'Der Mythos', in S. Dehnhardt (ed.) *Das Wunder von Bern*, Munich: Heyne.

—— (2004c) '"Berufsspieler sind Schädlinge des Sportes, sie sind auszumerzen . . ." Crux und Beginn eines deutschen Sonderwegs im europäischen Fußball: Die Amateurfrage im deutschen Fußball der Weimarer Republik', in W. Pyta (ed.) *Der lange Weg zur Bundesliga*, Münster, Lit.

Eichberg, H. (1998) *Body Cultures*, in J. Bale and C. Philo (eds), *Body Cultures: Essays on sport, space and identity* London: Routledge.

Eisenberg, C. (1999) '*English Sports' und deutsche Bürger*, Paderborn: Schöningh.

—— (2003) 'Möglichkeiten und Grenzen der Konsumgeschichte – das Beispiel des Sportkonsums', in M. Prinz (ed.) *Der lange Weg in den Überfluß: Anfänge und Entwicklung der Konsumgesellschaft seit der Vormoderne*, Paderborn: Schöningh.

Fest, J. (2004) 'Fußball ist niemals nur ein Spiel', *Frankfurter Allgemeine Zeitung*, 3 July.

Fischer, G. and Lindner, U. (1999) *Stürmer für Hitler*, Göttingen: Die Werkstatt.

Gehrmann, S. (2004) 'Der F. C. Schalke 04 und seine frühe Geschichte', in W. Pyta (ed.) *Der lange Weg zur Bundesliga*, Münster: Lit.

Giesen, B. (1999) *Kollektive Identität*, Frankfurt/Main: Suhrkamp.

Goch, S. (2003) 'Aufstieg der Konsumgesellschaft – Niedergang der Milieus?', in M. Prinz (ed.) *Der lange Weg in den Überfluß: Anfänge und Entwicklung der Konsumgesellschaft seit der Vormoderne*, Paderborn: Schöningh.

Gömmel, R. (2004) 'Der "Club" und sein Hinterland: Der 1. FC Nürnberg als Faktor fränkischen Regionalbewußtseins', in W. Pyta (ed.) *Der lange Weg zur Bundesliga*, Münster, Lit.

Harig, L. and Kühn, D. (eds) (1974) *Netzer kam aus der Tiefe des Raumes*, Munich: Hanser.

Herbert, U. (1989) 'Arbeiterschaft im "Dritten Reich"', *Geschichte und Gesellschaft*, 15: 320–60.

Herzog, M. (2004) '"Lautern ist eine große Sportfamilie!": Fußballkultur als Faktor städtischer und regionaler Identität', in W. Pyta (ed.) *Der lange Weg zur Bundesliga: Zum Siegeszug des Fußballs in Deutschland*, Münster: Lit.

Holtmann, E. (1998) 'Heimatbedarf in der Nachkriegszeit', in B. Weisbrod (ed.) *Von der Währungsreform zum Wirtschaftswunder*, Hannover: Hahn.

Jamme, C. (2004) 'Symbolische Bedeutungsansprüche der Kulturen', in F. Jäger and B. Liebsch (eds) *Handbuch der Kulturwissenschaften*, vol. 1: *Grundlagen und Schlüsselbegriffe*, Stuttgart: Metzler.

Knoch, H. (2001) *Die Tat als Bild. Fotographien des Holocaust in der deutschen Erinnerungskultur*, Hamburg: Hamburger Edition.

—— (2002) 'Gemeinschaft auf Zeit: Fußball und die Transformation des Nationalen in Deutschland und England', in Zentrum für Europa- und Nordamerika–Studien (ed.) *Fußballwelten: Zum Verhältnis von Sport, Politik, Ökonomie und Gesellschaft*, Opladen: Leske & Budrich.

Knüpfer, U. and Potthoff, R. (eds) (2004) *1954. Das Jahr in der WAZ*, Essen: Klartext.

Kühne, T. (1998) 'Zwischen Männerbund und Volksgemeinschaft: Hitlers Soldaten und der Mythos der Kameradschaft', *Archiv für Sozialgeschichte*, 38: 165–89.

Luckmann, T. (1988) 'Die "massenkulturelle" Sozialform der Religion', in H-G. Soeffner (ed.) *Kultur und Alltag*, Göttingen: Schwartz.

Maase, K. (2001) 'Schund und Schönheit: Ordnungen des Vergnügens um 1900', in K. Maase and W. Kaschuba (eds) *Schund und Schönheit: Populäre Kultur um 1900*, Cologne: Böhlau.

Mergel, T. (2000) 'Milieu und Region', in J. Retallack (ed.), *Sachsen in Deutschland*, Dresden: Verlag für Regionalgeschichte.

—— (2002) 'Überlegungen zu einer Kulturgeschichte der Politik', *Geschichte und Gesellschaft*, 28: 599.

Moeller, R.G. (2001) 'Heimkehr ins Vaterland: Die Remaskulinisierung West-deutschlands in den fünfziger Jahren', *Militärgeschichtliche Zeitschrift*, 60: 403–36.

Nielsen, S. (2002) *Sport und Großstadt 1870 bis 1930*, Frankfurt/Main: Peter Lang.

Oswald, R. (2004) '"Den Professionalismus entlarven und auslöschen": Der "Neue Weg" des Westdeutschen Spielverbandes, 1921–26', *SportZeiten*, 4: 33–53.

Paetzold, H. (1994) *Die Realität der symbolischen Formen: Die Kulturphilosophie Ernst Cassirers im Kontext*, Darmstadt: Wissenschaftliche Buchgesellschaft.

Preißler, D. (2004) 'Fußball im katholischen Milieu – DJK-Fußball in der Weimarer Republik', in W. Pyta (ed.) *Der lange Weg zur Bundesliga: Zum Siegeszug des Fußballs in Deutschland*, Münster: Lit.

Prinz, M. (ed.) (2003) *Der lange Weg in den Überfluß: Anfänge und Entwicklung der Konsumgesellschaft seit der Vormoderne*, Paderborn: Schöningh.

Pyta, W. (2004a) 'Der Beitrag des Fußballsports zur kulturellen Identitätsstiftung in Deutschland' in W. Pyta (ed.) *Der lange Weg zur Bundesliga: Zum Siegeszug des Fußballs in Deutschland*, Münster: Lit.

—— (2004b) 'Paul von Hindenburg als charismatischer Führer der deutschen Nation', in F. Möller (ed.) *Charismatische Führer der deutschen Nation*, Munich: Oldenbourg.

Raithel, T. (2004) *Fußballweltmeisterschaft 1954: Sport – Geschichte – Mythos*, Munich: Bayerische Landeszentrale für politische Bildungsarbeit.

Reckwitz, A. (1999) 'Praxis – Autopiesis – Text: Drei Versionen des Cultural Turn in der Sozialtheorie', in A. Reckwitz and H. Sievert (eds) *Interpretation, Konstruktion, Kultur*, Opladen: Westdeutscher Verlag.

—— (2000) *Die Transformation der Kulturtheorien*, Weilerswist: Velbrück.

Rödder, A. (2004) *Die Bundesrepublik Deutschland 1969–1990*, Munich: Oldenbourg.

Saldern, A. von (1992) 'Cultural conflicts, popular mass culture and the question of Nazi success: The Eilenriede Motorcycle Race, 1924–39', *German Studies Review*, 15: 317–38.

—— (1999) 'Sozialmilieus und Massenkultur in der Zwischenkriegszeit', in K. Kreter (ed.) *Stadt und Überlieferung*, Hannover: Hahn.

Schildt, A. (1999) *Ankunft im Westen*, Frankfurt/Main: S. Fischer.

Schneider, M. (1999) *Unterm Hakenkreuz: Arbeiter und Arbeiterbewegung 1933 bis 1939*, Bonn: Dietz.

Schulze-Marmeling, D. (1997) *Die Bayern: Vom Klub zum Konzern*, Göttingen: Verlag Die Werkstatt.

Schwarz, H.P. (1986, 1991) *Adenauer*, vol. 1: *Der Aufstieg: 1876–1952*; vol. 2: *Der Staatsmann: 1952–1967*, Stuttgart: DVA.

Seitz, N. (1987) *Bananenrepublik und Gurkentruppe: Die nahtlose Übereinstimmung von Fußball und Politik 1954–1987*, Frankfurt/Main: Eichborn.

—— (2004) 'Was symbolisiert das "Wunder von Bern"?', *Aus Politik und Zeitgeschichte*, 21 June: 3–15.

Siegrist, H., Kaelble, H. and Kocka, J. (eds) (1997) *Europäische Konsumgeschichte*, Frankfurt/Main: Campus.

Tomlinson, A., Markovits, A. and Young, C. (2003) 'Mapping Sports Space', *American Behavioral Scientist*, 46: 1463–75.

Wehler, H-U. (2003) *Deutsche Gesellschaftsgeschichte*, vol. 4: *Vom Beginn des Ersten Weltkriegs bis zur Gründung der beiden deutschen Staaten 1914 -1949*, Munich: Beck.

Wiedermann, S. (2002) *Franz Beckenbauer*, Düsseldorf: Dirk Lehrach.

Wolf, R. (1980) *Die heiße Luft der Spiele*, Frankfurt/Main: Frankfurter Verlagsanstalt.

Young, C. (2003) 'Kaiser Franz and the Communist Bowl. Cultural memory and Munich's Olympic Stadium', *American Behavioral Scientist*, 46: 1476–90.

Ziemann, B. (2003) 'Germany after the First World War – a violent society?', *Journal of Modern European History*, 1: 80–95.

2 Germany versus Austria

Football, urbanism and national identity

Roman Horak

The difference between the football nations Germany and Austria appears at first glance to be quite straightforward: on the one hand, we see a country that has won the World Cup several times, on the other we see a country that can count itself lucky if it qualifies once in a while for the finals of a world championship. However, the common cultural, political and social history of Germany and Austria – also with respect to issues of nationhood and nationality – is quite complicated. The respective evolution of the game of football (as a spectator sport) in each country must be seen as intertwined with – and even as a part of – that history.

I will argue that from the very beginning, football in Germany was destined to be a national affair and a part of the sports culture. In order to be effective, football needed to be 'Germanized', as Christiane Eisenberg has termed it, and this could only be accomplished with great difficulty. The idea of German gymnastics (the German variant of physical exercise culture) and the ideals of amateurism stood in the way of a broad popular-cultural acceptance of the game. Before it could become an element of the entertainment culture, football had to become embedded in the national consciousness in an important moment of national self-assurance. Winning the 1954 world championship, almost a decade before the (West) German *Bundesliga* (Federal League, 1963) was formed, firmly established the game as a national, German affair. By comparison, football in Austria was from the beginning a specifically Viennese affair. The creation of the first legitimate, established professional league on the Continent in 1924 – there may have been concealed professional practices elsewhere – testified to an urban culture that embraced the game of football in its two dominant forms: the double codification by the liberal middle class (symbolized by the coffee house) and the proletarian masses (symbolized by the Viennese suburbs) respectively.

The successes of the Austrian 'wonder team' in the early 1930s (essentially still a Viennese affair) already hinted at the gradual changes that were to take place after the Second World War: in the wake of growing national self-confidence in Austria, football underwent a transformation (particularly in the 1960s and 1970s) from a Viennese urban spectacle to a mainstream Austrian sport. The game now served – internally – as a place of confrontation between Vienna and the provinces and – outwardly – as an important visible emblem of national independence, particularly *vis-à-vis* Germany. It was then that the rivalry, which found its most pronounced expression in the lasting significance of the victory over the German national team at the World Cup in Argentina in 1978 (the 'Miracle of Cordoba'), came into effect.

In this chapter I will relate this Austrian story, with appropriate references to the development of football within German culture. In the first section, the different ways football arrived and was taken up in Germany and Austria will be outlined in broad detail; I will then turn to the formation of a particular Viennese urban and popular football culture. This will be followed by a discussion of the 'Austrification' of Viennese football culture, a process that reached its peak in the 1970s, and by a brief account of recent developments within Austrian football. In the conclusion, the chapter returns to the complex relationship between German and Austrian football and discusses how this relationship has haunted Austrian football culture.

Two beginnings

Football came from England to Germany at the end of the nineteenth century and did not always meet with enthusiastic approval. From the outset the game expressed and was inhibited by a deep tension between two conflicting body cultures. 'English sports' or 'German gymnastics' were the alternatives: 'do away with "Fusslümmelei"!' (soccer louts) (Planck 1898/ 1982) was the war-cry of concerned national youth organizers. However, there is more than a different exercise culture concealed in the contrasting natures of modern, achievement and record-oriented sports, and the philosophy and model of 'natural' gymnastics upheld by the Germans. The high-school teacher Karl Planck, cited above, also knew this and ended his pamphlet 'Fusslümmelei: Über Stauchballspiel und englische Krankheit' with a political message:

> We have learned to wield the sword, and just as we achieved national unity, we are now fighting a fiery battle to overcome class barriers so that a free people can live in a free land. . . .
>
>   Therefore, German people, today you are fertilizing the soil by the sweat of your brow, so that the seed of justice and of high human morals may grow; open your eyes, lest weed is mixed under your wheat by a friendly neighbour or by your own clumsy hand!
>
> (Planck 1898/1982: 41)

What we are seeing here – albeit in a somewhat encoded form – is an indication of the growing rivalry between the first industrial power, the colonial British Empire, and an aspiring, young Wilhelmine Germany. Thus it was imperialistic competitiveness that came to light in this secondary ideological arena, so defining the foundations of the reception of football in Germany. Although disapproved of by national elites and people of influence, football gained in popularity and became a 'parlour game' for the bourgeois middle class, as Eisenberg (1994) put it in the subtitle of her study; but it was not – at least initially – a working-class mass spectacle. Under the circumstances, its growing popularity was made possible primarily by being freed from the stigma of 'Englishism': the rules of the game were translated into German early on so that attacks by traditionalist-nationalist opponents of football, confronted by a German-language written code, increasingly missed their target. Thus, redefined as a German game, football was able to gain a foothold within the German Empire, despite the unpromising circumstances of its origins.

Initially, however, the game had no great impact on the masses: it was part of the bourgeois club culture that its early organizers, mostly aspiring office employees, modelled on student fraternities. The latter were also a source for the names of the teams – 'Victoria', 'Teutonia', 'Germania' – the most popular German club name was 'Deutschland' (Eisenberg 1994:197). Rituals were also imported from student culture, such as the students' ceremonial football drinking sessions, known as 'Salamander'. The establishment of the DFB (German Football Association) in 1900 caused things to change: the 'parlour game' became a 'competitive game', and as such football at last gained wider public recognition. In the years before the First World War its institutional base expanded considerably. In 1910 it was included in the training programme of the army, and in the following year the DFB joined the paramilitary-national 'Jungdeutschlandbund'. Football had become an all-German political affair.

The sport of football came to Austria in two different ways. An interesting point here is the fact that the reception the sport met with in Vienna and Graz respectively reflects almost precisely the problems discussed above (i.e. German gymnastics vs. English sport). Apparently the game had come to Graz, or so circulating football stories will have us believe, by way of a student who had been 'infected with the football bacillus' in the Prague environment of the founder of the DFC (German Football Club) Prague, who himself actually came from Frankfurt in Germany. In any case, it was the students who were playing football in Graz in the mid-1890s and who made the sport popular. The 'Akademisch-Technische Radfahrverein (ATRV)', a cycling club, initially provided the organizational framework, but it soon became apparent that it was unable to cope with the growing demand: 'The (then) flourishing fraternities saw a double danger in the fast development of football as a sport: students might have favoured the training and playing ground over the crammer, and "German" gymnastics as advocated by the athletics guru Jahn were not to be pushed to the wall by a sport that originated from England and used English terms such as goalkeeper, back, halfback, forward etc.', wrote the chronicler of Austrian football, Leo Schidrowitz (1951:15). In November 1898, the foundation of the 'Grazer Fussball-Verein' (Graz Football Association) and the incorporation of players who had left the ATRV by then marked the separation of football and gymnastics in Graz.

While the game of football came to the Styrian capital in a detour via Frankfurt and Prague, it found its way more directly to the metropolis of the Dual Monarchy. It was, in fact, members of the 'English colony' who began to play football in Vienna. Staff members of various Vienna-based English firms and a clergyman of the Anglican Church had already set up the 'Vienna Cricket Club' in 1892. When this was changed to the 'Vienna Cricket and Football Club' two years later, the game of football joining the more upper-crust game of cricket in the club's programme, it provided an expanded sporting base for the expatriate British community. The addition of football to the sporting agenda of such a club also demonstrated a shift in interests. Newspapers began to report on games, sport magazines began to take more and more notice of football, and the autumn of 1897 saw the introduction of the first serious football competition in Vienna, the so-called Challenge Cup.

In contrast to the 'Cricketers', the 'First Vienna Football Club', set up in 1894, was not an exclusive association and was not restricted only to UK citizens. Accordingly, the names of the 'Cricketers' team that played in 1895 in away games in Prague and Berlin were: R. Lowe sen., Thursfield, Blackey, Flavin, Gramlick, Early, Blyth, F. Lowe, Gandon, Shires, H. Lowe (Kastler 1972: 13). Three years later, five non-British players appeared in the 'characteristic line-up' of the First Vienna Club, although one of them had changed his name to John Mac and another had lived in England before coming to Vienna (Schidrowitz 1951: 27). The club was founded by the English gardener to Baron Nathaniel Rothschild, but also counted locals – as well as one Swiss national, one German and one Frenchman – among its members in the year it was established. Nevertheless, the direct English influence continued for some time: England as a football nation and role model continued to shape Viennese football culture.

The contrast to developments in Germany was pronounced, and there were no serious and successful efforts in Vienna to translate football's vocabulary into German. Even today, the classic football *aficionado* is far more familiar with the English terms than with their German translations. Terms such as 'penalty', 'hands', 'corner', 'out', 'cup', 'derby' and so on – albeit pronounced somewhat differently – are still part of the basic verbal inventory of the football fan in Vienna.

A further indication of the significance of the direct English influence on football in Vienna during this early period was the central role that the former professional of West Bromwich Albion, M. D. Nicholson, played. He came to Vienna as manager of the local branch of the Thomas Cook travel agency and from 1897 onward played for the Vienna Football

Club. In the following years it was he who was to make sure that English teams visited Vienna regularly and helped to popularize the game. Obviously, football was played in the most diverse parts of the Habsburg Monarchy. The reason for examining the Viennese beginnings of the game in greater detail is that a special urban football culture was to develop in the metropolis during the 1920s, a culture that not only enjoyed international success but was also to be of decisive significance for the future status of the sport in Austria.

Until the collapse of the Austro-Hungarian Monarchy in 1918, the game also functioned as the forum and funnel for national disputes concerning individual crown lands and ethnicities (Marschik 1997: 21–4, 1999a). In contrast to the situation in the German Empire, football could not serve as a nation-building element in the multi-nation monarchy. However, the club structure that developed was of significance, as were certain clubs – such as Slavia Prague and Hakoah Vienna – that carried political connotations, albeit in their local and regional contexts as league sides.

Football as a key moment of modern urban culture

From the 1920s in particular, Viennese football found its most fruitful terrain in the suburbs: this was where it became a mass spectacle, where it had its most faithful and devoted fans, and where its transformation into a modern spectacle began. No reliable statistics on the make-up of the spectator population exist; indirectly, some valid observations can be made, however, particularly with regard to the interwar period. In recent times, several essential theoretical studies have illuminated the nature of the culture of the proletarian suburb (see Maderthaner and Musner 1999); the game's primary location in this social space allows us to assume a homology of players and spectators. And the players – even those playing in the big clubs of the professional league between 1924 and 1938 – were mostly workers.[1] The suburbs championed the developing modern spectator sport of football but we also can detect pre-modern, atavistic characteristics demonstrating the persisting strengths of traditional culture. Local loyalties, closely tied to a defined territory, are hardly a modern phenomenon, but in the context of an emerging popular culture, such loyalties assume a modern form, such as when presented in the new mass media (i.e. the sports press).

It is these urban elements and their robust cultural profile that constitute the divergence from the situation in Germany. Viennese football broke from the narrowly defined paradigm 'sport', sacrificing in doing so the middle-class regulative ideas of fairness and physical fitness, and thus became a central moment in the Viennese popular landscape of taste. This was a twofold development, as I shall now show. In a first phase, the game conquered the space that was upheld by the 'masses'[2] as a spectacle that, on the one hand, attracted more and more spectators to the stadium and football field and took place locally and that, on the other hand, was a source for and subject of magazine reports, the variety theatre and cinema. These parallel developments contributed to the creation of a (predominantly male) land-scape of taste. We may put this – roughly speaking – in a 1920s time-frame. In the following decade – again oversimplified – the coding of the game changed and broadened. The game was now metaphorically elevated, and gained new social, cultural and political space. When the mass spectacle of football became the focus of feature pages, it changed its coding. Football in Vienna was no longer an affair involving just the lower classes; the game received a second, complementary Viennese-modern-urban definition. This double definition made it special and different from the 'national' coding that characterized the game of football in Europe at the time – although that differed in specific countries.[3]

'City club' and 'stuffy coffee house fumes' versus 'healthy suburb club' was the stylization/codification that kept the dynamics of Viennese (profes-sional) league football going. If 'SK Rapid' stood for proletarian toughness and the suburb, then 'Austria' stood for the city, coffee house and the liberal (Jewish) middle class. The coffee house, the true drawing-room of Viennese writers in the First Republic and plotting ground and venue for witty conversation and repartee, was a key site. Some of the many coffee houses that existed served as proper football coffee houses, a meeting place for officials, players and fans. The fact that 'Austria' was officially headquartered in various coffee houses of the first district fitted beautifully with the image the club liked to cultivate of itself.

Ehn and Strouhal (1998) describe convincingly how closely the rise of the Viennese coffee house was linked to that of the game of chess. The coffee house was an ideal stage for playing chess, a meeting point for the exchange of views and a venue for political discussions as well as everyday conversations; social differences were less visible in this 'corridor between public life and privacy' (Ehn and Strouhal 1998: 9). Witty feature writers writing about football could not get past the chess metaphor. In his bril-liant obituary on Matthias Sindelar, who died in January 1939 in mysterious circumstances, Alfred Polgar compared the footballer's way of playing with that of a chess player (see also Maderthaner 1992). Sindelar was the play-maker of the 'wonder team' that in 1931 defeated the German national team 6–0 in Berlin and 5–0 in Vienna. Rather than these two games it was the 3–4 defeat inflicted by England in December 1932 that was later stylized into a football myth. Germany was still not seen as a serious opponent; a Viennese team still played under the title of the national team. In the opposite positions redefined explicitly in the Austro-fascist era (1934–1938) of city versus countryside, that is to say of metropolis versus province, football clearly stood for Vienna against the 'idiocy of rural life' (Marx and Engels 1976: 488), or of the provinces. In contrast to the chess players' association that separated – along those lines – for political reasons (Ehn and Strouhal 1998: 54ff.), contradictions in football were not openly displayed.

With the arrival of National Socialism the tension between popular culture and feature writing, between suburb and coffee house, was broken. When the (Jewish) members of the literary coffee houses were murdered or sent into exile, the one facet of this culture for which the 'wonder team' was the climax and anticipation disappeared for good. But what happened to the other element of the football culture, based in the suburbs? It survived, it submerged, or it retreated for tactical-defensive reasons.[4] We find ties to suburban districts, for example, until well into the 1950s. Non-political explicit resistance was formulated, but now and then there was contradiction and insubordination. Both were clearly 'anti-Prussian' as Matthias Marschik (1999b) has shown. Assaults on the symbols and installations of the National Socialist state such as the rioting that took place in the autumn of 1940 at the games between Schalke 04 and Admira, and Rapid and Fürth were quite possibly directed against the Germans ('Piefkes') rather than the National Socialist system. Such protest was not about a political programme that had to be defended. It was simply the horizon of the suburb that stood up for itself in its own way – however powerless that may be – against the militaristic regimentation, and which happened to surface from time to time. During the game between Admira and Schalke – which was meant to be a 'game of conciliation' – growing irritation arose when the (Reichs-German) referee twice disallowed a – in the opinion of the spectators – legitimate goal by Admira. The indignation escalated more and more, and eventually led to wild scenes resulting in smashed windows and the beating of security guards. Even the 'state car of Gauleiter Baldur von Schirach in front of the stadium gate with smashed windows and cut tyres' (Schwind 1994: 114) had become the subject of outrage. However, one ought not and need not interpret these examples of insubordination as an explicit form of resistance against the Nazi regime. On the other hand, the public character of such an expression of disapproval meant the breakdown of discipline; that is to say, the breakdown of the one principle of authority/power that, while it is not specific solely to the authoritarian system, is virtually indispensable for the rigorous and non-negotiable upholding of that power.

Towards Austrification

The 1954 World Cup in Switzerland represents an important turning point in the relationship between the football nations Germany and Austria.[5] With this tournament, more precisely with the 6–1 defeat suffered at the hands of the underestimated Germans, the future world champions advanced to the position of new 'arch enemy' and began to take on the role previously played by the Hungarians (John 1997: 82). The defeat was so dramatic because it came as a total surprise. The writer and football enthusiast Friedrich Torberg called it the 'most devastating defeat since Königgrätz' (Lechnitz and Spitaler 1998: 93).[6] Afterwards, the playing style of the teams was seen as an expression of national differences but the Viennese characteristics (lightness, elegance) were still referred to by commentators in descriptions of one's own sense of being and, so to speak, coded as 'Austrian'. The detachment from Germany was also politically opportune – one of the cornerstones of Austrian post-war ideology with regard to the *Anschluss* to Nazi Germany in 1938 was the idea of Austria's role as victim. Keeping distance from the successor states, the FRG and the GDR, could do no harm here.

Internally, the general climate of consent, the emphasis on an 'Austrian' concept, was one shared by all political parties, and it was to extend to football. The national league, designed to represent clubs from all parts of Austria, has been in existence since the 1949–50 season. Although the Viennese clubs still dominated initially, a first step towards the 'Austrification' of the game had been taken (Horak 1994).

More significant changes were on the way. Already in 1961, Joschi Walter, the manager of FK Austria-Vienna, publicly presented the first plans for reform and hence the introduction of professionalism into Austrian football. The ideas that had eventually led to the installation of the *Bundesliga* in the FRG during the 1963–64 season served as his model. In March 1964, he was provisionally appointed the new ÖFB Federal Capitan and he was installed in the post in May 1964. Bela Gutmann, who had won the European Cup with Benfica Lisbon in 1961 and 1962, was appointed at his side as supervisor of the national team. Walter drew up a plethora of reformist ideas – the so-called 10 Point Programme – which were only adopted in part at the general meeting of the ÖFB. It was decided, furthermore, to introduce a National League responsible to the ÖFB with a reduced number of associations/clubs (twelve), and to reduce the quota of foreigners to two playing in the team at any one time, as well as introduce the classification of three types of players (amateurs, contractual and licensed players, whereby the latter could only be active at the top level of the game). The issuing of a national league licence was tied to different economic prerequisites that had to be fulfilled by the associations. But soon, in October 1964, Joschi Walter and Gutmann resigned. Walter 'felt himself to have been left alone with his reform programme by the state league, by the provincial associations, and even by the leading ÖFB officials. He evidently saw no possibility of realizing the most important points of his programme ... because of massive opposition from all sides' (*Welt am Montag*, 12 October 1964).

In fact the reduction in numbers in the upper league was never implemented, nor were the economic prerequisites ever checked in practice. Only the installation of the National League and the new Players'

Regulations were carried through in 1965. Walter distanced himself from these reforms which were associated with his name: he insisted on 'declaring publicly that not I but others had given birth to the regulations in their present form' (*Express*, 19 July 1965). Ever since these first attempts at modernization, Austrian football has oscillated back and forth between reforms and counter-reforms, but it was now on the way to becoming a truly national, Austrian phenomenon. In 1965 LASK (Linzer ASK) was the first team from the federal provinces to become Austrian champions: Vienna's domination of the sport was finally broken.

The risky business of modernization

Since these first attempts, the modernization of Austrian (and therefore also of Viennese) football continued to shift between reform and counter-reform. This process emphasized and speeded up the split between top level and lower level football in Vienna. Two clubs with international aspirations (Austria and Rapid) stand apart from other clubs that still embody elements of the old Viennese football culture (ties to the home district, local roots). But even these two big clubs are, due to their semi-professionalism, stuck within this structure. Although they tried to break away, they never really succeeded. An almost tragic example was provided by the club Rapid Vienna. The establishment of a Rapid Limited Company (in 1991) ended in disaster and led the club to the edge of bankruptcy; and it is still unclear how the attempts of Frank Stronach, an Austro-Canadian millionaire who de facto owned the club from the late 1990s, to transform Austria Vienna into a major European club will end.

It is not by chance that the first serious attempt to establish a big Austrian club that could come up to international standards occurred in the provinces. The history of the FC Tirol club, which was formed in 1986 and wound up in 2002, would not have been possible in Vienna. It is – still – hard to imagine that Rapid or Austria would change not only their club colours but also their name. This happened in Innsbruck without any difficulties. The FC Swarowski Tirol club, sponsored by the international Swarowski company, took over the first division licence of Wacker Innsbruck, employed Ernst Happel as manager, and was actually quite successful in the Austrian championship, although never on an international level. It attracted its supporters by creating an image of a club standing against the (historically) dominant Viennese football culture. It is not only motives concerning football which play an important part here; it is also the general anti-centralist, more precisely anti-Viennese, attitude of the spectators that is important. But this is only part of the story. Because of the image of professionalism and modernization – built up following the model of Bayern Munich – this new club attracted the representatives of the new middle class throughout the whole of Austria, even the Viennese, a class that was very much orientated towards success. The new club won the Austrian league twice but did not succeed internationally; glorious defeats such as a 1–9 in the second round of the 1990–91 European Cup against Real Madrid are still well remembered among Austrian football fans.

But it all got even worse. In June 2002, the club went bankrupt; it lost its licence and was relegated to the third division. In January 2005, the manager and two former presidents of the club were convicted and sentenced to one year and three years respectively in prison, though this was reduced to probation.

Football and nation-building processes

The 1970s were the historic period in which the football rivalry between Austria and Germany emerged most clearly. Politically speaking there were similar attempts to introduce social democratic reforms in both Austria and West Germany. But conflicts within Germany that had a profound effect upon the political climate of the country, such as the problems surrounding the RAF, the left-wing terrorists of the Bader Meinhof group, remained largely unrepeated in Austria. The emphasis on political independence became stronger than ever before and under Bruno Kreisky the country sought to go its own way in foreign relations. This is evident above all in the policies towards the Eastern bloc and the question of the Near East, which were carried out under the aegis of neutrality, as enshrined in the constitution. This independent line was adopted towards the North Atlantic Treaty Organization (NATO) but also especially towards the larger Western neighbours.

Within this context of neutrality and independence, the 'Miracle of Cordoba' was a major event: when the Austrian side beat the German team for the first time in almost half a century, football was irrevocably established as an integral element in national identity. The composition of the team itself revealed another change: while the Austrian players in the 1958 world championship were, with just one exception, all from Viennese clubs, in 1978 there were only four from the previously dominant metropolis. The 3–2 victory was seen as a vindication of 'Austria', even though the two decisive goals were scored by Hans Krankl, who at the time represented the archetypical personification of proletarian Viennese culture. Ever since the game, the final goal clinching the 3–2 victory is aired on television at every opportunity (whether appropriate or not), together with the radio commentary of reporter Edi Finger ('I'm going crazy . . .'), which is now also known widely even in Germany. The constant retelling and replaying of the moment and its interpretation indicate the importance of an event that goes far beyond the football pitch.

Four years later, during a preliminary round game at the 1982 World Cup finals in Gijon, Spain, the two teams helped each other in a scandalous goalless match, since universally decried as 'fraternization rather than fraternal strife', to advance to the next round. Many commentators read this as an indication of a changed national self-understanding and a 'normalization' of Austrian political cultures as well as a weakening of the dialectical tie with Germany (see, for example, Lechnitz and Spitaler 1998: 95–6). The indignation that the Austrian sporting public felt over the Gijon game, as well as the circumstances of later showdowns between the two nations, shows that German–Austrian football relationships are still oscillating today, at least within Austrian media discourses, between making overtures and maintaining detachment.

Notes

1 A newspaper article from the year 1937 estimates that two-thirds of the professional players came from the two classic working-class districts Floridsdorf and Favoriten (*Wiener Zeitung*, 12 December 1937). A few details on the working-class professions of the Rapid and Admira players round off the picture. The *Sport-Tagblatt* of February 1931 presented the following data: among the thirty players it mentioned we find six unskilled workers, three chauffeurs, three locksmiths, two tailors, two shoemakers, two salesmen, one second driver and one student. The list of other professions reads: car-mechanic, scaffolder, merchant, metal printer, railway worker, electrician, milliner, steel worker and plumber; one player who stated his profession as 'footballer' had seemingly not learned a trade (*Sport-Tagblatt*, 18 February 1931).
2 The discussion of the term 'mass' in a football context cannot be included here for lack of space; see Horak and Maderthaner 1997.
3 This process has been traced, focusing on the two typical exponents: the 'Tank' of the 1920s, Josef Uridil (SK Rapid) and the 'Papierene', Mathias Sindelar (Austria) of the 1930s (see Horak and Maderthaner 1996). Uridil is the tough working-class character, his nickname derived from the British military invention of the First World War: he stands for the 1920s and Rapid Vienna, the working-class club. Sindelar's nickname, 'the guy made of paper', evokes Austria and the 1930s paradigm – intellectuals, writers, the (Jewish) middle class.
4 Here I refer to Michel de Certeau's understanding of the 'popular' according to which the tactics of the powerless practically and contextually resist the strategies of power (see De Certeau 1984).
5 I would argue that Wolfgang Pyta overestimates the importance of football – as a moment of popular culture – in Germany before 1954 (see Chapter 1 in this volume).
6 This is the key symbolic moment of the Austrian–German relationship. In 1866, news of Prussia's dramatic victory over Austria at Koniggratz caused the papal secretary to exclaim, 'Casca il mondo!' ('The world is collapsing'). After the Battle of Koniggratz, nothing was the same again. Suddenly, the balance of power in Central Europe was overthrown; Germany unified itself around upstart Prussia, and the old Austrian Empire began its long slide towards the trash heap of history. In time, Koniggratz would be seen as the beginning of Europe's 'German problem', a problem that needed two World Wars to resolve.

References

Bausenwein, C. (1995) *Geheimnis Fußball. Auf den Spuren eines Phänomens*, Göttingen: Die Werkstatt.
Brändle, F. and Koller, C. (2002) *Goooal!!! Kultur- und Sozialgeschichte des modernen Fussballs*, Zurich: orell fueslli.

De Certeau, M. (1984) *The Practice of Everyday Life*, Berkeley: University of California Press.

Ehn, M. and Strouhal, E. (1998) *Luftmenschen: Die Schachspieler von Wien*, Vienna: Sonderzahl.

Eichberg, H. and Hopf, W. (1982) 'Fußball zwischen Turnen und Sport. Nachwort', afterword in K. Planck *Fußlümmelei: Über Strauchballspiel und englische Krankheit*, Stuttgart [original 1889]. Münster: Lit Verlag.

Eisenberg, C. (1994) 'Fußball in Deutschland 1890 – 1914: Ein Gesellschaftsspiel für bürgerliche Mittelschichten', *Geschichte und Gesellschaft*, 20(2): 181–210.

Eisenberg, C. (1997) 'Deutschland', in C. Eisenberg (ed.) *Fußball, soccer, calcio: Ein englischer Sport auf seinem Weg um die Welt*, Munich: dtv.

Eisenberg, C. (1999) *'English sports' und deutsche Bürger: Eine Gesellschaftsgeschichte 1800–1939*, Paderborn: Schöningh.

Fußball in Gegenwart und Vergangenheit (1976) 2 vols, Berlin (DDR): Sport Verlag.

Gehrmann, S. (1988) *Fußball – Vereine – Politik: Zur Sportgeschichte des Reviers 1900–1940*, Essen: Bouvier.

Giulianotti, R. (1999) *Football: A Sociology of the Global Game*, Cambridge: Polity Press.

Heinrich, A. (1994) *Tor, Tor, Tor: Vierzig Jahre 3:2*, Berlin: Rotbuch.

Heinrich, A. (2003) 'The 1954 Soccer World Cup and the Federal Republic of Germany's Self-Discovery', *American Behavioral Scientist*, 46(11): 1491–505.

Hopf, W. (ed.) (1979) *Fußball: Soziologie und Sozialgeschichte einer populären Sportart*, Bensheim: paed. extra Buchverlag.

Horak, R. (1994) '"Austrification" as Modernization: Changes in Viennese Football Culture', in R. Giulianotti and J. Williams (eds) *Game Without Frontiers: Football, Identity and Modernity*, Aldershot: Arena.

Horak, R. and Maderthaner, W. (1996) 'A Culture of Urban Cosmopolitanism: Uridil and Sindelar as Viennese Coffee-House Heroes', *The International Journal of the History of Sport*, 13(1): 139–55.

Horak, R. and Maderthaner, W. (1997) *Mehr als ein Spiel: Fußball und populare Kulturen im Wien der Moderne*, Vienna: Loecker.

Horak, R. and Spitaler, G. (2003) 'Sport Space and National Identity – Soccer and Skiing as Formative Forces: On the Austrian Example', *American Behavioral Scientist*, 46(11): 1506–18.

John, M. (1995) 'Sports in Austrian Society 1890s–1930s: The Example of Viennese Football', in S. Zimmermann (ed.) *Urban Space and Identity in the European City 1890–1930s*, Budapest: Central European University Budapest (Working Paper series).

John, M. (1997) 'Österreich', in C. Eisenberg (ed.) *Fußball, Soccer, Calcio: Ein englischer Sport auf seinem Weg um die Welt*, Munich: dtv.

Kastler, K. (1972) *Fußballsport in Österreich*, Linz: Trauner.

Lechnitz, F. and Spitaler, G. (1998) 'Eigentlich waren die Österreicher immer schon anders . . .', in M. Wassermair and L. Wieselberg (eds) *3:2 Österreich: Deutschland: 20 Jahre Cordoba*, Vienna: Doecker.

Lindner, R. and Breuer H.T. (1979) *'Sind doch nicht alles Beckenbauers': Zur Sozialgeschichte des Fußballs im Ruhrgebiet*, Frankfurt/Main: Syndikat.

Maderthaner, W. (1992) 'Ein Dokument wienerischen Schönheitssinns: Matthias Sindelar und das Wunderteam', *Beiträge zur historischen Sozialkunde*, 3: 17–24.

Maderthaner, W. and Musner, L. (1999) *Die Anarchie der Vorstadt: Das andere Wien um 1900*, Frankfurt/Main: Campus.

Marschik, M. (1997) *Vom Herrenspiel zum Männersport: Die ersten Jahre des Wiener Fußballs*, Vienna: Turia & Kant.

Marschik, M. (1999a) *Vom Idealismus zur Identität: Der Beitrag des Sportes zum Nationalbewußtsein in Österreich (1945–1950)*, Vienna: Turia & Kant.

Marschik, M. (1999b) 'Between Manipulation and Resistance: Viennese Football in the Nazi Era', *Journal of Contemporary History*, 34(1): 215–29.

Marx, K. and Engels, F. (1976) 'Manifesto of the Communist Party' (first published London 1848), in Karl Marx and Frederick Engels *Collected Works, volume 6: Marx and Engels: 1845–48*, London: Lawrence & Wishart.

Planck, K. (1982 first published Stuttgart 1898) *Fußlümmelei: Über Stauchballspiel und englische Krankheit*, Münster: Lit Verlag.

Schidrowitz, L. (1951) *Geschichte des Fußballsportes in Österreich*, Vienna, Wels and Frankfurt/Main: Traunau.

Schulze-Marmeling, D. (1992) *Der gezähmte Fußball: Zur Geschichte eines subversiven Sports*, Göttingen: Die Werkstatt.

Schümer, D. (1998) *Gott ist rund: Die Kultur des Fußballs*, Frankfurt/Main: Berlin Verlag.

Schwier, J. (2000) *Sport als populäre Kultur: Sport, Medien und Cultural Studies*, Hamburg: Czwalina.

Schwind, K. H. (1994) *Geschichten aus einem Fußballjahrhundert*, Vienna: Überreuter.

Seitz, N. (1987) *Bananenrepublik und Gurkentruppe: Die nahtlose Übereinstimmung von Fußball und Politik 1954–1987*, Frankfurt/Main: Eichborn Verlag.

Väth, H. (1994) *Profifußball: Zur Soziologie der Bundesliga*, Frankfurt/Main and New York: Campus.

3 A tale of two Germanys

Football culture and national identity in the German Democratic Republic

Markus Hesselmann and Robert Ide

> The word 'national team' should not be a taboo tonight, even though we know that there can't be two national teams from one nation.
>
> (Werner Schneider, West German TV reporter on the 1–0 victory of the GDR over the Federal Republic at the 1974 World Cup in Germany)

State of the nation: the GDR and its identity problems

Sport has long been seen as a defining factor in a nation's identity (see most recently Smith and Porter 2004).[1] 'The imagined community of millions', observed Hobsbawm (1992), 'seems more real as a team of eleven named people. The individual, even the one who only cheers, becomes a symbol of his nation himself.' In this respect, the German Democratic Republic was no exception. In his comprehensive study *Nation und Nationalismus in Deutschland. 1770 bis 1990*, the historian Otto Dann lists sporting successes as vital consolidating moments in the nation-building of the GDR:

> In its revised constitution of 1968 the GDR called itself a 'socialist state of the German nation'. Its political consolidation as a state was unmistakable by then and that was recognised at home and abroad: the national holiday, 7th October, found its broadest approval among the East German people; in 1969 the Protestant churches of the GDR left the Evangelische Kirche Deutschland (EKD); big successes in sports caused sensations abroad. After 1970 they were accompanied by political recognition as well.
>
> (Dann 1996: 340)

Sports recognition came first, then politics. In fact, it was a sports event that symbolically constituted the GDR as an independent state worldwide: 'In 1968 the GDR achieved the complete recognition of its National Olympic Committee so that at the Munich Games in 1972 it could appear

as a sovereign state for the very first time. It won third place behind the
USA and the Soviet Union. German unity, still upheld under an artificial
flag and anthem in Mexico 1968, was shattered there in front of the eyes
of the world' (Dann 1996: 343). The nation was born from the spirit of
sport.

The GDR needed sports as an identificational factor more than other
countries. This rather artificial nation[2] had many deficiencies in what Smith
(1993) lists as 'fundamental features of national identity': a historic territory or homeland, common myths and historical memories, a common mass
public culture, common legal rights and duties for all members, a common
economy with territorial mobility for members. In fact, the short history of
the GDR may be seen as a history of identity problems. Sports helped to
alleviate these problems to a certain extent, not only as 'panem et circensis'
('bread and races', as Roman satirist Juvenal put it) by way of distraction
from the manifold problems the young nation had to face, but also as a
matter of identification through athletic success. The number one sport
in Germany East and West was football, so it would only be logical to
use football above all other sports to that end. Spitzer (2004: 25) analyses
football as a 'primary object of identification for the construction of
GDR society'. Fuchs and Ullrich (1990: 92) recall that an 'unübertroffene
Massenwirksamkeit' ('unsurpassed effectiveness in relation to the masses')
was attached to football by leading politicians and that successes in this
immensely popular sport were even seen as strengthening economic production (Leske 2004: 96). In addition to these domestic effects, there was the
desire to strengthen identity by way of international recognition, an important aspiration for nations in general. Holmes and Storey (2004: 88) claim
that 'performances of national football teams can put countries on the map',
going so far as to say that the success of the Irish football team in the late
1980s and early 1990s 'made Ireland exist'. It is the aim of this chapter to
explore how far football was helpful in creating a national identity in East
Germany, and how far it failed. Further-more, it aims to show how, in an
ironic shift of meaning, football became a factor in shaping a regional East
German identity after reunification. Our findings show the – streamlining
or subversive – political potential of football.

There are some recent monographs on GDR football. To a great extent
they rely on Stasi and party documents to draw conclusions as to how
control was kept over football (Leske 2004; Spitzer 2004). This 'top-down'
approach necessarily puts the protagonists into focus: the players, the
coaches, the referees, the officials and not least the politicians surrounding
and using the game to their ends. Following Hobsbawm's claim, however,
that phenomena like national identity 'cannot be understood unless analyzed
also from below, that is in terms of the assumptions, hopes, needs, longings
and interests of ordinary people' (Hobsbawm 1992:10), our main aim was
to explore how the East German people felt and feel, i.e. those who
had no official roles in football and were neither mainstream communists

nor outspoken dissidents. To this end, we held a number of interviews with reliable eyewitnesses and gathered many scattered voices from popular publications on GDR football. We compared these views to the findings of published studies and available documents.

The pitch is greener on the other side: East German fan culture between Bayern Munich and Dynamo Berlin

Cultural, political and economic separation from West Germany was crucial in the creation of a GDR national identity after the building of the wall. In football, this proved particularly difficult due to the great interest within the GDR in West German clubs. Bayern Munich, Schalke 04, Hamburger SV, Hertha Berlin and Borussia Mönchengladbach had many followers east of the Elbe. Even Manfred Ewald, the notorious head of the GDR sports association DTSV, claimed that he had been a Schalke fan (Ewald 1994: 13). The printers at *Neues Deutschland*, the Party's official paper, would place their modest self-organized bets on the capitalist *Bundesliga*, while setting the articles on the slogan-ridden speeches of the communist nomenclatura, as Lothar Heinke, then journalist at *Der Morgen*[3] and a founder Union Berlin fan, recalls. The high viewing figures at Dynamo Dresden's Rudolf Harbig stadium are the exception that proves the rule: it was in this pocket of the Republic – widely dubbed 'Das Tal der Ahnungslosen' ('The valley of the clueless') – that Western television and therefore *Sportschau*, the West German equivalent of BBC television's *Match of the Day*, could not be received (Leske 2004: 92).

East German football fans put themselves at some risk for their passion for West German clubs. In *Football against the Enemy*, Simon Kuper (1994) recounts the case of a fan who was a member of an illegal 'Hertha society' in East Berlin. He supported Hertha Berlin, Bayern Munich and the West German national team and had to endure repression by the Stasi for his loyalties. His every move following his heroes' away games all over Eastern Europe had been documented. When his Stasi file was handed over to him after the fall of the wall, the official said to him: 'It's all about football!' In his well-written and deservedly prize-winning book, Kuper paints a rather clear-cut picture of the allegiances of fans in East Berlin as far as the Stasi club BFC Dynamo and the dissident club 1. FC Union were concerned: 'Dynamo were popularly known as Eleven Schweine' (eleven pigs) and 'when Union met Dynamo, the ground would be full with everyone supporting Union.'[4]

But events in East Germany were not as clear-cut as Kuper would have us believe. In an interview with one of the authors of this chapter, Thomas Brussig was asked to name his favourite football team in his youth. The famous novelist and playwright, whose books are now part of the German school syllabus, answered: 'I have to say, I have to admit it right here and now, I supported BFC Dynamo. At least in my childhood. When after 1979 the team won the championship every year I was not interested any more. ... I would feel better if I could say today that I never supported BFC. But that would be like Gregor Gysi saying he had nothing to do with the Stasi' (Brussig 2003). Matthias Schlegel, a Saxony-born journalist then working in Berlin for *Neue Zeit*,[5] would go to the Jahn stadium at Prenzlauer Berg and watch BFC Dynamo, 'just because I was living next door and I generally think that it is best to support the local club within walking distance'. In the recent fan compilation *Fußball-Land DDR* (Willmann 2004), the writer Jochen Schmidt tells us about his early life as a BFC fan, when he sneaked out of the living room as a boy while his father was watching West German *Sportschau* to watch East German *Sport aktuell* with the neighbour's son who was not allowed to tune into Western television. Andreas Gläser, acclaimed for his book *Der BFC war schuld am Mauerbau* ('The BFC is to blame for the Berlin wall') (2000), includes an auto-biographical initiation story which centres on his first away game with his beloved Dynamo Berlin. Contrary to a common belief these days, it was not only the children and relatives of Stasi officers who went to and supported Dynamo.

The orientation towards the West of many fans did not mean that the Oberliga itself was a dull and dry affair. Arguably the best account of what football meant in the GDR, particularly for young GDR people, was written by Christoph Dieckmann, now of the weekly newspaper *Die Zeit*. Dieckmann, still an ardent follower of FC Carl Zeiss Jena, maintains that there were 'three kinds of football' in the GDR:

> On Sundays at the Waldsportplatz you had the relegation battle in the Magdeburg district league, division C, between Traktor Dingelstedt with 'Boxer' Könnecke in goal and Stahl Elbingerode – 1–1 (after trailing at half-time). There was, and this wasn't bad either, Western television on Saturday nights at Uncle Rittmüller's on his country-style sofa: 1860 Munich with 'Radi', 'Peru' and Horst Blankenburg against Bayern – 2–1. But then on Saturday afternoons, four o'clock sharp on Radio GDR 1, you had the 'Oberliga link-up of the second halves of all seven matches in the football Oberliga of the GDR', as radio anchorman Herbert Küttner would solemnly announce. 'But first, the results of the junior Oberliga.'
>
> (Dieckmann 1999)

The potential was there. Brussig's, Dieckmann's, Gläser's and Schmidt's recollections show that a young generation of East Germans was willing to adopt the East German clubs as its own – in spite of the ever-present influence of the West. For a short period in the early 1970s, when 1. FC Magdeburg won the European Cup Winners' Cup in 1974 and the GDR *Auswahl* ('selection') beat West Germany's *Nationalelf* ('national eleven') at the World Cup in the same year, it seemed that East German football could probably be a major factor in shaping GDR identity. 'When Magdeburg won, that really thrilled me', Matthias Schlegel, who is now a man in his fifties, recalls. Many football fans rated this club success even more highly than the *Auswahl*'s big victory. The novelist Annett Gröschner, who was 10 years old in East German football's *annus mirabilis*, recalls 'that even girls became football fans then'. Gröschner (1999) wrote a book about the 'Heroes of Rotterdam', who beat favourites AC Milan in the final on 8 May: 'The celebrations of the people of Magdeburg were heard all over the town, cries of joy burst out of living room windows, even at the theatre the performance was changed and the victory was mentioned.' But then: 'On the next day, however, in the local paper, the *Magdeburger Volksstimme*, the main headline did not read "European Cup for Magdeburg", but "Celebration for Soviet heroes", and the main photograph was not of our boys but of the aged members of the state and Party leadership of the GDR paying tribute to the 29th jubilee of the day of liberation at the Soviet monument at Berlin-Treptow.' And when the official sports association yearbook *Das Jahr des Sports* was published, it dealt with the Youth Spartakiad at length, while covering the great football victory of 1. FC Magdeburg with only a few photographs (Seifert *et al.* 1975). Coach Hans Meyer, then at Carl Zeiss Jena, later at Mönchengladbach and Hertha Berlin, recalls a similar experience:

> When we lost the European Cup Winners' Cup final in 1981, nobody took any notice of us. We had beaten AS Roma, Valencia and Benfica Lisbon with a kind of *Bezirksauswahlmannschaft* ('district selection'). After such successes I should have grabbed some Deutschmark and told my players, 'Let's have a party'. But in the end the defeat by the heinous class enemy was held against us.[6]

The people's game always remained the most popular sport in East Germany, as it did in the West. But the communist leaders never really managed to develop a successful strategy for using that popularity for the national and socialist cause. East German football could have flourished. For a country of 18 million, it was relatively successful (Hesse-Lichtenberger 2002), but the leaders continually alienated the supporters. By the time Manfred Ewald realized that 'football has its own special value [–] individual-ism and fanaticism are often stronger than discipline and rationalism', it was too late. He was in resigned mood when this succinct analysis was published five years after the fall of the wall (Ewald 1994: 66). The creator of the sports miracle of the GDR admitted that he had failed to come to grips with football. The dialectics of football, its interplay of collectivism and individualism, had asked too much of him and the other GDR leaders. The ways in which 'scientific' training methods that had worked in other sports were falsely implemented in football have been well analysed in the literature, as has the conscious neglect of team sports in general on the basis that winning medals is much more difficult and infrequent than in individual sports (Leske 2004: 75–6). Doping, a method of increasing performance that could not be as easily applied to the complex ball and team sport of football as it was to individual athletics, has also been emphasized (Spitzer 2004: 55).

But it was not all down to training methods and medal planning. The specific cultural value of the people's game was also not understood by politicians and officials who defined themselves as champions of the proletarian cause. In their will to detach the new state from everything that represented the disgraced old Germany, they did not understand that tradition is an all-important factor in football culture. East German clubs were rigorously cut off from their past as 'bourgeois' organizations. Clubs such as VfB Leipzig, the first German champion in 1903, or Dresdner SC, the last wartime champions in 1943 and 1944, were stripped of their names and, as in the case of Dresden, rigorously put at a grave disadvantage (Hesse-Lichtenberger 2002: 282–3). In an attempt to link sports and recreation to the new socialist folklore of the *Betriebsgemeinschaften* (BSG, 'factory communities'), crude names were given to teams, of which 'Stahl Stalinstadt' (later 'Stahl Eisenhüttenstadt'), 'Rotes Banner Trinwillershagen' or 'Aktivist Schwarze Pumpe' were some of the most ridiculous examples. This was reversed to some extent in 1965 when more or less independent football clubs were reintroduced and the good old 'FC' reappeared in the names of many top clubs (Spitzer 2004: 18). Leske (2004: 166) sees this as the beginning of a modest GDR football tradition of its own; yet it was just another example of the constant changes in GDR football. It was not only the names that were confusing: whole clubs were moved from town to town in order to have a better allocation of top teams to the newly founded fifteen GDR districts. The northward 'transfer of the small Saxon team Empor Lauter to become Empor Rostock' and eventually Hansa Rostock is a striking case in point (Hesselmann and Rosentritt 2000). Vorwärts Berlin (to Frankfurt/Oder) and Dynamo Dresden (to Berlin) were treated in a similar fashion (Leske 2004). In short: identification with the local football club, the traditional basis of all football supporting, was not made easy in the days of the GDR Oberliga.

The classic case of football socialization, as described in *Fever Pitch* (1992) by Nick Hornby, where fathers took their sons to the match, was not the rule in East German football. 'Compared to Western clubs like Schalke, where generations of supporters flood into the stadium and young men inherit their season tickets from their fathers, this did not occur in our clubs', says Jürgen Heinsch, a former goalkeeper, trainer and talent scout at Hansa Rostock, the last East German champion and the only former GDR club that managed to compete in the Bundesliga for a number of years. In Heinsch's view the problem was that in the East German sports collectives there was no way for supporters to become members of their club or otherwise to become attached to it in any organizational form

(Hesselmann and Rosentritt 2000). This early deficit had been slightly amended with the reintroduction of the football clubs in 1965. As the SED district paper *Berliner Zeitung* wrote in December 1965: 'People interested in football shall now have the chance to join the new football clubs or Oberliga teams respectively as supporting members. Thereby the relation of football supporters to their clubs shall be shaped more closely and solidly' (Leske 2004: 167).

However, such an offer appealed more to mature and sedate supporters and less to the fan subculture. In the GDR, the latter was often seen as full of antisocial, 'negative decadent' elements (Leske 2004; Spitzer 2004) who were not willing to participate in the organized leisure activities of the official youth movement, the *Freie Deutsche Jugend* (FDJ). In the chronicles of the clubs such fans show up regularly as 'Rowdys' ('hooligans') who had to be expelled from the stadium because of misbehaviour (Hesselmann and Rosentritt 2000). The first traces of what could be seen as an independent fan culture may be found in the late 1960s and early 1970s (Fuge 2004). One of the few liberties left to GDR citizens was the right to travel freely, at least in their own country. An informal movement of *Schlachtenbummler* ('away supporters') took advantage of this and followed their clubs to away games. At the beginning of the 1980s, Hansa Rostock, like other clubs, attempted to organize their fans. *Zehnergruppen* ('groups of ten supporters'), were assembled, each with a club official at their head. They organized what were known as *Sportlerfahrten* ('athlete trips') to away games. Fans got cheaper GDR *Reichsbahn* tickets and could travel more easily. But the authorities were not really happy with these travelling supporters. 'They did not behave according to the socialist order', Axel Klingbeil, a seasoned Hansa fan, notes ironically. What he hints at are alcoholic excesses and fights with fans from other clubs, particularly in railway stations.[7] It was one of many examples of how attempts at streamlining GDR fan culture not only failed, but yielded the opposite of what was intended.

Even more illegal fan clubs were founded. Attempts by the FDJ to establish a hold in the fan scene were not very successful. As a Stasi memorandum noted:

> We must recognise that there is a remarkable number of fan clubs which are not registered with the football clubs/sports associations. Usually these are spontaneous amalgamations. In a number of cases these are not in line with the criteria of the German football association of the GDR for registration, and partially form a focus point for negative-decadent youths and young grown ups.[8]

Especially remarkable is the behaviour of the negative-decadent football following. In particular, followers of the punk scene, as it calls itself, try to establish a hold by way of aggressive behaviour and a certain inclination towards brutality. Behavioural patterns which follow Western models surface quite often, such as:

- glorification of the professional football of the FRG;
- taking over of *Schlacht-Gesängen* ('fan chants');
- sporting of symbols of Western European football clubs;
- mimicking the activities of the fan clubs of capitalist states.

In their typical bureaucratic language, the Stasi lament in the same document that the number of fan incidents which threatened calm and security at matches through violence or verbal abuse was not decreasing over the years. Spitzer (2004: 166) describes this document as the Stasi's 'declaration of bankruptcy' with regard to fan control. Fans who co-operated overtly with the officials were soon to be outcasts among their peers, as Klingbeil, the veteran of the illegal fan scene in Rostock, recounts. In an instance of Northern regional solidarity across the border with the class enemy, many of those fans also supported Hamburger SV. Such divided loyalty or 'double identity' (Spitzer 2004: 166) was also common for hardcore football fans in the East. The supporters of the underdog Union Berlin, for example, underlined their subversive standing by maintaining ties to Hertha Berlin and other clubs on the capitalist side of the wall (Leske 2004: 456).

When Sparwasser beat Beckenbauer: the two 'national teams'

It is commonly held nowadays that East Germans marvelled at the West German team and hated their own. The reality, again, seems to have been more multi-faceted, as responses to and memories of the GDR's 1974 victory over the FRG show. Thomas Brussig, an expert in East German mentality before and after the fall of the wall, summed up in our interview with him how East Germany felt from his point of view: 'That match triggered a vast polarization. Some people were strongly in favour of the West German footballers, others were completely against them. There were political reasons for that. The GDR defined itself, amongst other things, by way of its success in sports. Therefore those people who were against this state begrudged it the glory of that victory' (Brussig 2003). But there was an additional factor that should never be forgotten where football is concerned: 'It is always more fun to see the favourites stumble and the underdog win', says Brussig. And that allowed even critical East Germans to take sides with the GDR team who had, after all, met and beaten the European Champions and World Champions-to-be. That victory catered to a feeling of inferiority that somehow had always been there. Sandra Dassler, a journalist with a background in the Protestant Church of the GDR, comments: 'I was a Bayern Munich fan as a kid. But when we thought of our holidays in Hungary and those boastful West Germans with their Mercedes and our Trabant standing next to them, there was a natural sense of belonging to the underdog team. And that was the GDR.' Dassler also recalls that as a 13-year-old girl she was very proud of her country after that victory: 'We were playing in a handball youth tournament at the time in Meiningen, my home town in Thuringia, and the football victory was announced by the officials and celebrated by everybody.' Yet the return home was a huge anticlimax. She remembers becoming very angry at her father who told her coolly that the whole thing was fixed because the West Germans had tactically lost the game in order to be in the weaker group and to avoid Brazil in the next round of the tournament. Lothar Heinke, now a veteran reporter for *Der Tagesspiegel* in Berlin, was on holiday in Bulgaria during the World Cup 1974 and encountered many West German fans who were just too sure of victory beforehand: 'After the match, there was no great celebration by the East Germans, but there was an atmosphere among us of: "You West-Germans should have kept your mouths shut".' Not surprisingly, Brussig himself was for the GDR that night:

> That was absolutely clear for me. That is my country and I am for it. Strangely I was not interested in football at all up to that game. The match against the FRG was the first one that I saw in full length on television. I was eight years old then and at that age it is not easy to concentrate for 90 minutes. But I watched the match and I had the feeling that something important was happening.
>
> (Brussig 2003)

Again, as with club football, we see that the disposition for identification was there, but Brussig and many of his GDR countrymen did not watch much more after that. *Qualifikationsversager* ('qualification losers') is the attribute that the disillusioned coach in Brussig's play *Leben bis Männer* ('Life up to the men's team') uses for the constant lack of success of the East German *Auswahl* in important matches (Brussig 2001). After 1974 the GDR never managed to get to the finals of the World Cup or European Championships again. *Freundschaftsspielweltmeister* ('world champion in friendlies') was another nickname for the team that played (and won) a lot of matches against their socialist comrade nations in Africa and Asia, but always shunned a rematch against West Germany (Blees 1999: 132–3). Once again, politics repressed reasonable sports planning. In Thomas Brussig's career as a football fan, two factors put him off the game in the end: his favourite club BFC Dynamo won everything, his favourite country won nothing. In addition, there was the team that lost to the GDR in 1974 but went on to become world champions. It is a sports-historical irony that the best days of GDR football coincided with the blossoming of one of the best teams in football history right across the border. Despite the major blip, Beckenbauer *et al.* put Sparwasser in the shade.

When Hansa beat Bayern: the legacy of Oberliga and Auswahl

From the line-up in the last season of the Oberliga in 1991, only one club managed to survive for a couple of years in the first *Bundesliga*: FC Hansa Rostock. Dynamo Dresden and Energie Cottbus each made the first division for brief periods. Very few clubs could even establish themselves in the second division of the *Bundesliga* for long. The subsequent fate of the Oberliga clubs (shown below for the 2004–05 season) is very telling:[9]

1	Hansa Rostock	2	Bundesliga
2	Dynamo Dresden	2	Bundesliga
3	Rot-Weiß Erfurt		Regionalliga (third division)
4	Hallescher FC Chemie		Oberliga (fourth division)
5	Chemnitzer FC[10]		Regionalliga (third division)
6	FC Carl Zeiss Jena		Regionalliga (third division)
7	1. FC Lok Leipzig		Bezirksklasse (seventh division)
8	Stahl Brandenburg		Verbandsliga (fifth division)
9	Stahl Eisenhüttenstadt		Verbandsliga (fifth division)
10	1. FC Magdeburg		Oberliga (fourth division)
11	FC Berlin[11]		Oberliga (fourth division)
12	FC Sachsen Leipzig[12]		Oberliga (fourth division)
13	FC Energie Cottbus	2	Bundesliga
14	Viktoria Frankfurt/Oder[13]		Verbandsliga (fifth division)

Ironically, many East German clubs are playing today in a division called the 'Oberliga'. But since the West German league system has been implemented in the East, the word Oberliga stands for, as it did in West Germany, a number of regionally restricted fourth divisions. The past and present of East German football is well documented. Many books on the Oberliga, its clubs and the national team have appeared since the fall of the wall. There is also a well-established subcultural infrastructure with internet pages and fan magazines. That may come as a surprise given the loss of significance that the East German football clubs have gone through since reunification.[14] But East German football clubs still retain an important function in preserving East German identity. They do so even more the further we move temporally from reunification. Books such as *Fußball-Land DDR* (Willmann 2004) or *Die Geschichte der DDR-Oberliga* (Baingo and Horn 2003) have recently catered for an ever-increasing demand. Politically, that East German identity is voiced by the Party of Democratic Socialism (PDS), which is the post-communist successor of Ulbricht's and Honecker's Socialist Unity Party (SED) and very successful in regional elections in the five new Bundesländer. Economically, the eastern parts of Germany are far away from the 'blooming landscapes' that Chancellor Helmut Kohl had promised at reunification. The situation is far from rosy, with unemployment around 17 to 18 per cent in 2005, but there are some rays of hope coming from the modernization of the old industry. When car-makers Opel got into trouble in 2004, General Motors implemented rationalization measures in its West German branches, leaving the plant at Eisenach in Thuringia alone because, by comparison, it was very modern and productive. When in 2005 brewers Brau and Brunnen decided to streamline their production in Berlin, they decided to close down their old brewery in the West and expand the newer one in East Berlin. East German post-GDR self-conscience has also risen in cultural areas such as cinema (*Goodbye Lenin*, *Sonnenallee*), literature (particularly the works of Thomas Brussig) or pop music (Die Prinzen, Rammstein). Since the end of the 1990s, there has also been a trend towards kitsch 'Ostalgie' ('eastalgia'). Parties with Honecker look-alikes, T-shirts or cups with the GDR logo of hammer and compasses have been criticized as playing down the totalitarian state that the GDR without doubt was.[15] 'Es war ja nicht alles schlecht' ('not everything was bad') was a common saying in the years after the *Wende* and it has turned into something of a running gag when everyday life in the GDR is discussed nowadays. But many East Germans seriously reclaimed what they thought of as their right to their own biography, which had, in their view, been taken away by a perceived West German takeover. For many of them, football was an important part of this biography.

Ironically, the torch-bearer of East German football identity after reunification was a club that nobody really cared for in the days of the Oberliga. Hansa Rostock had a modest following in its northeastern home region. The club did not win a single league title in GDR times but it went places at exactly the right historical juncture. Rostock always had a solid basis of talented players and managed to build up a good team in the final years of the GDR. But the players were not real stars, so they were not bought up by Western clubs as soon as the wall came down, as happened to Hansa's much more prominent competitors for the two East German places in the Bundesliga such as Dynamo Berlin, 1. FC Magdeburg, Carl-Zeiss Jena or Lokomotive Leipzig. Dynamo Dresden also lost many good players, namely Matthias Sammer, but still started off promisingly under capitalism by making it directly into the *Bundesliga*. However, the Saxons soon fell victim to mismanagement by club officials who were mainly imported from the West. Things were different at Rostock: in the north-east, a certain continuity was maintained not only in the team but also in management. All through its years in the first and second *Bundesliga*, Hansa Rostock was looked after and run by former players of the club and politicians from the region. There was one significant exception: Hansa Rostock was the first East German team to rely on the expertise of a West German manager, a concept with which it largely stuck (Hesselmann and Rosentritt 2000). The former Werder Bremen and Germany player Uwe Reinders led the team from the Oberliga into the *Bundesliga* and managed three victories in a row at the start of the season. Hansa Rostock even surprised Bayern Munich at their own Olympic Stadium with a 2–1 win that year. At the end of the season, however, Rostock were relegated with Reinders already sacked. Yet the club achieved the unexpected, and came back three years later and stayed up for another ten years.

A team that had always had a rather regional appeal had now become the team for the whole of East Germany. When Hansa played away in Berlin at the vast Olympic Stadium, sometimes 20,000 supporters showed up, more than at most games in Rostock itself. This is because Berlin was within easier reach from all directions of the territory within the former GDR than Rostock. The famous East German rock group 'Puhdys' not only composed the anthem for the ice hockey team Eisbären, formerly known as Dynamo and a pivot of East German identity in their hometown Berlin, but also conceived one for Hansa Rostock, even though singer Dieter Birr admitted that he did not care much for football (Wittich 1998). And when they were in danger of relegation, the whole of the East supported Hansa: Gregor Gysi, a Berliner and by far the most popular PDS politician to date, said in 1999 in a statesmanlike tone: 'The players know what is at stake and therefore they will have the power to win.' Less optimistically, former GDR international Joachim Streich feared that 'it will get dark in the East for years to come' if Hansa ever got relegated. 'For the new Bundesländer, Hansa is the team to identify with,' he added. 'You can tell when fans in Magdeburg or Chemnitz cheer because Rostock are winning a match somewhere else' (Hesselmann and Rosentritt 2000: 206–7). On trips to away games, the Hansa fans themselves voiced their Eastern pride in ironical chants. West German train passengers looked bewildered when they heard 'Wir kommen aus dem Osten und wir leben auf eure Kosten' ('We come from the East and we're living at your expense'), by which they ridiculed the *Solidaritätszuschlag*, a special tax that subsidized the five new Länder. 'Wir sind die Jungs vom Getränkekombinat Hanseat' ('We're the boys from the drinking combine Hanseat') went another favourite chant that alluded to the nationalized industry of 'Volkseigene Betriebe' and 'Kombinate' in the GDR.

But the mutual identification faded over the years. When Energie Cottbus was promoted, there was another club from East Germany with more specific Eastern appeal due to its legendary trainer Eduard Geyer, the last manager of the GDR-*Auswahl* (and also, as it happens, a Stasi spy). Hansa itself did everything to establish a new image as a northern rather than an eastern club, not least by hiring a number of Scandinavian players. This spawned a certain internationalization. On Saturdays, Swedish fans nowadays 'commute' over the Baltic on ferries to spend the morning shopping in Rostock before watching Hansa at the newly built Ostsee (Baltic) Stadium in the afternoon. The merchandizing industry reacted quickly by bringing out blue and yellow scarves on which the very words 'Hansa Rostock' were supplemented by 'Sweden Power'.

How was integration and identification brought about in the national team of the united Germany? This got off to a bad start after Beckenbauer's megalomaniac remarks about Germany being 'unbeatable for years to come' made in the afterglow of winning the 1990 World Cup. When Denmark beat the united Germany in the final of the 1992 European Championships in Gothenburg, this was proof once again that merging two teams does not necessarily make one better one. Since 1992, the contribution from the former GDR to the national team has been as follows:

Sweden 1992	22 players	3 born in GDR
USA 1994	22 players	2 born in GDR
England 1996	23 players	3 born in GDR
France 1998	22 players	5 born in GDR
Belgium/Holland 2000	22 players	7 born in GDR
Japan/South Korea 2002	22 players	7 born in GDR
Portugal 2004	23 players	3 born in GDR

The role that East German footballers played in the national team since reunification transformed from humble beginnings to a veritable high towards the millennium. This, significantly, was the last year when talented players bred under the GDR system would have been in their prime, after ten years of football under more competitive capitalist conditions. It is proof of the quality of GDR football and particularly its education and scouting system that at times nearly one-third of the German team came from a quarter of the population (i.e. from the East). And there was quality to match the quantity. The key player in the team that won the 1996 European Champions was Matthias Sammer, who learned his football at Dynamo Dresden. And in 2006 – as in 2002 and 2004 – Germany's title hopes will rely on Saxony-born Michael Ballack.

Yet the recent decline is striking. Of the team at the 2004 European Championship in Portugal, only Ballack, Schneider and Jeremies were born in East Germany. This development is paralleled by the decline of East German club football outlined above. Formerly a model of good youth football, the East German clubs no longer produce any talented players. The reason for this is simple. In order to survive in the short term, they buy mediocre but experienced foreign players rather than take the risk of training and fielding their own youngsters. It was no surprise that the first *Bundesliga* team to field not one single German player in a *Bundesliga* match was Energie Cottbus (against VfL Wolfsburg in April 2001). It was another four years before this happened in the English Premier League. But when Arsenal relied solely on foreigners in its 5–1 defeat of Crystal Palace in February 2005, it was for a different reason: Arsène Wenger fielded a team made up mainly of French world stars because English players were not good enough for him. Eduard Geyer at Cottbus, by contrast, had to rely on a team of mediocre Eastern European mercenaries because German players were too expensive.

Notes

1 With examples solely from the Anglophone world, Smith and Porter (2004) and their contributors explore areas as diverse as 'Englishness and sport', 'Ethnicity and nationalism in Scotland' and 'Baseball, exceptionalism and American Sport'.
2 Following Anderson (1991), Gellner (1983) and Hobsbawm (1992), we are aware that all nations are cultural artefacts, not natural phenomena. Furthermore, it is understood that a group of people may gain, win or achieve the quality of becoming a nation by way of a specific form of behaviour. This is roughly how Max Weber put it at the beginning of the twentieth century (Weber 1997).
3 *Der Morgen* was the paper of the Liberal Party of the GDR (LDPD). It had the same printing house as *Neues Deutschland*, which was the paper of the Socialist Unity Party (SED).
4 For an account of the rivalry between Dynamo, champions ten times in a row after 1979, and underdog Union, see Mike Dennis (Chapter 4 in this volume).
5 *Neue Zeit* was the paper of the Christian Democrat Party (CDU) of the GDR.
6 Interview in *Die Zeit*, 26 July 2001, quoted according to Leske (2004: 79).
7 See also Mike Dennis (Chapter 4 in this volume).
8 Bundesbeauftragter für die Unterlagen des ehemaligen Staatssicherheitsdienstes der DDR: Zentrale Auswertungs- und Informationsgruppe des MfS Berlin 3543, MfS: Information Nr. 397/86 of 2 September 1986, pp. 1–6 (published in Spitzer 2004: 167).
9 Another East German club in the second division at that time were Erzgebirge Aue (formerly Wismut Aue).
10 Chemnitzer FC is the successor of FC Karl-Marx-Stadt. This is a rare case in which not only a football club but a whole city was 're-renamed' after reunification.
11 Trying to detach itself from its not so glorious past as a Stasi club, BFC Dynamo renamed itself FC Berlin after the fall of the wall, only to succumb to 'eastalgia' later on by reintroducing the name BFC Dynamo.
12 The new club Sachsen (Saxony) Leipzig came about via a merger of the GDR clubs Chemie Leipzig and Chemie Böhlen.
13 Viktoria Frankfurt/Oder is the successor of Vorwärts Frankfurt/Oder. The club was founded when the whole Vorwärts Berlin team was transferred from the capital to the town on the Polish border. For a succinct account of all the name and place changes in the history of GDR football, see Baingo and Horn (2003).
14 *Nordostfußball* and *fussball hautnah* are magazines cum internet pages. On www.fussballfanseiten.de a number of pages may be found even for lower league clubs: third division 1. FC Union Berlin, for example, is still popular enough to have twelve fan pages, 1. FC Lokomotive Leipzig, recently founded anew in the eleventh division, can boast three homepages.
15 When a Berlin furniture dealer sold coffee cups with GDR logos, the director of the Stasi jail memorial site in Berlin Hohenschönhausen, Hubertus Knabe, sent an open letter of protest to the dealer. See also Doelfs (2003) and Schoelkopf (2004).

References

Anderson, B. (1991) *Imagined Communities: Reflections on the Origin and Spread of Nationalism*, London: Verso.
Baingo, A. and Horn, M. (eds) (2003) *Die Geschichte der DDR-Oberliga*, Göttingen: Verlag Die Werkstatt.
Blees, T. (1999) *90 Minuten Klassenkampf: Das Länderspiel BRD – DDR 1974*, Frankfurt/Main: Fischer 1999.

Brüggemeier, F.-J. (2004) *Zurück auf dem Platz: Deutschland und die Fußball-Weltmeisterschaft 1954*, Munich: DVA.

Brussig, T. (2001) *Leben bis Männer*, Frankfurt/Main: Fischer.

—— (2003) 'Sich die ganze Welt vom Fußball her erklären: Thomas Brussig im Gespräch mit Stefan Hermanns und Markus Hesselmann', in R. Adelmann, R. Parr and T. Schwarz (eds) *Querpässe: Beiträge zur Literatur-, Kultur- und Mediengeschichte des Fußballs*, Heidelberg: Synchron.

Dann, O. (1996) *Nation und Nationalismus in Deutschland 1770 bis 1990*, Munich: C.H. Beck.

Dieckmann, C. (1999) '"Nur ein Leutzscher ist ein Deutscher": Fußball in der DDR', in Deutscher Fußball-Bund (eds) *100 Jahre DFB: Die Geschichte des Deutschen Fußball-Bundes*, Berlin: Sportverlag.

Doelfs, G. (2003) 'Produkte des DDR-Sozialismus auf dem Vormarsch: Bürgerrechtler warnen vor verklärender Ostalgie und Pop-Sozialismus – Kritische Auseinandersetzung mit Unrechtssystem gefordert', *Die Welt*, 13 April.

Ewald, M. (1994) *Ich war der Sport: Wahrheiten und Legenden aus dem Wunderland der Sieger*, Berlin: Elefanten Press.

Fuchs, R. and Ullrich, K. (1990) *Lorbeerkranz und Trauerflor. Aufstieg und 'Untergang' des Sportwunders DDR*, Berlin: Dietz.

Fuge, J. (2004) 'Von Fußballanhängern und schlachtenbummlern', in F. Willman (ed.) *Fußball-Land DDR: Anstoß, Abpfiff, Aus*, Berlin: Eulenspiegel.

Gellner, E. (1983) *Nations and Nationalism*, New York: Cornell University Press.

Gläser, A. (2000) *Der BFC war schuld am Mauerbau: Ein stolzer Sohn des Proletariats erzählt*, Berlin: Aufbau.

—— (2004) '1980', in F. Willmann (ed.) *Fußball-Land DDR: Anstoß, Abpfiff, Aus*, Berlin: Eulenspiegel.

Gröschner, A. (1999) *Sieben Tränen muß ein Club-Fan weinen: 1. FC Magdeburg – Eine Fußballegende*, Leipzig: Gustav Kiepenheuer.

Hesse-Lichtenberger, U. (2002) *Tor! The Story of German Football*, London: WSC.

Hesselmann, M. and Rosentritt, M. (2000) *FC Hansa Rostock: Der Osten lebt*, Göttingen: Verlag Die Werkstatt.

Hobsbawm, E. (1992) *Nations and Nationalism since 1780: Programme, Myth, Reality*, Cambridge: Cambridge University Press (Canto).

Holmes, N. and Storey, D. (2004) 'Who are the boys in green? Irish identity and soccer in the Republic of Ireland', in A. Smith and D. Porter (eds), *Sport and National Identity in the Post-War World*, London: Routledge.

Hornby, N. (1992) *Fever Pitch*, London: Victor Gallancz.

Kuper, S. (1994) *Football against the Enemy*, London: Phoenix.

Leske, H. (2004) *Erich Mielke, die Stasi und das Runde Leder*, Göttingen: Verlag Die Werkstatt.

Schmidt, J. (2004) 'Offenbar gab es doch keinen Schießbefehl', in F. Willmann (ed.) *Fußball-Land DDR: Anstoß, Abpfiff, Aus*, Berlin: Eulenspiegel.

Schoelkopf, K. (2004) 'Ostalgie-Boom im Möbelhaus: Umstrittener Handel mit DDR-Symbolen – Kritiker: "Verhöhnung der Opfer"', *Die Welt*, 27 February.

Schöpflin, G. (1995) 'Nationalism and Ethnicity in Europe, East and West', in C.A. Kupchan (ed.) *Nationalism and Nationalities in the New Europe*, Ithaca and London: Cornell University Press.

Seifert, M. (1975) *Das Jahr des Sports*, Berlin: Sportverlag.

Smith, A. (1993) *National Identity: Ethnonationalism in Comparative Perspective*, Reno: University of Nevada Press.

Smith, A. and Porter, D. (eds) (2004) *Sport and National Identity in the Post-War World*, London: Routledge.

Spitzer, G. (2004) *Fußball und Triathlon: Sportentwicklung in der DDR*, Aachen: Meyer & Meyer.

Weber, M. (1997) 'Die "Nation"', in *Schriften zur Sozialgeschichte und Politik*, Stuttgart: Reclam.

Willmann, F. (ed.) (2004) *Fußball-Land DDR: Anstoß, Abpfiff, Aus*, Berlin: Eulenspiegel.

Wittich, E. (ed.) (1998) *Wo waren Sie, als das Sparwasser-Tor fiel?*, Hamburg: Konkret Literatur.

4   Soccer hooliganism in the German Democratic Republic

Mike Dennis

Pitch invasions, attacks on referees, running battles between drunken rivals, clashes between police and young fans, racist chanting and railway carriages demolished. These kinds of incidents were not restricted to Western Europe but were part of a common culture of soccer violence which established itself on both sides of the Berlin Wall. Despite concerted efforts by the East German Ministry of State Security (MfS) and the police to curtail football-related disorder, disturbances rose from 960 in the 1986–87 to 1,090 in the following season.[1] These figures made unwelcome reading for the ruling party, the SED, and its security forces. Not only did soccer hooliganism damage the reputation of the German Democratic Republic (GDR) both at home and abroad, it was not even supposed to exist in a society which claimed to have eliminated its preconditions. According to the tenets of Marxist-Leninist ideology, antisocial behaviour was rooted in exploitative capitalism and the concomitant social misery of young working-class males. Why football violence and other forms of public disorder were prevalent under state socialism and how they developed in the GDR are the subject of this chapter. In exploring these and other pertinent issues in the history of GDR football, the chapter draws on declassified files held in the central and regional archives of the Federal Commissioner for the Records of the Ministry of State Security of the Former German Democratic Republic (BStU), the Berlin branch of the Federal Archive and the Saxon State Archive Leipzig. These materials, which include reports and analyses by the police, the MfS and the SED Central Committee Department for Sport, provide invaluable insights into official policy-making on, and perceptions of, the hooligan 'wars'. They are complemented by several recent studies of GDR football, the MfS and football hooliganism, notably those by Baigno and Horn, Braun, Dennis, Leske, Luther, Pleil, Spitzer, Waibel and Willmann. Published recollections by fans and former members of the hooligan scene, as well as the memoirs of sports functionaries, complete the source base.

The 'strange world' of GDR football

Although there were exceptions, notably the defeat of West Germany in the 1974 World Cup and 1. FC Magdeburg's triumph in the European Cup

Winners' Cup in the same year, the GDR national team and clubs failed to distinguish themselves in international tournaments. Despite this under-achievement and the attraction of West German teams, watching domestic football was a major pastime: attendances at first division (Oberliga) matches reached 2,516,000 in 1976–77 season, albeit falling below the two million mark in 1984–85. Popular interest was catered for by television and radio as well as by the daily press and specialist publications such as *Fußballwoche* and *Deutsches Sportecho*. Although, in some respects, GDR football was, to quote Ulrich Hesse-Lichtenberger (2000: 277), a 'strange world', most of its characteristics were found elsewhere behind the Iron Curtain (Duke 1995: 92–3, 95, 101). Clubs changed their names with bewildering frequency and were relocated in accordance with political criteria, players were 'dele-gated' to leading clubs and were called up as reservists to the army in order to weaken less privileged teams. In the absence of a transfer market, players were induced to change clubs by the bait of an apartment, a car and illegal payments above the basic salary. Journalists were under pressure to report favourably on Berlin Football Club Dynamo (BFC) and evidence has been uncovered of the doping of footballers when playing for the GDR and for their club in international tournaments (Spitzer 2004: 59–69). Referees, players, trainers and officials collaborated with the Stasi, SED organizations were attached to clubs to ensure ideological and political compliance, and BFC Dynamo, the Minister of State's favourite team, won the Oberliga for ten consecutive seasons, from 1979 to 1988, before an ever-diminishing home support.

Several of these features influenced supporters' behaviour. Passions were aroused by the advantage derived by clubs attached to a powerful sponsor and by the blatant favouring of BFC Dynamo by top referees. Local and regional rivalries were intense. The antagonism between SG Dynamo Dresden and BFC Dynamo may have had deep roots in Saxon and Prussian history but it was also fuelled by contemporary Dresden's resentment at the better provision of housing and consumer goods in the capital. When crowd trouble broke out over the referee's partiality towards BFC Dynamo at an Oberliga match in December 1978, Dresden supporters complained that 'we are cheated everywhere, even on the sports field' (Pleil 2001: 219). By a curious irony, both teams belonged to the Dynamo Sports Association, the umbrella sports association of the Ministry of State Security and the Ministry of the Interior. Erich Mielke, the autocratic and powerful Minister of State Security, who was also chair of the well-endowed Dynamo Sports Association, was determined that BFC would prevail over its Dresden comrades. The Saxon club's famous sweeper, Hans-Jürgen Doener, recalled that Mielke told the Dresden players at their championship celebrations in 1978 that it was now the turn of BFC (Luther and Willmann 2003: 70–1). The following season witnessed the start of BFC's long domination of the Oberliga, due in no small part to Mielke's patronage. An earlier and much disputed attempt to fast-track the Berliners to the title took place in

November 1954, when Mielke ordered the relocation of the SG Dynamo
Dresden players to Berlin, where they entered the Oberliga as the newly
formed SC Dynamo Berlin. The club was renamed BFC Dynamo twelve
years later. The tribal rivalry between the teams and their fans on the Spree
and the Elbe even spread to members of the Stasi's own Guard Regiment
in Dresden. In 1985, their behaviour at a match between the two teams
was likened by one Stasi officer to that of 'rioting fans'; some had cried
out 'bent champions!' ('Schiebermeister!') as BFC were leaving the pitch.[2]
Disturbances by spectators were endemic. Only three years earlier, one
Dresden fan had complained to a top SED functionary, Rudi Hellmann,
that rioting occurred in recent years only when BFC played in Dresden.
'Berlin rowdies,' he protested, 'had demolished the stadium and injured a
number of children . . . I am of the opinion that we are all citizens of our
republic and that chants of "Prussia" and "Saxony" by BFC supporters do
not belong in our stadia.'[3]

BFC's rise was also bitterly resented by 1. FC Union Berlin, their great
rivals in the capital. The 'Irons', who played in humble surroundings at
their stadium *An der Alten Försterei* in the Köpenick district had run through
several name changes before settling on that of 1. FC Union in 1966.
Although it won the FDGB cup two years later, it remained a yo-yo team.
Union's fans cherished its image as the eternal underdog and as a football
club rooted firmly in the working class, in contrast to the Stasi-sponsored
big brother across the city. (See the interviews with Union fans in Luther
and Willmann (2000: 103, 136) and in Farin and Hauswald (1998: 77–8).)
Their resentment at the delegation of leading players to BFC was com-
pounded by anger at referees' blatant bias in favour of Mielke's team. With
Union becoming a focus of hooligan attention, its home games against
BFC were transferred by the German Football Association (DFV) for reasons
of safety to the *Stadion der Weltjugend* from 1976 onwards. A situation
analogous to that in Berlin existed in Leipzig, where competition was
fierce between the city's foremost team 1. FC Lokomotive (Lok) Leipzig
and the underdogs at BSG Chemie Leipzig. The latter was regarded by its
fans as the 'local' team in contrast to Lok, which had been created in the
early 1960s on orders from above and was subsequently nurtured as one
of the GDR's elite clubs (Fuge 1997: 61, 74–5; Remath and Schneider
1999: 68–9).

The structure of GDR football was overhauled on several occasions, partly
to raise standards and partly as a result of the machinations of powerful
political leaders and interest groups at regional and central level. While
Erich Mielke, a member of the SED Politbüro as well as security minister,
is the best known of these leaders, his Politbüro colleagues Harry Tisch
and Egon Krenz were also involved in a game of political football. The
former had been head of the SED Regional Administration in Rostock until
he became chair of the FDGB, the trade union organization, in 1975. Krenz
had held the key post of SED Central Committee Secretary for Security,

Youth and Sport since 1983. Many political leaders took a keen interest in football and used their connections and resources to promote their favourite team and boost the prestige of their region or organization. This pattern is repeated elsewhere, especially at the level of the state enterprises and the large-scale economic units known as combines. In consequence, central control was weaker in football than in many other branches of sport. The main authorities for sport, the German Gymnastics and Sports Association (DTSB), the DFV and even the SED Central Committee's Department for Sport, were unable to dictate the development of GDR football and had to work in conjunction with, and sometimes against, these other interest groups. The DFV was a subsidiary of the DTSB, the overarching organisation for GDR sport. The ruthlessly energetic DTSB president, Manfred Ewald, was the mastermind behind the emergence of the GDR as a world leader in athletics, swimming, bobsleighing and many other sports. Football was a notable exception. In his memoirs, written after German unification, Ewald attributed the mediocrity of GDR football to undue interference by the political and economic functionaries at both central and regional level (Ewald 1994: 56–7), an opinion which was shared by the DFV.[4]

Given the inflated egos and the clash of interests, arguments were bound to erupt from time to time in the upper echelons of party and state. The standard of refereeing was a bone of contention. On one occasion, during the 1985 FDGB Cup Final between BFC and Dynamo Dresden, Harry Tisch was so incensed at the performance of Rossner that he protested to Mielke that such referees were damaging the credibility of the competition.[5] Rossner was later banned from refereeing international and Oberliga matches. Even the SED-controlled daily newspapers such as *Neues Deutschland*, the specialist sport press and the FDJ organ *Junge Welt*, were sometimes critical of referees for favouring Mielke's team. When *Junge Welt* found fault with referee Stumpf for awarding a late penalty to BFC in the game against 1. FC Lok Leipzig in March 1986, Mielke complained to Ewald and Hellmann that such scribbling undermined the standing of both BFC and the Dynamo Sports Association (*MfS und Leistungssport* 1994: 105). Had it been known that several top referees, Stumpf included, were Stasi informers, then the atmosphere among the dignitaries in the guest area as well as on the terraces would have been further inflamed. There is, it should be stressed, no evidence to show that referees were under direct instructions from the MfS to favour BFC (Leske 2004: 479–81; Spitzer 2004: 73–8).

While passions usually ran high at BFC games, particularly away from home, disturbances also occurred when other teams clashed. In 1982, 1. FC Union's ground was closed for two matches as a result of crowd trouble triggered by referee Habermann's decisions in the game against FC Vorwärts Frankfurt. The police had been forced to come to the rescue of Habermann, a frequent target of criticism for his partiality towards BFC (Luther and Willmann 2000: 114–15). Biased refereeing as a source of unrest is a thread running back to the very first major football-related disorder. When BSG Horch Zwickau beat SG Dresden-Friedrichstadt 5–1 in a match which decided the Oberliga title at the end of the 1949–50 season, their victory was attributed by rioting fans to unfair decisions by the referee against the Dresden team, for reasons which were related to what was in official eyes a 'politically incorrect' bourgeois club (Luther 2004: 9–10; Leske 2004: 109–10). Most of the Dresden players, including Helmut Schön, left the GDR for the West soon afterwards.

Football hooliganism kicks off

Although football matches in the 1950s and 1960s were venues for violence, antagonisms tended to be low-key, ritualistic and verbal. The return of 1. FC Union Berlin to the Oberliga in the 1970–1971 season, however, marked a new departure as the seriousness of incidents in connection with Union's clash with BFC turned football hooliganism into a societal issue worthy of the close attention of the MfS (Leske 2004: 432–4). While fan disorder continued throughout the 1970s, it would not be until the 1980s that violence became widespread with a concomitant spiralling state concern and engagement. Finally, from about the mid-1980s onwards, the infiltration of soccer by skinheads inaugurated a significant shift towards a more militant and less casual soccer terrace culture. At this stage it should be noted that there is no watertight definition of soccer hooliganism, partly because the term is sometimes used to encompass not only acts of physical violence but also disturbances of a lower order. Furthermore, whether or not certain acts are referred to as 'soccer hooliganism' is often dependent on whether they cover activities which, as in England, the government and the media may deem to be illegitimate. The East German police and Ministry of State Security, the enforcers of law and order, never shied away from attaching pejorative labels to violent football supporters and what they regarded as other deviant youth subcultures, whether punks or rock fans, skinheads or heavy metallers. They were all subsumed under the category of 'negative-decadent forces'. While the label was all-encompassing, a differentiation was made between the small minority or hard core of 'negative-decadent' fans and those supporters who did little more than chant provocative slogans. This distinction may be illustrated by the Leipzig regional police's breakdown of offences committed by 142 followers of 1. FC Lok Leipzig and BSG Chemie Leipzig during the 1986–87 season when over 71 per cent of the acts were committed by 16- to 22-year-olds.[6] Most of the incidents were low-key, that is, 'undisciplined actions' on public transport and elsewhere, such as drunkenness and urinating in public (60.5 per cent); insulting and provoking spectators, passengers on public transport and the police (14.1 per cent); and throwing fireworks and missiles on to the pitch (9.2 per cent). The most serious offences consisted of causing damage to train coaches, stadia and public facilities (7.7 per cent) and physical assaults on other fans, spectators and passers-by (8.5 per cent).

The voluminous documentation compiled by the Stasi, the police, the SED and the football authorities provides numerous illustrations of specific incidents. The taunting of opposing fans ranged from accusing BFC of being 'bent champions' to belittling them as 'Jewish pigs', 'Berlin Jews' and 'leaders of Turks'.[7] Chants which the authorities regarded as politically motivated were 'Stasi out!' and 'The fuzz are work-shy'.[8] The kind of vandalism which frequently occurred on public transport, at railway stations and in city centres is described in an official complaint lodged by a school group against the uncivilized behaviour of Chemie Leipzig fans during a train journey from Quedlinburg to Leipzig. Bottles were thrown at the pupils, the carriage was soon reduced to the state of a cattle truck, fans sprawled on the floor in a drunken stupor, some of the males exposed themselves and many sang Nazi songs.[9] In the same month, October 1987, when Stahl Brandenburg met 1. FC Karl-Marx-Stadt (Chemnitz), fireworks were set off in the stadium and damage to trams by 'negative-decadent' away supporters amounted to 5,000 GDR Marks. Simultaneously, about 300 fans of 1. FC Union were fighting with followers of 1. FC Lok Leipzig at the Berlin-Schönefeld railway station.[10]

Yet this should not have happened, for seventeen years earlier the MfS had devised an elaborate series of measures to prevent a repeat of the rioting by Union fans during the derby with BFC. The operation was designated OV 'Kraketer'. An OV (*Operativer Vorgang* – operational case or campaign) was the most highly organized type of operation conducted by the MfS against groups or individuals who supposedly posed a threat to the socialist order of the GDR. A less complex campaign, an OPK (*Operative Personenkontrolle*), was often the prelude to an OV. A differentiation was attempted between 'hostile-negative' and 'negative-decadent' forces. 'Hostile-negative' forces, such as the human rights and peace groups of the 1980s, were regarded as the more serious threat. They were allegedly political enemies who, in conjunction with Western imperialism, were pursuing acts aimed at destroying state and party. That the forces arrayed against the socialist system were seemingly so wide-ranging may be explained by the fragile legitimacy of the SED regime, the perception of Western imperialism as an omnipresent enemy determined to undermine the GDR, the authorities' deep-rooted distrust of East German youth and the determination of Mielke and his ministry to use every opportunity to expand their security empire. However, in the age of détente, the SED and the MfS had to pay greater respect to their domestic and international audience than they had in the 1950s. OVs and OPKs, it was realized, were an appropriate alternative to, albeit not a substitute for, overt forms of repression and were integral to the system of quiet or insidious repression, that is, the combating of subversive activity by 'softer' methods of control. The Stasi called this 'operational decomposition' (*operative Zersetzung*); political necessity was therefore the mother of an incongruous operational invention. With the aid of unofficial collaborators (IMs), the ministry's officers sought to divide, paralyse and isolate their targets in order to foil or stop hostile-negative actions. This was the aim of OV 'Kraketer'. Under the direction of Department XX of the MfS Administration of what was then called Greater-Berlin, IMs and the Stasi service units were instructed to draw up a list of the active supporters of 1. FC Union, to identify their political views, to uncover any links with the West and to discover who were the negative elements and their leaders. The Union players also came under close surveillance. Reliable IMs were to penetrate the inner circle of the 'negative' fans and, together with full-time officers, to keep watch over every Union game. In these ways, sufficient information was to be gathered in order to apprehend the key figures and to eliminate the problem as quickly as possible.[11]

This proved to be a Canute-like aspiration: in December 1971, trouble broke out once more at the Union–BFC encounter at the Berlin *Sportforum*. The eight persons arrested were described by the Stasi as 'unstable and of primitive intelligence'.[12] With disorder continuing at Union matches, Mielke urged Krenz, the Central Committee Secretary for Youth, State Security and Sport, to authorize action against what the Stasi boss called 'negative-decadent' youths whose behaviour was a threat to society. An MfS information bulletin accompanying Mielke's request noted that six 'negative-decadent' Union supporters had assaulted a GDR citizen and damaged the window of a shop in the East Berlin district of Lichtenberg. During the first half of the 1976 to 1977 season, twenty-three preliminary proceedings and seventy-four administrative penalty proceedings had been instituted.[13]

East Berlin was not the only centre of football-related disorder. Other towns and cities were affected too (Waibel 1996: 109–16). During the 1976 to 1977 season, the number of unruly fans attached to Lok Leipzig and Chemie Leipzig was estimated by the Leipzig regional police force at between 100 and 300. The bulk of offenders, about 80 per cent, were 15 to 18 years of age. A displacement of incidents, it was noted, had occurred from inside or in the vicinity of the stadium to the inner city and the main station. In 1976, nineteen preliminary criminal proceedings had been instituted against fourteen offenders, including five for rowdyism and two for vilification of the state. Forty-six administrative penalty proceedings were implemented to deal with minor forms of rowdy behaviour and damage to property.[14] While unpublished internal police and Stasi files are the main sources for these kinds of incidents, reports appeared from time to time in the media. For example, the authorities' growing concern was signalled by the publication in 1983 of a book on deviance among young people. The book revealed that supporters of FC Rot-Weiss Erfurt had caused trouble in Aue, Halle and Leipzig in 1979. Three fans were jailed for assault and for damage to property (Queißer 1983: 98–9).

Soccer violence and disorder in the 1980s

The failure of the Stasi, the police, the SED and the DFV to quell disturbances is attested by the detailed statistics compiled by these bodies from 1978 until the end of the 1989 season. A sample is to be found in Table 4.1, much of it derived from the Stasi's Central Operational Staff (ZOS). One of this organ's jobs was to assemble data and prepare critical analyses and surveys of incidents of public disorder. In its review of the period 1978 to 1981, it drew attention to a rise in the number and seriousness of football-related offences, above all at games involving 1. FC Union Berlin. Of the 472 arrests made between February and December 1980, 245 had occurred in connection with the 'Irons'. On the other side of the capital, little trouble had occurred at BFC matches due to a heavy police and steward presence.[15] Increasingly, ZOS and other bodies homed in on a hard core of 'negative-decadent' fans, the inveterate soccer hooligans. Numbers were relatively small, Union having only about 150 to 200 in 1986 (Leske 2004: 455). Aged predominantly between 14 and 22 years, it was members of the hard-core groups at Union and elsewhere who committed the serious acts of vandalism and assault described elsewhere in this chapter. Towards the middle of the decade, a significant radicalization occurred as the skinheads added a more explicit racism and lethal militancy to the hooligan scene. This is one of the reasons why the MfS Main Department XX concluded in 1988 that while the actual number of incidents showed a slightly downward trend, their intensity and seriousness was mounting.[16] It should be mentioned in parenthesis that this left an unfortunate legacy: once the controlling hand of the SED and Stasi had been removed with the disintegration of the communist regime, a wave of violence swept through many of the football grounds of East Germany (Leske 2004: 459–60).

The figures in Table 4.1, which represent an overview of arrests and legal measures, can be supplemented with data on the number and location of incidents and the clubs most affected. There were nine hundred and sixty recorded disturbances in the 1986 to 1987 season and 1,099 in the following season. In the latter period, more than half of offences were committed by the fans of HFC Chemie (188), 1. FC Union (171), FC Hansa Rostock (146) and FC Rot-Weiß Erfurt (126). 1. FC Magdeburg (88) and SG Dynamo Dresden (83) lagged some way behind. Not surprisingly, ZOS concluded that 'a decisive turning point had not been achieved in this area [public order]' despite numerous preventive and security measures.[17] As is apparent from the Leipzig regional police report mentioned above, vandalism and other acts of public disorder were by no means confined to the grounds. Thus in the 1987 to 1988 *Oberliga* season, 42 per cent occurred in the stadia, 35 per cent in the city or town where the game was being held and 23 per cent on the trains or property of the railway authority.[18]

The statistics in Table 4.1 do not provide a full picture, since there is reason to believe that some of the data were massaged by the police and

Table 4.1 Arrests and proceedings against offenders at Oberliga matches, 1984–89.

Season	Arrests	Preliminary criminal proceedings	Administrative penalty proceedings
1984–85	1,027	47	606
1985–86 (first half)	467	3%	40%
1986–87 (first half)	503	35	n.a.
1987–88	1,076	59	929
1988–89 (first half)	516	42	91
1988–89 (second half)*	80	6	49

Note
* Includes FDGB games.

Sources: Leske (2004: 441, 443, 447); BStU, ZA, HA XX, 221, 'Bericht über den Stand der Realisierung der Aufgabenstellung der Information des ZK der SED "Zur Lage auf den Fußball-plätzen und Vorschläge zur Gewährleistung von Ordnung und Sicherheit im Zusammenhang mit Fußballspielen"', Berlin (East), 30 December 1985, p. 37; BStU, ZA, HA XX, 221, 'Bericht über die Gewährleistung von Sicherheit und Ordnung bei Spielen der Fußball-Oberliga der DDR während der 1. Halbserie 1987/88', Berlin (East), 18 December 1987, p. 193; BStU, ZA, HA XX, 221, 'Bericht zum Stand der Sicherheit und Ordnung bei Fußballspielen im Spieljahr 1987/88', Berlin (East), 15 July 1988, p. 259; BStU, ZA, HA XX, 221, Appendix 1: 'Vorkommnisse/ Störungen bei Fußballspielen der Oberliga sowie Maßnahmen der DVP. 1. Halbserie 1988/89', n.p., n.d., p. 299; BStU, ZA, HA XX, 221, 'Berichterstattung über die Ergebnisse der Erhöhung von Ordnung und Sicherheit bei Fußballspielen', Berlin (East), 2 June 1989, p. 327.

the MfS before they reached the higher party authorities (Spitzer 2004: 94, 96). In what is anyhow a notoriously grey area, an examination of internal reports reveals that many incidents went unrecorded and arrests did not lead automatically to sentencing. Of the 467 persons arrested by the police in the first half of the 1985 to 1986 season, 109 were released after being cautioned.[19] Sometimes, as in the stadia and on public transport, the police were simply overwhelmed by the sheer scale of their task. One such case occurred at the Oberliga match in April 1988 between arch-rivals BFC and SG Dynamo Dresden. With serious overcrowding in the Dresden section of the ground and with tension rising, the police and MfS decided not to arrest fans who were destroying seats and shouting abuse at the Berlin team, since this would have only worsened the dangerous situation.[20] This was not an isolated occurrence. A supporter of Chemie Leipzig recalls that the police hardly dared intervene when brawls broke out in the *Georg-Schwarz-Sportpark* for fear of having thousands of spectators at their throats (Remath and Schneider 1999: 70). Public transport was another area where the police were overtaxed. Officers accompanying fans to away matches are known to have turned a blind eye to troublemakers on the trains, an indication that unruly behaviour was regarded by some officials as a normal football occurrence.[21] Finally, political decisions had a bearing on statistics. This was the case when the SED Politbüro instructed the security forces to smash the skinhead movement soon after the public furore following attacks by about thirty militant skinheads on visitors at an evening rock and punk concert at the *Zionskirche* in East Berlin on 30 October 1987. The inebriated skinheads had been at the 1. FC Union football game against Lok Leipzig earlier in the day.

Skinhead militancy

At the beginning of the 1980s, Western skinhead music, dress and militancy began to appeal to young East Germans, including the violent-oriented football supporters, as an alternative to the dominant political and ideological system and its institutional instruments such as the Free German Youth. Among the other nonconformist groups were punks, heavy metallers, Goths and New Romantics. Like the punks, the skinheads constituted an aggressive form of protest and, at least at first, were a cultural, not a conscious political tendency. However, by the later 1980s, a hybrid of xenophobia, hyper-nationalism and anti-communism had begun to take shape among a section of the skinheads. Among their targets were foreign contract workers from countries such as Mozambique and Angola. Their antagonism towards foreigners also coincided with mounting popular antipathy towards the Vietnamese, who were seen, especially in the industrial conurbation of the southern regions, as rivals for consumer goods in short supply. In December 1987, there were, according to MfS data, approximately 750 skinheads in the GDR and about thirty-eight small groups. East Berlin was the main centre and BFC and Union the two football magnets, not only for those from the capital but also for skinheads from the neighbouring Potsdam and Frankfurt/Oder regions. Typical meeting places were the semi-structured environment of pubs, youth clubs, discos, gyms and Oberliga football grounds. A common interest in football served as a link not only between skinheads across the GDR but also with those in Hungary, the Federal Republic and Czechoslovakia.[22] A spate of trips to football matches in neighbouring socialist countries by 'ambassadors' in black bomber jackets was, however, a highly unwelcome development for the SED. Such was the importance of football for the skinheads and other rowdies that Walter Süß has likened the protection afforded by the stadia to that provided by the Protestant churches for the alternative peace and ecological groups (Süß 1996: 12–13).

The skinheads were able to tap into and then influence the extreme right potential which pre-dated their appearance and had found expression in cries such as 'cyanide B for BFC' (see the interviews with Union fans in Luther and Willmann 2000: 130, 138). By the end of December 1985, about thirty or forty skinheads were associated with the two Berlin Oberliga clubs, many of them attached to the BFC fan club 'Anale Berlin'.[23] Its following made no secret of their glorification of fascism. In August 1985, fourteen members of the group assaulted people in Dresden and bawled out such fascist songs as 'My father was an SS-soldier'.[24] They were arrested and nine received prison sentences. Among other Oberliga teams which attracted skinheads were Lok Leipzig, FC Hansa Rostock and BSG Energie Cottbus. They were few in number, however, with only two to three skinheads turning up at the Stadium of Friendship in Cottbus.[25]

After a period of relative tolerance by the authorities, the MfS and the police carried out numerous operations to undermine and destroy the hard-core militant skinhead element. A crackdown was launched on the BFC skinheads in August 1987 and, three months later, against skinheads across the GDR after the *Zionskirche* incidents. Despite the many arrests, interrogations, deportations to the West and match bans, the skinheads were shaken but not crushed.[26] Indeed, the FDGB Cup Final between BFC and FC Carl-Zeiss-Jena at East Berlin's *Stadion der Weltjugend* in June 1988 was the scene of some of the most serious violence ever witnessed at a GDR football game. About 100 to 150 skinheads and other football hooligans gathered together in nearby Pankow before proceeding in formation to the match. They chanted fascist songs and clashed violently with other supporters.[27] Among the reasons for the survival of the skinheads is that they went underground temporarily and dressed in a less conspicuous manner in order to escape the attention of the security forces. More significantly, however, is that they did not stand in isolation but could fall back on the loose networks which they had formed with Western skinheads and East German youth groups, such as the 'negative' fans at Union and BFC. The Stasi was not oblivious to this development. In June 1988, Department XX/2 of the MfS East Berlin Administration identified a militant group of skinheads and a section of young fans who subordinated themselves at matches to the skinheads and, contrary to their usual behaviour, committed penal and a variety of minor offences.[28] This pyramid hierarchy of fans also comprised juvenile supporters who were attracted to skinhead culture, thereby creating what the Department called a 'reservoir of youthful followers'.[29] A secondary factor in the survival of the skinhead movement, as well as of the violent football fans, was the reluctance of MfS personnel to carry out their duties at BFC matches with the requisite devotion to duty.[30] This may have stemmed from the belief that such work was the province of the more lowly police rather than, as some police officers believed, the Stasi's softly-softly approach to BFC rowdies.[31]

Combating the hooligans

Despite concerted efforts by the football authorities, the SED and the security forces, especially from the end of the 1970s, football-related disorder remained a significant social problem. Myriad guidelines and recommendations, similar to those devised in the West, sought to quell antisocial behaviour by a more effective use of stewards at matches, restrictions on the sale of alcohol, football 'special' trains, better liaison between the police, the MfS and the Free German Youth, educational measures and the infiltration of the hard-core element by youthful informers. A series of punitive measures was also implemented, among them the closure of grounds, exclusion orders, fines, arrests and convictions. The Penal Code gave the police and the MfS plenty of scope for punishing offenders, above all the articles on rowdiness, public vilification and hindering state or social activity. Article 215 on rowdiness, for example, prescribed punishment of up to five years for anyone who, through disregard for public order or the rules of the socialist community, threatened or caused gross annoyance to people or malicious damage to objects or equipment.[32]

While all these measures were pursued throughout the 1980s, some received greater emphasis as a result of external pressures and events. After the disaster at Brussels' Heysel stadium in 1985, in which thirty-nine people were killed and many more injured, the GDR responded to FIFA guidelines with a more rigorous segregation of opposing fans by means of barriers and by the installation of higher perimeter fences. Safety, however, remained a serious problem: many of the GDR stadia were urgently in need of modernization, with the outbreak of fire in the wooden stands a real worry when fans set off fireworks and burned banners and newspapers. While the Bradford fire disaster in Yorkshire, England, a fortnight before Heysel, was a painful reminder of this kind of danger, there was a chronic shortage of funds to carry out the necessary ground redevelopment.

The cultivation of desirable traits by persuasion and example was a favoured method in the preventive approach to football unruliness. This entailed appealing to fans to behave in a manner deemed appropriate to socialist society, urging players to play the game fairly and arranging special sessions in schools and at the workplace for the discussion of public order issues. In addition, rowdies were 'named and shamed' in football programmes, the press carried reports on prison sentences as a warning to others and parents were informed of their offsprings' misdemeanours. However, since this low-key approach enjoyed only limited success,[33] more rigorous forms of control were implemented. Closed-circuit television was used to identify offenders, bans were imposed on miscreants, the sale of tickets was restricted and stewards were employed in greater numbers not only on special trains but also at the grounds. The stewards' tasks included enforcing the ban on alcohol and missiles in the stadia and helping to eject unruly fans. All these measures entailed a high level of co-operation between club officials, the police and the MfS.[34] Clubs were required to establish a separate working group for order and safety (*Arbeitsgruppe Ordnung und Sicherheit*) to oversee the various measures at local level, and in 1986 a commission attached to the Presidium of the DFV was set up for the direction of policy at central level. By the end of 1985 most clubs had established a working group, the membership consisting of representatives not only from the clubs themselves but also from organs such as the SED, the police, the Stasi and the FDJ.[35]

Stewards were one of the keys to the maintenance of public order. They were provided by the clubs as well as by the FDJ and other bodies. A target of between 150 to 200 stewards per Oberliga club was set.[36] While 'frisking' could be very thorough, as I came to realize on visits to Union matches, the stewarding system left much to be desired. The turnover among stewards was high, and 'negative-decadent' fans managed to infiltrate their ranks. Some stewards neglected their duties and, on occasions, became involved in disorderly acts.[37] BFC, which recruited its stewards from among its own youthful fans, as well as from the DTSB and the Central Administrative Office of the Dynamo Sports Association, did not always appreciate outside assistance. It was reported in 1988 that the DTSB stewards, most of whom were pensioners, had proved to be a disruptive influence on account of their drunken behaviour.[38]

The many fan clubs which sprang up during the 1980s were another means by which the DFV and the other organs responsible for football hoped to maintain law and order. In 1988, the Stasi estimated that there were 353 fan clubs in the GDR, with an average membership of between five and thirty-five. Dynamo Dresden had the most fan clubs (seventy-four),[39] and a ratio of one registered to four non-registered fan club members.[40] The authorities were highly suspicious of these clubs, since they regarded them as focal points for rowdies and as conduits for the highly undesirable Western fan culture, whether hairstyles, chants or fashion (Braun 2004: 440–1). However, after much hesitation, it was decided to try and use them in the campaign to control hooliganism. They were permitted to register as associations in accordance with the 1975 Decree on the Founding and Activities of Associations and encouraged to co-operate with the parent football club. While members of some fan clubs were undoubtedly attracted by incentives such as privileged access to players and tickets, going to club discos and football tournaments, others could not be reached, since they were spontaneous formations and were contemptuous of the notion of official registration.[41]

The leading SED and sports functionaries, sensitive to the reputation of the GDR, were determined that antisocial behaviour should not occur in full view of the international media at club matches in European competitions and games involving the national team. Matches between East and West German teams were especially problematic for the SED, since many young East German supporters openly showed their allegiance to clubs such as Bayern Munich and HSV. Frequent visits by Hertha Berlin fans to 1. FC Union Berlin matches and banners displaying messages such as 'Jena greets Uerdingen' were seen by the SED as unwelcome signs of an empathy with the clubs across the Wall. Even more crucially, chants of 'Germany, Germany' were interpreted as a rejection of the official SED position that the national question had been 'resolved' by the formation of two nations, one socialist and the other capitalist. The Stasi and the police went to great lengths to prevent manifestations of German national identity and violent incidents by GDR fans. At a quarter-final game in the European Cup between BFC and the holders Nottingham Forest in 1980, most of the tickets were distributed to Stasi officers and family members. In addition, 1,200 MfS officers, several hundred members of the Stasi Guard Regiment 'F. Dzierzynski' and 800 police were drafted in to control the crowd.[42] Unofficial collaborators (IMs) were also used at games, both in the GDR and in neighbouring socialist countries, as part of a plethora of counter-measures.

OV 'Kraketer' was an early example of the ways in which the Stasi used IMs to observe and infiltrate the 'negative-decadent' football scene of 1. FC Union Berlin. Surveillance, whether in an OV or an OPK, was usually comprehensive. Forty IMs and other kinds of collaborators attached to the Stasi District Service Unit Dresden-Stadt and fifty IMs of the local Criminal Police were deployed at Dynamo Dresden's home game against BFC in March 1987.[43] The radicalization of the hooligan scene in the mid-1980s added momentum to the Stasi's search for IMs among the hard core and other 'negative-decadent' fans. Such informers, it was envisaged, would help the ministry and the police to identify the leaders, their links with Western hooligans and skinheads and plans to cause trouble. Recruitment was difficult, as the hard core were dismissive of appeals to socialist convictions, opposed to snitching on their mates and were likely to 'betray' any approach by the Stasi. Material incentives served only to reinforce negative impressions of the MfS and the police. Given these difficulties, recruiting officers preferred to concentrate on those youths who were not already integrated into a 'negative-decadent' football group and who, potentially, had some respect for law and order. 'Atonement' for previous misdemeanours and financial and other material advantages were also used as bait.[44]

Explaining the inexplicable

The intensification and the greater sophistication of the state's operations notwithstanding, football-related antisocial behaviour survived in a system which, so the regime's ideologues asserted, had removed its basic preconditions. According to the standard interpretation, which was regurgitated in Stasi internal reports and the theses written by officers, soccer hooliganism was inherent within capitalism, not socialism. Typical of this approach is an analysis compiled in 1981 by the Central Operation Staff (ZOS) of the MfS, in which it was contended that the commercialization of the game drove profit-minded clubs in England and West Germany to search for instant success and the players, who were little more than commodities, into an aggressive style of play. Aggression on the field was replicated off it. At a time of growing social misery and unemployment among the working class, young people in particular sought in football a violent outlet for their frustrations with everyday life. The violence was exacerbated by the sensationalism of the media and the clubs' lack of interest in putting a stop to hooliganism.[45]

But how did the Stasi explain the outbreak of soccer-related disorder in the GDR? Its officers were often as bemused as social psychologists, ethnographers and sociologists adhering to a figurational perspective in the United Kingdom who tried to explain why certain individuals and groups had caught and transmitted the 'English disease' (Williams 2001: 45–50). As the ministry failed to uncover any direct steering of the skinheads and the hard-core soccer fans by imperialist agencies, it fell back on the notion of political-ideological diversion (PID) in the form of Western media transmissions, fan culture, the illegal distribution of football literature and personal contacts between East and West German fans. Certain sections of GDR youth were seen as particularly susceptible to this method of undermining GDR society. It was not simply a structural issue in that younger age groups were more prone to violence than older generations but that specific conditions in the family and at work predisposed them to a kind of behaviour at variance with the all-round socialist personalities beloved of SED propagandists. The type of family circumstances which, according to the MfS, was conducive to 'negative-decadent' behaviour was where parents failed to control their children's consumption of Western media,[46] and where homes were broken and relationships disrupted. It has also been argued by Bernd Wagner, an expert on right-wing extremism and youth violence in the GDR, that those football fans and others who were oriented towards violence came from the margins of society (Wagner 1995: 62). While further studies are required to test this kind of observation, preliminary research conducted between October 1987 and November 1989 by two sociologists attached to Humboldt University does not support the notion of 'abnormality'. Commissioned by the criminal police with the blessing of the MfS, the researchers concluded from their study of skinheads, punks and other subcultural groups that the level of qualifications, family status and general circumstances corresponded to a cross-section of society (Kinner and Richter 2000: 273, 279–80). Although they did not focus on football-related violence as such, the overlap between the hard-core football fans and skinheads suggests that their results may be of relevance in this area too. A study of the data on the social profile of the football hooligans, which is available in the files compiled by the DVP and the Stasi's Main Departments IX and XX, may contribute to a better understanding as to whether offenders were incorporated into or excluded from mainstream GDR society.

Some of the variables which GDR officialdom identified as significant for the genesis of football 'hooliganism' may also be found in social scientific and governmental publications in the West. An internal assessment originating in the Central Committee Department for Sport, with comments by Egon Krenz, highlighted the highly charged atmosphere at football matches, excessive drinking, the socialization of young fans into violence, the release from boredom with everyday life derived from the emotional 'buzz' of risk-taking, a 'primitive urge' to attract attention and enhance the status of the group, opposition to the police and a desire to demonstrate superiority and strength.[47] Although these features were, it was conceded, similar to those in the West, the official line continued to stress political-ideological diversion by the imperialist foe and the uncritical emulation of Western norms and behaviour by morally weak and easily influenced persons.[48] This tendency to overlook the specificity of conditions in the GDR was heavily criticized by Walter Friedrich, the head of the Central Institute for Youth Research in Leipzig. In a confidential memorandum to Egon Krenz in 1987, he argued that an exaggeration of the responsibility of the class enemy for the growing disenchantment of GDR youth with the socialist system was both simplistic and a barrier to the urgent need for a long overdue analysis of conditions in the GDR. Nor, he argued, should one interpret the verbal abuse of the security forces at football grounds as a political 'affront' and evidence of planned action.[49] He could have added that many of the football-related troubles stemmed not only from subjective decisions by referees but also from the popular perception that these reflected a politically driven discrimination. The SED leaders, as well as the Stasi, were unwilling, however, to grasp the nettle of self-analysis. It was more comfortable to blame external forces rather than examine the role played by social control as a trigger for disorder, by the friend-foe mentality of state propaganda, by the militarization of everyday life and by the aggressive masculinity which underpinned the 'cop culture' of the Stasi and police. This kind of intellectual rigidity not only led to an overemphasis on heavy security to curb football-related disturbances but, more significantly, it also helped to drive a wedge between the SED elites and young people, and so accelerated the collapse of communist rule.

Notes

1 BStU, ZA, HA XX, 221, 'Bericht zum Stand der Sicherheit und Ordnung bei Fußballspielen im Spieljahr 1987/88', Berlin (East), 15 July 1988, p. 259.
2 BStU, ZA, HA XX, 2701, 'Information', Berlin (East), 22 May 1985, p. 13.
3 SAPMO-BArchiv, DY 30/4981, Letter to Hellmann, Dresden, 30 April 1982, pp. 46–7.
4 SAPMO-BArchiv, DY30/4963, 'Einschätzung zum Leistungsstand und zur Leistungszielerfüllung im DFV der DDR', [1985], p. 206.
5 BStU, ZA, HA, 2701, 'Tonbandbericht IMS "Michael Hirsch" vom 3.7.1985', p. 15.
6 StAL, SEDBLLp, 1681, 'Lage zur öffentlichen Ordnung und Sicherheit bei Fußballspielen der Saison 1986/87', Leipzig, 11 August 1987, pp. 16, 18.
7 BStU, ZA, HA XX, 221, 'Auswertung des Sicherungseinsatzes zum Fußball-oberligaspiel BFC – Dynamo Dresden am 6.4.1988, 17.00 Uhr, im Friedrich-Ludwig-Jahn Sportpark', Berlin (East), 8 April 1988, p. 233.
8 SAPMO-BArchiv, DY 30/IV 2/2.039/251, 'Information zur Lage auf den Fußballplätzen der DDR und Vorschläge zur besseren Gewährleistung von Ordnung und Sicherheit im Zusammenhang mit Fußballspielen', [1984], p. 23.
9 BStU, ZA, HA XX, 2700, 'Eingabe wegen Bahnfahrt am 18.10.87 von Quedlinburg über Wegeleben nach Leipzig', 23 October 1987, p. 68.

10 BStU, ZA, HA XX, 221, 'Bericht über die Gewährleistung von Sicherheit und Ordnung bei Spielen der Fußball-Oberliga der DDR während der 1. Halbserie 1987/88', Berlin (East), 18 December 1987, p. 194.
11 The key documents are in BStU, ZA, HA VIII, 925, vol. 14, pp. 6–8, 12–14.
12 BStU, ZA, HA XX, 1039, 'Bericht', Berlin (East), 27 December 1971, p. 8.
13 BStU, ZA, ZAIG, 2731, Mielke to Krenz, Berlin (East), 10 October 1987, pp. 6, 20.
14 StAL, BT/RdBLp, 24808, 'Information zur Lage auf dem Gebiet der öffentlichen Ordnung und Sicherheit im Zusammenhang mit Fußballspielen in der Stadt Leipzig und auf dem Territorium der Deutschen Reichsbahn', Leipzig, 20 January 1977, n.p.
15 BStU, Außenstelle Frankfurt (O), BVfS Frankfurt (O), BdL, 1684, 'Zusammenfassende Darstellung zur Problematik der Ausschreitungen bei Fußballspielen im In- und Ausland, insbesondere für den Zeitraum von 1978 bis 1981', Berlin (East), June 1981, pp. 12–13, 35.
16 BStU, ZA, HA XX, 221, 'Berichterstattung über die Ergebnisse der Erhöhung von Sicherheit und Ordnung bei Fußballspielen', Berlin (East), 14 June 1988, p. 251.
17 BStU, ZA, HA XX, 221, 'Bericht zum Stand der Sicherheit und Ordnung bei Fußballspielen im Spieljahr 1987/88', Berlin (East), 15 July 1988, p. 259.
18 Ibid.
19 BStU, ZA, HA XX, 221, 'Bericht über den Stand der Realisierung der Aufgabenstellung der Information des ZK der SED "Zur Lage auf den Fußballplätzen und Vorschläge zur Gewährleistung von Ordnung und Sicherheit im Zusammenhang mit Fußballspielen"', Berlin (East), 30 December 1985, p. 37.
20 See the report in BStU, ZA, HA XX, 221, 'Auswertung des Sicherungseinsatzes zum Fußballoberligaspiel BFC – Dynamo Dresden am 6.4.1988, 17.00 Uhr, im Friedrich-Ludwig-Jahn-Sportpark', Berlin (East), 8 April 1988, pp. 233–5.
21 BStU, ZA, HA XX, 221, 'Gesprächsvermerk zu einer Beratung im PdVP Berlin', Berlin (East), 20 October 1988, p. 281.
22 BStU, ZA, HA XX, 898, 'Einschätzung über die in der DDR existierenden Skinheads bzw. Skinheadgruppen sowie über die Ergebnisse und Wirksamkeit der politisch-operativen Arbeit zur Verhinderung und Unterbindung der von derartigen Jugendlichen ausgehenden Gefährdungen der Sicherheit und Ordnung', Berlin (East), 16 December 1987, pp. 27–9.
23 BStU, ZA, HA XX, 221, 'Bericht über den Stand der Realisierung der Aufgabenstellung der Informationen des ZK der SED "Zur Lage auf den Fußballplätzen und Vorschläge zur Gewährleistung von Ordnung und Sicherheit im Zusammenhang mit Fußballspielen"', Berlin (East), 30 December 1985, p. 32.
24 BStU, ZA, HA XX, 5147, 'Information über Entwicklung von Skinhead's und Fußball-Fan-Clubs des FC Union und des BFC', Berlin (East), January 1986, p. 250.
25 BStU, ZA, HA XX, 221, 'Information über die Situation von Ordnung, Disziplin und Sicherheit im Zusammenhang mit öffentlichkeitswirksamen Sportveranstaltungen im Bezirk Cottbus im Verlaufe des Jahres 1987', Cottbus, 28 December 1987, p. 187.
26 BStU, ZA, HA XX, 221, 'Bericht zum negativen Fußballanhang des BFC Dynamo in der Spielsaison 1987/88 und zu den Ergebnissen der politisch-operativen Bearbeitung', Berlin (East), 13 June 1988, pp. 245–6.
27 BStU, ZA, JHS, 21493, Rainer Taraschonnek, 'Diplomarbeit zum Thema: Erfordernisse der Erziehung und Befähigung von inoffiziellen Mitarbeitern (IM) zur operativen Bearbeitung von rechtsextremistischen Erscheinungen unter Jugendlichen der Hauptstadt', 1989, p. 14; BStU, ZA, HA IX, 1303, 'Informationen', n.d., n.p., pp. 69–70.

28 BStU, ZA, HA XX, 221. 'Bericht zum negativen Fußballanhang des BFC Dynamo in der Spielsaison 1987/88 und zu den Ergebnissen der politisch-operativen Bearbeitung', Berlin (East), 13 June 1988, p. 243.
29 BStU, ZA, HA XX, 221, 'Einschätzung zum jugendlichen Anhang des BFC Dynamo und zur Erhöhung von Sicherheit und Ordnung bei Fußballspielen der 1. Halbserie 1988/89', Berlin (East), 29 December 1988, p. 306.
30 BStU, ZA, HA XX, 221, 'Bericht über die Erhöhung von Ordnung und Sicherheit bei Fußballspielen', Berlin (East), 22 June 1989, p. 329.
31 BStU, ZA, HA XX, 221, 'Gesprächsvermerk zu einer Beratung im PdVP Berlin', Berlin (East), 20 October 1988, pp. 279–80.
32 For a list and discussion of the measures which could be used for countering hooliganism, see the document compiled by ZOS in BStU, Aussenstelle Frankfurt (O), BVfS Frankfurt (O), BdL, 1684, 'Zusammenfassende Darstellung zur Problematik der Ausschreitungen bei Fußballspielen im In- und Ausland, insbesondere für den Zeitraum von 1978 bis 1981', Berlin (East), June 1981, pp. 29–38.
33 For example, the enterprises and the vocational colleges had little interest in helping out; see BStU, ZA, HA XX, 2700, 'Beschlußvorlage 10/85 für das Büro des Präsidiums des Deutschen Fußball-Verbandes der DDR. Betr.: Maßnahmen zur Erhöhung von Ordnung und Sicherheit bei Fußballgroßveranstaltungen', Berlin (East), 1 March 1985, p. 21.
34 BStU, ZA, HA XX, 2700, 'Richtlinie für den Ordnungsdienst bei Fußballveranstaltungen der Oberliga- und Ligamannschaften des DFV der DDR', Berlin (East), December 1977, pp. 16–17.
35 BStU, ZA, HA XX, 221, 'Bericht über den Stand der Realisierung der Aufgabenstellung der Information des ZK der SED "Zur Lage auf den Fußballplätzen und Vorschläge zur Gewährleistung von Ordnung und Sicherheit im Zusammenhang mit Fußballspielen"', Berlin (East), 30 December 1985, pp. 30, 34–5.
36 BStU, ZA, ZAIG, 3543, 'Informationn über einige aktuelle Erkenntnisse zu Fragen der Gewährleistung von Ordnung und Sicherheit bei Spielen der Fußball-Oberliga der DDR', Berlin (East), 2 September 1986, p. 3.
37 BStU, ZA, HA XX, 221, 'Bericht über den Stand der Realisierung der Aufgabenstellung der Information des ZK der SED "Zur Lage auf den Fußballplätzen und Vorschläge zur Gewährleistung von Ordnung und Sicherheit im Zusammenhang mit Fußballspielen"', Berlin (East), 30 December 1985, p. 31.
38 BStU, ZA, HA XX, 221, 'Einschätzung zum jugendlichen Anhang des BFC Dynamo und zur Erhöhung von Sicherheit und Ordnung bei Fußballspielen der 1. Halbserie 1988/89', Berlin (East), 29 December 1988, p. 307.
39 BStU, ZA, HA XX, 221, 'Bericht zum Stand der Sicherheit und Ordnung bei Fußballspielen im Spieljahr 1987/88', Berlin (East), 15 July 1988, p. 261.
40 BStU, ZA, HA XX, 221, 'Protokoll. Erfahrungsaustausch zu Problemen der Ordnung und Sicherheit bei Fußballveranstaltungen am 10.03.1988', Berlin (East), 28 April 1988, p. 218.
41 BStU, ZA, ZAIG, 3543, 'Information über einige aktuelle Erkenntnisse zu Fragen der Gewährleistung von Ordnung und Sicherheit bei Spielen der Fußball-Oberliga der DDR', Berlin (East), 2 September 1986, pp. 3–4.
42 BStU, ZA, HA XX, 1823, 'Kartenaufteilung zum Europa-Cupspiel BFC Dynamo gegen Nottingham Forest am 19.3.1980', Berlin (East), 17 March 1980, p. 55 and BStU, ZA, HA XX, 1823, 'Anlage 1', March 1980, p. 14.
43 BStU, Außenstelle Dresden, KD Dresden-Stadt, 13358A, 'Informationen über die Arbeitsergebnisse der zum Oberligafußballspiel SG Dynamo Dresden – BFC Dynamo am 14.3.87 eingesetzten IM', Dresden, 27 March 1987, p. 71.

44 See the dissertation written by an MfS officer: BStU, ZA, JHS, 21466, Dirk Kreklau, 'Diplomarbeit zum Thema: Die Gewinnung jugendlicher und junger-wachsener IM aus dem negativ-dekadenten Fußballanhang und die kontinuierliche Zusammenarbeit mit ihnen', 1989, pp. 4, 12, 18, 21–4, 29, 31.

45 BStU, Außenstelle Frankfurt (O), BVfS Frankfurt (O), BdL, 1684, 'Zusammenfassende Darstellung zur Problematik der Ausschreitungen bei Fußballspielen im In- und Ausland, insbesondere für den Zeitraum von 1978 bis 1981', Berlin (East), June 1981, pp. 6–10.

46 BStU, ZA, HA IX, 1039, 'Bericht', Berlin (East), 23 June 1970, p. 16.

47 SAPMO-BArchiv, DY 30/IV 2/2.039/251, 'Information zur Lage auf den Fußballplätzen der DDR und Vorschläge zur besseren Gewährleistung von Ordnung und Sicherheit im Zusammenhang mit Fußballspielen', [1984], p. 24 and 'Zur Information zur Lage auf den Fußballplätzen und den Schlußfolgerungen', [1984], p. 31.

48 BStU, Aussenstelle Frankfurt (O), BVfS Frankfurt (O), BdL, 1684, 'Zusammenfassende Darstellung zur Problematik der Ausschreitungen bei Fußballspielen im In- und Ausland, insbesondere für den Zeitraum von 1978 bis 1981', Berlin (East), June 1981, pp. 10–14.

49 SAPMO-BArchiv, DY 30/IV 2/2.039/248, Appendix to a letter to Krenz, 28 July 1987, pp. 59, 67.

References

Baigno, A. and Horn, M. (eds) (2003) *Die Geschichte der DDR-Oberliga*, Göttingen: Verlag Die Werkstatt.

Braun, J. (2004) 'Sportfreunde oder Staatsfeinde? Fußballfans im Visier der Staatsmacht', *Deutschland Archiv*, 37: 440–7.

Dennis, M. (2003) *The Stasi: Myth and Reality*, Harlow and London: Pearson/Longman.

Duke, V. (1995) 'Going to Market: Football in the Societies of Eastern Europe', in S. Wagg (ed.) *Giving the Game Away: Football, Politics and Culture on Five Continents*, London and New York: Leicester University Press.

Ewald, M. (1994) *Ich war der Sport*, Berlin: Elefanten Press.

Farin, K. and Hauswald, H. (1998) *Die dritte Halbzeit – Hooligans in Berlin-Ost*, Bad Tölz: Verlag Thomas Tilsner.

Fuge, J. (1997) *Ein Jahrhundert Leipziger Fußball: Die Jahre 1945 bis 1989*, Leipzig: Connewitzer Verlagsbuchhandlung.

Hesse-Lichtenberger, U. (2002) *Tor! The Story of German Football*, London: WSC Books.

Horn, M. and Weise, G. (eds) (2004) *Das große Lexikon des DDR-Fußballs*, Berlin: Schwarzkopf and Schwarzkopf.

Kinner, K. and Richter, R. (eds) (2000) *Rechtsextremismus und Antifaschismus*, Berlin: Karl Dietz Verlag.

Leske, H. (2004) *Erich Mielke, die Stasi und das runde Leder: Der Einfluß der SED und des Ministeriums für Staatssicherheit auf den Fußballsport in der DDR*, Göttingen: Verlag Die Werkstatt.

Luther, J. (2004) 'So rollte der Ball im Osten', in F. Willmann (ed.) *Fußball-Land DDR. Anstoß, Abpfiff, Aus*, Berlin: Eulenspiegel Verlag.

Luther, J. and Willmann, F. (2000) *Und niemals vergessen – Eisern Union!*, Berlin: BasisDruck.

Luther, J. and Willmann, F. (2003) *BFC: Der Meisterclub*, Berlin: Das Neue Berlin.

MfS und Leistungssport (1994) BStU, Reihe A: Dokumente, no. 1, Berlin: BStU.

Pleil, I. (2001) *Mielke, Macht und Meisterschaft: Die 'Bearbeitung' der Sportgemeinschaft Dynamo Dresden durch das MfS 1978–1989*, Berlin: Ch. Links Verlag.

Queißer, W. (1983) *Jugendstreiche oder Rowdytum?*, Berlin (East): Verlag Neues Leben.

Remath, C. and Schneider, R. (eds) (1999) *Haare auf Krawall: Jugendsubkultur in Leipzig 1980 bis 1991*, Leipzig: Connewitzer Verlagsbuchhandlung.

Spitzer, G. (2004) *Fußball und Triathlon: Sportentwicklung in der DDR*, Aachen: Meyer and Meyer Verlag.

Süß, W. (1996) *Zu Wahrnehmung und Interpretation des Rechtsextremismus in der DDR durch das MfS*, BStU, Reihe B: Analysen und Berichte, no. 2, Berlin: BStU.

Wagner, B. (1995) *Jugend – Gewalt – Szenen: Zu kriminologischen und historischen Aspekten in Ostdeutschland. Die achtziger und neunziger Jahre*, Berlin: dip.

Waibel, H. (1996) *Rechtsextremismus in der DDR bis 1989*, Cologne: PapyRossa Verlag.

Willams, J. (2001) 'Who You Calling a Hooligan?', in M. Perryman (ed.) *Hooligan Wars. Causes and Effects of Football Violence*, Edinburgh and London: Mainstream Publishing.

Willmann, F. (ed.) (2004) *Fußball-Land DDR: Anstoß, Abpfiff, Aus*, Berlin: Eulenspiegel Verlag.

Abbreviations

BDVPLp	Bezirksbehörde Deutsche Volkspolizei Leipzig (Regional Office of the German People's Police Leipzig)
BFC	Berliner Fußballclub (Berlin Football Club)
BSG	Betriebssportgemeinschaft (enterprise sports community)
BStU	Bundesbeauftragte für die Unterlagen des Staatssicherheitsdienstes der ehemaligen Deutschen Demokratischen Republik (Federal Commissioner for the Records of the State Security Service of the Former German Democratic Republic)
BT/RdBLp	Bezirkstag und Rat des Bezirkes Leipzig (Regional Assembly and Council of the Leipzig Administrative Region)
BV	Bezirksverwaltung (Regional Administration of the MfS)
DFV	Deutscher Fußballverband (German Football Association of the GDR)
DTSB	Deutscher Turn- und Sportbund der Deutschen Demokratischen Republik (German Gymnastics and Sports Association of the GDR)
DVP	Deutsche Volkspolizei (German People's Police)
FDGB	Freier Deutscher Gewerkschaftsbund (Confederation of Free German Trade Unions)
FDJ	Freie Deutsche Jugend (Free German Youth organization)
GDR	German Democratic Republic
HA	Hauptabteilung (Main Department)
HFC	Hallescher Fußball Club Chemie (Halle Football Club Chemicals)
IM	Inoffizieller Mitarbeiter (unofficial collaborator)

MfS	Ministerium für Staatssicherheit (Ministry of State Security, also Stasi)
OPK	Operative Personenkontrolle (operational personal check)
OV	Operativer Vorgang (operational case)
SAPMO-BArchiv	Stiftung Archiv der Parteien und Massenorganisationen der DDR im Bundesarchiv, Berlin (Berlin Branch of the Federal Archive of the Foundation for the Parties and Mass Organizations of the GDR)
SC	Sportclub (sports club)
SED	Sozialistische Einheitspartei Deutschlands (Socialist Party of Germany)
SG	Sportgemeinschaft (sports community)
StAL	Sächsisches Staatsarchiv Leipzig (Saxon State Archive Leipzig)
ZA	Zentralarchiv (Central Archive)
ZAIG	Zentrale Auswertungs- und Informationsgruppe (Central Assessment and Information Group)
ZOS	Zentraler Operativstab (Central Operational Staff)

5 Turkish immigrants in German amateur football

Dirk Halm

Introduction

Organized sport in Germany throughout the twentieth century was characterized to a large extent by migration (Blecking 2001). Yet migration did not really bring structural changes to the sport system, by, for example, establishing explicit integration programmes. Although there have been significant efforts to establish such programmes since the 1990s, the general approach to the problem of most amateur sport clubs in Germany is the (false) assumption that participation in sports has an integrative effect per se and no further purpose.

A more precise and differentiated view of intercultural contact in German sports raises doubts as to the validity of this optimistic point of view. This scepticism is particularly appropriate with regard to amateur sports, in which, unlike professional sports (where integration is achieved by way of the cheque-book and intercultural interaction is of a more professional character), club membership serves to fulfil a series of complex needs, namely:

> the securing of participation and access, which bring positional recognition; for moral recognition in discourses on values and norms; . . . and for the emotional recognition of collective identity in the context of community appropriation through group membership.
>
> (Klein *et al.* 2000: 289)

This chapter will present an overview of the situation, problems and prospects faced by immigrants in German club sports. It will refer to research the author has carried out in his capacities as a sociologist at the Centre for Turkish Studies, as well as to other current research.[1] The present work shares, or rather continues, one deficit in the existing literature on immigrant participation in sport in Germany insofar as it concentrates principally on amateur football. This is due primarily to the fact that the majority of organized athletic activity undertaken by immigrants is in football, followed at some distance by martial arts. Nevertheless, it would be highly desirable if future research were to include sports with lower levels of immigrant participation as well, as such data are necessary to determine the extent to which processes of integration and de-integration are sports specific. The same is valid as regards the participation of women, in particular Muslim women, in German club sports. They remain severely underrepresented and have barely registered in sports-sciences literature, a situation which is equally to be observed in the sports with the highest rates of immigrant participation, namely football and the martial arts.

In the 1990s, however, the thematic of sport and immigration was given considerably more attention in the German-speaking world than in preceding years, and this resulted in the closing of at least some gaps in research.[2] But all macro-sociological approaches to the thematic of the organizational development of immigrants in sport – in common with other sport-sociological approaches – are confronted with the difficulty of grasping the phenomenon of immigrant sport through secondary statistical data. The sports associations and clubs do not collect data on their members on the basis of nationality, which leaves researchers the task of gathering primary statistical data. Moreover, researchers are increasingly confronted with the basic problem that the background of immigrants manifests itself less and less frequently in foreign citizenship. Of the largest immigrant group living in Germany, the 2.5 million people of Turkish descent, 470,000 had German citizenship by the end of 2001 (Sauer 2001: 212).

The defining question, in this regard, is that of the integrative effect of immigrant sports in Germany, where particular emphasis is placed on the problematization and differentiation of the term 'integration'. This approach addresses, among other issues, one of the basic questions of immigrant sport and its organizational forms, namely the voluntary or involuntary character of the retreat into the 'parallel society' or 'ethnic niche'. This chapter will begin with a presentation of the organizational situation of immigrant sports, especially of football; on this basis, I will then address the determinants that are at work in the situation. Finally, I will turn to the analysis of the special problems and conflicts faced by immigrants in German amateur football with a view to developing scenarios for the future integration of immigrants into German amateur football.

The presentation is largely limited in its scope to the largest group of immigrants living in Germany, the Turks. This restriction finds its justification not only in regard to their quantitative significance, but also in the fact that the problems of integration of immigrants into German sports seem to gravitate frequently towards the Turkish immigrant community. This is due, on the one hand, to the culturally based 'physical foreigness', as Bröskamp (1994) puts it. On the other hand, it rests on the basis of general social indicators, which have a significant influence on behaviour and which, despite noticeable differentiation among Turks over the past few years, overall remain unfavourable in comparison with immigrant groups from the traditional guest-worker emigration states. In short, the social opportunities available to people of Turkish descent in Germany are still insufficient (Şen et al. 2001).

Organization of immigrants in German amateur football

Theoretical considerations

Owing to the integrative effect ascribed to sport, organized football and public opinion generally assume that the organization of immigrants in the German football system simultaneously implies the integration of immigrants into German sport. But even if we were to recognize this conclusion as fact, or at least as a normative postulation, we would not have gained much by doing so. We must first reach agreement on what integration really means, or what social structures might be the result of a successful integration process. In football, there are really several forms at play in this regard: the organization of Germans and immigrants in mixed clubs and teams; in mixed clubs with single-ethnicity teams; in single-ethnicity clubs with single-ethnicity teams; or in clubs with mixed-ethnicity teams. Are all of these forms expressions of integration in German football?

At first glance one could answer the question affirmatively; yet it is primarily *de*-integration that one observes in the general *non*-participation of immigrant women and seniors. Undoubtedly, the founding of single-ethnicity football clubs and teams is, in the eyes of many Germans, equally a sign of de-integration. This is informed by the conception of integration in German sports, which places great emphasis on mutuality and camaraderie. Participation alone is not an adequate condition for what may be considered successful integration. It is much more a question of what form the participation takes, i.e. whether in single-ethnicity or in mixed-ethnicity infrastructures. Perhaps the only statement that would meet with general agreement is that teams made up of Germans and immigrants, ideally in a 'German' club, are a sign of integration.

The conception of integration in sport is not the object of scrutiny here; indeed, it is a political and highly normative enquiry. The only sensible approach to assessing the validity of sport's conception of integration is to measure it against reality. How does the current integration situation in German football measure up against this standard?

Physical activity among immigrants

Before presenting a more precise view of single-ethnicity vs. mixed-ethnicity organization, we begin with a brief quantitative overview of physical activity undertaken by Turkish immigrants, arranged according to socio-structural characteristics (Table 5.1).

It is notable that the majority of those surveyed never engage in physical activity, while the proportion of non-active women is considerably higher than that of the men. Only 14 per cent of women engage in physical activity several times a week; for men the figure is 22 per cent. Even clearer than the distinction between the figures for men and women, however, is that found for levels of education and age. There is a relationship between advancing age and decreasing physical activity, and between higher levels of education and more frequent physical activity. The most striking contrast yielded by the study was that 81 per cent of those who did not graduate from secondary school never engage in physical activity, while the same is true for only 54 per cent of those with an *Abitur* (A level qualification).

The evidence thus presented is not surprising, and corresponds to that of the entire population, though at a lower overall level.[4] However, it is debatable whether these tendencies can be attributed to similar motives in regard to physical activity. Theoretically, it is possible to imagine a range of distinct preconditions among immigrants – for instance, a greater psychological distance from physical activity due to a different (culturally driven?) view of the body, which might explain the underrepresentation of women and senior citizens. Likewise it may provide some insight into the possible dominance of self-affirmation and social recognition as a driving motive for some young men, as compared with the gender-independent practice of the older generation of engaging in physical activity either primarily as a means of maintaining good health or as physical therapy. Football is of exceptional significance, particularly for male youths, in dealing with social transformation (Schmidt 1993), and social transformation, in turn, has different implications for different population groups, i.e. for immigrants and natives. Expectations and the potential for frustration are equally different.

Table 5.1 Physical activity and socio-structural characteristics for Turkish immigrants in Northrhine-Westphalia in per cent.[3]

		Physical activity			
		Never	*Once a month*	*Once a week*	*Several times a week*
Gender					
	Male	60.5	6.5	11.4	21.7
	Female	70.1	5.7	10.4	13.8
Age					
	Under 30	52.2	7.5	13.6	26.7
	30 to 44	68.2	6.1	12.3	13.4
	45 to 59	78.9	5.8	6.3	8.9
	60 and older	76.2	2.4	2.4	4.8
Education					
	Still in school	16.0	4.0	24.0	56.0
	No diploma	81.0	4.2	4.9	9.8
	Haupt-/Realschule	61.5	7.2	12.9	18.7
	Abitur	53.6	8.2	15.5	22.7

Single-ethnicity and mixed-ethnicity organization in amateur football

This chapter considers whether such differences in the motives underlying physical activity may also be responsible for the development of single-ethnicity teams and clubs. To begin, we shall consider the ethnic structures under which immigrants pursue club sports and the changes to which these structures have been subject in recent years.

The detachment of immigrants from physical activity is and has been reflected in the low degree of organization in sports clubs. The last general survey to include this question was carried out by the state sports association of Northrine-Westphalia (NRW) in 1990, and covered thirteen administrative districts and independent municipalities in the region. In the municipalities surveyed, on average the degree of organization (i.e. membership) in sports clubs was 6 per cent for immigrants, while the average for German citizens was 20 per cent.[5] This considerable difference shows that while amongst immigrants only those who practise sports regularly were club members, there was a much higher proportion of passive club members among the German population. Such data and their interpretation are subject to the proviso that no continuous assessment on the organization of immigrants in sports clubs was carried out; second, the available data that could show development over time describe different groups – people of Turkish descent, foreigners and Muslims. Under this proviso, however, it may be assumed that the degree of organization in sports clubs among immigrants (or those of Turkish descent, foreigners and Muslims) over the past two decades has remained comparatively constant (and indeed low). In view of the fact that the average length of residence of the classic guest-worker and his offspring has reached, on average, twenty years, it is plausible that the degree of organization among people of Turkish descent is higher than that for foreigners and Muslims; Turkish immigrants have, by and large, established themselves in Germany, with a mere 32 per cent aspiring to return to Turkey and one in five adopting German citizenship (Sauer 2001: 183–216). This corresponds proportionally to inclinations among Turks to join German clubs or to establish single-ethnicity organizations.

Overall, 47 per cent of immigrants are members of a club or association. Of those surveyed, one-third were members of German organizations (33 per cent) and one-third members of Turkish organizations (33 per cent).[6] Fifteen to 30 per cent of all immigrants with club membership were members of both German and Turkish organizations; 18 per cent were in either a German or a Turkish organization, of which each represented one-third of all organized immigrants. A quarter are members of one organization, 7 per cent of two organizations and 3 per cent of three or more organizations – indeed, of those who are members of German organizations as well as those who are members of Turkish organizations (Table 5.2).

Table 5.2 Organization of people of Turkish descent in NRW in German or Turkish clubs and associations in per cent.

German organizations	%	Turkish organizations	%
Labour union	16.7	Religious organization	18.3
Sports club	12.9	Cultural organization	9.1
Professional association	4.1	Sports club	6.8
Cultural organization	2.7	Educational organization	2.4
Political association/group	2.7	Ethnic/national group	2.1
Educational organization	2.1	Political association/group	1.5
Recreation club	1.8	Other	1.3
Other	1.8	Professional association	0.9
Religious organization	0.4	Recreation club	0.4
Ethnic/national group	–	Labour union	–

The German organizations in which immigrants, at 17 per cent, show the highest level of membership, are, as might be expected, the labour unions: union membership has traditionally been strong among all 'guest-worker nationals'. The unions have been, from the beginning, the institutions in which compatriots, colleagues and the like-minded could come together. In second place are the sports clubs, at 13 per cent of those surveyed. Distantly following at 4 per cent and 3 per cent are professional associations, cultural clubs and political groups, respectively. For members of Turkish organizations, on the other hand, the emphasis is clearly in the area of religion. Eighteen per cent of immigrants are members of religious organizations, while 9 per cent and 7 per cent are members of cultural clubs and sports clubs, respectively.

Klein and colleagues researched the quantitative development of single-ethnicity – not only Turkish – football teams from 1985 to 1997 in NRW, in the cities of Münster, Wuppertal and Duisburg. Their findings are in line with the trends described above, namely the organization of approximately one-third of club members of Turkish descent in single-ethnicity teams. In Münster, the percentage of single-ethnicity teams in local leagues rose in the years 1985 to 1997 from 4.7 per cent to 10.6 per cent, in Wuppertal from 13.1 per cent to 35.5 per cent, and in Duisburg from 18.0 per cent to 41.2 per cent (Klein *et al.* 2000). In view of the four-year interval between the 2001 figures on the ethnification in sports clubs by those of Turkish descent and the 1997 figures on segregation in football teams, it is noteworthy that the numbers do not clearly suggest a continuation of the ethnification process in club sports. Here we see a comparison of sports clubs in general with football clubs in particular, but, due to the dominance of football in immigrant sports, if ethnification in single-ethnicity teams had advanced at the same pace as was found in the study by Kothy *et al.*, one would expect this to appear in the analysis of statistics on the organization of immigrants in sports clubs for the period

1997 to 2001. Given this assumption, it would seem that the ethnification process in German amateur football decelerated considerably in the mid- to late-1990s.

Looking at the development of the self-organization of immigrants in general, this would not be surprising. The establishment of ethnic infrastructures – generally in the form of clubs – could, after about 1995, be considered largely complete (ZfT 1999). The dramatic increase in the number of immigrant organizations in the 1980s and 1990s was the result of the maturation of second and third generations of immigrants in the Federal Republic of Germany, which is to say 'immigrants' with no personal experience of migration and for whom the possibility of 'return' was largely immaterial. Meanwhile, the majority of Turkish immigrants no longer expect to return to their 'country of origin' (Sauer 2001: 199). With the intention of staying, engagement in Germany has grown along with the necessity of securing the fulfilment of specific long-term cultural needs in the land of residence. Moreover, the provision of own-ethnicity infrastructures has, at least in the conurbations, been solidified and has reached a certain degree of saturation. It may be presumed that in amateur football, the number of own-ethnicity teams will not increase drastically in the years to come, not least because the majority of own-ethnicity football clubs exist in close connection with cultural or mosque-based organizations.

Looking at the integration model of immigrant participation in football through integration into clubs and teams, however, the 1980s and 1990s saw the advent of some serious de-integrative developments in amateur football, which have become a concern at the district and national levels.

Causes of segregation in amateur football

Statistical framework of segregation and marginalization

The depiction of the development of own-ethnicity organization in amateur football still sheds no light on the causes of segregation. It merely shows that the improved infrastructure for the establishment of own-ethnicity football clubs enabled the fulfilment of an apparent demand for the founding of own-ethnicity clubs. As to the *motives* underlying these developments, two competing hypotheses may be put forward. The motives may consist in the belief among immigrants that they can best pursue their athletic aims – playing time, success, training opportunities – in own-ethnicity clubs; or, on the other hand, immigrants may be motivated primarily by sport-unrelated preferences along the lines of 'birds of a feather flock together'. Put another way, segregation in amateur football is either the result of the perception of inequality or discrimination, or it happens *despite* equality of opportunity. These alternative explanatory schools, in the end, are valid for all forms of own-ethnicity organization. That said, in the literature there is general agreement with the thesis that as the duration of immigrants' stay in the receiving society increases, the decision to remain with own-ethnicity clubs is a sign of inadequate opportunities in the receiving society, whereas in the first years those structures are valuable as spaces of orientation and sanctuary for recent arrivals (Heckmann 1998). This presents a fundamental dilemma for the institutions of immigrant self-organization. On the one hand, they need the ethno-specific cultural capital of being a minority to maintain and develop their influence. As a rule, it is only possible to win and mobilize clientele on the basis of ethno-cultural identity. However, as integration tends to undermine conservative ethno-cultural identities, such notions collide with vital interests within the ethnic organizations (ZfT 2000: 17). Whether it is the decision to stay in own-ethnicity clubs or discrimination by the receiving society that is ultimately to blame for lost chances is open to question.

How can the relationship between own/ethnicity organization and marginalization be represented? In 2001, the Centre for Turkish Studies carried out a telephone survey on club membership of 998 immigrants of Turkish descent (ZfT 2001) (Table 5.3).

Looking at age, length of residence and motive for immigration of immigrants in the most frequently named organizations, it is notable that the members of unions and religious organizations and, to a lesser extent, of cultural organizations, are older than average, have lived in Germany for a long time and are disproportionately former guest-workers. Members of sports clubs are noticeably younger. Not surprisingly, members of German clubs differ from those in Turkish clubs in that they have lived longer in Germany and were generally born in Germany.

Thus we see that one of the central motives for membership in Turkish organizations is the need for a religious connection that cannot be fulfilled by German clubs. Former guest-workers, in particular, who maintained the desire of returning to Turkey, joined religious and cultural organizations

Table 5.3 Membership in selected organizations according to socio-demographic variables in per cent.

	Age	Length of residence[a]	Former guest-workers[b]	Born in Germany[b]
Unions	40	24	30.1	15.4
German sports clubs	32	23	9.4	28.1
Turkish sports clubs	32	21	10.2	20.2
Turkish cultural organizations	37	23	23.1	25.3
Religious organizations	40	22	32.5	13.3
Total	36.4	21.4	18.5	21.2

Notes
[a] Median value in years.
[b] Proportion of organized members in per cent per line.

Table 5.4 Marginalization* and segregation** tendencies according to membership in German and Turkish organizations (median values).***

Membership	Marginalization index	Segregation index
German-only organization	11.98	7.51
German and Turkish organization	12.05	7.03
Turkish-only organization	12.60	6.57
Total	12.15	7.06

Notes:
* Median value scale from 6 = cultural belonging to 18 = cultural marginalization.
** Median value scale from 3 = pronounced segregation tendencies to 9 = no segregation tendencies.
*** Weighted according to age.

as well as unions quite early. The degree of membership in religious organizations and unions among younger generations, however, is considerably lower. Even among youths, however, the demand for native-culture organizations has not entirely dissipated (Table 5.4).

The indices on marginalization and segregation show that the interviewees who are members of German clubs only feel marginalized considerably less frequently and show segregationist tendencies less frequently than do interviewees who are members of Turkish clubs only.[7] Immigrants who are active in both German and Turkish organizations show up in the middle of both indices. As these calculations do not allow for an analysis of the causal relationships, it is impossible to say with certainty which variable is influencing the other. It is unclear whether membership in German clubs leads to a reduction in these tendencies, or if those who assert segregationist tendencies and feel marginalized prefer to join own-ethnicity clubs and thus strengthen the tendency. Both theses are plausible.

Empirical data on the causes of segregation

With increasing acculturation – most clearly observed in those of Turkish descent who were born in Germany – there has been a noticeable if weak trend away from own-ethnicity organization and towards German or mixed-ethnicity clubs. Nevertheless, even among youths, a not insignificant number remain in Turkish clubs or join them after leaving the youth programmes of German clubs. These findings raise the question of the existence of a possible 'Turkish' footballing identity, and further, of how such an identity may be modified in the acculturation process. An indicator in this regard is support of German and Turkish professional football clubs (Table 5.5).

Overall, the preference for Turkish club teams amongst those of Turkish descent in NRW is clear. This suggests a particular footballing identity – over 80 per cent of Turks favour teams from their country of origin, irresepective of level of education. A linear increase in the difference between lower and higher levels of education – towards sympathy for German clubs and teams – may be seen in the data, but remains at a very low level (Table 5.6).

Taking the improved access to education as indication of integration – and education is the precondition for participation opportunities which are, for their part, integral components of integration (Şen *et al.* 2001: 19) – the successful progress of the integration process calls for a recognition of 'Turkish' football player identity within the broader football cultures of Germany. This interpretation is supported by the consideration of the connection of age and club preference. Here, a lower age group – when the predominant part of one's lifetime would be spent in Germany – tends more towards acculturation than a higher age group. There appears to be almost no rejection of this preference for Turkish clubs and teams in the younger age groups (Table 5.7).

Table 5.5 Nationality of favoured club teams among people of Turkish descent in NRW according to level of education in per cent.[8]

	No diploma	Haupt-schule	Realschule	Fachober-schule	Gymnasium	Total
Turkish	89.7	83.6	85.5	81.6	80.6	84.4
German	8.2	12.6	13.2	12.8	18.1	12.7
Both	2.2	3.8	1.3	5.6	1.3	2.9

Table 5.6 Nationality of favoured club teams among people of Turkish descent in NRW according to age in per cent.[9]

Age	18–29	30–44	45–59	60+	Total
Turkish	85.0	82.5	82.0	94.9	84.2
German	11.8	14.3	16.0	5.1	13.1
Both	3.2	3.1	2.0	0.0	2.8

Table 5.7 Favourite teams of people of Turkish descent in NRW in per cent.[10]

Team	%
Galatasaray	39.0
Fernerbahce	29.6
Besiktas	9.1
Bayern München	2.2
Schalke 04	4.3
Dortmund	2.3
Trabzonspor	6.2
Other Turkish Teams	2.8
Other German Teams	4.3

Of relevance here is also the often touted integration and people-connecting power of the popular team Schalke 04, or Dortmund's Borussia, which appear much weaker than is generally accepted. Their popularity among people of Turkish descent has almost completely ceased. There is thus not much to detect of the so-called 'melting-pot' of the Ruhr valley industrial conurbation.

Is this apparent, deviating footballing identity of the German Turks actually the cause of segregation in own-ethnicity teams? To be able to make a conclusive statement about the cause and causal relations requires a non-standard method of surveying. In 2001, the Centre for Turkish Studies questioned sixty Turkish youths from youth 'B' team football regarding their club socialization. Of these, twelve players from a Turkish own-ethnicity team were questioned by means of biographical interviews (Halm 2002). The results from the interviews with the youths provide some indication of the general situation, despite the low number of cases.

The average duration of club membership among all those questioned comes to 6.6 years. With an average age of 15.1, this means an average entry age of 8.5. The average length of stay in a current club comes to 3.6 years. The Turkish youth 'B' team players could look back on real club socialization in football generally, as well as in a current club. The interviewed players from the segregated team could, at 7.7 years, point to a similar length of club socialization. This therefore rules out playing in a solely Turkish team as a motive for entrance into a club. At 2.0 years, the average length of stay in a current club is lower than in the total group because the youth division of the segregated team was still in a stage of construction – the youth 'B' team had just begun its 2001–02 season activity. What were the motives for the change of youth players in the same-ethnicity clubs? Here the motive structure produced by the biographical interviews appears to conflict. The players predominantly indicate having changed of their own free will, foremost because playing with the Turks would be more fun. Of the others, three of those questioned indicate having felt underlying or open discrimination whilst playing in German teams, a perception which is also always paired with the feeling that more fun may be had in an own-ethnicity team.

The causes for the segregation in own-ethnicity clubs are therefore complex. In no case, however, do the outlined results suggest a conclusion. Segregation in football is based foremost on the feeling of discrimination by German clubs and teams – even if it occurs. Just as important are the 'soft' factors of the participants in football – the club's environment, the understanding of sport – as well as the bidding structure, and the organization's sociological process as regards the stabilization of foreignness for the purposes of protecting their own club clientele. An evaluation of these results is not simple: on the one hand, it discharges the football system from the reproach of failing to integrate immigrants. On the other hand, it limits the football club's opportunities to serve the project of integration.

The partially own-ethnicity organization in German amateur football could become, in the long term, the norm, with all its resulting conflicts and problems. This will now be discussed in the following section.

Integration, disintegration and conflicts

Own-ethnicity teams and risks for intercultural understanding

As a rule, the football districts and associations perceive own-ethnicity teams as problematic.[11] It could be reasoned on the one hand that, in principle, segregation runs contrary to the view of sports in clubs ('sport connects', 'sport speaks all languages' and so on). From a social-psychological theoretical approach it may be surmised that this apprehension by the associations is not without foundation. The preconditions of this communication in football are in principle – and here the general perception is confirmed – justly reasonable, at least in ethnically mixed teams (Kothy 1997).

An examination of scientific findings on the effects of intercultural contact suggests certain conditions promoting inter-ethnic convergence and distancing (Amir 1969) (Table 5.8).

The conditions promoting communication are present to a far greater degree with the meeting of Germans and immigrants on mixed-ethnicity teams than with the meeting of two own-ethnicity teams where distance-creating conditions prevail. Inter-ethnic competition and involuntariness of contact are elements hindering communication. They come into effect especially with the meeting of own-ethnicity teams, during which the communication-promoting elements of contact regularity, high intensity of contact, mutual advantages of contact and possible realization of a common goal are absent. Statistically, these negative preconditions lower the amount of participation of own-ethnicity teams in conflicts due to rule-breaking. The doubling of the previously outlined trend of immigrants playing on

Table 5.8 Preconditions of communication in an intercultural contact.

Convergence	Distancing
• Equal social status	• Competition in the contact situation
• Heightened social status of the ethnic minority	• Involuntariness of contacts
• Promotion of social climate	• Loss of status of a group through the contact
• Regularity of contacts	• Dissatisfaction with the social class
• High intensity of contacts	• Incompatibility of cultural standard
• Mutual advantages of contact	• Lower social status of the ethnic minority
• Realization of a common goal[12]	

Source: Adapted from Amir (1969).

own-ethnicity teams from 1985 to 1997 greatly affected the proportion of the participation by these teams in disciplinary hearings: in Münster, the proportion rose during this same time period from 11.1 per cent to 43.4 per cent – meaning half of the immigrants up before disciplinary committees came from own-ethnicity teams, even though only one-tenth of the immigrants in Münster are even organized into own-ethnicity teams. In Wuppertal the proportion rose from 41.3 per cent to 70.7 per cent and in Duisburg from 26.3 per cent to 55.3 per cent (Klein *et al.* 2000: 289). As a rule, the district and football associations statistically point to a high proportion of participation by immigrants in rule-breaking relative to their participation in active play. Thus it is not without foundation that they see the own-ethnicity immigrant teams as a problem case and disruptive factor. This notwithstanding, however, nothing has yet been said about 'guilt' or 'responsibility' for the existing problem. The own-ethnicity team at least catalyses conflicts involving rule-breaking. We turn now to a detailed structure of conflict in the following section. If the own-ethnicity club organization is so difficult to influence, how far can the conflict potentiality of the own-ethnicity team be positively influenced?

Cultural difference vs. social interaction

Among the conditions hindering communication in intercultural contact, social psychology has identified the 'incompatibility of cultural standards'. Does one solve conflicts by strengthening own-ethnicity teams, i.e. the existing, different understandings of sport? Or do more complex mechanisms take over here, which are not explained by individual attitudes and behaviour, but rather by certain patterns of social interaction? Both alternatives are theoretically conceivable.

As a basis for his convergence on the problematic of cultural difference in sports, Bernd Bröskamp established, with recourse to Pierre Bourdieu's cultural sociology (1987), the concept of 'physical foreignness', namely an understanding of different socially mediated attitudes towards physicality between people from different cultural backgrounds. Bröskamp conducted nineteen interviews with teachers from Kreuzberg, who verified the significance of – as he called it – 'physical foreignness' in sports instruction (Bröskamp 1994: 67). In the case of the majority of Turkish girls and boys, he showed significantly different associations to their own bodies in relation to their fellow students, and showed which of these entirely differing ways could lead to conflict: because of the required sports clothing, for instance, girls of Islamic belief ran into conflict either with their families or with their classmates, who felt that gymnastics in street clothing was not sporty. Conflicts regarding participation in athletic or swimming instruction would often be dealt with simply by the family via means of suppression. The Turkish students would reject the team shower, and Turkish boys would reproach fellow students for their excessive involvement, especially in football. This last point corresponds with the conflicts in the encounters of German and Turkish football teams formulated by Bröskamp (1994: 172):

> The question can be raised based on varied cultural views about what degree of physical hardiness is adequate. Concerning the participants (rather the Germans) the question is whether that which is happening here is sports at all (or not just 'kicking' or simply 'bodily injury'). . . . The reverse question can be raised (rather with the Turkish athletes) whether the members of the opposing team – they who complain to the referee of the hard physical effort (they 'whine' like 'women' and 'children') are actually men. Finally, the strictness towards maintaining neutrality and authority by the (mostly) German referees could be altered if they let themselves be influenced (or appear to be), and instead of fulfilling their role of fairness they may find reason to speculate and to stand on the side of the other team.

The sports physician Jens Kleinert points not only to differences in playing behaviour, but also in dealing with injuries. While the pain threshold of different athletes hardly varied, pain tolerance and coping with pain appeared to vary not only according to age and gender but also according to cultural affiliation (Kleinert 2000: 70). This seems to give a plausible explanation for the immigrants' attested harder manner of playing. In contrast, other results also show that the original social preconditions which drive young Germans and comparable young Turks are very different. On the football field, many of the young Turks seem to seek recognition for that which, as a yet disadvantaged group, is denied them in other areas of life. For them, competition in football seems to be a comparatively serious opportunity, which allows little room for an understanding of football as a sport for the purpose of fitness (Halm 2001: 260–7) (Table 5.9).

The Centre for Turkish Studies enumerated problematic attitudes towards football which were based on the evaluations of a list of statements by sixty youth 'B' team players from Essen. Apparently, the youths go with commitment to work, which is combined with relatively strong emotional involvement – there is less agreement with the statement 'Defeat creates a problem for me' with an average value of 2.33, and much more agreement with 'After victory I am euphoric' with a value 1.33. Yet physical effort and acceptance of injury were expressed with a value of 1.25: 'Healthy roughness is a part of football'. The distribution of answers is not remarkable for the total group. What is significant is the relatively strong agreement – with an average of 1.75 – that the referee blows his whistle for too many petty incidents. Potential conflict manifests itself herein.

In the above-listed statements we are dealing with sets of attitudes which together correlate with each other. Most important here is the connection

Table 5.9 Conflict-prone attitudes towards football by Turkish youth 'B' team players in Essen total 60.

	Healthy roughness is a part of football (%)	Defeat creates a problem for me (%)	Referee's blows (calls) too petty (%)	For success injury is unavoidable (%)	After victory I am euphoric (%)	When in pain, clench your teeth (%)
Agree	49.2	35.3	47.5	29.3	55.0	51.7
Strongly agree	37.3	37.3	32.2	37.9	30.0	33.3
Strongly disagree	10.2	20.3	18.6	15.5	11.7	10.0
Disagree	3.4	6.8	1.7	17.2	3.3	5.0
Total	1.68	1.98	1.75	2.21	1.63	1.68
Own-ethnicity teams average*	1.25	2.33	1.67	2.08	1.33	1.42

Note
* Scale from 1 to 4 (1 = Agreement, 4 = Rejection of the statement).

between emotional involvedness and approval of a rough style of playing – 93.1 per cent of those who agree entirely with the statement that a healthy hardiness is a central part of playing also agree completely or strongly with the statement 'After victory I am euphoric'. These results confirm the thesis that the search for social recognition leads to strong emotional commitment on the playing field, which in turn leads to risky behaviour by the players. While this thesis is supported by the factual correlation between commitment and play behaviour, the reference to seeking social recognition remains a plausible consideration since the interviewees are socio-economically so uniformly structured – namely as predominantly underprivileged – and sufficient cases of privileged youths would be found, as in the random sample, to prove that the commitment on the playing field actually correlates negatively to the social opportunities in other areas of life. A strong argument for connecting the seeking of social recognition and strong emotional commitment is the relative homogeneity of the socio-economic structure, as well as that of the understanding of sports in the target group. It is a noteworthy fact that a relatively strong commitment from the Turkish youth on the football field, and with it the connected risk of injury, have deep-running social and socio-psychological causes consisting of very complex interrelations.

The initial state of reported research suggested that 'cultural' factors could influence the understanding of sports, especially the ways of dealing with pain. Yet one argument in particular spoke against the truth of this theory with reference to the interviewees. In the absence of a comparable group of Germans, one has to employ more speculative arguments and analyses. Presuming that one motive for entry into the own-ethnicity club is to play with peers of the same age group and of the same ethno-cultural background, the different way of dealing with pain on own-ethnicity teams must appear a stronger trend than with the Turks who play on mixed-ethnicity teams and who have had a far-reaching acculturation process. Concerning agreement with the statement 'When in pain, clench your teeth', the total number of interviewees with a value of 1.68, and the twelve segregated players with a value of 1.42, are not positioned so far apart that grounds for the significance of cultural attitudes regarding ways of dealing with pain could be deduced. The interviewees were, moreover, presented with the statement, 'Turks play with more effort than the Germans'. Here the answers were also inconsistent, with a balance of agreement and rejection (Table 5.10).

How is this distribution to be interpreted? First, that there is no obvious 'cultural consensus' among Turkish players regarding a typical way of playing which could be designated by especially great effort. Furthermore, one may ask whether a cultural factor underlies the differences of perception expressed in Table 5.10. The affirmation of the existence of a typically Turkish way of playing may indeed stem from the observation of facts, which in the end have the social causes described above. It should be considered whether agreements with the statement stems from players' own self-image. It is thus appropriate to evaluate the statement that Turks are characterized by greater effort in relation to the duration of stay in Germany. A connection could be provided by the assumption that with a shorter stay in Germany there remain stronger cultural differences. As a matter of fact, there are no significant correlations between a shorter duration of stay and the sense of difference in the understanding of the player's approach to the game. Of the nine who were not born in Germany, five agreed or agreed strongly, four disagreed or disagreed strongly. However, it must be pointed out with regard to these results that due to the low number of cases, those who were not born in Germany had only limited representation here. Second, the argument conducted here does not presume the existence of a 'third generation return' which would contrast, through

Table 5.10 Agreement with the existence of greater effort by Turkish players.

	Frequency	%
Agree	17	28.3
Strongly agree	15	25.0
Strongly disagree	14	23.3
Disagree	14	23.3
Total	60	100

the traditional attitudes of immigrant youth, with the established second generation of immigrants.[13] Even if this were the case, this development in the own-ethnicity team in Essen is not to be registered in respect to a provable cultural difference in sports understanding as opposed to the Turkish players on the German teams – the distribution of the answers is far too similar here.

In this context it is clear that the majority of those interviewed display a surprisingly similar attitude to the youths from the own-ethnicity team as regards their understanding of sport. In the own-ethnicity team there seems to be, at least in this case, no particular problem or potential for frustration in an especially aggressive manner of play or similar expression. These findings contradict the frequently circulated estimation of the own-ethnicity team as being especially prone to conflict, insofar as the members of the non-segregated Turkish team are, in an individual perspective, hardly to be differentiated. Since here the whole is more than the sum of its parts, one cannot come to definite conclusions about the final conduct of the team on the field. Perhaps the explanation for the apparent contradiction of these findings is found in the analysis of Klein and colleagues among others. Apparently, group dynamic processes that the local surveys did not account for have to be reckoned with.

Strategies for supporting the integrative potential in amateur football

Which strategies for improved activation of the integrative potential in German amateur football do these findings suggest? In the team sport of football there is a mix of cultural difference, struggles for resources and social recognition. Players, managers, referees and officials are each confronted with specific conflicts. The differentiation between own-ethnicity and mixed teams is also important. The meeting of own-ethnicity teams especially creates conflict potential due to the existence of poor conditions for intercultural communication. The fact that own-ethnicity organizations have hardly had any youth departments at their disposal for many years – and as a result the athletic socialization for Germans and immigrants began, as a rule, on common teams – appears not to have halted the trend towards own-ethnicity teams. The return of immigrants can be explained only partly by athletic discrimination. If the opportunities for club football to influence ethnification prove to be insignificant, however, then it must be seriously considered whether the conditions that particularly hinder communication cannot be changed in the athletic contact – in the sense of minimizing conflict. The intensity of competition would be especially worth considering here. Doubtless it contradicts the essence of football to pass off thoughts of competition on to a wider front – with a view to boys' football, the question must be asked whether the strong ambition of the young Turks would have to be redirected in order to encourage and thereby be able to create a freer space for intercultural common ground and communication.

At first glance, if these recommendations and views on conflict potential in encounters between own-ethnicity teams in amateur football may seem paradoxical – since the own-ethnicity club needs to be seen as normal in an immigrant society – it is also due to their unconditional acceptance on behalf of the football districts and organizations. Improved representation of immigrants on the regional and club level also needs to be achieved. This would have two immediate effects: first, a stronger participation of immigrants would, on the one hand, significantly reduce objectively unfair handling by referee and courtroom arbitrators; on the other hand, it would dampen the immigrant's subjective and possibly unjustified feeling of discrimination, whereby pointing the finger at 'the Germans' would lose its meaning. Only when this acceptance creates the foundation for the greatest possible co-operating own-ethnicity team will the preconditions for mid- and long-term improvements exist to enable the integrative potential of amateur football. This new integrative potential would then express itself less in a return of own-ethnicity club founding, but rather more in the entry of Germans into segregated immigrant clubs. That such a development could actually come to fruition is already apparent today. In particular, immigrant clubs can, as regards club management (for example, the maintenance of relations with district and association), contribute to the professionalization of immigrant clubs, which for their part often have little experience, report problems with the allocation of facilities and have difficulties with youth programmes. In turn, the Germans would, especially in areas with high immigrant populations, ensure their access to sport infrastructures.

Notes

1 The Centre for Turkish Studies works cited in the following are ZfT 1996, 2001; Halm 2001, 2002.
2 In addition to the above-cited contributions of Klein et al. and Blecking, see especially Bröskamp (1994), Halm (2000), Pilz (2000), and, in addition, Auernheimer (1988) and Heckmann (1992).
3 Telephone survey of 998 Turkish households; see Halm (2001: 260).
4 These results confirm the findings from some five years before (ZfT 1996: 6). The deficits compared to the German population in 1994 were to be observed less among those in each group who played sports frequently, but rather among the Turks who seldom took part in sport – a group that, at under 10 per cent, hardly existed. Evidently there has been no demonstrable change with regard to the frequency of physical activity of Muslims in Germany in the latter half of the 1990s. This is notable, since the Turkish population in Germany was at the same time undergoing rapid social transformation and differentiation processes (see Şen and Goldberg 1994). The tendencies stated here, based on a comparison of Muslims and Turks at different times, may be considered acceptable in this context, as the Turks make up three-quarters of the total Muslim population in Germany. Of the three million Muslims living in Germany, 2.5 million are of Turkish descent.

5 Compare the results of the LSB NW in ZfT (1996: 8).
6 Following results from ZfT (2001: 113–17). In this study, 998 people of Turkish descent in NRW were surveyed by telephone in autumn 2001.
7 'Marginalization' and 'Segregation tendencies' were indexed by means of questions on personal perceptions of social, economic, political and cultural opportunities.
8 Telephone survey of 998 immigrants of Turkish descent in NRW in 2001, evaluation of 699 valid responses.
9 Telephone survey of 998 immigrants of Turkish descent in NRW in 2001, evaluation of 699 valid responses.
10 Telephone survey of 998 immigrants of Turkish descent in NRW in 2001, evaluation of 714 valid answers.
11 Since the end of the 1990s there has been a careful reconsideration by the umbrella organization that amounts to an acceptance of own-ethnicity organizations. This is documented in a position paper by the Landessportbund Northrhine-Westphalia on Migration and Sports from the year 2000.
12 With a view to intercultural contact, Kothy specifies the point made by Amir as 'work for a common goal' (Kothy 1997: 71). The unfulfilled common goal in sports can lead to frustration and the weakening of inter-ethnic group cohesion.
13 For this theory on the German-speaking area, see Heckman (1992: 172), Nauck *et al.* (1997: 477) and Nieke (1991: 16). Recent results seem to show a differentiation in the passing third generation and indicate that the 'third generation return' is predominantly relevant for a segregated minority among the migrants; compare also Şen *et al.* (2001: 118).

References

Amir, Y. (1969) 'Contact Hypothesis in Ethnic Relations', *Psychological Bulletin*, 5: 319–42.
Auernheimer, G. (1988) *Der sogenannte Kulturkonflikt: Orientierungsprobleme ausländischer Jugendlicher*, Frankfurt/Main and New York: Campus.
Blecking, D. (2001) *Polen – Türken – Sozialisten: Sport und soziale Bewegungen in Deutschland*, Münster: Lit.
Bourdieu, P. (1987) 'Programme pur une sociologie du sport', in P. Bourdieu *Choses dites*, Paris: Minuit.
Bröskamp, B. (1994) *Körperliche Fremdheit: Zum Problem der interkulturellen Begegnung im Sport*, St Augustin: Academia.
Halm, D. (2000) 'Theorien zu interkulturellen Konflikten im Sport', *Zeitschrift für Migration und Soziale Arbeit*, 3–4: 48–52.
—— (2001) 'Interkulturelles Konfliktmanagement: Endbericht zum Projekt', in *Migrationsbericht des Zentrums für Türkeistudien 2002*, Münster: Lit.
—— (2002) 'Vereinssozialisation und Gesundheitsvorsorge bei türkischen B-Jugend-Fußballern: Ergebnisse einer empirischen Untersuchung', *Zeitschrift für Migration und soziale Arbeit*, 3–4: 92–8.
Heckmann, F. (1992) *Ethnische Minderheiten, Volk und Nation: Soziologie interethnischer Beziehungen*, Stuttgart: Enke.
—— (1998) 'Ethnische Kolonien: Schonraum für Integration oder Verstärker der Ausgrenzung?', in Friedrich-Ebert-Foundation (ed.) *Ghettos oder ethnische Kolonie? Entwicklungschancen von Stadtteilen mit hohem Zuwandereranteil*, Bonn: Friedrich-Ebert-Foundation.

Klein, M.L., Kothy, J. and Cabadag, G. (2000) 'Interethnische Kontakte und Konflikte im Sport', in R. Anhut and R. Heitmeyer (eds) *Bedrohte Stadtgesellschaft*, Weinheim: Juventa.

Kleinert, J. (2000) 'Was lehren uns die Leiden der Athleten?', in *Quadratur Kulturbuch 3 – Sportwelten*, Duisburg and Köln: 70–4.

Kothy, J. (1997) 'Konfliktdimensionen interkultureller Kontakte im Fußballsport', in J. Kothy and M.L. Klein *Ethnisch-kulturelle Konflikte im Sport*, Hamburg: Czwalina.

Nauck, B., Kohlmann, A. and Diefenbach, H. (1997) 'Familiäre Netzwerke, intergenerative Transmission und Assimilationsprozesse bei türkischen Migrantenfamilien', *Kölner Zeitschrift für Soziologie und Sozialpsychologie*, 49: 391–419.

Nieke, W. (1991) 'Situation ausländischer Kinder und Jugendlicher in der Bundesrepublik Deutschland: Vorschule, Schule, Berufsausbildung, Freizeit, Kriminalität', in K. Lajios Konstantin (ed.) *Die zweite und dritte Ausländergeneration: Ihre Situation und Zukunft in der Bundesrepublik Deutschland*, Opladen: Leske U.B.

Pilz, G. (2000) *Fußball und Gewalt – Auswertung der Verwaltungsentscheide und Sportgerichtsurteile im Bereich des Niedersächsischen Fußballverbandes Saison 1998–1999*, unpublished manuscript.

Sauer, M. (2001) 'Die Einbürgerung türkischer Migranten in Deutschland: Befragung zu Einbürgerungsabsichten und dem Für und Wider der Einbürgerung', in A. Goldberg, D. Halm and M. Sauer *Migrationsbericht des Zentrums für Türkeistudien 2002*, Munich: Lit.

Schmidt, W. (1993) 'Kindheit und Sportzugang im Wandel: Konsequenzen für die Bewegungserziehung?', *Sportunterricht*, 1: 24–42.

Şen, F. and Goldberg, A. (1994) *Türken in Deutschland: Leben zwischen zwei Kulturen*, Munich: Beck.

Şen, F., Sauer, M. and Halm, D. (2001) 'Intergeneratives Verhalten und Selbst-Ethnisierung von türkischen Zuwanderern: Gutachten des ZfT für die Unabhängige Kommission "Zuwanderung"', in *Migrationsbericht des Zentrums für Türkeistudien 2002*, Münster: Lit.

ZfT (1996) *Teilnahme von Menschen ausländischer Herkunft, insbesondere muslimischer Frauen, an den Angeboten der Sportvereine in der Bundesrepublik Deutschland*, Essen: ESpo.

ZfT (1999) *Bestandsaufnahme der Potentiale und Strukturen von Selbstorganisationen von Migrantinnen und Migranten türkischer, kurdischer, bosnischer und maghrebinischer Herkunft in Nordrhein-Westfalen*, Düsseldorf: Schriftenreihe der Landesregierung.

ZfT (2000) *Die Ablehnung und Akzeptanz infrastruktureller Einrichtungen der türkischen Minderheit durch die aufnehmende Gesellschaft und Konfliktkonstellationen individueller, infrastruktureller und regionaler Desintegrationspotentiale* (= ZfT-aktuell Nr. 83), Essen.

ZfT (2001) *Integration und Segregation türkischer Migranten in Nordrhein-Westfalen: Results of the third multiple-subject survey commissioned by the Ministerium für Arbeit und Soziales, Qualifikation und Technologie NRW*, unpublished manuscript.

6 The future of football is female!?

On the past and present of women's football in Germany[1]

Gertrud Pfister

Introduction

'The future of football is female', declared FIFA president Joseph Blatter after the women's football World Championship in 1995. Whether or not his prediction will turn out to be correct will be discussed in the second part of this chapter. Football has a future in Germany, not least because of the World Championship which will take place in Berlin in 2006. In Germany, football is definitely on the agenda today, with books on football being published, discussions held and exhibitions planned. Politicians, artists and scholars are certainly talking about and reflecting on football – but about 'proper' football, i.e. the male version.

From the very start, football and masculinity were closely intertwined. In the 1880s, English students, businessmen and sailors imported football into Germany, where it was looked upon as being such an aggressive, exhausting and dangerous game that anxious physicians and educationists wanted to see football banned, especially for boys. But this opposition could not stop the enormous popularity of the game. Certainly by the end of the First World War football had become Germany's national sport, awakening both the interest and the national feelings of the (male) population (Pfister 2003a). Football provided (and still does provide) a stage upon which male attributes and behaviour such as toughness, strength and a fighting spirit are not only expected but also demonstrated and rewarded. The football stadium is a place where – whether on the pitch or in the stands – men can be men and act like 'real' men, and where fans can identify with players and imagine themselves as heroes (see, for example, Dunning 1986; Marschik 2003). Fighting for possession of the ball, the 'sworn brotherhood' of eleven players, the chanting and singing on the terraces (*'Deutschland vor – noch ein Tor'* ['Germany in the lead – another goal we need']), the playing of the game live and its coverage by the mass media, the speeches, texts and pictures, the numerous associations, symbols and myths – all this contributes towards the glorification of masculinity and national superiority. The language of football likewise belongs to the world of men, a world full of metaphors depicting the game as a battle and the players as soldiers and heroes attacking and defending, striking and shooting and, in the end, either claiming victory or suffering defeat.

For a very long time women did not exist in this world, since football was totally incompatible with femininity. The exclusion and later the marginalization of women in football contributed at the same time to the construction and presentation of gender differences, and thus to the repro-duction of a gender order based on gender duality. The question arises as to whether the growing popularity of women's football in recent years has changed the world of football and whether, in general, it signals a change in the gender arrangements prevailing in society. In this chapter, I recon-struct the history of women's football in Germany, analyse the initiatives for and the opposition to the participation of women in this 'unfeminine' sport, and describe the opportunities as well as the challenges for female football players today. In conclusion, I will discuss the prevalent discourses and reconstructions of gender in and through football.

From German gymnastics to sport and football – men's spheres

Backgrounds and contexts – women and physical activities

The development of women's soccer in Germany can only be understood against the backdrop of the social order and the gender arrangements of the time, and in the context of the developments of movement cultures such as *Turnen* and sport. *Turnen* (German gymnastics) developed at the beginning of the nineteenth century as a reaction to social and economic changes as well as to the military and political challenges of the period. The aim of the *Turner* movement was to liberate Germany from French occupation, to overthrow the feudal order, and to overcome the division of Germany into small kingdoms and principalities and form a German nation state. *Turnen* was developed by men and for men. The exclusion of women can be explained, on the one hand, with the political and military aims of *Turnen* and, on the other, with the role of women in the nine-teenth century – a role which denied them, among other things, political rights, university education and academic professions. Legitimised by the theory of the polar differences between the 'natures' and the characteristics of the two sexes, women were considered the 'weaker sex' and their activ-ities restricted to the home, the family and motherhood. Because of the myth of the 'weaker sex' and women's 'predestination' as wives and mothers, the participation of women in strenuous and dangerous exercises was unthinkable (Pfister and Langenfeld 1980, 1982).

From the 1830s onwards some physical education teachers provided courses in gymnastics for girls with the promise of improved health and enhanced grace, but it was not until the end of the 1880s that adult women began to take up *Turnen*. They founded women's gymnastics associations or formed women's sections in men's *Turnen* clubs, where, however, they were denied the same membership rights as the male *Turner*. Girls' and women's gymnastics followed the principle of 'heads up and legs down' and, for the most part, consisted of simple and easy exercises on apparatus and gymnastic exercises (Pfister 1980).

By the end of the nineteenth century, English sports had spread to Germany. In stark contrast to *Turnen*, sport emphasized competition, quantifiable performance and records, thus giving rise to a serious conflict between the *Turner* movement and advocates of sport. It was a question not only of values and tastes but also of power and influence: whereas the *Turner* propagated the training of the whole body, the inclusion of the (male) masses and nationalism, sport was about specialisation, top performances and international competitions and comparisons (Pfister 2003b). The *Turner* concentrated their attacks on football, which was denounced as being un-German, unaesthetic and dangerous. While the number of female members joining *Turnen* clubs increased towards the turn of the century, sport was still considered to be particularly 'unfeminine'. Nevertheless, women, too, were overcome by the growing fascination with sport and dared – at first individually – to take up various sports from cycling to skiing.

In most sports women were confronted with specific problems, reflecting established opinions with regard to the abilities and competences of the so called 'weaker sex' on the one hand and the expectations which society had of women (and also of men) on the other. Swimming was problematic because women in bathing suits supposedly undermined public morals and offended the laws of propriety. And, since rowing was believed to be too strenuous for them, women rowers were restricted to competitions in style which focused on exact movements rather than on speed. Athletics was looked upon as especially unfeminine because it was competition-oriented and thus allegedly exceeded women's physical as well as mental capacities.

In Germany, the First World War had far-reaching consequences, bringing about fundamental changes to the political, social and economic situation. The political and economic problems and the related insecurity and crises of identity which followed Germany's defeat created a climate favouring manifold and, in part, contradictory developments in all areas of life. For women, these changes brought with them new opportunities: they now had access to university education and academic professions, and in 1919, through universal suffrage and the right to vote, they gradually gained political influence and power. Fashion freed women from corsets and long skirts, and the abolition of traditional norms and values gave women access, at least as long as they were single, to the labour market. However, this does not mean that the gender hierarchy had disappeared. Women mostly worked in low-paid occupations in factories or offices and, upon marrying, entered a new state of dependence, this time on their husband as the head of the family. However, it must be added that the expectations which society had of women and the circumstances of their personal lives were dependent to a great degree on their social backgrounds and the attitudes of their surroundings. Although women's ideals and roles were various and ambivalent, the staunch belief in the unchangeable 'natures' as well as the pre-ordained order of men and women dominated popular wisdom (Frevert 1995).

During this period, increasing numbers of German women started to take part in physical activities, leading to a heated debate on the question of whether women ought to be allowed to take up sports which demanded strength, endurance or aggressiveness and whether it was appropriate for the 'weaker sex' to play in contests. The majority of educationists, physicians and journalists as well as sports officials rejected the participation of women in competitions, arguing that women did not have the necessary physical and mental capacities. Sports competitions were condemned for being not only unaesthetic but also a threat to women's health, especially to their ability to have children, and thus for being in contradiction to women's 'natures' (Pfister and Langenfeld 1982). As one can see from the programme of the early modern Olympic Games, the spectrum of the sports accessible to women was very small. Upper-class activities such as tennis or golf were accepted as well as sports like swimming because of the alleged health benefits. Athletics remained a contested terrain and it was only in 1928, after a lengthy dispute between the International Women's Sport Federation, the International Amateur Athletic Federation and the International Olympic Committee that women were first allowed to take part in Olympic athletic events (Pfister 2000).

'Ladies' play football – but only in other countries

Even more than athletics, football belonged to that category of sports which, according to popular belief in Germany, 'is not suited to the female disposition; it looks anomalous and deforming and therefore should be left to the male of the species' (*Sport und Gesundheit*, 1932, 1: 11). This, however, did not stop women in other countries such as England and France trying out football as a game for their own enjoyment. As early as 1894, a British Ladies' Football Club was inaugurated and only a year later various women's teams were playing matches against each other in England before thousands of spectators, both male and female (Lopez 1997; Pfister *et al.* 1998). Accompanied by the nationalist fervour of the First World War, women's football reached a zenith when football matches were organised between women's teams in order to raise money for charity. In 1921 there were around 150 women's football teams in England. In France, too, teams were founded during the First World War (Prudhomme 1996). In 1917 the first women's football championships were held and in 1922 two Football Cup competitions were introduced. In the 1920s, moreover, numerous matches took place not only between French teams but also against women's teams from other European countries. This comparatively tolerant attitude towards women's football in England and France is partly due to the exceptional circumstances prevailing during the First World War, but it may also be attributed to specific constellations of sports politics, not least to the existence of and competition between various women's sports organisations in these countries.

Opposition to women's football in Germany

The general development of women's sports as outlined above, the labelling of sports as either 'male' or 'female' and, not least, the opposition to aggressive types of sport as well as competitive sports were the determining factors in shaping the opportunities, or rather the barriers, for girls' and women's participation in football. At the end of the nineteenth century the introduction of physical education for girls and their integration into the 'games movement' provided the first opportunity for them to play football. This movement, which in the 1880s propagated outdoor sports out of concern for the health of the German nation and its ability to defend itself against an aggressor, also sought to attract girls and women because of the widespread belief that 'strong offspring can only be born of strong mothers'. Among the activities that were recommended for girls were ball games such as 'football in the round' in which the ball was only allowed to be moved by kicking it with the feet. Like the typical games of the 'games movement', this type of football game completely lacked both a competitive impulse and any orientation towards performance. It was perhaps this game which Heineken was referring to when, in 1898, he claimed that 'for many years football has been played by girls, too, and they enjoy playing it' (1993: 226).

An advocate of women's football was also to be found among the first female doctors who were in favour of physical fitness for women. In order to build up strength and stamina, Anna Fischer-Dückelmann (1905) even went so far as to recommend football for women, provided that they wore the right clothing. There is no evidence that this unconventional advice was ever followed.

In spite of repeated reports in German sports journals of football matches being played between teams of women in England and France, there was never any question in Germany of the football field becoming a place for women. 'All types of sport which go beyond a woman's natural strength such as wrestling, boxing or football are unsuitable; furthermore, they are unaesthetic and unnatural' was, for example, how Willy Vierath expressed it tersely in his book *Modern Sport*, published in 1930. According to another author, German women disapproved of football, first, because the 'rough way' in which the game was played was contrary to women's sensibilities and, second, because the game was not suited to the 'build of the female body' (*Sport und Sonne* 1927: 24).[2] In similar vein, an article in a women's magazine called the *Damenillustrierte* commented in 1927: 'Women may be playing football in England and America but it is to be hoped that this bad example is not to be followed in German sport' (Special Issue, *Frauensport*, p.7).

Because of the stigmatisation of football as an unnatural and unfeminine game for women as well as the critical voices about women's football in other countries, very few women in Germany dared to play the game.

There are a number of reports that individual sportswomen – for example, women handball players or the eccentric actress and later pilot, Antonie Strassmann – did try out football as a game. As far as we know, however, there was only one initiative to form a women's football team: in 1930 a women's football club in Frankfurt was founded with thirty-five members, all of them young women, who trained regularly on Sundays on the Seehofwiese in Sachsenhausen (Schreiber-Rietig 1993).

In a magazine called *Illustriertes Blatt* (27 March 1930) one of the few favourable reports about this initiative was published. The astonishingly positive article included the following comment: 'The lady footballers . . . intend to play a cheerful, combative kind of football. Whether it will be worse than hockey, we will have to wait and see. . . . It will be interesting to see what will come of this venture.' Other sports journalists had an entirely different view of this, describing women's football as a show of 'abominably bad taste' comparable to 'fairground sideshows' and, generally, putting them on a level with women wrestlers. The press reports of this 'scandal' caused a public outcry and the women's football club ceased its activities in 1931 (Schreiber-Rietig 1993).

Women's football had absolutely no chance of success in an age when gender differences were given great emphasis – among other things because the intrusion of women into men's domains like the labour market was perceived as a threat to traditional gender arrangements.

In contrast to Germany, a women's football movement arose in Austria and even an Austrian Ladies' Football Union was founded which, however, was disbanded by the authorities in 1938 after Germany's annexation of Austria (Marschik 2003). Under the National Socialists, who liked to highlight gender differences, women's football had to be stamped out since it offended their notion of gender segregation.

Initiatives after the Second World War

Although the lack of food and housing made the daily struggle for survival very difficult, people began to take a renewed interest in sport (and especially football) immediately after the war had ended. From August 1945 onwards football matches were organised in German cities nearly every Sunday, and from November 1945 even league games were played in some regions. Besides providing excitement and distraction, football paved the way for Germany's return to 'normality', and an important milestone in this phase – as well as being a source of new self-esteem – was the 'Miracle of Berne', the legendary victory of 'our boys' in the 1954 football World Championship which – after all the uncertainty caused by the war, the country's defeat and years of internment in POW camps – enabled men to identify with new and positive ideals of masculinity (http://www.wunder-von-bern.de).

In the 1950s West Germany's economic upswing and the normalisation of everyday life was accompanied by a striving for a normalisation of gender relationships, too. In other words, men and women were expected to assume their traditional roles once more, a development which was legitimized by the re-establishment of the theory of 'gender polarity'. In the various sport discourses, too, emphasis was placed on gender differences and the myth of the 'weaker sex' was kept alive, especially by the medical profession. In spite of all this, a number of women did begin to play football. In the early 1950s, for example, the wives and girlfriends of the Tennis Borussia football team in Berlin held New Year's football matches at which – according to press reports – the spectators amused themselves exceedingly (Brüggemeier 2000: 300). Thus eventually, the German Football Federation (*Deutscher Fußballbund* – DFB) was forced to consider the question of whether or not to recognise women football players. Its reaction in 1955 was one of total rejection, forbidding its clubs from either founding women's sections or putting their grounds at the disposal of women's teams.[3] Nevertheless, in 1957, in the *Journal WFV-Sport*, the journal of the West-German Football Federation, 'neglected football dames' and 'lonely football wives' confronted the DFB with a 'revolutionary demand: "Equal rights for all! We want to play football, too!"' (*WFV-Sport*, 7, 11 April 1957). In 1957 there was even a women's international between West Germany and Holland in the Kornwestheim Stadium near Stuttgart. Many spectators were attracted to the stadium by the promise of a highly amusing and entertaining afternoon. Although it appears that the women played quite creditably, some reports of the game contained descriptions of the women covered in mud but failed to mention the result (*Christ und Welt*, 19 September 1957). In the same year a match took place between a women's team from West Germany and one from West Holland in the Dante Stadium in Munich in front of 14,000 spectators. While the sports reporters spoke enthusiastically about the victory of the West German team, the spectators, the majority of whom were men, seem to have had a less sporting and less gentlemanly view of things: 'The men clapped and slapped their thighs, bursting out laughing whenever a player slipped and fell on the grass.' The same article also mentions a West German Ladies' Football Association with twenty-two affiliated clubs; unfortunately, however, no further information is available about this association.[4] The author of the article then put forward the proposal that the DFB should incorporate women's football and take it under its wing in order to stop sensationalism and profiteering, and prevent women's football from sinking to the level of women's wrestling. Banning women's football was pointless, the author went on, and did not make any sense, since ideals of femininity had changed and women had proved themselves in many other types of sport.

The demands of women football players and their (few) supporters did not succeed in inducing the DFB to change its mind. On the contrary, in 1958 it was again unanimously confirmed that grounds, apparatus and referees were not to be put at the disposal of women's football teams (Diem 1978).

The DFB was able to back up its decision with medical arguments ranging from certain anatomical characteristics such as 'knock-knees' and the difficulty of conditioning female muscles, to the 'diminished ability to reproduce' and the 'masculinisation' of women football players (*WFV-Sport*, no. 11, 13 June 1957). A medical review commissioned by the DFB likewise warned of the dangers to which women allegedly exposed themselves while playing football (Fechtig 1995: 25). Opponents of women's football even gained the support of the renowned philosopher F.J.J. Buytendijk, who in his psychological study of football published in 1953 remarked that:

> Football as a game is first and foremost a demonstration of masculinity as we understand it from our traditional view of things and as produced in part by our physical constitution (through hormonal irritation). No one has ever been successful in getting women to play football. ... Kicking is thus presumably a specifically male activity; whether being kicked is consequently female – that is something I will leave unanswered.
>
> (Buytendijk 1953: 20)

Thus, because of the DFB's negative attitude, women were only able to play football 'unofficially' in recreational teams throughout the 1950s and well into the 1960s. Despite this lack of support, however, several women's football teams and clubs had been founded by the end of the 1960s, for example, *Oberst Schiel*, a club formed by a women's team in Frankfurt (DFB 1983; Fechtig 1995: 31; Ratzeburg and Biese 1995: 21). At Borussia Berlin, too, a regular team was formed in 1969 by players' wives along with a number of women handball players; this team went on to gain second place in the (still unofficial) municipal championship in 1971 (http://www.tennis-borussia-frauen.de/dt-hist.htm).

Women playing football – processes of institutionalisation

Women's football becomes 'official' in West Germany

In the late 1960s, the DFB could no longer react as it pleased to what it perceived to be an undesirable development; it was also forced to take account of the changing social conditions.

In West Germany the 1960s were a period of almost revolutionary social upheaval in which, for example, women's levels of education increased, leading to a growing integration of women into the labour market. At the same time, a new women's movement arose which contributed to a new image and to a new self-awareness of women, who no longer identified with the 'weaker sex'. One of the most important changes was the invention of methods of birth control, which allowed women greater choice with regard to both their bodies and their futures. In this climate of 'women's liberation' the DFB was forced to change its policies, and in 1970, at the DFB's national conference in Travemünde, 'ladies' football' was finally officially recognised. The reason for this change of heart was, as Hannelore Ratzeburg (the best-known of the DFB's women officials) noted, the federation's fear of losing control over the women's football movement (DFB 1983; Ratzeburg and Biese 1995: 21).

A pioneering role was also played by women's football initiatives abroad. In Italy, for instance, a first unofficial World Cup tournament was held in 1970, which was watched by 35,000 spectators and in which a selection of women players from German clubs took part (Ratzeburg 1986; Fechtig 1995: 31). A reporter from the *Münchner Abendzeitung*, who accompanied the women, wrote:

> Just before setting off for the World Championship in women's football, Helga Walluga, aged 28 from Bad Neuenahr, the German eleven's striker, went to the hairdresser's to have her hair smartly permed. Then she joined her twelve giggling team mates in the bus. . . . There was trouble, too, when the reporters wanted to visit the changing rooms while the women were in them. The German women had tried, they said, to keep their bosoms out of the limelight in order to be able to return safely to the haven of matrimony afterwards. . . . Unfortunately the prettiest team lost.
>
> (Brändle and Koller 2002: 225)

In short, the journalist ended up writing a 'humorous' (i.e. belittling) description of a spectacle which was supposed to be funny because of its absurdity.

Since women's enthusiasm for football could no longer be suppressed, it was thought that they ought at least to be 'kept on the right track' by means of suitable guidelines. Thus the DFB's Games Supervisory Committee developed a set of rules on how the game should be played by women's teams: for example, women were to play two halves, but only of thirty minutes each; they were to use the same specification of ball laid down for men's youth teams; they were not allowed to have studs in their boots; and advertising on jerseys was banned because it allegedly drew the spectators' gaze to the players' bosoms. In the years that followed, however, these rules proved to be superfluous, if not senseless, and were successively abolished (DFB 1983:12–4; Ratzeburg and Biese 1995).

The rise of women's football in West Germany

In the 1970s, women's football in West Germany made huge progress: in 1971 the first knockout competitions were organised; in 1972–73 championship matches took place in the regional football associations of the German federal states; and in 1974 the first national championships were held (Fechtig 1995: 35). In 1980–81, club cup matches were introduced in which all women's teams could take part, regardless of the league in which they played (*DFB-Vereinspokal*). Since then, selected regional teams (*Landesauswahlteams*) with the best players of each German federal state have competed for the DFB Women's Federal Cup (*Frauen-Länder-Pokal*). In 1985–86, regional leagues in the West German federal states were introduced and in 1990 a national league was established with two divisions of ten teams each. Since 1997–98 twelve teams have formed a national league with a single division in an attempt to concentrate women's football on the best clubs and thus raise standards of play (Ratzeburg and Biese 1995: 21–3). In 2004, finally, a second national league with two divisions was established, not least in order to put women's football on a broader base and give young players the opportunity to play in higher grade matches (http://www.ich-spiele-fussball.dfb.de).

In the 1980s, major breakthroughs were achieved by women's football at the international level and West German women numbered among the best and most successful players in the world game. The first unofficial World Championship in women's football, held in Taiwan in 1981, was won by a German club team, SSG 09 Gladbach, whose members had to finance the trip to Taiwan themselves. Subsequently, in 1982, an 'official' national team was formed from the country's best players and in the same year the German women's eleven played their first international against Switzerland, which they won five to one (http://www.ich-spiele-fussball.dfb.de).

Women's football in East Germany

Football fever also spread to girls and women in East Germany, where a highly efficient and centralised sports system had been established with the aim of gaining political recognition through success in sports. All available resources were invested in those athletes and sports with the greatest potential to win medals in world championships and the Olympic Games (Pfister 2000). After the first women's football team was founded at the Technical University of Dresden in 1968 on the initiative of a Bulgarian student, women's football spread quickly during the 1970s and by 1981 there were 360 women's teams playing football in the GDR (Pfister 2002).

Regarded as a leisure pastime and thus as a recreational sport, women's football was not officially recognised and supported as a top-level competitive sport. In 1979 a working group on women's football was set up which extended the organisation of women's football to the regional and national levels. In the same year competitions took place for the first time to find the best team, but official championships were not held, even though the working group repeatedly demanded the organisation of leagues at all levels as well as official championships (Meier 1995).[5]

In the course of the 1980s women's interest in football decreased, partly because the players were confronted with problems which were similar to those faced by female players in West Germany, i.e. since football was looked upon as a men's sport, female players were not taken seriously and they often had to fight against inadequate conditions in training and matches. However, the main problem was the decision of leading GDR sports functionaries not to class women's football as a top-level sport and give it the corresponding support. This meant that East German women were excluded from international competitions. The scarce resources, especially the hard currency that was so valuable to the state, could not be allowed to go into a sport which was not accepted by the public and which did not have the potential to win medals.

It was not until the late 1980s that an upper league with two divisions was introduced and not until 1990–91 (i.e. after German reunification) that the East German Football Association established a national league and formed a national team (Meier 1995). Incorporated shortly afterwards into the DFB, the East German Football Association became the Regional Association North East, and 'finally gave women's football the recognition for which it had fought for 21 years' (Meier 1995: 37). Players from the former East Germany were then assimilated into West German women's football, organised as it was by the DFB. The GDR's best team, Turbine Potsdam, is today one of the few top teams that comprise the women's *Bundesliga*.

The discrimination against women football players in East Germany can only be properly evaluated if it is seen in the context of widespread public fascination with the game, as well as the many different privileges accorded to the GDR's male players. Although East German football was not very successful internationally, male players were greatly favoured by the state and the ruling party, and were supported in spite of the unfavourable cost–benefit ratio, which otherwise played an important role in the promotion of a particular sport.

Developments after German unification

The integration of East German players was of great benefit to women's football in Germany, which has since been very successful at the international level. The West German women's national team had already won the European Championship in 1989, and the German women continued their run of victories in the years 1991, 1995, 1997 and 2001. In 1991 the first official World Championship was held in China, where the German team took fourth place. In the second World Championship tournament in Sweden in 1995 the German team lost to Norway in the final, thus becoming runners-up in the tournament (http://www.ich-spiele-fussball. dfb.de). The players were proud to play for their country and dreamed of participating in the Olympic Games. Sylvia Neid, one of the best German players of this period, even described participation in the Olympics as her life's goal (*Spiegel* 45, 1994, p. 193). This dream came true in 1996 when women's football became an Olympic discipline at the Atlanta Games. In the 2004 Games in Athens, the German team won the bronze medal.

Germany is world champion

The 1990s saw a radical change in the way women's football was played. The players' athletic abilities and competences improved along with their technical and tactical skills, thus increasing the tempo of play and making systematic and strategic sequences of passes possible. The football played by the top teams in the women's *Bundesliga* is characterised today by clever tactics and creative footwork.

German players proved that they could play excellent football at the 2003 World Championship in the USA, where they managed to eliminate a strong US team and won the final 2–1 against Sweden after Nia Künzer's header in extra time. The 26,000 spectators in the stadium experienced a game that had been full of excitement right up to the final whistle. The reaction in Germany was overwhelming. The DFB's president, Gerhard Mayer-Vorfelder, sang the team's praises, the German chancellor and the German president sent their congratulations, and FIFA president Joseph Blatter spoke of 'a new dimension', 'tremendous progress' and 'football of the highest order'.[6] The media poured on the superlatives and about 12.5 million football fans followed the match on television. On their return to Germany the players were given a reception in the Emperor's Hall of Frankfurt Town Hall and cheered by the jubilant crowd when they appeared on the balcony – a tradition hitherto reserved for the men's national team.

Suddenly women's football was being taken seriously – it was no longer 'Wiegman, Prinz and Co' but Germany; and now Germany was world champion. What would have been unthinkable (or even the object of mockery) twenty years before was suddenly something quite natural. Women's football evoked national emotions and processes of identification. But it was not just the World Championship title, it was the quality of the game, rather, which gave women's football the long-awaited stamp of respectability. After showing a certain amount of nervousness in the first half, the players proved that they were capable of playing attractive football of a high standard, both technically and tactically (http://fifaworldcup.yahoo.com/03/en/t).

Can one draw the conclusion that, through their achievements and triumphs, women have now finally conquered one of the most prestigious male domains, the game of football?

Women football players – still a minority

In spite of the successes of the national team, female players still form a small minority of members in the DFB, which, with its 6.3 million members, is the largest sports federation in Germany. In 2004 there were 857,220 female members enrolled in the DFB, 635,072 of them women and 222,148 girls (i.e. under 16 years of age). This means that women make up 14 per cent of DFB membership. Whereas the number of women members decreased slightly from 2003 to 2004, the number of girls in the DFB increased by about 7,000 over the same period. The DFB attributed this rise of young members to the success of the women's team in the World Championship tournament (http://www.dfb.de/dfb-info/eigenprofil/index.html). However, these impressive figures do not mean in any way that more than 850,000 girls and women play football in Germany, since it must be taken into consideration that the DFB also caters for other types of sport such as aerobics and 'keep fit' classes. Since only 3,466 women's and 3,400 girls' teams are registered with the federation for taking part in competitions, it may be assumed that only 10 per cent of the women and around 30 per cent of the girls enrolled in the DFB play football. What then are the reasons for the large under-representation of football players among the women members of the German Football Federation?

Opportunities and challenges for women's football

The continuing development of women's football and its record of success in the past should not be allowed to obscure the fact that women football players have always been confronted with various problems and that this is possibly still the case today.

Power in the hands of men

A problem that is still as topical and as serious today as it ever was is the lack of women in executive bodies (Linsen 1997). From the very beginning of women's football, decision-making bodies were made up of men and it was extremely difficult for women to assert claims or push through demands. Monika Koch-Emsermann, a player and coach from the early days of women's football, remembers that 'just about everything [that she proposed] was turned down' (*Caracho*, 1, 1986, p. 23).

The growing popularity of girls' and women's football is due in part to the establishment of women's committees and the appointment of officials in charge of girls' and women's football within the DFB and its regional associations. Hannelore Ratzeburg (who in 1977 was the first woman to be made a member of the DFB's Games Supervisory Committee), together with the bodies responsible for girl and women members and the individuals appointed in the period that followed, initiated numerous projects and schemes in order not only to establish women's football as a recognised sport but also to ensure its continuing growth and development. However, the lack of female members in the DFB's governing bodies has still not changed today: in 2004 there was not a single woman among the fourteen members of the presidential committee, its highest body. The DFB's executive board, its next highest body, is made up of the twenty-four heads of the various sections; the only woman represented on this board is the head of the women's football section. Thus, although it is understood and even accepted that women should take an active part in women's affairs, as soon as they aspire to a role in men's football, they are seen as a threat and meet with strong opposition. The example of Britta Steilmann illustrates the mistrust that women face when they take over managerial positions in football. Britta Steilmann, the daughter of a businessman and sponsor of Wattenscheid 09 football club, took over the club's marketing and public relations work, thus becoming Germany's first woman football manager. There was subsequently a great deal of resistance in the club and among the fans, not only to the woman who wanted to 'lay down the law' in a male domain but also to her unorthodox ideas and methods (*Spiegel* 11, 1994, pp. 182).

Coaches

The further development of girls' and women's football also depends to a large extent on the work of committed coaches. In the early days of women's football these were exclusively male. It was not until 1985 that the first woman applied for a licence as a football coach. By the end of 1994, twenty-four women had obtained the highest licence, the 'A' licence, and five had qualified as football 'instructors' with a diploma (Ratzeburg and Biese 1995: 48). In German sports more widely, women are greatly under-represented among coaches: the higher the level of qualification of the coaches and the performance level of the athletes, the lower the percentage of female coaches. Here, it must be also taken into consideration that in many sports, including football, the majority of coaches work in a voluntary capacity parallel to their professional work. Very few coaches have a permanent, full-time position; and these are predominantly men (Cachay and Bahlke 2003). This is true of all sports with the exception of 'female' sports such as rhythmic gymnastics.

In 2001 only 0.8 per cent of football coaches with an 'A' licence and 1.2 per cent of football 'instructors' were women (Cachay and Bahlke 2003: 64). Whereas it seems quite natural that men should coach women's teams, female football coaches work solely with women's teams. In contrast to many other sports, though, women also coach teams at the highest level in football: in the 2001–02 football season, for example, six women (four coaches and two assistant coaches) and eighteen men were employed in the twelve women's *Bundesliga* clubs.

The reasons for the low proportion of women coaches are various and complex, ranging from their training, which is oriented towards men's experiences and competences, to women's motivations and decisions as well as their personal circumstances (Kugelman and Sinning 2004). Nevertheless, there is seemingly more success than in most other sports in persuading experienced women football players to take up a career in coaching. Moreover, this could have a positive influence on the development of women's football, since well-known and successful coaches can serve as role models. A good example of this is Tina Theune-Meyer, who in 1996 was the first woman to take over the position of national coach. The German team's World Championship title in 2003 bears testimony to her competence and professionalism and, indeed, she was the first woman in the world to lead a football team to the title. In spite of this, it is still difficult today to find coaches, whether male or female, for girls' and women's football teams.

Fostering new generations of players

It has always been difficult to motivate talented girls to take up football. In girls' physical education football plays only a minor role – if it plays a role at all. Even in co-ed classes an informal kind of gender segregation often takes place, with boys playing football and girls doing gymnastics. The indifference of most schools to girls' football is a crucial problem, since most girls are unable to develop skills in controlling a ball, either in the family or in kindergarten. Girls' lack of skill in ball control, especially when playing football, is thus not compensated for at school (www.ich-spiele-fussball.de/schule/unterricht). In the whole of Germany there is only one DFB training centre for women's football and this is a boarding-school at which girls go to school and are able at the same time to take part in football training (*Berliner Zeitung*, 11/12 October 2003, p. 3). There are signs that the girls at the centre will go on to form a new generation of top-level football players (*Berliner Zeitung*, 11/12 October 2003, p. 3). On the other hand, women's football is not generally very high on the list of girls' sporting preferences, and playing football is certainly not 'in' in the same way as horse-riding or ballet are. Besides, many parents are not exactly thrilled when they learn that their daughter has discovered a liking for football (Pfister 1999). (After the final of the 1995 World Championship in women's football Gero Bisanz commented: 'We have seen that football is a sport for women and I hope that many parents will give up their aversion to girls playing football' [*Die Welt*, 20 June 1995].) As a result, it is very difficult to put together girls' teams and even more difficult to keep them together. Teams that do exist often suffer from fluctuation and lack of continuity.

According to Kugelmann and Sinning, the reason for this large under-representation of girls in football and their lack of interest in it is the orientation of the game to male interests, competences and lifestyles: 'The football culture staged for the media and by the media as well as the way football is learned and played at school and in clubs is traditionally domin-ated by male behaviour and male perceptions' (2004: 135). The techniques of teaching football and the training instructions, for example, fail to take into account the fact that girls have often had no previous experience of the game. With this didactic consideration in mind, Kugelmann and Sinning have developed guidelines for a kind of football training which also appeals to girls and to different groups of girls with various interests.

It is still to be seen whether any lasting changes have occurred in girls' attitudes to football after the World Championship triumph. What has changed in the run-up to the 2006 men's World Cup, however, is the DFB's attitude towards fostering new generations of players as well as towards girls' football. In 2002, partly in view of the 2006 World Cup in Germany, the DFB developed a strategy for fostering young players and introduced a scheme for sponsoring new talent on a scale that had never been seen before anywhere in the world. Three hundred and ninety training centres with 1,200 coaches were established all over Germany, catering for 22,000 young players between the ages of 10 and 17 years. Only 3 per cent of these players are girls and, currently, a research project is looking into the reasons for their under-representation (http://www.claudia-kugelmann.ag. vu/s7.html). In 2005 the DFB launched a 'DFB Football Programme for Girls' with the aim of getting more girls to take up football. The addressees are not only the girls themselves but also parents, teachers and instructors (i.e. those groups which play a key role in promoting girls' football). In this project, strategies are developed, brochures are devised, contact networks are established and clubs are urged to form girls' football teams (*DFB-Journal* 2004, p. 4; www.ich-spiele-fussball.de).

Professionalisation of women's football?

It is conspicuous that most of the teams in the women's *Bundesliga* come from small towns and unknown clubs with few financial resources. In the past, the players frequently complained that women's teams 'played second fiddle' in their clubs, even when they were much more successful than the men's teams. The clubs' lack of interest in women football players resulted in numerous instances of discrimination, from the allocation of pitches to financial backing. 'We are the flagship of our club', commented a player in a small town in Westphalia, 'but, even still, when it comes to handing out funding, we're always at the end of the queue' (Linsen 1997: 256). Even in large and famous clubs like Bayern Munich, women are still disadvantaged today: 'At FC Bayern women's teams are treated as though they were "C" youth teams', a former Bayern Munich player reported in 2003 (*Berliner Zeitung*, 11/12 October 2003, p. 3).

Moreover, the hand-outs paid to German women players for winning international matches have been shamefully small. After winning the European Cup in 1980, each member of the men's team received a bonus of 30,000 Marks while the women of the team which won the European Championship in 1989 were each presented with a coffee set. In 1995, however, things improved, and the women eleven's victory in the European Championship was rewarded with 3,000 US dollars. In 2003, moreover, after winning the World Cup, the women received €6,000 from German Sport Aid and €9,000 from the DFB (*Die Zeit*, 22 December 2003, No.1, http://www.zeit.de/2004/01/10_2f12_2fRottenberg).

In contrast to their male counterparts, women football players still have amateur status today. Whereas in the mid-1990s women players in the USA were already earning up to US$150,000 a year and great sums were being paid in Japan's professional women's league, playing women's football in Germany has always been and is still more or less an unpaid pastime.[7] Most *Bundesliga* players are either students or full-time employees and train four or five times a week in the evenings. Because of the lack of funding as well as the 'double burden' of women players through football and work, top-level training is still scarcely possible even today. It is small wonder that Germany has become an exporter of female football players: from 1990 onwards, after winning the European Championship, the first German players were asked to play as professionals in Italy, and in the following years some of the best German women players went as 'legionnaires' to other countries and gave added strength to teams in Italy and the USA (*Kicker* 1990, p. 64; *Der Spiegel* 45, 1994, p. 193). In 2001 three top players, among them Doris Fitschen, played in the newly founded professional league (WUSA) in the USA (*Der Spiegel* 24, 2001, p. 162).

The DFB took the first step towards the professionalisation of women's football with the establishment of a women's *Bundesliga* in 1997–98, but its aim of finding sponsors for this league could not be achieved. Thus the clubs have had to fend for themselves, with the consequence that most of them are chronically short of money since they lack both revenues and sponsors. Several clubs have had to withdraw their teams from the league after failing to find any financial backing (*Die Zeit*, 22 December 2003, http://www.zeit.de/2004/01/10_2f12_2fRottenberg).

'There's more money in every one of the men's regional leagues than there is in the whole of women's football', commented a player in 1997 (see also *Berliner Zeitung*, 11/12 October 2003, p. 3). Today the financial resources of the teams in the women's *Bundesliga* range between €100,000 and €300,000; this is a lot of money compared to the situation in the 1990s but still too little to pay the players more than their expenses. Consequently, even if clubs are proud of the achievements of their women's teams, this does not guarantee good or even adequate conditions, since even today only a few clubs have adequate resources and infrastructure to support and market their women's teams adequately. Since 1998, four *Bundesliga* teams have left their clubs and founded their own associations in the hope of improving their marketing chances and shaping a more professional environment. They seem to have been successful in their venture, since they have been able to 'sign on' the best women players and attract the most spectators.

After the World Championship in 2003, demands for the professionalisation of the *Bundesliga* became louder. At the same time, experts doubted that the clubs could establish professional structures, not least because there is still relatively little interest in women's football and therefore it is difficult, if not impossible, to find sponsors. Even now, women's *Bundesliga* games attract no more than an average of some hundreds of spectators (see for example, *Berliner Zeitung*, 14 October 2003, p. 28). All the same, the absolute number of spectators at women's *Bundesliga* games rose from 50,000 in the 2002–3 season to 70,000 in the 2003–04 season – although this was due more than anything else to the increased interest of spectators in the three best teams.

The following comment in the *Berliner Zeitung* characterises the situation in women's football: 'The games of the women's *Bundesliga* are still played in a ghost-town setting ... and the majority of the players will continue to pursue their sport as a hobby' (*Berliner Zeitung*, 13 October 2003, p. 31). The general view is that the clubs will first have to '"feel their way" towards professional structures' (*Bundesliga-Magazin* 2004–05, p. 6, http://www.ffc-frankfurt.de/c/cms/upload/blm/BLM_06+07.pdf). Even so, semi-professionalism does seem possible today in the best teams.

Women's football in the public sphere

As mentioned above, one of the greatest problems facing women football players from the very beginning has been the lack of public interest. Women's football matches were virtually played in private, so to speak. In 1993, for example, women's football was shown only three times on television for a total duration of four hours and twenty-one minutes. In 1995, the year of the qualifying games for the European Championship, approximately five hours of women's football were broadcast (Mende 1995: 6). In the print media, too, women's football scarcely existed (Kröger 1996). And in 1997, games of the women's *Bundesliga* were shown on television 'in clips lasting no more than seconds' (www.uebersteiger.de). The lack of public interest is also one of the complaints regularly raised by women football players: 'There is scarcely any interest in top-level women's football – unless something quite fantastic happens', Sylvia Neid told the *Spiegel* magazine (*Spiegel* 45, 1994, p. 193).

Whereas in the 1970s and 1980s the media repeatedly made fun of women's football, most reports today are objective, constructive and even enthusiastic. However, the coverage given to women's football is still extremely rare, especially in everyday football reporting, which continues to focus on the men's *Bundesliga*. Even the women's football World Championship in 2003 was no exception. The semi-final against the USA was watched on German television by a mere 650,000 viewers – compared to the audience of around 30 million the previous day which followed the Saturday *Bundesliga* matches in the ARD's traditional *Sportschau* ('Sports Review') programme (http://www.dw-world.de/dw/article/0,,987016,00.html). A journalist commented on this as follows: 'Women's football remains the stepchild of an overbearing father – men's football – at least as far as the interest of audiences and economic power are concerned' (ibid.).

However, we must not forget that the coverage of women's sport in general plays no more than a marginal role. According to a study conducted by Hartmann-Tews and Rulofs (2002), women's sport is given 12 per cent of the sports coverage of selected German print media. Television, too, concentrates on a few sports and mainly men's sports, not least because this provides a clearly defined target group (i.e. men between 16 and 49 years of age) for the advertising industry. As a consequence, women's football continues to be played mainly out of the public gaze. The final of the women's World Cup was an exception, and it is debatable if the popularity of this game signals a new trend. After the victory in the World Championship, at any rate, there was consensus among journalists that the 'Californian Rocket' would not bring women's league football, the sport of a tiny minority, into the public gaze (see, for example, *Berliner Zeitung*, 14 October 2003, p. 28). That their scepticism was well founded could be seen in the coverage of the women's matches during the Athens Olympics: the 8–0 victory of the German team over the Chinese women was given a 4cm-long text on page five of the *BILD* newspaper's sports pages (*Emma*, September/October 2004, p. 13).

Who does not know German football players like Bayern stars Oliver Kahn, Michael Ballack and Co? Today, *Bundesliga* stars have even become the heroes of girls' dreams. But who knows what team Kerstin Garefrekes or Petra Wimbersky play for? Like the 'invisibility' of women's matches, the fact that female football players are not idols in the same way as male players are has negative consequences in two respects. On the one hand, there are no female role models for girls; on the other, women's football cannot be marketed. Without well-known names and faces the decisive incentive for audiences to switch on the television set for a football game and the interest of potential sponsors is missing. For this reason, all the initiatives for promoting girls' and women's football endeavour to make the best players visible and their names familiar (http://www.ich-spiele-fussball. dfb.de). The motto is: 'The country needs idols.' One of these idols may be Nia Künzer, a member of the World Championship team, whose 'golden goal' in the final was voted 'Goal of the Year' by 36.7 per cent of viewers, making her the first woman in the history of the ARD's *Sportschau* to receive this honour.

Women's football makes use of various media today in order to gain publicity and visibility, and several women's football magazines have been founded, only to be withdrawn from the market some time later. However, *die elf* or *FFMagazin* are journals which have been published since 2004 and which report extensively and knowledgeably about the game and the players. Moreover, a stylish women's *Bundesliga-Magazin* has appeared since 1999 which serves as a joint presentational brochure and 'visiting card' for all the *Bundesliga* clubs. The aim of the magazine is to 'give women's football a face and turn it increasingly into a product with a brand name', thus making it more attractive for the media, the fans and sponsors (*Frauenfußball Bundesliga-Magazin* 5, 2004–05, p. 1). In addition, the internet provides clubs, teams and players with the opportunity of presenting themselves on a platform which is accessible to an unlimited public.

Furthermore, the 'DFB Football Programme for Girls' mentioned above has launched an attractive website with the intention not only of providing information and knowledge but also of binding loyal fans, arousing interest in new ones and awakening the desire to emulate the stars. The pictures and biographies of the players of the national and the *Bundesliga* teams are meant to trigger processes of identification (http://www.ich-spiele-fussball.dfb.de).

In various respects, sports coverage, football and gender are interrelated and interdependent phenomena. First of all, the fans and spectators are predominantly male, even if women seem to have become more interested in football in recent years. Because of the lack of opportunity of identifying with the players, however, it is small wonder that girls and women make up only a small percentage of football fans. Consequently, sports reports are oriented towards male audiences – and these are predominantly interested in men's football. Furthermore, the overwhelming majority of sports journalists are male, the percentage of women among them being under 10 per cent. And, more often than not, the few female sports journalists that there are do not cover football, since, particularly in this sport, they are often confronted with mistrust, doubts about their competence and even rejection. A woman radio reporter, for example, was asked by a well-known *Bundesliga* coach about her qualifications before he gave her an interview (*Spiegel* 11, 1994, p. 183). And when, at the end of the 1980s, the German WDR radio station's head of sport, Sabine Töpperwien, worked for the NDR, another public broadcasting station, her colleagues tried to put her in the 'women's corner' and make her report on gymnastics. She refused to do so and subsequently became the first woman to commentate on *Bundesliga* games live on the radio (*Anstoss*, 1, 2004, p. 27–9). Players, journalists and audiences are in the same boat, so to speak, and contribute in their different ways to the constant reproduction of gender structures and practices as well as to the presentation of football in the media as a men's sport.

To a certain extent women's football is caught in a vicious circle. The lack of interest shown by the media and, as a result, by the general public leads to a corresponding lack of interest among sponsors, which in turn hinders the professionalisation of women's football and prevents it from getting the public attention it deserves. Many steps have already been taken to lift women's soccer out of obscurity: the success of the German national team, the marketing efforts of the *Bundesliga* clubs as well as the initiatives of the DFB will certainly contribute to a greater acknowledgement of this sport. Even so, as far as its marketing is concerned, women's football is still in a dilemma: 'For real women it is too mannish and for real men it is too womanish. . . . The sponsors who are interested in women are put off by the football and the ones who are interested in football are put off by the women' (*EMMAonline*, http://www.emma.de/632065710772500.html). Here, though, there are signs of change and several players have been able to sign contracts with advertisers (for example, Nia Künzer and Steffi Jones are to be seen in coffee adverts for Nestlé). However, stereotypes of women football players, their image and, generally, the construction of gender in football are further important barriers that prevent women's football from becoming more popular.

Gender deconstructions?

Playing football, doing gender

Women's football is a product of, as well as, a driving force behind the gender order, which is embedded in institutions, conveyed by gendered scripts, enacted in interactions and appropriated by individuals. Here, gender is to be understood as a social construction that is based on the dichotomous categories of male and female (Lorber 1994, 2000; Connell 2002).

Gender is always something we present and do; and gender is the enactment of various ambivalent gender images which reproduce the gender arrangements of a given society. Since gender 'is always there' (even if for the most part subconsciously) and the gendered scripts are always present, the attributes and the behaviour patterns of men and women are perceived, interpreted and judged differently – even when they do the same thing (e.g. play football).

Sport always involves the presentation of the body as well as of abilities and skills which have masculine and feminine connotations. Sport also involves the enactment of identities and images. Thus sport is an activity in which physical differences as well as gender differences are produced and presented in a particularly visible way. Doing sport is therefore always to some degree 'doing gender'. Hence, for the players, playing football means presenting themselves as women and men with more or less emphasis on masculinity or femininity. This also means that the definitions and social contracts on which sport is constituted, as well as the associations and evaluations which are connected with sporting activities, are created through discourse, constructed socially and influenced by the gender order. Depending on the images and ideals presented in it as well as on the norms and stereotypes and the behaviour patterns required by it, each sport has a distinctive culture which is produced by society, the media and the participants, and which is reflected in the self-awareness and the images of the sportsmen and women who play this particular sport. Since, in accordance with the prevailing gender arrangements, certain forms and cultures of movement connote masculinity while others connote femininity, sports develop either a male or a female image; and women and men develop preferences for certain sports and skills in certain disciplines in accordance with gendered social norms, values and expectations. The experiences and emotions conveyed by sport are, in turn, filtered through gender identity and thus serve to reinforce this identity (Klein 1997).

Football is clearly a place of enacting masculinity. The exclusion or – later – the marginalisation of girls and women from football has to do with the labelling of the game. So why, then, is football labelled 'male'? As mentioned above, from the late nineteenth century onwards football was considered in Germany to be competition-oriented, strenuous, aggressive and potentially dangerous. Thus playing football was totally incompatible with the prevailing ideal of femininity (Pfister 1993). The myth of football as an aggressive sport as well as the glorification of strong and hardy men has obscured the fact that the game can also be played in an entirely different way.

Even today football is only 'real' football for the fans when the game is rough and aggressive. Most fans and even the women players interviewed in various projects agree that football is still the same male sport it has always been (see, for example, Linsen 1997). It may be used for the production and demonstration of 'male' attributes such as strength, power and aggression. Several studies have pointed out how sport is used for the production and demonstration of masculinity. This is especially true of soccer and, to an even greater extent, to American football, which is a clear demonstration of the 'male' attributes mentioned above. Michael Messner (1994: 22) describes 'doing gender' in American football in the following terms:

> Football, based as it is on the most extreme possibilities of the male body ... is clearly a world apart from women, who are relegated to the role of cheerleaders/sex objects on the sidelines. ... In contrast to the bare and vulnerable bodies of the cheerleaders, the armoured bodies of the football players are elevated to mythical status and as such, bear

testimony to the undeniable 'fact' that here is at least one place where men are clearly superior to women.

As Eric Dunning was able to show, using rugby as his example, sport gains particular importance as a source of male identity in times when a shift takes place in the balance of power between the sexes (Dunning 1986). Rugby and football teams along with their fans can – through their rituals and enactments – be interpreted as male bonds, alliances constituted above all on the exclusion of women and the rejection of both femininity and all the qualities related to it, such as gentleness and mildness (Völger and Welck 1990). Thus women who play football have transgressed the socially fixed boundaries between the sexes, posing a threat to gender ideals and myths. This is the reason why women's football is viewed sceptically, marginalised or even rejected; and this is especially the case when women players orient their style of play to men's football. Women who play rough and aggressive football do not fit into the dichotomous gender arrangements and therefore awaken misgivings and tension. After the World Championship victory, the DFB president deplored: 'You can't change the rules so that fighting for the ball becomes gentler' (*Berliner Zeitung*, 14 October 2003, p. 28).

It should also be noted that in Germany, as in many other countries, football is a national sport. National sports and myths of masculinity are interwoven in a special way: 'A specific male identity is produced and maintained in the national sport of any given society. This explains why the national sport in every society is not only a male preserve ... but is also bound up with sexual claims, needs and anxieties' (Klein 1983: 18). This helps to explain why, even at the turn of the twenty-first century, women meet with resistance when they wish to play football on men's football pitches. In spite of all the enthusiasm after the women's World Championships, sports journalists doubt very much whether women's football will become a genuine national sport. All in all, the experts predict that it will be difficult for women's football to win over the hard-core fans for any length of time, to shed its image as a 'men's sport' or even to contribute to a deconstruction of gender. However, the 'metrosexuality' and 'gender play' of stars like David Beckham may help to popularise the new and alternative constructions of masculinity and thus make room for new constructions of femininities in football.

The image of female players

Women playing football present images that deviate from traditional feminine ideals. These feminine ideals, however, still play a very important role in football – perhaps not on the pitch but certainly in the private lives of the stars, accounts of which saturate the pages of the tabloid press. In the world of football the mass media focus on the male stars and the wives they have either just abandoned or married, the girlfriends they have had for years or for days and their secret or not-so-secret mistresses. In answer to the question of who the eleven most important women in German football were, *BILD* newspaper wrote: 'The wives and girlfriends of the national team' (*Emma*, September/October 2004, p. 13). They are presented as the 'other sex', as erotic and attractive status symbols – and get much more public attention than do female football players, who radiate too little of the glamour that today's media demand of stars and starlets, including such sports idols as tennis player Anna Kournikova. American players like Brandi Chastain of the World Championship team have adapted to market principles, posing semi-nude for men's magazines. However, it is questionable whether this has helped to make women's soccer more popular in the USA, for even here women soccer players do not have a particularly good image, even though sixteen million girls and women play it. In the popularity hierarchy of the American high school, kids playing it is not exactly an advantage for girls: an old car, glasses, liking arts, being intellectual, not wearing the right clothes and being a member of the soccer team – single or in combination – are sins which make a girl 'undateable' for boys and an outcast for the other girls: (*Spiegel* 24, 1999, p. 221). Accordingly, the Women's United Soccer Association, the professional league founded in 2001, was not able to survive for very long, failing to generate adequate public attention and interest to sustain its sponsorship base.

With their bodies, their movements and their clothes, women football players send out a signal that they do not fit into the traditional ideals and stereotypes of femininity. Thus, being different, they are described as 'she-men' – which is to be seen in the many discussions in internet forums as well as in conventional media coverage (see, for example, *Welt am Sonntag*, 23 May 2004). And comments on women spectators may be found along the lines of: '1,500 spectators and 1,440 of them she-men. And that's exactly the reason why this sport will never be as popular as some people would like.'[8] Women football players are – at least until now – no role models; and here Alice Schwarzer, editor of the feminist journal *Emma*, and German football player Doris Fitschen are in complete agreement. In an interview Fitschen emphasised that only highly attractive athletes in 'attractive sports' can earn the big money and become top stars. The importance of appearance and appeal is something that other women players are indeed aware of. After the World Championship victory, Silke Rottenberg said, 'I used to think: the main thing is that I can play football. But for a few years now I've thought it's more important not to appear quite so masculine' (http://www.zeit.de/2004/01/10_2f12_2fRottenberg). Most soccer players, though, do not want to fit into current ideals of beauty. At the same time, most players reject traditional models of femininity and have developed their own definitions and constructions in order to be able to combine playing football with their lives as women (Pfister 1999; Pfister and Fasting 2004). Therefore, most of them refuse to serve as 'objects of male desire', Sylvia Neid, for example, rejecting a highly lucrative offer from *Playboy* magazine to pose for nude photos (*Spiegel* 45, 1994, p. 193). Such responses show that femininity and strength are no longer as contradictory as they once were, an argument also made by Heywood and Dworkin in their book *Built to Win* (2003), in which they describe how – on account of changes in ideals and images – strong and successful athletes such as the soccer player Mia Hamm have become idols of at least a part of the American population. According to the *Berliner Zeitung*, the World Championship managed to become a popular event in spite of the fact that 'often rather brash women are to be seen scudding along the turf and many of the players refuse to observe the basic principles of marketing'. Is this a signal for the change of taste and a change of gender ideals in German society?

Homophobia

The image of women football players as well as their experiences are decisively influenced by homophobia, which is not directed exclusively at homosexual athletes but also at sportsmen and women who are suspected of being homosexual because they to do not conform to the traditional gender arrangements. This is especially true of soccer players because they have intruded upon a traditional and prestigious male domain (see, for example, Griffin 1998).

The results of the interviews conducted in the project 'Sport in Women's Lives' back up the assumption that women football players experience homophobia, regardless of their sexual orientation (Pfister 1999). The players interviewed talked quite openly about the topic of homosexuality, reporting that in all teams there were lesbian players but that this was in no way detrimental to either the solidarity among the players or the quality of their football. Some of our interview partners admitted to having a homosexual orientation during the interviews so that homophobic sentiments were relatively rare. Nevertheless, there were interview partners who felt that players who openly showed their sexual orientation had a harmful effect on the team, the club and the sport. Further, there were frequent reports in the interviews of homophobia in the football environment – among coaches, officials and spectators. All top-level players remembered situations in which homophobic attitudes were displayed, and some players related that they had been called 'mannish' and labelled lesbians. Several women also reported threats by managers and coaches that they would 'quit the job' if lesbians were allowed to the join the team.

The example of Martina Voss is illustrative of the extent to which homosexuality is taboo and of the damaging consequences that offending against 'compulsory heterosexuality' may have. As she reported to the *Spiegel* magazine, Voss was expelled from the national team without being given any official reason five months before the start of the Olympic Games in

Sydney after she had admitted to a lesbian relationship with another player (*Spiegel* 29, 2003, p. 160). Some of the interviewed players in the study mentioned above also claimed that showing affection towards another woman had to be avoided since the mere suspicion of being a lesbian could lead to being 'thrown out of the team'. Similar consequences were feared by players who were 'outed' as lesbians, for example, by taking part in the 'Gay Games'. And when in a radio interview the famous Green politician, Daniel Cohn-Bendit, described the World Championship team as the 'national lesbian eleven', 'the telephone lines of the NDR radio station were jammed – you can't say such a thing, can you?' (*Anstoss*, 1, 2004, p. 18).

Making homosexuality a taboo is one of the most important and effective strategies of homophobia. The consequence for lesbian players is that they conceal their feelings, their thoughts and their private lives. The pressure bearing down on lesbian athletes can have a harmful effect on their self-confidence and their self-image as well as on their sporting performance. Homophobia can have a decisive influence on a sport. Football is still a sport with a 'male' image, meaning that, while male football players connote heterosexuality (and today perhaps also various kinds of masculinity), women players connote masculinization and homosexuality. And the fact that women's football has relatively little attraction may be related – at least partly – to this widespread homophobia: it may be assumed that the image of women's football as a 'lesbian sport' is detrimental not only to the willingness of girls to take up football but also to the willingness of parents to let their daughters play the game. It is this argument, at any rate, that is used to great effect by clubs and associations to prevent the 'outing' of their women players. In general terms, too, making homosexuality a taboo is a way of preventing the deconstruction of gender arrangements, based as they are on the duality of gender and on heterosexuality.

Women's football and the construction of difference

Since the nineteenth century, women and football have been constructed and described as contradictions. From the beginning, football was a gender marker and produced gender differences partly by assigning competence in the sport to men and denying the same competence to women. Doubts about the abilities of the players have always belonged to the repertoire of arguments put forward by opponents of women's football. In 1986, for instance, the football idol Paul Breitner expressed the opinion that women players 'were wrecking the game of football' (*Characho*, 1, 1986, p. 23). In the above-mentioned interview-study with female soccer players, nearly all the players mentioned prejudices which referred not only to their competence as soccer players but also, as mentioned above, to their appearance and femininity (Pfister 1999).

Today, in a period of 'political correctness', it is not done to simply dismiss women football players on the basis of old prejudices. However, one exception to this is the famous football coach Max Merkel, self-styled 'custodian of the art of football', who in 2003 claimed that women's football had nothing to do with football at all; it is 'a strain on the eyes. . . . How painful it is to have to watch this sort of game in slow motion – the women going into a sliding tackle with their strapping legs. And pulling at each others' jerseys, which just about cover what's left of their womanhood' (*TAZ*, 27 September 2003, http://www.taz.de/pt/2003/09/27/a0180.nf/ text.ges,1). By belittling the players' skills and casting aspersions on their femininity, Merkel restores order to the hierarchy of the sexes, that football underpins. That Merkel is not alone in his opinions is shown by the comments made about women's football in the various internet chat rooms, which range from 'Nobody gives a damn about women's football' to 'Women are scared of the ball'. In Germany, where football is part of the culture, women's football remains a kind of subversive culture that provokes emotional opposition.

A further question continues to be whether women should play football like men or rather a separate form of women's football. But there is still no consensus today about the extent to which the men's game differs from that of the women and whether it is necessary or even desirable for women to play the game in exactly the same way as it is played by men.

After the official recognition of women's football in 1970, special rules were drawn up first of all to ensure a 'women's style of play'. Football played by women was required to be a 'very elegant game, pleasing to watch. They should not be rough and stubborn when fighting for the ball since that does not suit them at all' (*WFV-Sport*, 11, 10 June 1971). To put women's football in an appropriate framework, instructions for training and playing were published, for example, in *WFV-Sport*, the journal of the West-German Football Federation, where it was emphasised again and again that female players could not and should not emulate their male counterparts: 'It is here that the training of techniques, especially those of kicking the ball, differs from the men's training. The ball is not to be kicked with the same force and intensity that men use, for example when shooting at the goal or clearing. [The women] will play or pass the ball to each other' (*WFV-Sport*, 11, June 1971). Elsewhere it stated: 'Women, of course, are not like Günter Netzer or Fritz Walter. All the same, they, too, can learn this sophisticated shot' (*WFV-Sport*, 20, 21 October 1971; Naul 1989).

Slowly but surely, women's football developed into a sport which was to be taken seriously, improving continuously as the players who had trained consistently from their childhood gradually grew into the women's teams. Today there is no question about the tactical skills of top-level women players. Nevertheless, women agree that they could not and should not emulate male players. 'It's just the man–woman rivalry that pushes them.

And that's exactly what we don't want in football', said Birgit Prinz, one of the best women players, in an interview (http://www.stern.de/sport-motor/sportwelt?id=518842&p=2&nv=ct_cb). The DFB and the *Bundesliga* clubs are trying to establish women's football as a brand of its own, in which emphasis is placed on women's skills. According to the manager of the Frankfurt Women's Football Club, there is 'more playing and less fouling' (Morbach 2001: 7). In spite of all the statements that have been made, women are aware that they are measured according to male standards and that the constant comparisons always include a judgement. The highest praise that can be given to a woman is that she plays like a man – for example, Oliver Kahn. That this is belittling is all the more evident when the tables are turned and the Bayern Munich and German national side's goalkeeper Oliver Kahn is described as a second Silke Rottenberg.

As a rule, the comparisons are unfavourable for the women; for instance, when it is pointed out that women would not have a chance even against third-rate men's teams (http://www.politikforum.de/forum/archive/9/2003/11/4/39343). Even though the *Berliner Zeitung* criticised the comparisons made between men's and women's football, it stayed within the discourse of gender difference: 'The men are head and shoulders above the women players, which invites comparisons with the weaker sex. That the women simply don't stand up to such a comparison is self-evident. It may be true that the national team would have a hard time surviving in the men's regional league' (*Berliner Zeitung*, 13 October 2003, p. 31).

In *Anstoss*, the DFB's prestige magazine published in the run-up to the football World Cup in 2006, Klaus Theweleit, author of the cult book *Men's Fantasies* published in 1977 and professed football fan, wrote: 'Women's football is now in the ascendancy. . . . Technically speaking, the differences are not very great, and women handle the ball well. What is missing is strength and energy in running and tackling' (*Anstoss*, 1, 2004, p. 23). And even if a supporter of women's football like Daniel Cohn-Bendit claims that the women's style of play is more aesthetic since in men's football many of the sequences of passes are spoiled because of the increased tempo of the game, this implies – whether intended or not – that women's football is the 'other' version of football (*Anstoss*, 1, 2004, p. 19).

Like no other area of our society, sport serves to generate differences and make them visible – and this includes gender differences. This is also true of football which, although modifying existing gendered images and scripts by integrating women, still perpetuates dichotomous patterns of perception and judgement through its emphasis on gender differences. As already pointed out in various contexts, football is one of the sports in which gender discourses flare up but which also may change. The question is whether – and, if so, to what extent – the women football players themselves are involved in deconstructing gender.

Doing gender – the perspectives of the players

The players – biographies and attitudes

In the interviews conducted as part of the project 'Sport in Women's Lives' (Pfister 1999) as well as the biographies published on the web pages of the German *Bundesliga* players show typical patterns with regard to their biographies, their socialisation and their self-awareness. Most of the players learned football on the streets or in parks as children, often spurred on and given lessons by fathers or brothers, but sometimes also against their parents' will. For the project, ten top-level players and ten players at the 'sport for all' level described how they became committed football players. Seventeen of the twenty players interviewed, mentioned the importance of 'boys on the street' or brothers for their football careers. A recurrent theme in all the accounts is that the girls were accepted as footballers by the boys because they were as good as or even better than many of the boys. They were often the only girls allowed to play with the boys and were accepted as 'mates'. One player reported that she fitted in so well with the boys that 'there were many who didn't even know that I was a girl!' (Pfister 1999: 102). Almost unanimously, these were girls who defined themselves as 'tomboys'. One respondent's comment was typical: 'I was a part of the gang; in a way I was a boy'. Another player mentioned having similar feelings: 'I always wanted to be a boy because girls were not allowed to climb trees, be a member of a gang, play Cowboys and Indians, play soccer and be involved in all these exciting adventures'.

Not only the biographies but also the attitudes, experiences and motivations of the soccer players showed many similarities. They all derived a tremendous amount of pleasure from playing the game; they enjoyed a feeling of control, enjoyed the excitement of 'being physical' and enjoyed playing together. Probably the most frequently mentioned aspect of their experiences was the pleasure they gained from being together, their connectedness as women and as a team. 'If you play an individual sport you can only be glad for yourself. If you are in a team, it is a wonderful feeling when you have an important match and especially if you get a goal. It doesn't matter who scores the goal but, when the ball is in the net, we all throw ourselves on the ground and hug each other – this is great, this being and belonging together' (Pfister 1999: 143). Despite the male tradition and image of football, the women players seem to have created a female space in which they clearly enjoy sharing and supporting each other. These women share the meanings that they attach to the game and express very similar feelings of enjoyment. In addition, they present an 'active physicality' very similar to that discussed by Woodward (1996) in her study of women who do windsurfing, another male-dominated and male-defined sport. She argues that windsurfing involves entering a privileged masculine world and an active physicality which contravenes norms of feminine embodiment. Through windsurfing we challenge the oppressiveness of femininity and the privileges of masculinity and push at the boundaries of gender (Woodward 1996: 30).

Playing football is connected with specific ideals of the body and movement. Here, there prevails a more functional attitude to the body in which it is not appearance that is important but rather exertion, sweating, endurance, strength, toughness and competition. Besides technical and tactical skills, competition means aggressive body contact – woman fighting against woman. According to statements made in the interview study mentioned above, the players love the running and the fighting, and the game with its challenges. They like competition because of its intensity – competition is the 'real game', since it is connected with the fascination, thrill and experience of success (Pfister 1999). Thus female soccer players seem to have developed a specific type of physicality which contradicts traditional female conceptions of body and movement.

Devising new concepts of femininity

According to Judith Lorber (1994, 2000), the gender order can be deconstructed, i.e. decoded and modified, when people cross the boundaries of the gender norms, refuse to assume traditional roles and, instead, devise new concepts beyond the duality of gender. This is possible, not least because gender is not a simple, one-dimensional construction but rather a process in which various dimensions and categories (e.g. biological gender, sexual orientation, gender identities and gender images) can combine to form different 'mixtures'. An individual, for example, may have female genes and be a lesbian, mother, nurse and football player. Lorber proposes that we write new 'scripts' and play new roles, combining and mixing male and female 'gender markers' such as clothes and movements. In many respects this is precisely what top-level women football players do. On the one hand, they challenge the ideologies of femininity prevailing in the dominant sports culture by intruding upon the male domain of football. On the other hand, the women change – at least to a certain degree and partly in a subversive way – traditional interpretations of masculinity and femininity by refusing to identify with the stereotypes, expectations and ideals of womanhood or to conform to conventional images of femininity in terms of appearance and behaviour. This is clearly revealed in the interviews conducted as part of the project 'Sport in Women's Lives' (Pfister 1999). Irrespective of their sexual orientation, all the women interviewed were critical of the prevailing ideals of beauty and femininity, but all also agreed that they were women and, moreover, happy to be women. The majority of them, though, also described how they had acquired female identities in lengthy and ambivalent processes. 'I always played with the boys and I wished dearly to be one of them. All these girls – they were so boring', reported one of the players (Pfister 1999). Some of the women related how greatly they were in conflict with the expectations of their social surroundings and how they eventually reconciled themselves to being women – women with their own definition of womanhood. 'Today I'm so glad I'm a woman. I'm free to decide what to wear and how to behave. Sometimes I even use lipstick', declared one player in her interview (Pfister 1999). Many of the women admitted to having multiple, multi-layered or variable gender constructions, without passing a negative judgement on it or experiencing it as something problematic. On the contrary, they seem to be able to cope effortlessly with multi-dimensional and changing gender identities and images. They adjusted their appearance, their behaviour and their speech to the social context and to the people with whom they inter-acted. Several of the players interviewed described themselves as 'powerful' and self-assured – attributes that they considered entirely positive – and did not feel threatened by gender stereotypes which gave these attributes a masculine connotation. One of the German women interviewed described herself as a 'mixture of gentleness and steel'. The fact that they did not fit into either gender category had no negative consequences for them; on the contrary, they seemed to enjoy playing with gender stereotypes and regarded 'gender play' as a sport.

Football plays an important role in the construction and enactment of gender, since it transforms the body and behaviour. Maria expressed this as follows: 'When a woman plays a competitive sport, she will never look like a mannequin. The body builds muscles, and you can argue whether this is feminine, but I think it looks good' (Pfister 1999). Anna affirmed: 'I've learned to be tough, to fight. On a football pitch you can't be just a nice girl' (Pfister 1999). At the same time, the women – even those who regarded 'masculinization' on the football field as something positive – were well aware that muscular bodies and aggressive behaviour in everyday life, which is marked by gender duality, are not always judged favourably. Judith Butler (1990) coined the term 'gender troublemakers' to denote individuals who, actively opposing the prevailing gender order, redefine gender and enact gender differently. Several of the women players we interviewed seem to be such 'gender troublemakers', developing – at least to a certain degree – femininities which deviated from the socially accepted ideals but without acting in a 'typically male' fashion, feeling like men or renouncing their womanhood. Their reports suggest a disintegration of the extreme polarities of masculinity and femininity. In an article entitled 'Using Gender to Undo Gender', Judith Lorber (2000) observed that it was astonishing how 'the more things change, the more they stay the same'. When one considers both the lack of attention paid to women's sports, especially women's foot-ball, by the mass media, and the gender hierarchies existing in sports organisations all over the world, one cannot but agree with Lorber's observa-tion. The alternative gender constructions of women football players can, though, be interpreted as a first step in a general direction which, according to Lorber, ought to lead to a resolution of gender differences that have for too long been deeply established in a patriarchal culture.

Notes

1 Parts of this chapter have been published in: *Football Studies* 4 (2001): 41–58; F. Hong and J.A. Mangan (eds) (2004) *Soccer, Women, Sexual Liberation: Kicking off a New Era*, London: Frank Cass; D. Jütting (ed.) (2004) *Lokal-globale Fußballkultur*, Munich/Berlin: Waxmann.
2 Unfavourable comments on football in other countries are to be found, for example, in an article in *Sport und Gesundheit* (1938), 9: 18; see also Marschik 2003; Meier 2004.
3 See the typed report of Hans Hansen in the name of the board of consultants of the DFB (15 November 1969). This paper contains an overview of the decisions of the DFB concerning women's football and the proposal for a resolution on behalf of the acceptance of women's football. A copy of this paper was sent to me by Liselott Diem (letter from 25 July 1978). Cf. Ratzeburg and Biese 1995.
4 *WFV-Sport*, 7, 11 April 1957: see also *Sport im Spiegel*, 14 June 1957; this is a manuscript in the Carl-und-Liselott-Diem Archive at the German Sports University Cologne, Liselott-Diem-Collection File 334.
5 'Best team' competitions were not officially recognised as championships; they neither led to prizes nor awards, nor did they entitle those selected to take part in international contests. The players were thus deprived of the privileges connected with 'official' championships.
6 http://fifaworldcup.yahoo.com/03/en/031013/1/duq.html (accessed 27 September 2005); see also the other comments on this webpage.
7 *Frankfurter Rundschau*, 14 May 1995, p. 18; *Der Spiegel*, 45, 1995, p. 191; *Berliner Zeitung*, 237, 11/12 October 2003, p. 3, about the players of Turbine Potsdam.
8 See e.g. the discussion in the webpage of the top player Ariane Hingst: http://www.ariane-hingst.de/gaestebuch.php (accessed 27 September 2005).

References

Anstoss (2004) Vol. 1, edited as a special project by the Football Globe 2006 FIFA World Cup.
Brändle, F. and Koller, C. (2002) *Goooal!!! Kultur- und Sozialgeschichte des modernen Fußballs*, Zurich: Orell Füssli Verlag.
Brüggemeier, F.J. (ed.) (2000) *Der Ball ist rund*, Essen: Klartext.
Butler, J. (1990) *Gender Trouble*, New York: Routledge.
Buytendijk, F.J.J. (1953) *Das Fußballspiel: Eine psychologische Studie*, Würzburg: Werkbund-Verlag.
Cachau, K. and Bahlke, S. (2003) *Trainer . . . das ist halt einfach Männersache: Studie zur Unterrepräsentierung von Trainerinnen im Spitzensport*, Köln: Strauss.
Connell, R.W. (2002) *Gender*, Cambridge: Polity Press.
Deutscher Fußballbund (DSB) (ed.) (1983) *Damenfußball – Grundlagen und Entwicklung*, 2nd edn, Frankfurt/Main: Dt. Fußballbund.
Diem, L. (1978) 'Frauen-Fußball – ein Stück Emanzipation?', *Das Parlament*, 22–23 June, p. 11.
Dunning, E. (1986) 'Sport as a Male Preserve: Notes on the Social Sources of Masculine Identity and its Transformations', in N. Elias and E. Dunning (eds) *Quest for Excitement: Sport and Leisure in the Civilizing Process*, Oxford: Blackwell.
Fechtig, B. (1995) *Frauen und Fußball: Interviews, Porträts, Reportagen*, Dortmund: Ed. Ebersbach im eFeF-Verlag.
Fischer-Dückelmann, A. (1905) *Die Frau als Hausärztin*, 2nd edn, Dresden and Stuttgart: Süddeutsches Verlags-Institut.

Frevert, U. (1995) *Mann und Weib, und Weib und Mann: Geschlechter-Differenzen in der Moderne*, Munich: Beck.

Griffin, P. (1998) *Strong Women, Deep Closets: Lesbians and Homophobia in Sport*, Windsor: Human Kinetics.

Hartmann-Tews, I. and Bettina, R. (2002). 'Ungleiche Repräsentation von Sportlerinnen und Sportlern in den Medien?' in G. Pfister (ed.) *Frauen im Hochleistungssport* (S. 27–41), Sankt Augustin: Czwalina.

Heineken, P. (1898; 2nd edn 1993) *Das Fußballspiel: Association und Rugby*, Hannover: Ed. Libri Rari Schäfer.

Heywood. L. and Dworkin, S. (2003) *Built to Win: The Female Athlete as Cultural Icon*, Minneapolis: University of Minnesota Press.

Klein, G. (1997) 'Theoretische Prämissen einer Geschlechterforschung in der Sportwissenschaft', in U. Henkel and S. Kröner (eds) *Und sie bewegt sich doch*, Pfaffenweiler: Centaurus.

Klein, M. (1983) *Sport und Geschlecht*, Reinbek: Rororo.

Kröger, M. (1996) *Frauenfußball in der öffentlichen Diskussion – Entwicklungen und Veränderungen seit 1970*, unpublished thesis, University of Berlin.

Kugelmann, C. and Sinning, S. (2004) 'Wie lernen Mädchen Fußball-Spielen', in C. Kugelmann, G. Pfister and C. Zipprich (eds) *Geschlechterforschung im Sport*, Hamburg: Czwalina.

Linsen, K. (1997) 'Frauen im Fußballsport – zwischen Anspruch und Wirklichkeit', in U. Henkel and G. Pfister (eds) *Für eine andere Bewegungskultur*, Pfaffenweiler: Centaurus-Verl.-Ges.

Lopez, S. (1997) *Women on the Ball*, London: Scarlett.

Lorber, J. (1994) *Paradoxes of Gender*, New Haven, CT: Yale University Press.

—— (2000) 'Using Gender to Undo Gender', *Feminist Theory*, 1(1), 79–96.

Marschik, M. (2003) *Frauenfussball und Maskulinität*, Münster: Lit.

Meier, D. (1995) 'Frauenfußball in der DDR', in H. Ratzeburg and H. Biese (eds) *Frauen Fußball Meisterschaften*, Kassel: Agon-Sportverlag.

Meier, M. (2004) *Zarte Füßchen am harten Leder . . ., Frauenfußball in der Schweiz* Frauenfeld: Huber.

Mende, W. von (1995) 'Frauenfußball und die Medien', *dieda*, 6: 6–8.

Messner, M. (1994) 'Sports and Male Domination: The Female Athlete as Contested Ideological Terrain', in S. Birrell and C. Cole (eds) *Women, Sport, and Culture*, Champaign: Human Kinetics.

Morbach, A. (2001) 'Es tut sich was', *Der Fußballtrainer*, 52(8): 5–8.

Mosse, G. L. (1996) *The Image of Man: The Creation of Modern Masculinity*, New York: Oxford University Press.

Naul, R. (1989) 'Sportwissenschaftliche Analysen zum Frauenfußball', in Naul, R. and Schmidt W. (eds) *Beiträge und Analysen zum Fußballsport*, Chusthal-Zellerfeld: dvs.

Pfister, G. (ed.) (1980) *Frau und Sport*, Frankfurt/Main: Fischer-Taschenbuch-Verlag.

—— (1993) '"Der Kampf gebührt dem Mann . . .": Argumente und Gegenargumente im Diskurs über den Frauensport', in R. Renson *et al.* (eds) *Sport and Contest*, Madrid: INEF.

—— (1999) *Sport im Lebenszusammenhang von Frauen*, Schorndorf: Hofmann.

—— (2000) 'Women and the Olympic Games', in B. Drinkwater (ed.) *Women in Sport*, Oxford: Blackwell.

—— (2002) *Frauensport in der DDR*, Cologne: Strauß.

—— (2003a) 'Fussball als Erinnerungsort: Zur Globalisierung des Fußballsports an der Wende vom 19. zum 20. Jahrhundert', in R. Adelmann, R. Parr and T. Schwarz (eds) *Querpässe: Beiträge zur Literatur-, Kultur- und Mediengeschichte des Fussballs*, Heidelberg: Synchron Wissenschaftsverlag der Autoren.

—— (2003b) 'Cultural Confrontations: German Turnen, Swedish Gymnastics and English Sport – European Diversity in Physical Activities from a Historical Perspective', *Culture, Sport, Society*, 6 (1): 61–91.

Pfister, G. and Fasting, K. (2004) 'Geschlechterkonstruktionen auf dem Fußballplatz', in D. Jütting (ed.) *Die lokal-globale Fußballkultur*, Munich and Berlin: Waxmann.

Pfister, G. and Langenfeld, H. (1980) 'Die Leibesübungen für das weibliche Geschlecht – ein Mittel zur Emanzipation der Frau?', in H. Ueberhorst (ed.) *Geschichte der Leibesübungen*, vol. 3/1, Berlin: Bartels & Wernitz.

Pfister, G. and Langenfeld, H. (1982) 'Vom Frauenturnen zum modernen Sport. Die Entwicklung der Leibesübungen der Frauen und Mädchen seit dem Ersten Weltkrieg', in H. Ueberhorst (ed.) *Geschichte der Leibesübungen*, vol. 3/2, Berlin: Bartels & Wernitz.

Pfister, G., Fasting K., Scraton, S. and Vasquez, B. (1998) 'Women and Football – A Contradiction? The Beginnings of Women's Football in Four European Countries', *The European Sports History Review*, 1: 1–26.

Prudhomme, L. (1996) 'Sexe faible et ballon rond. Esquisse d'une histoire du football féminine', in P. Arnaud and T. Terret (eds) *Histoire du Sport Féminin*, vol. I, Paris: L'Harmattan.

Ratzeburg, H. (1986) 'Fußball ist Frauensport', in S. Schenk (ed.) *Frauen-Bewegung-Sport*, Hamburg: VSA-Verlag.

Ratzeburg, H. and Biese, H. (1995) *Frauen Fußball Meisterschaften*, Kassel: Agon-Sportverlag.

Schreiber-Rietig, B. (1993) 'Die Suffragetten spielten Fußball', *Olympisches Feuer*, 2: 36–41.

Vierath, W. (1930) *Moderner Sport*, Berlin: Oestergaard.

Völger, G. and Welck, K.V. (eds) (1990) *Männderbande Männerbünde*, 2 vols, Cologne: Rautenstrauch-Joest-Museum.

Woodward V. (1996) 'Exploring the gendered experiences of windsurfing women – Can women be "real windsurfers"?', paper presented at the LSA Conference: The Big Ghetto – Gender, Sexuality and Leisure, Leeds, 16–20 July 1998.

7 The Europeanization of German football

Alexander Brand and Arne Niemann

Introduction

Although 'football' has still a somewhat exotic status as a subject of interest in political science, there is a growing body of literature which tries to outline the important political dimensions of the game. This tendency is more evident in globalization debates, where football is taken to be one of the most globalized phenomena (Foer 2004). Some authors have also tried to establish a link between European integration and the development of football on the continent (Missiroli 2002). In this chapter, we analyse the impact of European-level governance – the case law of the European Court of Justice and the Community's competences in the area of competition policy – on German football. In the broader context, additional factors are considered which relate less clearly to the European integration process, such as the development of the Champions League or the emergence of transnational groupings such as the G-14. Taken together, these processes add up to the ongoing 'Europeanization' of German football.

The concept of Europeanization

Research on Europeanization has gradually increased since the mid-1990s and has developed into an academic growth industry over the past decade. While the term 'Europeanization' has been taken up by most (sub-) disciplines in the humanities and social sciences focusing on Europe, it is arguably in the area of political science scholarship dealing with European integration that the concept has been used most widely. In this latter field alone, the term 'Europeanization' is used in a number of different ways to describe a variety of phenomena and processes of change (Olsen 2002). Most frequently, Europeanization is understood as the process of change in the domestic arena, in terms of policy substance and instruments, processes and politics as well as polity and institutions resulting from European integration or the European level of governance more generally (Ladrech 1994: 69; Radaelli 2000: 3).

The current Europeanization research agenda faces several challenges. These may be described and systematized along terminological, theoretical, methodological and empirical dimensions. This chapter concentrates mainly on the empirical dimension. Empirical work on Europeanization has proliferated in recent years. An important set of questions revolves around the instruments, institutions, actors and mechanisms that induce and resist change (and may explain national variation in responding to European-ization pressures). Our empirical analysis highlights a rather neglected aspect in the literature: the societal/transnational dimension of Europeanization. This dimension encapsulates two elements: (1) the *level and sphere* of change; (2) the type of *agency* generating or resisting change. Hence by societal/ transnational dimension we mean, on the one hand, the fact that regu-lation and jurisdiction from Brussels is likely to induce some adaptational pressure not only at the political level but also in societal contexts (e.g. the realm of sport), and for our purpose, football. On the other hand, to speak of a transnational dimension of Europeanization aims at capturing some trends, which may be traced in analysing how societal actors are either acting towards attempts at regulation by the EU (e.g. football associations and clubs after the Bosman ruling) or creating transnational spaces and institutions in Europe themselves (e.g. the UEFA-Champions League, the so-called 'G-14') that in turn impact on the governance of football.[1]

The Bosman ruling and German football

Some important trends in German football during the past decade may be interpreted as symptoms of an ongoing Europeanization. This is because a whole complex of trends – the rapid influx of foreign-born players, various attempts to restrict their numbers as well as to promote young German talents, and the search for a new 'transfer regime' – has its roots in the seminal 'Bosman ruling' of the European Court of Justice (ECJ) in 1995. 'Bosman', in this regard, is not only the one legal case every football player and fan knows (Foster 2000: 39). The ruling and its antecedents, which have been described in detail elsewhere (Croci 2001; Parrish 2003; Weatherill 2003), together with the relatively active role of the European Commis-sion in the realm of sports during the 1990s, also had a tremendous impact upon German football.

The provisions in the Treaty establishing the European Community, secondary legislation, Community policies and decisions all had an increasing impact on sport throughout Europe in the past decade, although 'sport' has never been among the core competences of the EC/EU (Ducrey *et al.* 2003: 32). Traditionally, football in all its aspects has been regulated by a set of autonomous, interrelated organizations: football clubs, national leagues and associations, several regional federations and one worldwide football federation (Croci 2001: 2). During the 1990s, however, football came to be recognized as an economic activity by leading European insti-tutions such as the European Commission and the European Court of Justice, and thus as an activity that had to be regulated, like any other industry, according to the rules of the Community.

The Bosman ruling of the ECJ in 1995 in essence consisted of two general findings derived from EU law concerning the free movement of people within the European Union and competition law, which of course drew on the former. The two findings were: first, the traditional transfer system with transfer fees to be paid for out-of-contract players infringed upon the right of every European (worker) to move freely under Article 48 of the Treaty of Rome (TEC) and thus had to be abolished; and second, 'nationality restrictions' as a means to limit the number of foreign players in a football club were ruled illegal insofar as they discriminated against players from countries within the European Union (Foster 2000: 42).

Football in Germany has been affected by both aspects, although one could claim that the latter has had a more 'visible' effect for the whole football community. Rendering illegal any general nationality restriction implied the abolishment of the so-called '3 + 2 rule' which allowed a European team to field three foreign players and in addition two 'assimilated players' (foreign players who had played in the relevant country for at least five consecutive years). Abolishing this rule and opening up the market to players from all other countries within the EU would in itself amount to an increase in the number of foreign-born players in German football. The German Football Association (DFB), however, liberalized even further and expanded the right to play football in Germany without being considered a foreigner not only to EU residents (so-called *EU-Ausländer*) but to all players living within the fifty-one other member states of the European Football Association (UEFA). Thus after 'Bosman' the status of *EU-Ausländer* really meant *UEFA-Ausländer* in German football, and EU resident meant UEFA resident. This applied, however, to the two professional leagues only.

How can we account for such an extension, which has been exceptional in Europe? One line of argumentation refers to the special socio-political situation in Germany after re-unification. From this perspective, the DFB and its leading actors were still influenced and impressed by the dramatic political changes in Europe and the 'unification' of the continent that had taken place a few years before. They simply 'did not want to erect new walls or barriers', especially towards national associations in Central and Eastern Europe, which had strong ties to the DFB.[2] In a similar vein, some actors were convinced that the ongoing process of European integration would sooner or later render any differentiation between certain types of Europeans meaningless anyway.[3] Although the extension may show, in the words of DFB president Dr Theo Zwanziger, that 'football sometimes is more political than people think',[4] there was also an element of pragmatic (and even visionary) thinking to it, because the decision taken by the DFB in the end prevented non-EU European footballers from taking legal action against discrimination.[5] Another interpretation is that this extension created a larger market for German football clubs to sign players, especially players from Central and Eastern Europe, which for the most part proved cost-saving in the short term. Given the fact that after 'Bosman' a central source of financing for clubs – transfer fees for out-of-contract players – ceased to exist, and that German clubs were (and are) subject to a relatively strict licensing procedure, which means they had (and have) to pursue sound economic policies, opening up the market, especially towards Eastern Europe, also had a 'compensation effect' for German football clubs, since signing players from Poland or the Balkans was in general less expensive.[6] Both explanations – the socio-political climate as well as the clubs' interest in improving their position among European competitors – may be seen as complementary rather than mutually exclusive.

It is hardly surprising that this decision led to a surge of players coming from all over Europe to Germany. Table 7.1 points to the increase in foreign players, especially UEFA-*Ausländer*, in the First Bundesliga.

At the beginning of the 1990s – before 'Bosman' – the shares of the respective groups (German-born players, UEFA residents and non-UEFA

Table 7.1 Number of players fielded in the German 1. Bundesliga

Season	Players Bundesliga	German-born	Share (%)	'UEFA residents'	Share (%)	'non-UEFA residents'	Share (%)
1992/93	394	326	82.7	48	12.2	20	5.1
1993/94	415	332	80.0	53	12.8	30	7.2
1994/95	424	341	80.4	55	13.0	28	6.6
1995/96	428	346	80.8	60	14.0	22	5.1
1996/97	457	345	75.5	96	21.0	16	3.5
1997/98	444	293	66.0	128	28.8	23	5.2
1998/99	461	295	64.0	133	28.9	33	7.2
1999/00	440	270	61.4	128	29.1	42	9.5
2000/01	475	274	57.7	160	33.7	41	8.6
2001/02	469	248	52.9	167	35.6	54	11.5
2002/03	467	231	49.5	177	37.9	59	12.6
2003/04	469	237	50.5	168	35.8	64	13.6
2004/05	429*	208	48.5	166	38.7	55	12.8
Increase in size 92–04 (%)	9	–36.2		246		175	
Increase in size since Bosman	~0	–39.9		176.6		150	

Note
1992–2004, * = as of December 2004, split according to German-born players, UEFA residents, and players from other continents ('Non-UEFA residents') and their total share; increase in the number of players within these groups from 1992 to 2004 and from 1995 to 2004 (since the 'Bosman ruling' of December 1995 and the decision of the DFB only took effect in 1996, data from 1995 have been taken as reference point). Data obtained from IMP AG Ismaning/Germany.

residents) exhibit a fairly stable pattern. After 'Bosman' and the decision of the DFB to count all players from UEFA member states as EU residents, we can clearly detect some important changes in the composition of players in the *Bundesliga*. First, the share of German-born players has steadily decreased up to today's level of less than 50 per cent. Second, the share of UEFA residents as well as the share of players from other continents has substantially increased, although the share of non-UEFA residents remains relatively small compared to that of UEFA residents. Although the decision to open the market to all Europeans has been rather liberal, the DFB did not fully liberalize. The number of players from other continents which a professional club could field in any one match remained limited to three; since 2001 for reasons of international competitiveness it has been lifted to five.[7] However, in October 2004, the German Football League (DFL) took the decision to cut back the quota again: to four players in 2005 to 2006, and to three players in 2006 to 2007.

The increase in foreign players in national leagues has been just one of the presumed consequences of the 'Bosman ruling'. In the German case, especially with regard to its implementation through the DFB, this aspect has gained much prominence, perhaps even more than the presumed dramatic rise in transfer fees or the rise in salaries, because German clubs often could not keep up with their English, Italian or Spanish competitors.[8] Moreover, the rise in transfer fees and salaries that also took place in Germany during the 1990s may be explained only partially with reference to 'Bosman', since the income of the clubs also exploded during this period, mainly due to the returns from the sale of TV and broadcasting rights (Kipker 2002: 11).[9] In contrast, the consequences of 'Bosman' for the share of German-born players in German football have been widely discussed, especially in relation to the impact on German talent and the German national team. One could, for instance, argue that other football associations and leagues in Europe did not expand their definition of 'EU resident' precisely because they wanted to restrict the influx of foreign players, thereby protecting young players who would be eligible for national teams. In Germany, 'Bosman' and its extension to all Europeans arguably led to problems for the development of young players. As Gerhard Mayer-Vorfelder, president of the DFB, recently put it: 'Our decision was just to treat all citizens of UEFA member-countries like EU citizens. I now believe that this decision was wrong. . . . How can we expect young German forwards to develop in the *Bundesliga*, if seventy per cent of all forwards are foreign-born. And it is not true that the best players will always prevail.'[10]

If one interprets the shortage of young and talented German football players, which – the runners-up spot in the 2002 World Cup notwithstanding – became obvious at the end of the 1990s, either as a consequence of 'Bosman' and its implementation in Germany or as the result of a certain neglect on the part of the clubs, the carefully directed development of young and talented players eligible for German national teams has become a real concern of the DFB in the wake of 'Bosman'. What is more, the DFB – in accordance with the DFL – is attempting to steer this development by establishing certain rules for professional and amateur clubs, which aim at developing and protecting young and talented German players as far as possible within the limits of public national and European law. For instance, every club in the *Bundesliga* has to maintain a training centre for young players (*Nachwuchsleistungszentrum*) in order to comply with the licensing rules. The professional teams also have to sign at least twelve players who are eligible for German national teams (although there is no ceiling for the overall number of players). Amateur clubs linked to professional teams had until now to field at least six eligible players younger than age 24, three of them younger than age 21; from the 2005 to 2006 season onwards, these clubs will become full U23 teams (which means that only three players aged 23 or older can be fielded). Parallel to these measures, the number of non-EU players in amateur teams has been cut back from up to six (2002) to three (2004). This kind of steering policy within the association is complemented by the policies of the German Ministry of the Interior, which in 2002 issued a directive that in effect ruled out the possibility of a non-EU player getting a work permit in Germany unless he is signed by a team in the (first or second) Bundesliga. In 2003, the follow-up to this directive specified that non-EU players must be signed to play in the first team and must not play in the amateur teams of the professional clubs.[11]

The 'Bosman ruling' also stated that the traditional transfer system had to be completely revised, since the core of this system – the payment of transfer fees for out-of-contract players – had been found to infringe the right of free movement within the EU. The ruling itself posed a lot of questions, because among other things it did not consider transfers within member states of the EU and made no specifications concerning transfers of European but non-EU players between two clubs within the EU. Since the transfer system was internationally agreed upon and laid down through FIFA, it became clear during the second half of the 1990s that this part of 'Bosman' was not just (EU- or UEFA-)European business, but could and had to lead to a revision of the whole international transfer system. First and foremost the European Commission pushed this view, starting from the perspective that football constituted a normal business activity to be regulated according to competition law. On the other hand, the national and regional associations as well as FIFA tried to promote the view that football and sport fulfil peculiar social functions and therefore had to be treated differently. As Parrish (2003) has shown, these and other actors (such as clubs, leagues, media, lawyers) have formed so-called 'advocacy coalitions' to promote their views in the negotiation process. Although the Commission finally pushed FIFA/UEFA to the table by threatening another ruling through the ECJ in 2000 (Croci 2001: 7), the 'new transfer regime' agreed upon in 2001 showed that the European Commission in some parts had loosened its demands and abandoned its purism. This is especially true with regard to contract stability (vs. 'normal' periods of notice), which has to be guaranteed except for exceptional situations, and the introduction of a new system of training compensations (as a 'quasi'-transfer fee) for players aged under 23 to encourage and reward the club's input into training them (Weatherill 2003: 68). This change in attitudes on the part of the European Commission requires explanation.

One could reason, first of all, that the Commission has been persuaded by the arguments concerning the peculiarities of organizing football and the presumed consequences of a fully liberalized transfer regime put forth through UEFA/FIFA (and the DFB as well). Indeed, some leading German actors interpret the negotiation process with the Commission to some degree as a successful act of lobbying in the sense of creating more awareness within the Commission for possible disastrous consequences of strict liberalization (e.g. inoperability of leagues due to highly volatile player markets).[12] There are indeed some indicators that underscore this reasoning, since the Commission gradually reformulated its position throughout the 1990s, as may be seen in the so-called Helsinki Report on Sport from 1999 (Brown 2000: 139). Second, several national football associations, not least the German DFB, have tried to lobby their respective governments and especially their heads of government in order to exert some political pressure on the institutions of the Community, mainly in the form of public statements. In this respect, the joint statement of Gerhard Schröder and Tony Blair in the run-up to the Nice Summit 2000 – which expressed their concerns regarding a radical restructuring without enough consideration given to the peculiarities of football (Meier 2004: 14) – was contributed to by several meetings of the DFB, representatives of leading German clubs and the German Chancellor, in which the 'football community' successfully specified possible adverse implications of a fully liberalized transfer regime for the most popular sport in Germany.[13] Undoubtedly, the common stance of national governments exerted indirect political pressure on the European Commission, which can act with some degree of autonomy but certainly does not take its decisions in a political vacuum.

In sum, the 'Bosman' ruling undoubtedly changed the structures and the landscape of German football. Concerning the make-up of the *Bundesliga* it has become above all less German, more international, and more European in a wider sense. Through the decision of the DFB to count all citizens of UEFA member states as EU residents, German football has become more 'Europeanized' than required through the Commission and the ECJ. Other processes have shown as well that 'Europeanization' through European jurisdiction and institutions is far from being directed by Brussels alone. The Europeanization of German football thus seems to be more dialectical than commonly assumed.

Broadcasting rights and the Bundesliga marketing system

Over the past decade, the transformation of the broadcasting sectors has had a significant impact on professional football in most European countries, including Germany. The sharp growth in the number of actors on the demand-side of the market after the advent of private television in Germany in the mid-1980s, combined with the difficulty of increasing the supply of truly attractive football events, led to very considerable increases in the prices charged for *Bundesliga* broadcasting rights (at least until the 'Kirch-crash'),[14] a development that has also been witnessed, to varying degrees, in the rest of Europe. Overall, broadcasting has been a key element in the larger scale commercialization of football in recent times. This commercialization of sports (and above all football) in Europe has decisively fostered the intervention of EU institutions and Community law in the sector. The EU Commission's preoccupation with football has been driven by its need to monitor the much more important broadcasting sector, in which it seeks to preclude practices that facilitate incumbents to impede new entrants to the market (see Weatherill 2003: 74).

One of the most contentious issues concerns the marketing system of broadcasting rights. An established commercial practice in European football, as well as the European sports sector more generally, is the central marketing and joint sale of broadcasting rights on behalf of individual participants. This system, which currently applies to both free-TV and pay-TV broadcasting of the football *Bundesliga*, offers prospective buyers only the opportunity to compete for one package which comprises a league's entire output. Purchasers are unable to conclude deals with individual clubs. Such collective selling is an equalizing arrangement through which revenues are distributed more evenly than in a decentralized model. In the latter system the allegedly more attractive clubs would take significantly more of the pie (at the expense of smaller clubs). The main argument in favour of the collective system is that it helps sustain vibrant (inter-club) competition,[15] a crucial element of any sporting activity. For example, broadcasting rights for the *Bundesliga*, the English Premier League and the UEFA Champions League are marketed centrally by the DFB/DFL, the FA and UEFA, respectively. In 1999, the DFB requested an exemption from EU anti-trust rules with regard to the central marketing of television and radio broadcasting rights for professional football matches in Germany. From the perspective of EU law two issues are important here: first, whether the prevention of clubs from entering into individual agreements with broadcasters amounts to a restriction of competition and thus falls within the scope of Article 81 (1) TEC; second, whether the collective selling of broadcasting rights is necessary to ensure the survival of the financially weaker participants in the league. If the above-mentioned solidarity argument is accepted, an exemption under Article 81 (3) from the application of Article 81 (1) TEC may be granted (Parrish 2002: 9).

Under the German collective selling system, the DFB leases the broadcasting rights to the DFL which also markets the rights. The DFL redistributes the revenues gained from the broadcasting contracts to the clubs. The contracts in question in the DFB request for exemption from Article 81 concern the rights to show first and second division Bundesliga games. The DFB/DFL claim authority to enter into such contracts as the main organizers of the competitions. The application for derogation from Article 81 was substantiated with reference to the solidarity function which the central marketing system supposedly fulfils by redistributing funds (fairly) among clubs. It should be mentioned that this stance is accepted by most officials from the DFB and DFL as well as the vast majority of clubs. Among the thirty-six professional German football clubs, only Bayern Munich, Borussia Dortmund and Bayer Leverkusen favoured a decentralized marketing model, given their potential to raise substantially larger revenues. They also claimed occasionally that total generated income would be higher[16] under a decentralized system, sporadically making threats about their exit options, such as a European breakaway league. During the course of discussions all clubs eventually accepted the collective selling system. However, it was revealed later that Bayern Munich mainly came on board because of a 'secret' marketing treaty with the Kirch-Group, which had secured the rights for the period 2000 to 2004. In this agreement Bayern Munich was compensated for lost revenues by forgoing individual marketing arrangements. As a result, the club *de jure* agreed to the central marketing model, while *de facto* securing the financial status of a decentralized system. This may be regarded as the introduction of elements of decentralized marketing through the back door (Kruse and Quitzau 2003: 13–14).

In the DFB request for an exemption from EU anti-trust rules, the DFB and the DFL made a considerable effort to influence matters. They sought mainly to assert their preferences via UEFA. DFB president Mayer-Vorfelder was well placed in that respect as a member of the UEFA Executive Committee and the Executive Committee Working Group on matters related to the European Union. Within the UEFA framework DFB officials also participated directly in talks with representatives from the European Commission, members of the European Parliament and national ministers responsible for sports. In addition, direct relations were cultivated on the part of the DFB with the Commissioners Reading and Monti. The DFB also used UEFA as a channel mainly because the latter was (simultaneously to the DFB case) involved in talks with the Commission as it had applied for an exemption from Article 81 concerning the collective marketing of commercial rights to the UEFA Champions League. Lobbying (via UEFA) has retrospectively been viewed as an effective means.[17] Rather than applying direct (political) pressure, it was important in the talks with the European Commission and other EU circles to bridge certain knowledge gaps and to widen decision-makers' basis of information and to specify the implications of a vigorous application of Community anti-trust rules to professional football in Germany. Moreover, a certain amount of political pressure spilling over from the Bosman case and the subsequent discussions concerning transfer rules[18] provide an additional rationale for the Commission's decision to exempt the new system for marketing *Bundesliga* broadcasting rights. These logics must also be seen against the background of growing anxieties on the part of the Commission in recent years to show respect for the social and cultural benefits of sports (Weatherill 2003: 52–3, 75, 93–4).

Overall, the new marketing system for *Bundesliga* broadcasting rights that was first accepted by the Commission in July 2003 contains the main demands made by the DFB. The new model has been described as 'essentially a centralized system of marketing broadcasting rights with some decentralized elements on the fringes'.[19] Collective marketing of TV rights will broadly continue. However, broadcasting via mobile phones and the internet will become liberalized from 2006 to 2007, so that clubs will be in a position to market their home games via these media.[20]

The impact of the Champions League

So far we have predominantly looked at the adaptational pressures stemming from the European Union and the transnational and specifically German responses towards these pressures. In contrast, this section deals more with transnationally induced changes which have a significant bearing on the policies, structures and attitudes governing German (professional) football. The most important factor in that respect is the UEFA Champions League (and to a lesser extent the UEFA Cup). Since the early 1990s there has been increasingly strong pressure on UEFA from the big European clubs and media groups to expand European club-level football competition in order to exploit its commercial potential. UEFA welcomed these ideas because they entailed the possibility of (further) raising its profile and status. As a result, UEFA enlarged the European Champion Clubs' Cup in 1992–93 to include a league format, which was subsequently called the Champions League. Again on the initiative of the media companies and the largest European clubs, the league format was expanded in 1997. This allowed for the participation of the runners-up of the larger national leagues and increased the number of matches played, thus raising revenues.

The Champions League has become a real focal point for the more competitive Bundesliga clubs, a development paralleled across other European football leagues. The rationale is twofold. First, the participation in the Champions League is financially very lucrative. For instance, in the 2002–03 season Borussia Dortmund earned 33.7 million EUR (27.1 per cent of its total revenue) by (merely) reaching the second group stage in the Champions League. And in the 2000–01 season Bayern Munich gained 41.25 million EUR – almost twice as much as through total national TV revenues – by winning the Champions League that season. It may be argued that, due to different domestic TV market(ing) conditions, participation in the Champions League is even more important for the top German clubs than for their English, Spanish or Italian rivals in order to stay competitive on the European level, given the different and less lucrative domestic TV marketing conditions in Germany. English clubs can draw on huge earnings through their massive national broadcasting contracts. Top Italian clubs can raise very considerable revenue because the pay-TV sector is decentralized.[21] And in Spain both free- and pay-TV are marketed on an individual basis, which benefits the most attractive teams disproportionately.

Second, the Champions League has also become a focal point for the bigger German (and other European) clubs since its development into a top brand. Part of the success story is that in 2003–04 it contracted eighty-two TV partners in about 230 countries and islands and was able to increase its worldwide audience/broadcasting quota by (another) 9 per cent. In addition, Champions League matches have generated a higher average attendance than games in the highest domestic leagues in England, Germany, Spain, Italy and France.[22] Another indicator for the development of the Champions League brand is the continuity and fidelity of its sponsors: Ford, Mastercard and Amstel have all sponsored the Champions League either from the outset or shortly after. Sony is also developing into a long-term partner. These companies all seem to regard their substantial contributions as profitable investments. A different sign of successful brand-building is the award of the TV industry's 'Oscar' in March 2004 to the Champions League by the Broadcast Design Association for the best European overall image in the sports business. Of course, these 'soft' factors again have substantial positive financial implications for clubs taking part in the Champions League, for example, in terms of sponsoring and merchandising. Overall, our interviewing of officials at the bigger *Bundesliga* clubs has revealed that – due to the above developments – the Champions League brand and its monetary implications have generated for them a very substantial appeal. Clubs such as Borussia Dortmund and Bayer Leverkusen are aware that their performances in the Champions League have considerably raised their images nationally and internationally, and that they owe their membership in the G-14 forum primarily to it.

The G-14

In the past decade, new forms of European transnational networks within European football have evolved, most prominent of which is the so-called G-14. The G-14 – sometimes labelled the 'European club of the rich'[23] – is a self-selected and self-recruiting interest group of initially fourteen, but by the beginning of 2005, eighteen, top European football clubs. Its legal structure is that of a European Economic Interest Group (EEIG), which means that it is embedded in the instruments of the Community for facilitating and encouraging transnational cooperation between firms. The idea of forming such a group was born in 1997–98 by club representatives in informal meetings. Of great importance for the final formation of the G-14 was the proposal of the Italian media organization Media Partners in 1998 to establish a (breakaway) European Super League in order to generate higher revenues than under the scheme of the Champions League. Media Partners even complained to the European Commission that UEFA's prevention of such a breakaway league amounted to an abuse of a dominant position from the perspective of Community competition law (Parrish 2002: 11). Although UEFA countered by changing the format of the Champions League that appeased the big clubs, the grouping took further steps to formalize itself and, in 2000, constituted itself officially as the lobby group 'G-14'. In 2001, it opened an office in Brussels. The choice of location reflects the growing awareness that the European Union has become a centre of gravity for matters of football.[24] In the case of the G-14, it also reflects the fact that the European Commission has been interpreted by the big clubs as a potential ally in reforming football in line with the 'business perspective' (Ducrey *et al.* 2003: 34).

Interestingly, since the G-14 has not been recognized by either UEFA or FIFA as an official organization, the European Commission allowed the G-14 to explain its position as 'employer' of footballers in the talks between FIFA and the Commission about a new transfer regime in 2001. UEFA, not surprisingly, has a somewhat distanced relationship to the G-14, but recent developments hint at its attempt to strengthen ties with European football clubs either to accommodate or to weaken it. In this regard, the UEFA Club Forum was established in 2002 as an expert panel – with the status of an advisory body – with representatives of 102 European clubs as members. Similarly, the European Professional Football Leagues (EPFL), which as an association of fifteen professional leagues was founded in 1998, has recently become more vocal as it tries to establish itself as the fifty-third association within UEFA. On the basis of these developments a complex and important web of transnational networks and relationships has been established within the realm of European football, mainly through and with reference to the G-14 grouping. The G-14 itself represents a qualitatively different type of transnationalism from those of UEFA or FIFA, since the latter are constituted through national associations (Lehmkuhl 2004: 182). The transnational character of the G-14, on the other hand, is based more on personal relationships between top executives who have frequent contact with each other and act on the basis of interests which largely overlap. Moreover, national interests tend to dissolve[25] in contrast to UEFA where national interests from time to time seem to be more important.

Three German clubs are members of the G-14: Bayern Munich (from its inception), Borussia Dortmund (invited to join in 1999), and Bayer Leverkusen (2002). If one groups the votes in the General Assembly of the

G-14 by nations, the three German clubs in total rank fourth. At the Management Committee, the *de facto*-leading organ of the G-14, the 'German contribution' came in the form of vice-chairman Karl-Heinz Rummenigge, who has been regarded as the 'ambassador of the G-14' because of his involvement with Bayern Munich, the DFL, UEFA and FIFA. Since September 2004, Michael Meier of Borussia Dortmund has been vice-chairman of G-14's Management Committee. Thus, German football clubs play an important role in the G-14. But German football has also contributed to some counter-trends to the G-14. For instance, the strengthening of the EPFL has been partially pushed by leading actors of the DFL, since they wanted to remodel UEFA on the successful German example (the league as part of the association). To sum up, there is no unidimensional 'German role' within these processes of growing transnationalism in the European context.

Conclusion

Any attempt to capture the Europeanization of German football has to pay attention to two interrelated dynamics: a large part of the Europeanization dynamics may be classified as EU-Europeanization (i.e. the pressures originating from the EU level and leading to dialectical processes of adaptation in the various football associations). In addition, there are transnational dynamics, which emanate from football clubs within Europe and from the actions of the European football association UEFA as well as other private actors, driven in large part by economics and markets. As for EU-Europeanization, through 'Bosman' and its implementation, German football has become more 'Europeanized' than required through the European Commission and the ECJ. Other processes in German football have also shown that 'Europeanization' through European jurisdiction and institutions is far from being a one-way street. Although the EU can exert some adaptational pressure, there have always been attempts to seek ways to escape some of the consequences of adaptation (e.g. protective measures for young players) or to weaken the pressure itself (e.g. through persuasion and lobbying in the cases of a new international transfer regime or the marketing of broadcasting rights). On the other hand, there is some activism in (top) European club football which merits attention. The past decade has indicated important changes to the formats of football competitions and to the realm of its actors. With the introduction of the Champions League and the formation of new groups and networks besides the established and traditional associations, another dimension of 'Europeanization' has emerged. The growing articulation of common interests in transnational venues may be seen as an extension of and/or reaction to the 'Europeanization' processes initiated by European institutions. Leading German football clubs have – together with their European counterparts – played an important role in these processes.

Notes

1 At this point, however, it is also important to specify what we do *not* mean by 'Europeanization'. For instance, the asserted cross-cultural impact of prominent players in the sphere of football (Head 2004) is not captured by our concept of Europeanization. Neither are strictly 'cultural' aspects of football nor questions concerning the way it is being played (Vasili 1994).
2 Interview with the managing president of the German Football Association (DFB), Dr Theo Zwanziger.
3 Interview with the president of the DFB, Gerhard Mayer-Vorfelder.
4 Interview with the managing president of the DFB, Dr Theo Zwanziger.
5 Currently, the ECJ is preparing a ruling concerning discrimination against a European but non-EU professional player, who is seemingly restricted from playing by a nationality clause in Spain. Whether there will be a 'Simutenkow ruling' and whether this will expand the 'Bosman ruling' is not clear at the moment. See *Der Spiegel*, 12 January 2005.
6 See the *Frankfurter Allgemeine Zeitung*, 26 June 2004.
7 See *Kicker*, 2 July 2001.
8 The most expensive transfers in German football up until the end of 2004 were those of Amoroso to Borussia Dortmund (officially 17.5 million EUR) and of Makaay to Bayern Munich (18.75 million EUR), which rank at positions 92 and 80 in the list of the most expensive transfers ever. See the ranking at www.transfermarkt.de.
9 The *Bundesliga* has been an exception to the rule among big European leagues because the ratio of salary payments and returns did not change substantially. See Deloitte and Touche (2003).
10 See *Kicker*, 19 February 2004 (translation by the authors).
11 *Kicker*, 27 January 2003; EU player in this regard means a player born within a member state, where the rights concerning the free movement of labour do apply (this still excludes new member states such as Poland and Hungary).
12 Interview with the president of the DFB, Gerhard Mayer-Vorfelder.
13 Interview with the president of the DFB, Gerhard Mayer-Vorfelder.
14 The Kirch-Group which acquired the *Bundesliga* rights for the period 2000 to 2004 went bankrupt in April 2002. The price for *Bundesliga* broadcasting rights increased from 4 million EUR in 1988 to 169 million EUR in 1999–2000. Kirch paid 355 million EUR for 2000–01. The value has decreased to 291 million EUR per season since 2002–03.
15 A number of clubs in the *Bundesliga* crucially depend on the income earned from the *Bundesliga* broadcasting rights (*Frankfurter Allgemeine Zeitung*, 8 April 2002).
16 The literature, however, seems to contradict this point (e.g. Weatherill 2003: 77).
17 Interview (anonymous), January 2005.
18 For example, statements by Gerhard Schröder and Tony Blair as well as provisions in the Amsterdam Declaration emphasized the need for the bodies of the European Union to listen to sports associations when important questions affecting sports are at issue.
19 Interview with Dr Christian Hockenjos, Director of Administration and Organization, Borussia Dortmund.
20 For full details, see, for example, European Commission (2003). Closely related to the issue of collective marketing is the issue of exclusivity (i.e. the sale of exclusive broadcasting rights). For analysis of this issue see Brand and Niemann (2005).
21 According to one source, Juventus Turin made 93 million EUR through pay-TV during one season (interview with Karl-Heinz Rummenigge, CEO of Bayern Munich).

22 Between 1992–93 and 2003–04, the Champions League generated an average attendance of 37,073, more than any national football league during that period. When analysing individual seasons, national league games were attended by more spectators only in 2001–02 (Premier League), 2003–04 and 1995–96 (*Bundesliga*). Data available online: http://European-football-statistics.co.uk/attn.htm.
23 *Frankfurter Allgemeine Zeitung*, 1 December 2004.
24 In 2003, UEFA opened an office in Brussels as well to keep in touch with the EU.
25 Interview with Dr Christian Hockenjos, Director of Administration and Organization at Borussia Dortmund; see also Ducrey *et al.* (2003: 60).

References

Brand, A. and Niemann, A. (2005) *The Societal/Trans-national Dimension of Europeanisation: The Case of German Football*, paper presented at the 46th International Studies Association Convention, Honolulu (Hawaii), March.

Brown, A. (2000) 'European Football and the European Union: Governance, Participation and Social Cohesion – Towards a Policy Research Agenda', *Soccer and Society*, 1: 129–50.

Croci, O. (2001) *Taking the Field: The EC and the Governance of European Football*, paper presented at the 7th ECSA–USA International Conference, Madison (Wisconsin), May–June.

Deloitte and Touche (2003) *Deloitte Annual Review of Football and Finance*, London: Deloitte and Touche.

Ducrey, P., Ferreira, C.E., Huerta, G. and Marston K.T. (2003) *UEFA and Football Governance*, Project Work, Neuchâtel: CIES.

European Commission (2003) *New Marketing System for Bundesliga Broadcasting Rights*, Press Release IP/03/1106, Brussels, 24 July.

Foer, F. (2004) 'Soccer vs. McWorld', *Foreign Policy*, 140: 32–9.

Foster, K. (2000) 'European Law and Football: Who's in Charge?', in J. Garland, D. Malcolm and M. Rowe (eds) *The Future of Football – Challenges for the Twenty-First Century*, London: Frank Cass.

Head, D. (2004) 'Europeanization Through Football: The Cross-cultural Impact of Juergen Klinsmann and Sven-Goeran Eriksson from a British Perspective', *European Journal for Sport and Society*, 1: 23–33.

Kipker, I. (2002) 'Sind Salary Caps im europäischen Fußball umsetzbar und sinnvoll?', *Sportökonomie*, 1. Online. Available: http://www.ak-spooek.de/html/dez2.HTM (accessed 1 December 2004).

Kruse, J. and Quitzau, J. (2003) *Fußball-Fernsehrechte: Aspekte der Zentralvermarktung*, Universität der Bundeswehr Hamburg, Fächergruppe Volkswirtschaftslehre, Diskussionspapier 18.

Ladrech, R. (1994) 'Europeanization of Domestic Politics and Institutions: The Case of France', *Journal of Common Market Studies*, 32(1): 69–88.

Lehmkuhl, D. (2004) 'Der lange Schatten staatlichen Rechts: Verrechtlichung im transnationalen Sport', in B. Zangl and M. Zürn (eds) *Verrechtlichung – Baustein für Global Governance?*, Bonn: Dietz.

Meier, H.E. (2004) *Von Bosman zur Kollektivvereinbarung? Die Regulierung des Arbeitsmarktes für Profifußballer*. Online. Available: http://www.uni-potsdam.de/u/ls_verwaltung/Forschung/Von%20Bosman%20zur%20Kollektivvereinbarung_.pdf (accessed 1 December 2004).

Missiroli, A. (2002) 'European Football Cultures and Their Integration: The "Short" Twentieth Century', *Culture, Sport, Society*, 5: 1–20.

Olsen, J.P. (2002) 'The Many Faces of Europeanization', *Journal of Common Market Studies*, 40: 921–52.
Parrish, R. (2002) 'Football's Place in the Single European Market', *Soccer and Society*, 3: 1–21.
Parrish, R. (2003) *Sports Law and Policy in the European Union*, Manchester: Manchester University Press.
Radaelli, C. (2000) 'Whither Europeanization? Concept Stretching and Substantive Change', *European Integration online Papers* 4. Online. Available: http://eiop.or.at/eiop/texte/2000–008a.htm (accessed 1 October 2004).
Vasili, P. (1994) 'The Right Kind of Fellows: Nigerian Football Tourists as Agents of Europeanization', *The International Journal of the History of Sport*, 11: 191–211.
Weatherill, S. (2003) '"Fair Play Please!" Recent Developments in the Application of EC Law to Sport', *Common Market Law Review*, 40: 51–93.

8 German football – a media-economic survey

The impact of the KirchMedia Company on football and television in Germany

Lothar Mikos

As in other European countries, the nature of football as the people's game in Germany has changed radically since the Second World War. The transformation of football is the result of social changes in Western societies. On the one hand, these changes are based in the economic and social processes of late capitalism, and are influenced, on the other, by the media and their role in society. There is a 'deep mediation of everyday life' (Bjondeberg 2002: 162) in the so-called network society (Castells 2000) that is characterized by forms of 'reflexive modernization' (Beck *et al.* 1994). This deep mediation of everyday life will naturally affect football too. Indeed, the professionalization of sports is linked to the process of mediation and globalization. The global sports/media complex (Jhally 1989) is part of the transnational flow of cultural artefacts in a global media world and the transnational flow of money in a global economy. In every European country football is part of such changes, and is in one way or another related to global media and global money. From the 1950s until the 1980s there was still a close connection between football and television. This was the era of public service broadcasting, and the relation between football and television could be seen as cultural. In the 1980s new media players entered the field and the deregulation of broadcasting in Europe led to an increasing commercialization. The relation between football and television from this time on could be seen as purely economical. In this context, the KirchMedia Company had an enormous impact on football and television in Germany. When the company went bankrupt in 2002, this led to a crisis in German football with many clubs struggling to survive.

The early years – football in the age of public service broadcasting

The evolution of television as a mass medium in Germany is linked to popular cultural practices such as football. The early years of public service broadcasting in the Federal Republic of Germany (FRG) saw two major live events: first, the coronation of the United Kingdom's Queen Elizabeth II in 1953; second, the 1954 Football World Championship in Switzerland. The sales of television sets in the FRG increased rapidly during the tournament and the month after the German team had won the Cup. In January 1954 there were 11,658 television sets in Germany, many of them in pubs; in December 1954, by contrast, there were 84,278 television sets, many of them in private houses (Mikos 2002: 29). The industry had to work hard to satisfy customer demand. The magazine *Der Spiegel* reported on 7 July that year that the exciting live screenings of the World Cup had caused a big run on television sets. The stocks of manufacturers such as *Telefunken*, *Saba* and *Mende* were sold out. *Philips* shifted 1,000 television sets in just fourteen days – an enormous number considering that a year before there had been only 1,117 TV sets in the whole of the FRG. The manufacturer *Saba* advertised its model *Schauinsland W III* with the words: 'You can take part directly in this event that we are all awaiting with great suspense!' (Mikos and Nutt 1997: 172). The football fan and prospective television set owner was promised that neither tickets nor the weather need be a worry.

Pubs were the most popular venue for watching the World Cup. Sometimes up to 150 viewers crowded into individual pubs during the live transmission of the games. They had to pay for tickets, but got a free beer. On average, between ten and twenty viewers watched the games together in private homes, and between sixty and seventy in pubs or as 'window-shoppers' huddled around the shop windows of television dealers. Even in the German Democratic Republic (GDR), more television sets were sold than ever before, particularly in the regions where the public service broadcasting of the FRG could be received. The broadcasting of the 1954 World Cup also marked the advent of the European Broadcasting Network, later known as the EBU (European Broadcasting Union).

The first live transmission of sports events in Germany had taken place during the 1936 Olympic Games in Berlin. Several competitions were broadcast to so-called 'Fernsehstuben', public venues where it was possible to receive signals. In November 1936 the first football match, an international between Germany and Italy, was transmitted. It was a foggy day and the heavy cameras were barely able to follow the ball. It was therefore another three years before the transmission of another game, again an international between Germany and Italy. During the Second World War there were several transmissions, although very few people could follow them on television. This situation changed with the start of regular television operations in 1952. In August, a local match in Hamburg between the Hamburger SV and Altona 93 was transmitted, followed a few weeks later by a game between FC St Pauli and Hamborn 07 (Hickethier 1998: 77). In 1953 regular live transmissions of *Oberliga* matches on Sundays began. Even then television had to pay for the transmission rights. The *Nordwestdeutsche Rundfunk* (Northwest German Broadcasting Network) paid the clubs between 1,000 and 2,500 Marks per match (Grosshans 1997: 38). The same development took place in parallel in the GDR, where matches of their *Oberliga* were transmitted on Sundays (Hickethier 1998: 189;

Friedrich and Weickert 2003). In the Federal Republic there was a crisis when the clubs complained about a drop in the number of supporters and fans attending matches in the stadiums. They held television responsible for this crisis and some football associations demanded a general prohibition of transmissions at the weekend. In October 1958 German television (*Arbeitsgemeinschaft der Rundfunkanstalten Deutschlands*, ARD) and the German Football Association (*Deutscher Fußball Bund*, DFB) signed a contract that permitted the transmission of one club match and overall only two games per month, but not on Sundays.

The end of the 1950s saw a technological invention that radically changed the transmission and coverage of football and other sporting events: the VTR. This new technology allowed television to show sports events not only in live form but also in edited versions after the event itself. The pressure of competition between the live event in the stadium and live transmission was no longer relevant. In July 1961, the invention of the VTR led to a regular highlight programme. The *Sportschau*, broadcast on Sunday evenings, followed the same concept as the BBC's later acclaimed *Match of the Day* (1964). Concurrently in Germany, the professionalization of football was making big advances. The 1963 to 1964 season was the starting point of the *Bundesliga*, Germany's first professional league. The first day of play on 24 August also saw a new TV programme, *Das Aktuelle Sport-Studio* with recorded highlights of the matches and interviews with managers and star players. It was aired on the second PSB network, the *Zweite Deutsche Fernsehen* (ZDF), late on Saturday evenings. The two networks, ARD and ZDF, started negotiations with the German Football Association to fix the fees paid to football by television companies. In spring 1965 the deal was fixed, with the two networks paying 127,000 Marks for the 1965 to 1966 *Bundesliga* season (Grosshans 1997: 48). The *Sportschau* (ARD) showed between three and five matches, all the results and the tables at 6 o'clock in the evening. The *Aktuelle Sport-Studio* (ZDF) presented an average of four matches four hours later. The two recorded highlight programmes gained enormous audiences, which of course led to an increase in the fee payable in subsequent years (Table 8.1).

Table 8.1 Seasonal fees for football rights in Germany (several sources).

Bundesliga season	TV rights (in DM)
1966–67	0.13 m
1967–68	0.81 m
1968–69	1.68 m
1969–70	2.30 m
1974–75	3.60 m
1979–80	5.88 m
1984–85	10.00 m
1987–88	18.00 m

Until 1988 it was the case that the public service broadcasting networks bought the rights to the German *Bundesliga*. The increasing fees make clear how important football was to television. The situation changed when commercial TV networks joined negotiations with the German Football Association for the first time, and the deregulation of broadcasting in Germany had reached football.

The deregulation of broadcasting in Germany and the rise of KirchMedia

As in other European countries, new private media consortiums came on the scene in the 1980s 'to exploit the technological opportunity presented by satellite and cable transmission' (King 2003: 97). In 1984 commercial television started in the FRG. Private networks, like public service broadcasting, are integrated within Germany's complicated federal system. Before this could be accomplished, technical, legal and political issues had to be resolved. A decision by the federal Constitutional Court in 1981, known as the 'FRAG' decision, stipulated that private-sector broadcasting was essentially constitutional since the public airwaves fall under the sovereignty of the individual *Länder*. This cleared the way for media legislation at the level of the *Länder* to permit the licensing of private networks. In addition, due to advances in cable and satellite technology, the technical groundwork for distributing more television channels was also already in place. As early as November 1980, the minister-presidents of the *Länder* had agreed to test the feasibility and acceptance of cable television in four pilot projects, which were to be accompanied by scholarly studies. The pilot projects were financed by a portion of the radio and television fees collected by the *Länder*. On 1 January 1984, the age of private television, financed entirely by advertising revenue, began in Germany with the launch of a pilot cable project in Ludwigshafen and the founding of West Germany's first commercial television network, *Satelliten Fernsehen GmbH (SAT.1)*. *RTL plus*, which had until that point been transmitting from Belgium, also began broadcasting in Germany. A Munich pilot project started three months later, followed in June and August 1985 by pilot projects in Dortmund and Berlin.

In the years that followed, more and more private networks were added, broadcasting their programmes with varying success. Networks with complete programme schedules attained a larger audience than those with specialized programming. In the 1990s numerous private networks were founded with the result that today Germany has some forty networks that can be received nationwide as well as numerous regional networks and local stations. Some of these networks' programmes, however, can only be seen by subscribers on digital television. The first network to be financed through subscription fees rather than advertising was Premiere, which introduced pay-TV into Germany on 28 February 1991. The new networks mainly belonged to large publishing companies such as Axel Springer, Heinrich Bauer, Holtzbrinck and the WAZ group (*Westdeutsche Allgemeine Zeitung*), but also to media conglomerates such as Bertelsmann and the film distributor Leo Kirch.

In licensing private television networks, government agencies were to ensure that the interests of individual companies in several networks did not result in a monopoly of influence over public opinion, since private-sector television is constitutional only if market conditions guarantee a plurality of opinion. Nonetheless, because operating private television networks is an expensive business, some concentration occurred (Table 8.2). As a result, in 2001 there were three major television strands:

1   the public networks;
2   networks belonging to the KirchMedia concern of film distributor Leo Kirch; and
3   networks belonging to the Bertelsmann group.

This division of the German television market was destabilized when the KirchMedia concern went bankrupt in 2002. Leo Kirch's influence on the German television market has had a great impact on the relationship between football and television.

Before the rise of commercial television in Germany, Leo Kirch was a film distributor who sold the TV rights of films to the two public networks. He enjoyed a near monopoly in this market. The deregulation of broadcasting opened up obvious new prospects for his business. He started as a shareholder in the private channel SAT.1, and year by year worked on further establishing his media concern with several commercial channels. To be successful in the television market channels needed good content in the form of popular programmes. Series, films, game shows and sports

Table 8.2 Network families in Germany in 2001.

Public service broadcasting	Kirch	Bertelsmann
ARD	SAT.1	RTL
ZDF	ProSieben	RTL II
3sat (culture)	Premiere World (pay-TV)	Super RTL (children)
Arte	Kabel 1	Vox
Kinderkanal (children)	N 24 (news)	
Phoenix (documentary)	DSF (sports)	
3rd Programme (regional)	H.O.T. (shopping)	
	Neun Live	
	Local stations in Berlin, Munich and Hamburg	
Market share		
42.7%	25.8%	24.7%

such as football guaranteed high ratings and market shares. Kirch and his company KirchMedia owned 12,000 films and 40,000 hours of TV series. They sold the TV rights to their own channels and, from 1996 on, to their digital pay-TV. KirchMedia and Kirch pay-TV had built a chain of in-house exploitation by which they could force the prices for TV rights for other participants on the market such as the TV channels of the Bertelsmann Group or public service broadcasting.

As in other European countries, the deregulation of broadcasting in Germany had a significant impact on football and the transformation of the game under the conditions of commercialization. Dobson and Goddard's (2001: 81) account of the British market is also true for Germany:

> The arrival of two satellite broadcasters BSB and Sky in the late 1980s signalled a significant shift in the relative bargaining power of the football industry as the seller of broadcasting rights and the television companies as buyers. The BBC–ITV duopsony was gone for good, and the television companies were competing against one another to acquire broadcasting rights far more intensely than ever before.

In 1988 for the first time the German Football Association sold the TV rights to the *Bundesliga* to a private company, the UFA, owned by the Bertelsmann Group. They negotiated a fee of 135 million Marks for the next three seasons. UFA sold the rights to the private channel RTL and to the two public networks ARD and ZDF. ARD's *Sportschau* was able to show coverage of three matches at 6.20p.m., RTL's new programme *Anpfiff* owning the rights to show four matches between 7p.m. and 10p.m., with ZDF's *Aktuelle Sport-Studio* giving short summaries of all nine matches at 10p.m. But RTL had the right to decide which matches should be summarized in the ARD's *Sportschau*. After three years the deal was extended for another season, and then, in 1992, KirchMedia entered the fray. The agency ISPR, owned by KirchMedia, bought the *Bundesliga* TV rights for five seasons until 1996–97, the German Football Association receiving the enormous fee of 700 million Marks (Table 8.3).

In 1996 KirchMedia started a pay-TV channel, *DF1*, that merged in 1999 with another pay-TV channel owned jointly by KirchMedia and the

Table 8.3 Seasonal fees for football rights in Germany (several sources).

Bundesliga season	TV rights (in DM)
1988–89	40 m (UFA/RTL)
1989–90	45 m (UFA/RTL)
1990–91	50 m (UFA/RTL)
1991–92	55 m (UFA/RTL)
1992–93 to 1996–97	700 m (ISPR/SAT.1)
1997–98 to 1999–2000	540 m (ISPR/SAT.1)
2000–01 to 2003–04	3,000 m (KirchMedia)

Bertelsmann Group, called Premiere. The merged companies became Premiere World. In order to launch pay-TV in Germany, a widely popular product was needed to attract subscribers, and the success of football programmes made football the most desirable product. However, in a country where the audience is able to receive nearly forty free TV channels it is very difficult to establish pay-TV. The level of subscriptions remained poor. From the 1997–98 season onwards, the rights for free TV and pay-TV were bought by the agency ISPR and KirchMedia. KirchMedia tried to establish the exclusive rights for live transmissions of the *Bundesliga* for their pay-TV. They sold the rights for recorded programmes to their own channel SAT.1, but to protect the success and revenue of the pay-TV channel they decided to air SAT.1's football programme at 8.15p.m., rather than at 6p.m. as before. The result was an enormous decrease in the programme's market share and great public protest by supporters, fans and politicians. After a few weeks KirchMedia and SAT.1 decided to show the programme at 7p.m. It was a victory of football and television as cultural practice over the exploitation of the game and TV as sources of economic profit.

The beginning of the end for the KirchMedia company came in July 1996 when the company bought the TV rights for the 2002 and 2006 World Cups, paying the enormous sum of 2,800 million Swiss Francs. They invested in a prospected business that was dependent on the realization of pay-TV. The idea was to show the matches exclusively on their pay-TV channels, but unfortunately German and European politicians subsequently strengthened the rights of broadcasters to show sports events of national importance to viewers for free. After buying the TV rights to Formula 1 in 1999 and getting involved in several deals that were far from perfect (e.g. with Rupert Murdoch to save his pay-TV channel Premiere World which had heavy annual losses of about 900 million Euro), various of Leo Kirch's companies went bankrupt in the spring of 2002. The main reason for the insolvency of KirchMedia was 'the poor level of subscription to their pay-TV platform Premiere World' (Boyle and Haynes 2004: 100) that had paid around 3,000 million Euro for the broadcasting rights to the *Bundesliga* between 2000 and 2004. At that time the German Football League (DFL), which was collectively responsible for selling the *Bundesliga* broadcasting rights from 2001, had not yet received the full sum for the 2002–03 season because the KirchMedia Company was paying by instalments. The German Football League and the clubs of the first and second Bundesliga became aware for the first time of a possible financial loss. KirchMedia's bankruptcy was followed by a (financial) crisis in German football.

Television, KirchMedia and the financial dependence of German football

From the early 1990s, when KirchMedia bought football broadcasting rights, the German Bundesliga and the teams of the two national leagues received a lot of money from television for the first time. Because of the pay-TV vision of KirchMedia, they could rely on a growing income from TV rights. At the same time the TV channels were unable to finance football fees from advertisements, focusing on the enormous sums they were receiving from television. Budgets rose and, in terms of business, they became professional companies. However, their organizational structures remained unchanged: the same presidents and club secretaries who had learned their trade in the pre-professionalization era struggled to manage big budgets. They spent a lot of money on expensive players and paid them large salaries which they guaranteed for several years in the belief that more and more money would flow in from television. The annual salaries of players in the first *Bundesliga* rose from 60.3 million Euro in the 1988–89 season, when the broadcasting rights were sold for the first time to a commercial channel, to 240 million Euro in 1998–99. (Friedrichsen and Möllenbeck 2002: 40). But that boom was about to go bust. The clubs' dependence on television money becomes apparent when we look at the share of TV money in relation to the clubs' overall budgets (Table 8.4). The smaller clubs and those which were not so successful were highly dependent on TV money.

Major clubs such as Bayern Munich, Borussia Dortmund, Bayer Leverkusen and FC Schalke 04, who were active in Europe in the UEFA Cup and the Champions League, had other sources of income such as sponsoring, merchandizing, tickets and TV money from European competitions. The smaller clubs with smaller stadium capacity were more dependent on the national TV money. But revenue depends on success. The TV fees were transferred to the German Football League which paid them on to the clubs according to certain rules. Eighty per cent of the TV fee for a season went to the clubs of the first Bundesliga, 20 per cent

Table 8.4 TV as source of income, 2000–01.

Club	Share of TV money in overall turnover (%)
Bayern München	13.9
Borussia Dortmund	17.5
Bayer Leverkusen	22.7
Hamburger SV	27.4
1.FC Kaiserslautern	30.2
FC Schalke 04	33.3
VfB Stuttgart	35.0
Hertha BSC Berlin	37.0
1.FC Köln	38.2
1860 München	43.6
Werder Bremen	43.6
Energie Cottbus	47.6
Hansa Rostock	52.0
VfL Wolfsburg	54.5
SC Freiburg	60.7

to those of the second. Half of the fee was paid to the clubs as a fixed sum, the amount calculated according to the average success over the previous three years. The other half was paid according to a team's position in the table at the beginning of a given match day. The base sum was 6,074 Euro, the club at the bottom of the table receiving this unit, the clubs at the top receiving this times eighteen (because there are eighteen clubs in the first *Bundesliga*), i.e. 109,336 Euro per match day. The smaller clubs were caught in a vicious circle. The less successful they were, the less money they received from television; the less they were shown on television, the less income they received from merchandising and sponsoring. At the same time, therefore, the television money occupied a higher share of the overall turnover.

The collapse of KirchMedia led to a reduction in fees paid for broadcasting rights. The German Football League did not receive the 460 million Euro they expected for the 2003–04 season, receiving instead only 290 million Euro. From 2002 on, the clubs had to give up around 180 million Euro per season. In 2003 the PSB channel ARD bought the *Bundesliga* broadcasting rights for free TV for only 60 million Euro per season. From 2003 the ARD reactivated their *Sportschau* to cover the *Bundesliga* in recorded summaries. The rights for live transmission on pay-TV were bought by the former Kirch channel Premiere World, now owned merely by a fund, for 145 million Euro. The sports channel DSF bought the rights for two Sunday matches for 12 million Euro, and the second PSB channel ZDF paid 10 million Euro for the right to show summaries of all Saturday matches in the late evening on their *Aktuelle Sportstudio*. Thus, while all clubs received significantly less money from TV, they still had long-term contracts with their high-salaried star players. Many clubs had to sell players or renegotiate the contracts at lower salary levels. Formerly successful clubs such as Borussia Dortmund had real problems. In 1997 Dortmund won the Champions League, playing at European level, in the Champions League and the UEFA Cup over the subsequent years. They received a lot of revenue from ticket sales at the Westfalen Stadium (capacity around 80,000), sponsoring, merchandising and TV fees. They bought expensive players such as the Brazilian Marcio Amoroso and paid them very high salaries. In 2003–04 they missed the qualification for the Champions League and were eliminated at an early stage from the UEFA Cup. The reduction in revenue was followed by increasing debts. At the beginning of 2005, debts had reached 180 million Euro and the club was threatened by bankruptcy. One reason for the financial crisis of German football after the collapse of KirchMedia and the reduction of revenue from TV rights was the unprofessional structure of the executive committees in clubs. Most presidents and secretaries managed their clubs as they had done in more amateur times. They missed the opportunity to change the organizational structure of the clubs and turn them into professional enterprises. This was vital in times when football had become a professional and commercial business with major budgets.

Professional football in the sport/media complex

The transformation of football since 1945 took place in times of radical changes in Western societies. 'De-traditionalization', commercialization, individualism, globalization, postmodernism, network society are all catch-phrases that have been used to describe these social changes. Football as a cultural practice is deeply rooted in society. Thus football, too, is affected and transformed. The increasing role of mass media in societies of reflexive modernity fostered the tendencies of global information exchange, communication and, most importantly, capital. Sports in general and football in particular were transformed into professional businesses dependent on financial capital from the media. Football became wholly enmeshed in what Sut Jhally (1989: 78), with reference to the specificities of the US context, has called the sports/media complex:

> This can be (briefly) justified in two fundamental ways: (1) Most people do the vast majority of their sports spectating via the media (largely through television), so that the cultural experience of sports is hugely mediated; and (2) from a financial point of view, professional, and increasingly college, sports are dependent upon media money for their very survival and their present organizational structure.

The transformation of football from amateurism to professionalism and commodity product illustrates this very clearly. Inventions of new European competitions like the Champions League were only possible because there was enough money from television to support them. Introduced in 1992–93, the Champions League functions like a slot-machine for successful clubs (see Morrow 2003: 22–31). On the other hand, football is divided into a super-professional sphere that comprises the most successful teams on a European level (clubs such as AC Milan, Real Madrid and Manchester United), a mid-range professional sphere of clubs that participate in European competitions from time to time, and then the whole spectrum of less successful clubs that compete only on a national level and are dependent on national TV money. None the less, football is still a cultural product,

> and its meanings and significance are not wholly defined by its political economy. People in pubs or domestic lounges, as well as at live games at various levels of performance, can chant, sing, shout, speak and respond in their own appropriate way as, with varying degrees of freedom and choice, they negotiate the expression of a particular cultural identity through the public culture of the game. But at the top level, football represents more and more graphically the triumph of the universal market, and whenever it is watched – live or in its transmitted forms – it is an increasingly commodified cultural product in a structured environment of an intensifying exclusive type.
>
> (Sugden and Tomlinson 1998: 98)

Football as television can only be successful because of its cultural and social qualities: 'Football is powerful programming because it has established itself in the urban cultural traditions of Europe' (King 2003: 102). In this sense, football is not dependent on television money, rather television is dependent on football for successful programming.

The collapse of KirchMedia in Germany and ITV Digital in Great Britain illustrates the risks of late modern financial capital and investment in sports and new media technologies. The rise of cable, digital and satellite television, the internet and mobile communication has pumped huge amounts of money into sports and football. But if there is no audience for all these new technical devices and services, as witnessed in the poor level of subscription for Kirch's digital pay-TV, there will be no revenues. Football has truly become a commodity and 'the communicative space of football has become increasingly global in the new media age' (Boyle and Haynes 2004: 158), but the meaning and significance of football is rooted in the cultural practices of local and regional traditions. After the collapse of KirchMedia, there is still *Bundesliga* football in Germany, albeit with less money from television but with the same cultural power its tradition in Germany always afforded it. A media concern went bankrupt, but football is still alive, even if commercialization and mediaization had changed it.

References

Beck, U., Giddens, A. and Lash, S. (1994) *Reflexive Modernization: Politics, Tradition and Aesthetics in the Modern Social Order*, Cambridge: Polity Press.

Bjondeberg, I. (2002) 'The Mediation of Everyday Life: Genre, Discourse and Spectacle in Reality TV', in A. Jerslev (ed.) *Realism and 'Reality' in Film and Media*, Copenhagen: Museum Tusculanum Press.

Boyle, R. and Haynes, R. (2004) *Football in the New Media Age*, London and New York: Routledge.

Castells, M. (2000) *The Rise of the Network Society*, 2nd edn, London: Blackwell.

Dobson, S. and Goddard, J. (2001) *The Economics of Football*, Cambridge: Cambridge University Press.

Friedrich, J.A. and Weickert, S. (2003) 'Die Standardsendungen des DDR-Sportfernsehens: Ein erster Ansatz zur Periodisierung der Entwicklung der Programmsparte Sport', in J.A. Friedrich, L. Mikos and H-J. Stiehler (eds) *Anpfiff: Erste Analysen zum DDR-Sportfernsehen*, Leipzig: Universitätsverlag.

Friedrichsen, M. and Möllenbeck, S. (2002) *Kommerzialisierung des Sports: Zur Medienfinanzierung des Profifußballs*, Stuttgart: Hochschule für Medien.

Grosshans, G.T. (1997) *Fußball im deutschen Fernsehen*, Frankfurt/Main: Peter Lang.

Hickethier, K. (1998) *Geschichte des deutschen Fernsehens*, Stuttgart and Weimar: Metzler.

Jhally, S. (1989) 'Cultural Studies and the Sports/Media Complex', in L.A. Wenner (ed.) *Media, Sports, and Society*, Newbury Park, CA: Sage.

King, A. (2003) *The European Ritual: Football in the New Europe*, Aldershot: Ashgate.

Mikos, L. (2002) 'Freunde fürs Leben. Kulturelle Aspekte von Fußball, Fernsehen und Fernsehfußball', in: J. Schwier (ed.) *Mediensport: Ein einführendes Handbuch*, Hohengehren: Schneider Verlag.

Mikos, L. and Nutt, H. (1997) *Sepp Herberger: Ein deutsches Fußballleben*, Frankfurt/ Main and New York: Campus.

Morrow, S. (2003) *The People's Game? Football, Finance and Society*, Basingstoke and New York: Palgrave Macmillan.

Sugden, J. and Tomlinson, A. (1998) *FIFA and the Contest for World Football – Who Rules the Peoples' Game?*, Cambridge: Polity Press.

9 A game of nations?

Football and national identities

Sanna Inthorn

National identity and media representation

The importance of national identity to the media representation of football is widely documented. National sports events are annual viewing rituals in the broadcasting calendar. While we sit in front of our television sets at home, they give us the sense of belonging to a wider imagined community (Anderson 1991; Scannell and Cardiff 1995). Watching an annual sporting highlight, such as the German *Bundesliga* final, we can imagine ourselves in temporal and spatial unity with every other member of our national community. The arrival, first, of video and then of digital recording technology has arguably challenged the extent to which sporting events can still make us feel part of the nation. After all, the sense of temporal unity is challenged once we no longer watch sports at the time it is broadcast. Yet the media representation of national identity does not rely solely on simultaneous viewing by the national community (Brookes 1998). Regardless of whether we watch a recording or a live broadcast, the media text itself reminds us what it means to belong to 'our' nation. The syntax of the game of football also lends itself perfectly to the creation of such identities. It is based on the very essence of collective identity formation: the defining of borderlines between in-groups and out-groups (Giulianotti 1999: 10, 32). In football reporting, a nation's common interest, shared culture and character are emphasized, and are used as markers of difference that distinguish it from other nations (Brookes 2002: 89). Stereotypical images are a frequent characteristic which defines 'our' and 'other' nations. Such national images may be found in the representation of both players and fans. Examples are the 'fiery' and 'volcanic' Italians (Blain *et al.* 1993: 79–80), and the slightly less exciting but reliable Germans, who, so media coverage would have it, are the personification of discipline, dedication and hard work (Blain *et al.* 1993: 69). Central to this discursive construction of national identity is the notion that the world of football can be divided into distinct national styles of play.

There are, of course, different ways of playing the game. Yet while these styles change regularly, the perception of a nation's style of play does not.

The image of a constant national style corresponds to what Christian Bromberger calls a 'stereotyped image, vested in tradition, that the community gives itself and wishes to show to others' (cited in Lanfranchi and Taylor 2001: 191). A national style of play is used to say something about the nature of a people, what they are like and how they want to be seen (Lanfranchi and Taylor 2001: 191). This concept of a collective style often corresponds with the representation of fan behaviour. The image of emotional Southern nations on the pitch, for example, is matched by the image of their 'naturally' emotional and highly joyful fans (Blain *et al.* 1993: 94). The sense of a homogenous nation, united not only in support of the national team but also by a shared national character, emerges in the process of the construction of different, contrasting and potentially conflictual national cultures.

The image of a national character is but one key element of the discursive construction of national identity (Wodak *et al.* 1998). Further elements of this discourse are the ideas of a national culture and the national past (ibid.), both of which may be found in football reporting. References to national dress, language and food, for example, create the sense of distinct national cultures (Brookes 2002: 83), while references to past wars in particular emphasize nations' rivalries and relationships. British media coverage of the 'old classic', Germany versus England, in the past has been riddled with such references. Football becomes a form of 'war minus the shooting', in the classic Orwellian formulation of 1945 (Orwell 1970: 63): in this discourse, past glories of English (/British) victories and threats of German aggression are evoked (Garland and Rowe 1999; Maguire *et al.* 1999). The tabloid press in particular makes ample use of war rhetoric, with the *Daily Mirror*'s headline 'Achtung Surrender!' (24 June 1996) possibly being the most infamous English example to date. A nation's past glories are associated with the battlefield, and transplanted into the sports sphere and the football pitch. If a current team fails to live up to examples set in a 'golden age', a nostalgic discourse emphasizes the nation's past as a point of positive identification with the nation (Brookes 2002: 101). To sum up, it may be argued that media discourse constructs a sense of national identity by placing different nations in direct opposition to each other. The distinction of one nation from the other is sustained by references to national character, culture and past.

Other studies have discussed how this image of a homogenous nation, constructed through the sports media, tends to be gendered (Giulianotti 1999: 158) and ethnically exclusive (Carrington 1998; Dimeo and Finn 1998). Football reporting hides these social divisions by constructing the concept of a homogenous national identity. Football stars are often key symbolic figures in this discursive construction of the nation. Sports stars whose personal histories fit the cultural identity of a particular era and its moral ideals become symbols of national identity. They become national heroes (Faure 1996: 86) and their identity often serves to hide social tensions and divisions. In 1998, for instance, Zidane became the symbol of a united French nation (Marks 1998), similar to Raymond Kopa who became symbolic of the myth of well-integrated immigrants in the 1950s (Lanfranchi and Wahl 1996: 117). This chapter initially explores how national identities are 'imagined' (Anderson 1991) as homogenous, so constructing idealised versions of a national culture, character and history. The discussion is based on a qualitative analysis of German public service television coverage of Euro 2004. The sample includes support programmes, such as panel discussions and portraits of teams and players by the national state broadcasters ARD and ZDF, for the opening ceremony (12 June 2004) and the following matches: Czech Republic–Germany (23 June 2004), Latvia–Germany (19 June 2004) and Germany–Holland (15 June 2004). The discursive construction of national identities is, of course, not restricted to these elements of media coverage. Yet support programmes are a main carrier of interpretation of a game, and indeed a whole tournament. It is in such programmes that broadcasters tell us a coherent 'story' of what is going on. They define what is 'good' and 'bad' sporting performance, and explain the event with the help of ethnic and cultural stereotypes (Tudor 1981). Support programmes are therefore a particularly rich source of discursive constructions of national identities.

German media texts and the pictures from Portugal

A sample of German media texts provides a particularly interesting basis for the discussion of national identity, as explicit identification with German national identity has never been straightforward. During the 1998 World Cup, German media struggled with the wave of nationalism that international football tournaments often evoke. News discourse defined democracy and liberalism as key elements of German identity, which became the antithesis to the nation before 1945 (Inthorn 2002). Yet despite the representation of a nation that 'had learnt its lessons from the past', football reporting at the same time presented the ethnic community as the 'natural' and acceptable form of a nation. Media discourse sustained a concept of national identity that was also supported in news reports on citizenship reform and political rhetoric (ibid.). Football reporting thus needs to be understood within a wider social, political and global context (Blain *et al.* 1993; Garland and Rowe 1999: 85; Maguire *et al.* 1999; Maguire 1999).

Social and political developments, though, are not the only factors we need to keep in mind in the analysis of constructed forms and representation of national identity. Global, profit-driven football and media industries have challenged the extent to which football in the media can continue to be a meaningful and significant source of identification with the nation. Indeed, instead of an unease of identification with the nation, in 2004 a relative lack of concern with the national dimension was discernible. A central challenge to the extent to which football can still be a reference point for national identity is player migration. Foreign players have a strong presence in football leagues across the world. Moreover, a growing number of players are members of national teams in countries in which they were neither born nor have been resident for a long time (Brookes 2002: 84). One consequence of this development has been a decrease in the range of different football styles. Once the Brazilians play like the Europeans, it seems doubtful whether media discourse can sustain the idea of distinct 'national styles'. The globalization of media sports is fuelled by communication technologies that allow us to watch international football leagues while physically remaining in the context of our locale. German visitors to a pub in Britain are likely to find someone with whom to swap opinions about the German *Bundesliga*. The economics of media sport have also led to a rise in the number of international tournaments, particularly at club level. As a consequence of this development, for some fans the identification with their local club becomes more important than identification with the national team (King 2000). What matters most is success at a European level. To meet this goal the presence of foreign talent at home is often considered to be crucial (ibid.). Presence of 'home-grown' talent seems less important than international success. Further, fans whose allegiance seems mainly to focus on the local club often express a sense of European cosmopolitanism (ibid.). This may not erode completely football's contribution to fans' sense of national identity, but it nevertheless makes the dividing lines between 'us' (our nation) and 'them' (the other nations), seem less sharp.

Another consequence of the world-wide commercialization of sport is the creation of the sports star as transnational, global citizen (Giardina 2001). Some sports stars enjoy a flexible transnational celebrity status, on to which audiences of all nationalities can project their own local meaning and values. The star becomes a blank canvas on to which the characteristics of any nation may be painted. Such stars' identities are not confined to the narrative of one national identity, and their marketability is not at all limited to a single geographic area. They can endorse products worldwide and are sought out by transnational corporations, such as Omega and Adidas (ibid.).

While under threat from globalizing media and football industries, the concept of the nation, though, might be saved by its financial profitability, in the persisting public interest in particular stars as national figures. This chapter taps into the debate and asks whether the nation still matters in media coverage of international football tournaments. It explores the tensions between the persisting representations of national identities on the one hand, and the challenges posed to it, by the presentation of football as a global game, on the other. Following an analysis of discursive constructions of national identity through references to national character, culture and past, the discussion focuses on the representation of stars. Specifically, the chapter explores whether stars' performances are associated with a display of national identity, or whether they are presented more as transnational celebrities emblematic of an increasingly globalized football industry.

Representing the (German) national character

In the run-up to each game, both ARD and ZDF interrupted studio debates with short clips to introduce the host country Portugal, individual players and teams that would play against Germany. Not unlike programmes on bargain holidays and house-hunting abroad, they presented snapshots of a culture, such as key moments in history, or examples of national cuisine. Before the German team met their Czech opponents in Lisbon, the ARD's Ursula Hoffmann, from within a 'palace full of history' (ARD, 23 June 2004), introduces us to Portugal's Moor history. In another example of the discursive construction of national identity, before the 'classic' Germany versus Holland, ZDF commentator Dieter Nuhr jokingly describes Holland as the land of cheese:

> There is of course more to Holland than cheese and caravans. Holland is ... (he pauses) ... I mentioned cheese already, didn't I? I think there is probably more to it but, quite frankly, who cares?
> (ZDF, 15 June 2004)

The Germans, we learn, have other cuisine to be proud of. A subsequent report that 'samples the mood in Germany' presents a few shots from a sports bar. After a tracking shot over a display of sausages and mash, we see the bar's owner who proudly identifies the menu as 'Bockwurst, typically German – for the game Holland–Germany'. Underpinning reports such as these is the assumption that every nation has its very own, distinct, national culture. The discursive construction of the nation here is supported through the use of stereotypical images of national culture. Not all of them are presented in a serious, or factual way, which might influence audience reception of such stereotypes. Yet regardless of the extent to which people truly believe Holland to be the land of cheese or not, it may be argued that by drawing on such cultural stereotypes the discourse sustains the idea that nations can be identified by their own cultural traits, which distinguishes them from others.

Next to the concept of national culture we find the idea that nations have their very own national character. Reporter Michael Steinbrecher puts the question to studio guests Lothar Matthäus and Rein Van Duijnhoven: 'Why can't we do this [play football in a different way]? Is there a biological reason?' (ZDF, 15 June 2004). His query is not so much a question as a statement: the Germans are different from other nations. The underlying argument is further sustained in a short quiz on different nation's attitudes:

Steinbrecher:	There are a couple of quotes. When you hear them you ask yourself, who might have said this? 'I want my team to give everything, I want them to pull themselves together. . . .' Did a German say this, or a Dutch?
Matthäus:	Well, I would say that's a German.
Steinbrecher:	Yes. . . . Are the Germans different after all, despite all clichés?
Matthäus:	It has something to do with training.

(ZDF, 15 June 2004)

Despite Matthäus' point about players' training and despite a hint at the artificial and superficial nature of stereotypes, in this exchange the old image of the Germans as battle machines comes through. It is echoed in several reports and studio debates. For instance, in an interview before the match against Holland, the player Friedrich sees the 'German virtues' as elements that add up to a winning formula: 'Battling on and sticking together' (ZDF, 15 June 2004). The other side to this image of a people, who fight on like war machines, is the idea that they can never, ever relax. Before the match against the Czech Republic, reporter Andreas Becker suggests that the Germans, unlike the Czechs, find it difficult to relax: 'The Czechs,' he muses, 'don't seem to take anything at all seriously, one of many strengths they possess, in contrast to the Germans' (ARD, 23 June 2004). Taken in isolation, this example, as indeed most other references to German players' attitude, could be interpreted as part of a discourse that merely constructs the image of an homogenous identity among German players. They do not suggest that players, fans, and indeed Germans in general share the same mindset. They could be 'mere' evidence of the discursive construction of a German football 'school'. However, references to a German 'mentality' may also be found as part of arguments that seek to explain why Germans get along with each other, and not with members of other nations. Before the German and the Dutch teams meet on the pitch once more, Dutch player Van Duijnhoven and former German national player Matthäus debate the German players' 'mentality' (ZDF, 15 June 2004). Commenting on the team spirit in Dutch clubs and German *Bundesliga* teams, Van Duijnhoven suggests that 'the mentality in Germany is different' from Holland where players tend to socialize as a group. In response, Matthäus argues that bonding and socializing at club level is difficult in Germany because there are 'many nationalities'. In the national team, he announces, things are different: 'There is bonding' (ZDF, 15 June 2004). A common attitude is defined as 'natural' among members of the same national collectivity. Therefore, what is part of a style of play, or attitude towards the game, simultaneously becomes a marker of national identity. The national team becomes representative of the nation at large. It is distinguished from other nations on the basis of national character.

Central to the setting up of such oppositions between 'our' nation and 'other' nations are references to the national past. In the run-up to the match against Holland, the ZDF (15 June 2004) dedicated a whole report to the ways in which German–Dutch relations, on and off the football pitch, are defined by collective memory. In particular, it is the Dutch memory of German occupation that is identified as a source of constant friction. Such references to a history of rivalry and wars fought against each other, similar to British media references to the Second World War during Euro '96 (Garland and Rowe 1999), evoke the idea of a collective past and collective national identity. This picture of Dutch–German relations is complex. Embedded in the same report, which shows vox pops of Dutch citizens suggesting that their view of Germany is still framed by the collective memory of war, we get to see more playful examples of Dutch–German differences. We learn about the 2002 German website www.ihrseidnichtdabei.de, in which German fans ridicule their Dutch counterparts. We also hear of Carlo de Vries, singer of the Dutch hit 'De Zakkenvöller', a humorous 'attack' on the German coach Rudi Völler. Such comments take the edge off the claim that Dutch–German relations are shaped primarily by the memory of war. Yet what they do not do is limit the way in which the idea of a national culture serves as a constitutive element of a distinct national identity. References to the Second World War, even in arguments that suggest the diminished legacy of this time, nevertheless support the idea that nations have a distinct past.

Further, examples of 'normal' football rivalry between fans of neighbouring countries sustain the idea that one nation can be distinguished from another because of cultural differences. This notion of cultural difference is sustained further by nostalgic retrospectives of the nation's golden days of football glory. While discussing the German team's chances for Euro 2004, reporters don't raise false hopes: 'German strikers simply don't manage to get the ball into the net', says Bernd Schmelzer on ARD (23 June 2004). On ZDF (15 June 2004) Michael Steinbrecher presents an internet poll which suggests that almost 50 per cent of the German public think that the German team will not make it past the first round. Yet amidst dismay, or resignation, there is the allusion to a better past which all Germans supposedly identify with – past successes of the German team are repeatedly mentioned. Gerd Delling, for instance, introduces the Czech Republic as 'Germany's favourite opponent' (ARD, 23 June 2004), because in the history of German–Czech games, Germany had so far managed to claim ten wins and two draws (but was to lose this match to a second-string Czech side). A key figure in this nostalgic discourse is former member of the national team, now football commentator, Günter Netzer, who together with ZDF co-presenter Delling frequently exchanges banter over his time in the *Bundesliga* and the national team. His experience as a professional player in the key era of German football history serves as an example to explain and compare current football situations, such as the make-up of the German team. Netzer describes them as 'all of them good lads, but no stars', an analysis to which co-commentator Delling responds jokingly with 'almost like in the good old days of Werder [Bremen]' (ARD, 12 June 2004). The role of Netzer's persona as reference point for the discursive construction of the national past suggests that football stars might take a key role in the construction of the nation. In the following section, a second function of star personae will be explored: the transnational star as symbol of a globalized football industry. It is in this role that stars pose a potential challenge to the concept of football as a game of nations. An international tournament might no longer be explained to us mainly through references to national, ethnic and cultural stereotypes, but through references to a global sports industry.

German stars of Euro 2004

In 2004 there were two major stars in the German team: FC Bayern Munich's goalkeeper Oliver Kahn and midfielder Michael Ballack. Their product endorsement for international companies is evidence of their transnational celebrity status: Ballack has had contracts with Adidas-Salomon, Coca-Cola, McDonald's and Sony (managermagazin.de, 14 June 2004). Kahn, who with 8.84 million Euros' income from advertising ranks among the ten best-earning German players (ibid.), featured in campaigns for Adidas and is the face of Japanese company Noloan.[1] In these adverts the players do not function as a symbol of German national identity, but as symbols of successful athletic performance. The Adidas campaign 'Predator Experience', for example, presented Ballack as one of several 'Predator Stars',[2] next to other international stars such as Beckham and Zidane (Adidas United Kingdom 2004). His national identity is not central to the branding of the company, but his performance as a player, and masculinity, are. A look at adverts for German companies and German branches of global businesses suggests that Ballack's and Kahn's personae as football stars matter most even in adverts that target a German audience. Both players featured in adverts for the electricity company Eon, and in 2004 Burger King Germany launched the 'Burger King Kahn Aktion' (Pressemappe Burger King, 15 May 2004). The official slogan for Kahn's Burger King campaign was: 'Two who walk through fire' ('Zwei die durchs Feuer gehen'). This slogan alluded to the tough nature of the goalkeeper's job, and possibly to the publicity surrounding the breakup of this particular keeper's marriage. His identity as a German plays no signifying role. Thus, even though Kahn functions as a star of audience recognition within Germany, the advert does not use his image to symbolize specific qualities of German national identity. This is not to say that German football stars can never be used as symbols of national or regional German identity. Kahn is also 'the face of the FC Bayern'[3] for mineral water by Adelholzener, a company run and owned by nuns in Bavaria.[4] Promotional material for this company clearly constructs a sense of local identity. The company slogan promises 'the pure power of the Alps' ('Die reine Kraft der Alpen'). A webcam on the company website shows, as a caption reads, 'the Alps in good weather', and hyperlinks take us to information about the history of the convent. The company image is firmly placed within a narrative of a Bavarian natural idyll and religious tradition. Thus in his product endorsement for this specific company, Oliver Kahn functions as a symbol of Bavarian identity. His affiliation with FC Bayern Munich roots him in the locale, a link which the company can exploit. Therefore, it may be suggested that German football stars can feature as both transnational, and nationally/regionally specific, celebrities. Their personae may be used as a symbol of German culture, but also as transnational brands. In the role of the latter they are a symbol of an international, global game, in which football talent and star performance matter more than being representative of national characteristics.

In their coverage of Euro 2004, neither ARD nor ZDF uses the two players as symbols of German identity. Ballack appears in the role of international football star. In studio debates his individual qualities as a player are compared with other stars, such as Zidane. The comparison is not one between different national virtues, but between individual players' qualities. Similarly, Kahn's performance is not used as a display of German qualities. The narrative underpinning reports on Kahn is one of a star in his twilight years. Despite Kahn's waning success, both players are represented as members of an international league of 'superstars'. In the run-up to the opening ceremony, ARD (12 June 2004) indulges in a little star-gazing: 'Only our stars can take us on the road to Lisbon' announces the voice-over, as we see pictures of both Kahn and Ballack next to Zidane and Beckham. The report cuts back and forth between scenes from the German training camp and images taken from a recent Adidas advertising campaign. The image of the two German players is thus placed in a context of international football and a global, commercial industry. Back in the ARD studio, Delling picks up the narrative of a commercial football media:

> Superstars – maybe that's something to do with this present age of the mass media. In 1972 we had incredibly many stars, but were there any superstars?
>
> (ARD, 12 June 2004)

Thus a clear distinction is drawn between football today and football in an age gone by. Commercialization and media industries are defined as central to the game today and key to the emergence of football 'superstars'. Of course, in 2004 football stars were not an entirely new phenomenon. In response to Delling's query, co-commentator Netzer lists what he calls the 'player personalities' (*Spielerpersönlichkeiten*) of 1972, among them Franz Beckenbauer and Gerd Müller. Similar to the star persona of Netzer, references to former players, such as Beckenbauer and Müller, are part of a nostalgic construction of the national past. German football heroes are central to the story of the nation that is being told. Yet such national heroes have a different function from the concept of the football 'superstar' that Delling alludes to in the ARD. National heroes, such as Beckenbauer, do not function as symbols of a commercialized football industry to the same extent as the modern 'superstar'. Thus football stars serve as both symbols of the nation and also as symbols of a commercialized football industry. In 2004 the German team had only a few 'superstars' in its ranks, and it is mainly Kahn and Ballack who served as symbols of this 'football media age'.[5]

Other teams, such as Holland, had more star potential than Germany. In their coverage of these teams, both ARD and ZDF focus on these players, discuss their talents and, crucially, refer to them as stars, or superstars. On ZDF, a report on the Dutch team suggests that the amount of security and television cameras in front of the hotel befits 'popstars' (15 June 2004), and on ARD we see 'shy', 'global football star' ('Weltstar des Fußballs') the Czech Nedved being presented with a football shirt at a Milan fashion show (ARD, 23 June 2004). These players become defined as individual stars of global recognition. They are not symbols of national virtues, but of a globalized football industry. Thus, while not wishing to argue that stars have ceased to function as symbols of national identity, analysis of selected German media coverage of Euro 2004 suggests that what has emerged is a discourse that defines football as a global game in which transnational stars and their distinct talents matter. In this discourse football is no longer a game of nations, but a competition of individual talent. Studio debates about the German team's chances are underpinned by the assumption that it is stars, not collective qualities, that matter. A report on Ballack begins with a tracking shot that moves from the feet upwards to the player's head. 'The feet, the legs, the upper body, the head, the figure, of the German game', says reporter Begener's voice-over (ARD, 23 June 2004). An individual and his personal qualities are placed centre stage. Even though Ballack is 'the head' of the German game, he is not presented as a symbol of collective German values. Individual star performance becomes the focal point of a discourse that defines football as a globalized business. Expert commentary provided by Dutch player van Duijhoven before the match against Holland feeds into the same argument: 'The Dutch team is dispersed across the whole of Europe. Therefore they are all personalities. No one wants to sit on the bench' (ZDF, 15 June 2004). The argument emerges that player migration has turned football into a game of 'personalities'. Feeding into the discourse that defines football as a global game, rather than as a game between distinct national collectivities, is the argument that the demands of a global football industry have altered the previously (seemingly) homogenous 'ethnic make-up'[6] of various teams. In his report on the Czech team, the ARD's Andreas Becker informs us that 'the Czechs have not concerned themselves with the Germans. The reasons are obvious.' In the next shot of a press conference with the Czech team, we get to hear what these reasons are: '[Germany's] Kuranyi is half Brazilian. Klose is half Jugoslav' (ARD, 23 June 2004). The image of the Germans as united and homogenous is challenged. By underpinning their support programmes with references to such consequences of globalization, broadcasters tell the 'story' of a game that today needs to be understood in the context of global media sports industries, no longer solely through the concepts and constructs of national identity.

Concluding comments

This chapter began by asking whether the nation still matters in media coverage of international football tournaments. It argued that football reporting potentially is a revealing source for the discursive construction of national identities. Yet is also suggested that a globalized football and media industry poses potential challenges to the ways in which the game evokes images of national culture and identity. The emergence of football stars with transnational celebrity status was identified as a central challenge to the discursive construction of the nation. The chapter then set out to explore the possible tensions between the construction of national identities on the one hand, and the representation of football as a global game of transnational celebrities, on the other.

The analysis of support programmes on ARD and ZDF suggests that despite all potential threats to the persistence of national identities, football reporting is still a major source for the imaging of the nation. German national identity was constructed through references to national culture, history and character. Some qualms over such practice could be seen. Reporters seemed to be aware that football reporting tends to operate with simplifying but easily comprehendible stereotypes. 'Biological reasons' were rejected, yet nevertheless cultural differences between nations were upheld. Nations were defined as opposites to each other, since differences in national character, informed by national cultures, were identified. Yet concepts of national identities were not the only tool used to explain the tournament to audiences at home. Support programmes further 'explained' the story of Euro 2004 by defining football as a globalized and commercialized game. Instead of presenting stars as representatives of collective national virtues, support programmes evoked the image of transnational celebrities. The story of football today became the story of 'pop stars', and not nations. Thus a complex picture emerges: on the one hand, we can see the persistence of national identities as an explanatory framework for football reporting. Media discourse makes sense of international sporting events by drawing on stereotypical images of national culture and character. By drawing on these stereotypes, sport reporting discursively constructs a sense of national identity. Yet on the other hand, we see the construction of star personae as transnational celebrities. Stars are defined as central to the game. They are represented as an expression of the current nature of the sport industry to which they belong. Football reporting interprets a tournament for us, the audience at home, by referring to football as a global and commercialized industry.

It is doubtful whether the globalization of media sport can be adequately explained as a process whereby cultural roots and cultural diversities are replaced by a homogenous, global culture. Despite examples of global culture, such as the transnational star, the concept of national identity has not been completely jettisoned in sports media discourse. Despite a globalized football and media industry the nation still functions as a central point of identification. The economics of media sport themselves mean that it is financially lucrative for media organizations to target and address audiences as distinct national communities. National broadcasters, pay-per-view and pay-TV all either sell advertising space in their (national) markets, or adapt the promotion of their own products to nationally specific markets (Brookes 2002: 85). Further, while some stars may be transnational, and the embodiment of globalization in action, others are still marketed in terms of their national identities (Giardina 2001).

This study can hardly propose that one image, the world of nations, will eventually give way to the other image, football as a game of international superstars. It is impossible to establish in a single, small-scale and limited qualitative study whether one discourse is more prominent than the other. What the analysis can do, though, is point to the presence of both discourses and suggest that for now they are negotiated within the same context, at the same time. While sport remains the site of discourses that express heterogeneity of national identities, at the same time it is a site where cultural symbols converge in a mediated global world.

Notes

1   See the company website at http://www.noloan.com/main.html.
2   Own quotation marks.
3   Own quotations marks.
4   See the company website at http://www.adelholzener.de/fileadmin/frames/index. html.
5   Own quotation marks.
6   Own quotation marks.

References

Adidas United Kingdom (2004) 'Football downloads 2004'. Online. Available: http://www.adidas.com/verticals/football/com/03_do.asp (accessed 8 February 2005).

Anderson, B. (1991) *Imagined Communities: Reflections on the Origin and Spread of Nationalism*, London: Verso.

Blain, N., Boyle, R. and O'Donnell, H. (1993) *Sport and National Identity in the European Media*, Leicester: Leicester University Press.

Brookes, R. (1998) 'Time, National Identity and Television Schedules in the "Postbroadcast Age"', *Time and Society*, 7(2): 369–81.

—— (2002) *Representing Sport*, London: Arnold.

Carrington, B. (1998) '"Football's Coming Home" But Whose Home? And do we Want it? Nation, Football and the Politics of Exclusion', in A. Brown (ed.) *FANATICS! Power, Identity and Fandom in Football*, London: Routledge.

Dimeo, G. and Finn, G.P.T. (1998) 'Scottish Racism, Scottish Identities', in A. Brown (ed.) *FANATICS! Power, Identity and Fandom in Football*, London: Routledge.

Faure, J. (1996) 'National Identity and the Sporting Champion: Jean Borotra and French History', in R. Holt, J.A. Mangan and P. Lanfranchi (eds) *European Heroes: Myth, Identity, Sport*, London: Frank Cass.

Garland, J. and Rowe, M. (1999) 'WAR MINUS THE SHOOTING? Jingoism, the English Press, and Euro 96', *Journal of Sport & Social Issues*, 23(1): 80–95.

Giardina, M.D. (2001) 'Global Hingis: Flexible Citizenship and the Transnational Celebrity', in D.L. Andrews and S.J. Jackson (eds) *Sport Stars: The Cultural Politics of Sporting Celebrity*, London: Routledge.

Giulianotti, R. (1999) *Football: A Sociology of the Game*, Cambridge: Polity Press.

Inthorn, S. (2002) 'The Death of the Hun? National Identity and German Press Coverage of the 1998 Football World Cup', *European Journal of Cultural Studies*, 5(1): 49–68.

King, A. (2000) 'Football Fandom and Post-national Identity in the New Europe', *British Journal of Sociology*, 51(3): 419–42.

Lanfranchi, P. and Taylor, M. (2001) *Moving with the Ball: The Migration of Professional Footballers*, Oxford: Berg.

Lanfranchi, P. and Wahl, A. (1996) 'The Immigrant as Hero: Kopa, Mekloufi and French Football', in R. Holt, J.A. Mangan and P. Lanfranchi (eds) *European Heroes: Myth, Identity, Sport*, London: Frank Cass.

Maguire, J. (1999) *Global Sport: Identities, Societies, Civilizations*, Cambridge: Polity Press.

Maguire, J., Poulton, E. and Possani, C. (1999) 'Weltkreig III. Media Coverage of England versus Germany in Euro 96' *Journal of Sport and Social Issues* 23(4): 439–454.

Managermagazin.de (14 June 2004) 'Fußballmillionäre: Kick and Earn'. Online. Available: http://www.manager-magazin.de/koepfe/artike1/0%2C2828%2C303653%2C00.html (accessed 20 January 2005).

Marks, J. (1998) 'The French National Team and National Identity: "Cette France d'un "bleu métis"', in H. Dauncey and G. Hare (eds) *France And the 1998 World Cup*, London: Frank Cass.

Orwell, G. (1970) 'The Sporting Spirit', in S. Orwell and I. Angus (eds) *The Collected Essays, Journalism and Letters of George Orwell. Volume IV: 'In Front of Your Nose'*, Harmondsworth: Penguin.

Presse Mappe Burger King (15 May 2004) Presse Mappe. Online. Available: http://www.presseportal.de/story.htx?nr=557898&firmaid=35558 (accessed 20 January 2005).

Scannell P. and Cardiff D. (1995) 'The National Culture', in O. Boyd-Barrett and C. Newbold (eds) *Approaches to Media: A Reader*, London: Arnold.

Tudor, A. (1981) 'The Panels', in T. Bennett *et al.* (eds) *Popular Television and Film*, London: Open University Press.

Wodak, R. Cillia D.R., Reisigli N., Liebhart, K., Hofstätter, K. and Kargl, M. (1998) *Zur diskursiven Konstruktion nationaler Identität*, Frankfurt/Main: Suhrkamp.

10 Fandom and subcultural media

Jürgen Schwier

Fan culture in change

For Trekkies and soap addicts, for followers of hip hop, folk music, basketball or football, fan cultures in the digital age are accessed via and derived from the media. At the same time, however, soccer fans are increasingly developing their own media activity through which they articulate their demands and in particular their need to participate. By means of their own homepages, webzines and network campaigns, individual and specialist factions within the fan scene use the World Wide Web to produce a 'media public' from below, to come into contact with like-minded people and to promote their interests and ideas. Thus the internet increases the scope of action open to fans.

Characteristic of this change in fan culture in Germany are groupings of critical football fans, who, according to Aschenbeck (1998) and Schwier (1998), combine passion for the game and their own club with a thoughtful and sceptical attitude to that club's politics and to the commercialization of football as a whole. Indeed, the whole trappings of match day (atmosphere, arrival and departure, celebration) seem to be almost as important to them as the actual game itself. Following the slogan 'Reclaim the Game', critical football fans, via self-defined democratic processes, ultimately want to influence the development of football, and the fan culture belonging to it, from below. Moreover, because they are characterized by a mixture of irony and passion, media competence and the will to participate hitherto hardly found among football supporters, Giulianotti (1999) describes such critical fans aptly as 'post-fans'.

Based on the results of an empirical study (Schwier and Fritsch 2003), this chapter will argue that the use of digital media and the 'networking' of supporters may be interpreted as a symptom of, and at the same time as a motor for, transformational tendencies in fan culture. Our study attempts primarily to trace the differences, commonalities and interactive dimensions of the heterogeneous 'internet presence' of fans. Consequently, the major question will focus on the processes that construct meaning and how these affect the medial contexts in which they are embedded.

Distinction and participation

The media activities of football fans are characterized in principle by demarcation and co-operation. Alongside the obvious assertion of distinction, through the digital documentation of differences in taste between separate factions of the fan scene, the internet activities at the same time try to promote the solidarity of all engaged football fans in the often-attested 'Fight for the Game'. They also aspire to articulate the purpose of participation. The experiential horizon of cyber-fan culture and its processes of empowerment are determined by the complex interrelation between the demonstration of group identity in contradistinction to alternative models of fandom on the one hand, and the ordinary demonstration of cultural differences – in opposition both to the hegemonic forces in football and to 'fair-weather fans' – on the other. The following statement, which is typical of the online fan activist, indicates furthermore that demarcation underlines substantial aspects of their own self-understanding: 'We, the generation Lucifer, will further try to gather those around us . . . who see their own small world on the home terraces. . . . We don't need to act like a cloned heap each week and deliver a mad show for the internet or for new collages' (http://www.generation-luzifer.de; trans.).

Football fan groupings may be regarded as distinctive subcultures in which the production of the fans' own activities and preferences in the World Wide Web play an important role for the development of group identity and the quest for an authentic style of fandom. In the endless drive to be the 'best fans', internet presences have become virtual arenas that stand alongside songs, chanting groups and home-terrace dances on the social stage on which each faction presents itself – with varying nuances – as especially authentic, humorous, creative, passionate and original. The critical comments of 'Generation Lucifer' on the online presentation of fans' behaviour, cited above, show simultaneously that the contestation of style brought about by the new medium has become more confusing and more unstable. In the fast-growing ultra-movement, for example, groups can increase their capital in the scene, at least in the short term, through comments on different forums and the reproduction of spectacular fan-block choreography on their homepages. In this context it is still largely uncertain whether the range and quality of online activities correspond with the real appearance of the respective group of fans in the stadium.

The subtle distinctions between the various forms of development of fandom can, however, be documented on the digital stage through multimedia. In ways similar to those discovered by Wheaton and Beal (2003: 172–3) in the niche magazines of alternative sport, internet presences of fan groupings always form a part of the fight for sovereignty of interpretation in the field of football, and offer both insiders and prospective customers a stock of knowledge that is typical for the scene. The acquisition of such knowledge can both prove affiliation to, and extend the capital of, the subculture.

The football fans examined display a corresponding will to participate in the discursive field of football and to co-operate in the politics of their own club. Beyond the extremely different interpretations of fandom among active football supporters, there seems to be a fundamental agreement about the fact that fans have to become more interested in the organization and production of the game and should intervene if they do not want to lose their influence on the sport altogether. More precisely, they should concern themselves with on-game planning, security concepts, ticket allocation, marketing measures or the management of the local stadium.

Through their online activities, fans create their own popular cultural capital that stands mainly in an ambivalent relation to professional football's prevailing constellation of power. On the one hand, fans want to co-design the 'football experience' and sometimes to participate in the decision-making processes of the clubs and organizations from within, while on the other hand they detach themselves from the media-sport-complex and by communicating their protest push the parameters of the system and its concomitant mentality to the limit. Fan groups conceive of themselves as a voice for the interests of football followers and as faithful trustees of 'real football', which they want to protect against the onslaught of commercialization. From their point of view, commercialism is inextricably bound up with processes of transformation within the stadium itself – from real fans standing on the terraces to passive consumers sitting on expensive seats (see BAFF 2004). The tension between the commercial penetration of popular culture and its potential for obstinacy and empowerment expresses itself clearly and in a keen and vital way in the field of football, because football by its very nature lends itself so readily to expressivity and the articulation of emotions and worldviews. Football brings intensive feelings into play – and the opportunity to put utopian desires on the agenda. This very emotional involvement in the discursive field of football stimulates the desire to participate and commit. Thus the productivity of the fans acts back upon the original (Fiske 1997: 62).

The interactive dimension

As the internet represents a suitable communication platform for football fans, it is hardly surprising that a lively discussion culture has already firmly established itself on website forums. It is generally held that electronic language deforms not only linguistic usage, but also language itself. Fans involved in online discussions communicate at the interface between speech and writing (Gurak 2004; Storrer 2001). This is much in evidence in the current stylistic devices used by fans: jargon, insider intonation, short cuts, emoticons, associative references, word-creation and so on. Numerous contributions to the forums are spontaneous, casual and unedited. That is where the impression of verbal linguistic usage – in written form – comes from. In this context, communication on the internet brings about a change in language: 'Electronic language changes the way texts are dealt with, it makes them mobile, but elusive as well, distances them from concepts such as contemplation and dependability that they had developed in book culture' (Simanowski 2002: 10; trans.). Panellists in fan forums try to create coherence, referring to previous speakers by quoting and/or explicitly addressing them. However, at the same time a general problem of online discussions becomes evident: the more participants there are taking part, the more difficult it is to follow the discussion; often the group divides itself into several discussion strands or drifts away from the original subject. We hypothesize therefore that sophisticated panellists know about cutting and pasting and employ such procedures – considering, correcting and, at the very least, shortening their texts – *before* they publish them in the forums. Their experience helps them to maximize the possibilities of online communication. Contributions from beginners, however, are often redundant, awkward and, therefore, less effective.

In essence, discussion in the forums centres on the usual subjects of fandom (among other things the self-image of the scene, the commercialization of football, violence and repression). The majority of fans write about football as a social stage: human bonding and agonistic distancing. Football fans also argue about values that have validity in other social connections: solidarity, justice, loyalty, morality, mutuality, group affiliation, envy, reward and punishment. At the same time, they maintain the normal rules of give and take, reacting with protest, refusal, criticism and indignation if these are abused. They distinguish between fact and fiction and expose counterfeiters and cheats. Football fans therefore act in this context with a 'social brain module' (Schwier and Fritsch 2003: 147–68). Inherent in these written negotiations about value and meaning is a tension. On the one hand, authors aim to increase their status and distinction by clever position-taking and creative and profound comments. They want to stand out. On the other hand, they are seeking a connection to the community, to which they recommend themselves as worthy allies and co-operative partners. They want to be integrated. These parallel processes embed themselves into an elusive interplay of alliances and loyalties.

On the one hand, the discussions in fan forums tend to be part of authentic communication. Here and there different roles are assigned: the agitator, the negotiator, the opportunist, the loudmouth, the nut-case. In the course of an online discussion, which can extend over several weeks, participants will serially occupy these roles. At the same time, it is possible for a participant to change role and strategy (sometimes several times) – for instance, from a consent-oriented stance to an isolated radical position. According to Simanowski (2002: 10), theatrical elements may be attributed to the act of electronic writing since the reproduction of senders and receivers and the habitual role-play between them gives the entire act the character of a performance. On the other hand, debates in digital media run according to their own rules. The anonymity of the internet allows factors such as dominance and hierarchy to lose their importance. The balance of power between producer and recipient – and also that within the community – flattens out. Nevertheless, everyday-life rules of inter-personal understanding, although moderated, are valid in the World Wide Web: whoever has already participated in the panel for a longer time and has made a name for themselves among the other panellists assumes and emits more authority and credibility. Consequently, they are able to influ-ence both the agenda and its communicative regulations. Compared to discussions in face-to-face communication and to traditional media inter-changes, the range of power is smaller. One reason for this is that in a (semi-)anonymous network, panellists who wish to attain power do not possess the same means to discipline and self-control that can be used in face-to-face-communication or in traditional communication via the media. It is not possible to flash a strict look to prevent invalid utterances. There is no authority to hedge or devaluate an opinion before it is articu-lated. Furthermore, means of non-verbal communication, such as volume, intonation and visual contact, do not apply.

An attempt at classification

While football fans can neither determine the outcome of a match nor invent their own game, they are reliant on the discursive field they observe. Fan groupings, by necessity, make use of the resources the football industry and the media offer them, but correlate them productively with their own life background, biographical experiences, needs, passions and yearnings. Via headstrong, delightful, sometimes refractory and contradictory processes of meaning creation, fans package together their own cultural practices. Supporters pick up what football and the media have to offer as working material for their own symbolic productivity. Against this background, the online activities of active football fans may be interpreted as meaning-generated and participation-orientated. Different factions of the fan scene admittedly also place emphasis on different mental perspectives in the World Wide Web. Acting on the basis of our analysis of media football fans, we can distinguish four versions. These will be outlined in the following sub-sections as (1) online activities among critical fan factions, (2) the 'internet presence' of fun-based factions, (3) online magazines of intellectual factions, and (4) online activities of ultra factions.

Online activities of critical fan factions

The webpages of critical football fans are generally characterized by a desire to enhance an active, independent, fundamentally democratic and multi-cultural fandom. The use of the internet is aimed at profiling the growing fan culture, the mobilization and display of solidarity of football supporters, and gaining the attention of the media at large. On closer inspection, two main trends may be observed. There is an internet presence of fan groups that concentrate on football-specific subjects (e.g. the initiative 'Pro Fans', the webzine *Schwatzgelb*) and one that goes beyond this by posing socio-political questions (e.g. 'Schalker Fan-Initiative', 'Bündnis aktiver Fußballfans'). While the latter initiatives and fanzines had already been mostly formed offline during the 1990s before, around the millennium, exploiting the special opportunities of the internet, the former were web-based right from the beginning.

The best-known example of this trend is the inter-club initiative 'Pro Fans', which by now has counterparts in more than thirty football clubs and is recognized as a point of contact by the media as well as by the Deutsche Fußball Liga and the Deutsche Fußball Bund. The idea behind this online campaign – known originally as 'Pro 15:30' – came about during a discussion between fans from different clubs in a forum of the internet portal *Stadionwelt*. The campaign 'Pro 15.30' is well known for having successfully implemented internet-based protest in the field of football and sees itself as a representative of specific fan interests. Overall, the future prospects of this project will depend on the continued dedication of their active members and the further expansion of their base (see König 2002: 67). While the original focus of their activities centred on resisting a growing trend for the media to determine kick-off times, the campaign is now primarily concerned with the so-called 'criminalization' of football followers. Via a widely expanded educational discourse, it tries to make the general public aware of acts of discrimination and wrongful stadium prohibition. Club-oriented internet presences and webzines of this type, as well as the campaign 'Pro Fans', seek dialogue with representatives of the football system in order to create local improvements for supporters. Sport is seen more as a politics-free space, which leads to the assumption that the extensive exclusion of political topics from online communication is supposed to guarantee the gathering and solidarity of all fans under the club banner.

Contrasting with this are groupings such as BAFF (Bündnis Aktiver Fußballfans) and the Schalker Fan-Initiative as well as fanzines like the *Übersteiger*, which were founded as a response to hooliganism and right-wing extremist tendencies in national league stadiums about a decade ago. They deal intensively with current political questions and social problems. For this faction, football is seen exclusively though the lens of the organization (see BAFF 2004). Disputes about social inequalities, violence, racism, right-wing extremism or anti-Semitism are therefore an integral part of their contributions to football discourse. In this particular context, critical fandom sees itself in the avant-garde of stadium-goers and intervenes to create opportunities for football supporters to become involved in politics or in the decisions of clubs and associations. It articulates justifiable positions and interests for all fans in the mass media.

The citizens' initiative model is hereby frequently activated to influence and infiltrate institutions. Besides the organization of demonstrations, the fans' engagement in a democratic and tolerant fan culture leads to social projects and political formations such as fan congresses and involvement in club committees (see Berg 2002). From the point of view of this faction, independent sport-political activities and independent fan work are essential for long-term sustainability. Fan projects traditionally arranged 'from above' are now supplemented by individual initiatives in which full-time fans' representatives organize projects for and between fans. Some of these initiative groupings are already on their way to becoming professionalized.

Internet presences in the fun-oriented fan faction

The fun-oriented fan faction does not seek to counter the complete capitalization of sport via protest campaigns, but turns instead to hedonistic annexation tactics which caricature the supposed seriousness of football. As well as homepages and webzines (blutgraetsche.de is a key example) that aim to provide a humorous and/or satirical view, we might think in this connection of the online activities of the Groundhopper. These internet presences provide an almost ideal opportunity, for fans who love to communicate and express their opinions, to publish their own texts, in which they observe the soccer industry with humour, irony, scorn and mockery. Carried along by the sheer delight of producing their own meanings and nonsense, the operators, authors and users of such forums become a 'fun guerrilla' that rejoices in the play and concerns itself mainly with producing the next punch line. Members of the groundhopping movement report on webpages about the sensual experience of being on the way to and enjoying the atmosphere in various stadiums. The majority of these online texts show groundhopping also to be a mixture of adventure, expedition, passion for football, pioneer romanticism and party culture. These texts go beyond the mere description of the strains of travel, fan-block choreography and meetings with residents: they are examples of a communicative self-expression that is both an enterprising and a polyglot version of fan culture and fandom.

The humorous, ironical or satirical online texts on the sport as well as the practices of the groundhopping scene may to a certain extent be interpreted as a way of satisfying unfulfilled cultural needs whereby 'the dividends are paid in the form of humour and recognition within the community by kindred spirits with the same tastes' (Fiske 1997: 57; trans.). What concerns participants in the fun-centred fan faction primarily is therefore their own community; such fans are self-contained and are only partially concerned about public attention.

Online magazines of the intellectual fan faction

For several years new fanzines such as *Der tödliche Paß* ('The Killer Pass') or *11 Freunde* have followed on from the intellectually stimulating, humorous and playful British tradition. The editors and authors are almost without exception academically educated football fans, who, by their own admission, 'look out from the fan-block to the football field and at the same time take up a point of view' (http://www.11freunde.de; trans.). These webzines are, however, neither a mouthpiece of the active fan scene nor a genuine component of critical fandom. None the less, they certainly sympathize with the perspective of the fans in their subtle, critical and entertaining reportage on football events.

The fanzine *When Saturday Comes* and the category of football literature traditionally associated with Great Britain are the role models of this individual faction. The magazines differ from other multimedia and subcultural forms of football reporting, on the one hand through their sophisticated linguistic level and, on the other, through their treatment of subjects that are otherwise hardly handled on- or offline (among other things: the transformation of football in Eastern Europe; football and pornography; a trade union study about coaches in the professional game; or reviews of documentary films). The makers of these fanzines see it as their goal to establish a form of sport journalism that is both fan-orientated and suitable for the presentation of football as a cultural topic. The primary recipients might be those 'cosmopolitan fans' that Giulianotti (1999: 104–5) describes as younger, well-trained and financially strong members of the average social class. They enjoy the comfort of today's stadiums, albeit with some scepticism, and still cling to the search for a mythical, 'real genuine' football (Spitaler and Wieselberg 2002: 198).

These media outlets have over time, it seems, adopted the mantle of intelligent and intellectual devotional works that originally belonged to the editorial self-image of the quality press. The *11 Freunde* in particular seems to have taken on a mediating role between the communicative self-products of the fan scene and the sports reports of the national quality press, i.e. they take up debates begun by other fanzines and fan campaigns and selectively transmit the point of view articulated by football fans to the (online) sports pages of *Der Spiegel*, the *Frankfurter Allgemeine Zeitung* or the *Süddeutsche Zeitung*.

Online activities of the ultra-faction

The ultra scene, which has only been an active part of the scene in German football stadiums since the 1990s, conceives of itself basically as an autonomous youth movement and as a new, fanatic and fanciful form of fandom (Gabriel 2004). In this context especially, online activities have contributed decisively to the networking and quick polarization of the movement. The central idea of ultra philosophy is the maximizing of a common experience in competition with other groups of supporters. Obviously there are different interpretations of what is appropriate in achieving loud, creative and attention-seeking support. While some groups concentrate on spectacular fan-block choreography, large banners, the making of original 'double brackets' (the name given to banners attached to poles at both ends) and the presentation of these activities on their websites, other ultras maintain the tradition of the so-called 'Bengalo' actions or participate – partly in co-operation with hooligans – in violent acts in the environs of the stadium. There is a world of difference, for example, between the motto of the Düsseldorfer 'Lost Boyz' – 'Sometimes antisocial – always antifascist' – and the battle-cry of the 'Ultras Gelsenkirchen' – 'Our terrace – our pride – our club' – which at least restricts itself to a display of anachronistic male stereotyping such as territorial behaviour.

Under the broad and shifting label 'Ultra', left-wing as well as right-wing symbols are used. The usual avowed intent not to discriminate against minorities does not mean, however, that the supporters or functionaries of another club are not under threat. Ultras do not form a homogeneous or closed subculture. As the following excerpt from an online text by the Osnabrück 'Violet Crew' shows, self-definition of ultra groups is characterized by its minimalism: 'Being ultra has nothing to do with whether you are a member of a group, and now less than ever with what clothes you wear in the stadium . . . ultra means to give everything for your club . . . to go to great trouble to maintain fan culture, and not to let yourself be suppressed by authorities and "unreasonable rules"' (http://www.ultras-deutschland.com/ultras/osnabrück.html; trans.). This faction's websites prove that being ultra is defined by an inner attitude – both to the club, its following and fandom in general. The ultra movement aims primarily to strengthen the common bonds of belonging in the fan scene and to insert itself into a position of leadership within this process. It is not surprising therefore that numerous ultra groupings act as informal umbrella organizations for particular fan clubs (e.g. http://www.clubnr12.de). Two factors, therefore are essential for inclusion in the ultras: an apolitical stance, as often flaunted on their internet sites, and club loyalty fuelled by high-octane passion for football that transcends political convictions. While there is no homogeneous stance towards violence, online, at least, an anti-racist position is a dominant discourse: 'Ultra negates – Racism splits! Kick it out! It is not the colour of your skin that counts but the way you think' (http://www.schickeria-muenchen.de; trans.).

All in all, it is assumed that that the webpages of the ultra scene situate the movement in the 'Vorderbühnen' (Goffman 1983: 100–28), while insiders go to the 'Hinterbühnen' (Members' area) and there exchange knowledge that is not supposed to be made public. In this context, the relationship between the associations of the national league and the ultra movement seems ambivalent. On the one hand, the colourful presence in the fan terraces is welcomed as a positive image factor; on the other hand, the actions of these distinctly and self-proclaimed independent groups evade control and resist any canalization by the clubs.

The meaning horizons of fandom

Online activities focus primarily on subject areas that already featured in the 1990s as hot issues for printed fanzines: resistance to the commercialization of football, efforts to keep the terraces from being shut down, debates about developments in the fan scene and the game at large, reports about away games (Aschenbeck 1998; König 2002; Schwier 1998). Moreover, the layout of numerous websites as well as their focus on the text are reminiscent of the vision behind niche magazines. The new medium, however, increasingly exploits to its advantage technical possibilities such as updating, hypertext and interactivity. In this way audio, video and hypertext undoubtedly improve the narrative self-portrait of the fan scene in comparison with printed fanzines. A regular update of the contents, as well as the interactive online forums, moreover, gives the users a greater sense of proximity, which encourages them in turn to make their own contributions and experience a sense of authorial involvement. The struggle for an independent fan culture and influence on the way football is developing is a common denominator in this area. I shall summarize these activities below with a primary focus on the central aspect of commercialization. First, however, it is important to outline two further aspects that are generally present in media discourses of sport: gender and ethnicity (Schwier 2000: 108–11).

Even if internet presences are usually designed to point out the distinction of one group *vis-à-vis* another, nearly without exception these webpages construct the masculine subject as the authentic, 'real' football fan (Dembowski and Scheidle 2002). Thus, several online texts describe the members of their own group as 'Jungs' ('lads') and in so doing show a tendency towards an inherited masculine role pattern or power fantasy. On the other hand, by the use of terms relating to the feminine gender they also express online their low regard for rival teams or their fan group. In this connection, it is not untypical for the Dortmund webzine *Schwatzgelb* to herald Schalke 04 as 'Mädls aus Herne West' ('girls from Herne West'). The latent macho and disparaging tone of language used in some online texts makes one suspect that the authors have mainly masculine users in mind when they are writing. It should be noted, incidentally, that women participate in no short measure in critical fan campaigns as well as in fan- and webzines, but it is men, on the whole, who produce the vast majority of the texts, photographs and video sequences on the websites. For example, at the end of 2003, out of more than thirty contact persons listed in the 'Pro Fans' initiative at the individual clubs, only one representative was female (at 'Pro Fans St. Pauli').

Football fans thus present themselves primarily as media objects in the World Wide Web that operate within a masculine sphere. At the same time they also stress their anti-racist stance, in content and in tone. All the aforementioned factions have a strict prohibition of xenophobia and racism in common. Some ultra groupings are active members of international and anti-racist unions, but they limit their stance to the subject of football, referring to their alleged apolitical character: 'We are neither nationalists nor antifascists, neither progressive nor conservative – we are the union of active FC Bayern fans' (http://www.clubnr12.de/politik/index.html; trans.). In contrast to this, the critical fan scene points out the socio-political implications of their engagement that reaches beyond the game: 'Small-mindedness and stupidity are a fertile soil for racism. You need different people to form a team. And this is how we imagine society, many different people presenting a team that likes to play together' (http://www.demballegal.de/index.php; trans.).

The developing economy of football should – together with the break-through of new media technologies – contribute to the formation of active fan networks which then serve as a mouthpiece for all those football fans who refuse to oppose the creeping integration of the game into the recreation industry. Boyle and Haynes (2004) have come to a comparable evaluation concerning the English fan scene: 'Fan websites, or e-zines, are created from a labour of love motivated by passion and heavily tied to the construction of cultural identities. . . . The dispersal of new media production has therefore opened up a whole new communicative space for football fans' (Boyle and Haynes 2004: 141–2). It is not only German and English fan movements that use the World Wide Web as a central forum to criticize the commercialization of the game and fight for the preservation of the fan culture. The homepages of fan groupings and webzines inform their readers extensively about corresponding tendencies both in the domestic football market and in other European countries, enable exchange in online forums, force mobilization, promote, all in all, a feeling of community among football supporters and foster the co-operative cause of publicity-effective initiatives. Thus a largely autonomous fan zone has been created on the internet that is not *a priori* reliant on the supply of classical sports journalism (Schwier and Fritsch 2003).

Wherever and whenever the media-sport-complex (Schauerte and Schwier 2004) pushes forward the commercialization of football, the internet presences of fans try to articulate their resistance against such developments. This does not prevent them, however, from putting devotional items that signal membership and support (T-shirts, scarves, CDs) on to the fan article product market. Merchandising at present is naturally part of the fashion and style competition between projects such as *11 Freunde*, the 'Schalker Fan-Initiative' or the 'Übersteiger'. The creation of meaning by the fan groups produces scene products whose branding seems to be especially successful, albeit within a strictly limited reach. Fan groups and webzines known to supporters use their image to gain an edge in competition and naturally increase their own market value by the sale of dedicated commercial merchandise.

As communities of interpretation, active football supporters deal with the cultural project 'football' as intensely and with as much enjoyment as they would with any other hobby, but the space they inhabit has room for manoeuvre and potential that is currently also being exploited for processes of empowerment. The 'Pro Fans St. Pauli', for example, took part in a competition called 'Fan Movie' organized by Coca-Cola. The self-produced film by the fan campaign (http://www.p96.de/pro1530</pro-fans-stpauli.mov) expresses opposition to marketing strategies and emphasizes the negative effects such pressure puts on football and fandom itself ('bought fan culture'). The latter example illustrates that football fans articulate their own interests via mediated forms of action, and produce and point up cultural differences. Fans are in no way helplessly dominated and 'exhibitioned' by the strategies of the media-sport-complex; rather, with their unpredictable practices, they can evade rules, product logics or system constraint. One can participate in the commercial campaign 'Fan Movie' promoted by the firm Coca-Cola like the 'Pro Fans St. Pauli' – by, as De Certeau would say, 'doing something with it' (De Certeau 1988: 60). By creating their own meanings, football supporters move around almost like supple pathfinders in the jungle of social control and poach on the ground of the football industry. The everyday guerrilla tactics of the actors form, for De Certeau (1988: 69–76), a net of anti-discipline following from a logic of confusion and difference that improves with the creative and opportunistic exploitation of loopholes in control. Online activities mirror, among other things, the will of the fans to make a difference in the (football) world. If the different fan factions continue to work away at diversions within the media-sport-complex, pointing the culture in alternative directions to the dominant culture of that complex, their engagement will have a chance of achieving the hoped-for improvements in football. The passions shared by, and the bonds established between these factions can provide a basis for real interventions. Such hopes, now also virulent in the World Wide Web at large, are recurrent, persistent and resilient in the world of football fandom. They cannot be simply brushed aside, and are increasingly identified and articulated in the media-based activity and agency of individuals and interest groups.

References

Aschenbeck, A. (1998) *Fußballfans im Abseits*, Kassel: Agon-Sportverlag.

BAFF (ed.) (2004) *Ballbesitz ist Diebstahl*, Göttingen: Verlag Die Werkstatt.

Berg, B. (2002) 'Dem Ball is' egal, wer ihn tritt: Die Schalker Fan-Initiative', in G. Dembowski and J. Scheidle (eds) *Tatort Stadion*, Cologne: PapyRossa.

Boyle, R. and Haynes, R. (2004) *Football in the New Media Age*, London: Routledge.

De Certeau, M. (1988) *Kunst des Handelns*, Berlin: Merve (*The Practice of Everyday Life*, Berkeley: University of California Press 1984).

Dembowski, G. and Scheidle, J. (eds) (2002) *Tatort Stadion: Rassismus, Antisemitismus und Sexismus im Fußball*, Cologne: PapyRossa.

Fiske, J. (1997) 'Die kulturelle Ökonomie des Fantums', in SpoKK (eds), *Kursbuch JugendKultur*, Mannheim: Bollmann.

Gabriel, M. (2004) 'Ultra-Bewegungen in Deutschland', in BAFF (ed.) *Ballbesitz ist Diebstahl*, Göttingen: Verlag Die Werkstatt.

Giulianotti, R. (1999) *Football: A Sociology of the Global Game*, Cambridge: Polity Press.

Goffman, E. (1983) *Wir alle spielen Theater*, Munich and Zurich: Piper (*The Presentation of Self in Everyday Life*, New York: Doubleday, 1959).

Gurak, L.J. (2004) 'Internet Studies in the Twenty-first Century', in D. Gauntlett and R. Horsley (eds) *Web.Studies*, London: Arnold.

König, T. (2002) *Fankultur: Eine soziologische Studie am Beispiel des Fußballfans*, Münster and Hamburg, London: LIT.

Schauerte, T. and Schwier, J. (eds) (2004) *Die Ökonomie des Sports in den Medien*, Cologne: Halem.

Schwier, J. (1998) 'Fanzines – Szenezeitschriften jugendlicher Fußballfans', in J. Schwier *Spiele des Körpers: Jugendsport zwischen Cyberspace und Streetstyle*, Hamburg: Czwalina.

—— (2000) *Sport als populäre Kultur: Sport, Medien und Cultural Studies*, Hamburg: Czwalina.

Schwier, J. and Fritsch, O. (2003) *Fußball, Fans und das Internet*, Baltmannsweiler: Schneider.

Simanowski, R. (2002) *Interfictions: Vom Schreiben im Netz*, Frankfurt/Main: Suhrkamp.

Spitaler, G. and Wieselberg, L. (2002) 'Think Global, Act Local, Kiss Football', in M. Fanizadeh, G. Hödl and W. Manzenreiter (eds) *Global Players – Kultur, Ökonomie und Politik des Fussballs*, Frankfurt/Main: Brandes and Apsel.

Storrer, A. (2001) 'Sprachliche Besonderheiten getippter Gespräche: Sprecherwechsel und sprachliches Zeigen in der Chat-Kommunikation', in M. Beißwenger (ed.) *Chat-Kommunikation*, Stuttgart: ibidem.

Wheaton, B. and Beal, B. (2003) '"Keeping it Real": Sub-cultural Media and the Discourses of Authenticity in Alternative Sport', *International Review for the Sociology of Sport*, 38: 155–76.

11 Selling sex or dealing with history?

German football in literature and film and the quest to normalize the nation

Paul Cooke and Christopher Young

During the European Championship of 2000, Coca-Cola's 'Eat football, sleep football, drink Coke' advertising campaign crystallized the central position the game had achieved within the European popular imagination. For this soft-drink manufacturer at least, football (and by extension Coca-Cola) was to be viewed as part of Europe's very lifeblood. And it would seem that the company was not alone in this view of the game. As we shall discuss in this chapter, in Germany, as in the UK, there has in recent years been an explosion of interest in football – an explosion which has had a real and significant impact on the literature and film of both countries. What is interesting, however, is that within these cultural discourses we find football used in a far more complex, metaphorical manner than we see in the advertisements of global companies such as Coca-Cola. As German cultural theorists Gebauer and Lenk (1988: 149–50) note, everyday discourses of sport per se (such as one finds in newspaper coverage, television commentary and punditry, common parlance or advertising) are generally marked by habitualized narratives which have lost their interpretative freedom. However, in more aesthetically oriented arenas such as literature and cinema, a greater level of autonomy is maintained. This, in turn, allows artists to produce their own frameworks: 'the fascinating thing about sports literature is its freedom vis-à-vis sport itself' (ibid.). It is precisely the contours and texture of such interpretive frameworks, built on, but transcending football, that this chapter seeks to address.

Our specific focus is the cultural representation of football in Germany since the publication there of Nick Hornby's bestselling football diary cum memoir *Fever Pitch* (1992). As we shall explore in more detail below, although Hornby's book examines attitudes to football in the UK, it is a text which has also had a major impact abroad.[1] Within the German context, the success of *Fever Pitch* set the seal on the shift which the country's film and literary culture was undergoing at the time. During the Cold War, Germany's film-makers and writers, on both sides of the

Iron Curtain, were often presented, and indeed constructed themselves, as the nation's conscience, rigorously interrogating political and social attempts to come to terms with the Nazi period and the reality of national division. With unification in 1990, there was a feeling from some quarters of the cultural press that artists should now give up any attempt at social engagement (see, for example, Anz 1995). Thus, as Germany's political and intellectual elites were beginning to suggest that the nation might at last view itself once again as a 'normal' member of the international community and draw a line under its problematic past, within cultural debates, this call for 'normalization' (a key buzzword of the time: see Taberner 2005) was to manifest itself in a new, depoliticized form of art. Particularly since the mid-1990s, many of Germany's most popular writers and film-makers have indeed appeared to heed this call, adopting a mode of artistic production which eschews the overt political engagement of earlier generations and focuses instead on relationships and the personal sphere. In literature, this has brought with it a widespread rejection of the complex esoteric aesthetic forms one finds throughout twentieth-century German literature – from Thomas Mann to Günter Grass. Instead, authors are now praised for having discovered a *neue Lesbarkeit*, or a 'new readability', i.e. a simpler style that puts more emphasis on telling a good story than narrative experimentation, often foregrounding the self and the individual as well as a confessional mode. As such, these authors are generally seen to be strongly influenced by US and UK writers, of which Hornby is an oft-cited example (Hage 1999). Similarly, in the world of cinema, the concept of film as a sphere of public debate, an idea that characterized the work of Rainer Werner Fassbinder and Wim Wenders, central figures in the 'New German Cinema' of the 1960s and 1970s, has been overshadowed since unification by a trend towards film as entertainment. This is likewise often viewed as a shift towards a more Anglo-Saxon aesthetic and goes some way towards explaining the recent ability of some German film-makers and actors, such as Tom Tykwer and Franke Potente, who rose to international prominence as the director and lead actress of the techno-fuelled youth film *Rola Rennt* (*Run Lola Run* 1998), to find work in Britain and America.

In order better to contextualize this shift in German culture, as it is manifest in the representation of football, we begin with an analysis of the game's place in British cultural life. As we shall see, football in the UK often functions as a cipher for the viscissitudes of interpersonal relationships or as a landscape for existential crisis. Then, turning to the representation of football in Germany, we find that there are indeed increasing points of contact between German and British cultural aesthetics, as well as an exploration of the private sphere. Nevertheless, the legacies of the German past remain an important focus for writers and film-makers, the texts discussed here ultimately pointing, perhaps, to the limits of German normalization which their very existence ostensibly seems to declare.

Football in British culture since the 1990s

The 1980s had represented probably the greatest slump in football's fortunes since its establishment as a professional sport. With hooliganism at its zenith, a long stand-off with the Prime Minister Margaret Thatcher and her plans for exclusive entry to stadia via a membership card scheme, along with the twin stadium disasters involving Liverpool supporters at Heysel in Brussels (1985) and Hillsborough in Sheffield (1989), numbers attending football matches plummeted. This led to a decline in sponsorship revenues, and ultimately took its toll on the standard of the domestic league as well as performances on the international stage. The beginning of the 1990s, however, saw an extraordinary reversal of football's fortunes, as several factors came together (Tomlinson 2001). First, England – beyond all expectations – almost won the 1990 World Cup in Italy, only just losing out to Germany on penalties in the semi-final of a tournament that had been full of glamour (fine stadia, operatic music, fashion), drama (England footballer Paul Gascoigne's tears of vulnerability caught in close-up), and mixed television audiences (the percentage of female viewers rose from 7 per cent in 1986 to 44 per cent in 1990).[2] Second, football clubs followed the recommendations of the post-Hillsborough Taylor Report to convert their stadia into all-seater arenas. This eventually led to a less threatening atmosphere, an increase in mixed spectatorship and an upsurge in sponsorship and television revenues. At the same time as these structural changes were underway, football became a focal point of the shift in British popular culture from the 'New Man' (oversimplifying: soft tones, grooming, embrace of fatherhood), to the 'New Lad' (grooming, gadgets, beer and sport). This development in the social construction of masculinity has been characterized as the New Lad's disambiguation of the New Man's lifestyle-product-driven femininized masculinity (Nixon 2001).

Against this background, many cultural representations of the game in Britain since the 1990s have tended to lay a thematic premium on the glamorous, aspirational side of football life and, in particular, the status of individual players as cultural, or specifically sexual icons. The more outlandish elements of this development may be seen in magazines such as *Loaded*, often portrayed as the flagship of 'New Ladism', which roll together soft-porn, expensive lifestyle tips and football talk into a heady mix of aspirational consumerism,[3] or in the recent hit television serial *Footballers' Wives*, a kind of twenty-first-century British reply to *Dallas* that ran such a gamut of sexual proclivity that in 2004 the Archbishop of Canterbury, Rowan Williams, attacked it in his Easter message to the diocese of Canterbury. However, the most obvious example of this shift is the rise to global commercial stardom of David Beckham, considered by some to straddle perfectly the fence between New Man and New Lad, his good looks and prowess within the masculine environment of the football pitch being balanced by the apparently blissful domesticity of his existence as a husband and father (for further discussion see Cashmore 2002; Cashmore and Parker 2003). In 2004, Beckham's iconic status reached its climax when *David*, Sam Taylor-Wood's ninety-minute film of him sleeping after morning training at Real Madrid, was exhibited at London's National Portrait Gallery, drawing excited comparisons with Johnny Depp and Clint Eastwood from normally sober sports journalists. But, just months later, Beckham's star fell dramatically – tellingly after a sex scandal involving a former PA served as the prelude to his missing two vital penalties for England in the 2004 European Championships, events which dented both his sensitive New Man and his footballing New Lad credentials respectively.

In much popular culture, then, we find a hyper-commercialized version of the game which markets competing versions of masculinity.[4] In the literary and filmic representations of football in Britain, it is this shift in the representation of masculinity and, more importantly, its concomitant impact upon both gender relations and individual sexuality which are a major concern. Gurinda Chadha's internationally successful film *Bend it Like Beckham* (2002), for example, uses football and the (at the time still unshaken) god-like status of the England captain to explore changing attitudes to gender and sexuality in Britain, comparing the experience of a second-generation Asian girl and a lower-middle-class white girl, as they attempt to emulate their hero and carve out a footballing future for themselves. Although ostensibly about the problems facing those involved in English women's football, particularly young Asians, the film engages only very superficially with the social issues it raises (Bradshaw 2002). It is, instead, fundamentally a generic romantic comedy which simply uses football as a landscape for its universally applicable rites-of-passage narrative about two girls coming to terms with their relationship to the opposite sex, each other and their family: it 'effaces the everyday hardships and struggles of daily life in favour of a reformulated, faux progressive New Labour vision of race, gender and class relations' (Giardina 2003: 78).

Although a hit across Europe, *Bend it like Beckham* was particularly successful in Germany, probably due to its inclusion of a sequence set in Hamburg, a result, no doubt, of the film's funding partly coming from the city's Film Council (Filmförderung Hamburg). More broadly influential, however, has been Nick Hornby's *Fever Pitch* (1992). In a similar fashion to Chadha's film, *Fever Pitch* has as much to do with gender relationships, and particularly the representation of masculinity, as it does with football. As such, what might again be read as a critique of British societal developments instead becomes a means for its author to explore his individual psychological development.[5]

Fever Pitch is the confessional memoir of a long-term Arsenal fan, the narrative of which culminates in the team's League Championship win in 1989. His specific obsession with the team is then, like *Bend it Like Beckham*, used as a backdrop for a universally applicable rites-of-passage story, which tells of a boy from a dysfunctional family growing up in the suburbia of the

English southeast and his journey from childhood to young adulthood. As one might expect from a graduate in English from Cambridge University, Hornby constructs a consciously 'literary' narrative. In the tradition of writers such as Günter Grass or Salman Rushdie, he indulges in bouts of magical realist causality, in Hornby's case with the club's new Scottish striker Charlie Nicholas. He even contrasts his experience with no less a poetic luminary than T.S. Eliot's J. Alfred Prufrock. While the interminable tedium of Prufrock's tragic life is 'measured out in coffee spoons', for Hornby, Arsenal fixtures serve a similar function. However, Hornby's primary literary forebear is Viennese, the text self-consciously constructed as a 'Freudian drama' (1992: 17). Women, all anonymous apart from his mother – with whom he 'enacts a weird little parody of a sitcom married couple' on match days (1992: 52) – are the very antithesis of enabling agents. They keep him from the maternal womb of football, even when suggesting that after having children he might like to share a season-ticket with his partner so that she may alternate childcare and match attendance with him.

Of course, although the writer makes use of a high-cultural literary and psychoanalytical tradition, his work is deliberately populist. Thus we need not necessarily take such motives seriously. In fact, we may even choose to ignore them as a deliberate smoke-screen that either masks further psychoanalytical tensions or elaborately window-dresses the fact that football is a hard commercial, and exclusively male preserve (an example of what Lacan meant about male symbolic dominance with his famous apodictum: 'There is no such thing as a sexual relation'). But their presence on the surface of the text is undeniable, and typical of the relationship between football and sex/gender in the British transformation and representation of the game from the 1990s onwards.

Representing football in German culture: Hornby by another name?

Hornby's text has had a major influence on football writing in Germany. For example, Bodo Berg's *Mehr als ein Spiel* (*More than a Game*) – a personal memoir about supporting Schalke 04, the club's unexpected successful UEFA Cup campaign in 1997,[6] and the founding of Germany's first anti-racism fan initiative (*Schalker gegen Rassismus*) – has numerous global parallels with *Fever Pitch*, and the Werkstatt publisher's subtitle for the volume (*Aus dem Leben eines Fußballfans*) makes an obvious marketing play with that given to the German version of Hornby's text by publishing house Kiepenheuer and Witsch (*Die Geschichte eines Fans*). On the surface, women either play a similarly hindering role (a friend's wife prevents Berg and his closest fan group from travelling to the 1990 World Cup in Italy and participating directly in Germany's victory) or are punished for their own active involvement in the game (while Astrid from the delicatessen can safely provide fuel for the fans' initiative in the form of *Schnitten* (p. 72), Yvi breaks her finger playing in goal during the Polish exchange (p. 97)).

Clearly, Berg's publisher is aware of the marketability of Hornby in Germany, taking the British text as the norm for contemporary football writing and foregrounding how *Mehr als ein Spiel* has ostensibly adopted it. However, beyond the surface, the sexual economy of *Fever Pitch* stands in a completely different relation to Berg's text. While Hornby relies on an *explicit foregrounding* of sexual relations as a *structuring principle*, Berg's interests really lie elsewhere. In part, following football for Berg acts as a means by which sexual deviancy is smoothed over. On moving to a new district in Gelsenkirchen, the young Berg receives his first black eye from a one-armed 20-year-old nicknamed Kimbel – renowned for smashing up telephone boxes with his stump – for refusing to be made up by him with lipstick (pp. 30–1). Several decades later, on the road with Schalke, Berg finds emotional accommodation with two men, one dressed in morning suit, the other in a wedding dress, entering a disco after a gay wedding: 'Of course, this is Barcelona here, not Gelsenkirchen', Berg insists (p. 105). In the heterosexual realm, there is no tension between sexual activity and football. Whereas Hornby confesses that football has turned him 'into someone who would not help if [his] girlfriend went into labour at an impossible moment' (p. 106) and rejects the orgasm metaphor as wholly inadequate for expressing the pleasure of winning the League Championship (p. 230), Berg uses sport to impress girls (e.g. joining a boxing club, p. 37), and then gladly abandons sport to fully indulge his pleasure with the ladies: 'So bye to boxing and over to the girls and a really wild and wonderful time, which helped us over the loss of sport' (p. 38). After watching Germany lose the 1986 World Cup final, he wanders through the streets with his unopened magnum of champagne, which he conveniently manages to deposit in the fridge of an unmarried mother, over whom he barters briefly with a friend with whom he watched the match, before discovering that 'there are other pleasant things [to do] as well as win the World Cup' (p. 59). The precise wording is a clear indication that sex and football are complementary for Berg in a way that they could never be for Hornby, any tension that might exist between the two realms being completely removed.

Christoph Biermann's *Wenn du am Spieltag beerdigt wirst, kann ich leider nicht kommen* (1995) begins by quoting the opening lines from *Fever Pitch*: 'I fell in love with football as I was later to fall in love with women: suddenly, inexplicably, uncritically, giving no thought to the pain or disruption it would bring with it' (p. 12). That said, it is utterly lacking in the tension between football and women that characterizes Hornby's narrative. By the second subsection of his opening chapter, Biermann sees football as a completely alternative arena that protects men from the vicissitudes of the heart (p. 17). His narrative is interlaced with pictures of death (a corpse at Heysel) and sexuality – but these either float free from the narrative, neither underpinning nor driving it, or are marginalized verbally or visually. A sexually charged picture of a bare-breasted Jochen Abel, arms spread and ribs protruding in Christ-like pose as fans gaze upon him adoringly (p. 31), is punctured by Biermann's comment that the striker reminded him of Mowgli from the *Jungle Book* (p. 30). A picture of a male streaker at the Grotenburg-Kampfbahn in 1978 (p. 59) is striking for the fact that the male member has shrunk back into the body – this most bodily of images seeming to suggest football's status as a sexless enterprise. Significantly, Biermann's equivalent of Hornby's symbolic realm is not the single stadium, but 'an ideal stadium' constructed by discussions with fans, which make up the second part of the book, in a journey through the Federal Republic (p. 69).

As our analysis of Berg and Biermann suggests, while sex is an important part of these narratives, its treatment is radically different from UK football literature. There is one exception: Ronald Reng's *Der Traumhüter* (2002), marketed by Hornby's German publishers Kiepenheuer & Witsch as the best football book since *Fever Pitch*. The fictional narrative tells the rags-to-riches story of goalkeeper Lars Leese, who rose from the amateur German *Kreisliga* to the top of the professional game. At the summit of his career, however, he is shocked by men-only Christmas parties where the after-dinner entertainment ritual consists of the apprentices having sex on stage with prostitutes; where midwinter training consists of a week's sex-tourism on the Balearic Islands; and where young girls hang around the home training ground to administer oral sex to first team members. Yet *Der Traumhüter* is the exception that proves the rule. It is not set in Germany, but at Barnsley United during the club's time in the English Premier League in 1997 to 1998. Indeed, the amazement and detachment with which Reng and Leese tell their tale underlines the complete disjuncture of sport and sex in the representation of football in Germany.

Normalization, German football and dealing with history

Although German publishers make much mileage out of the points of contact between Hornby and these German football texts, and although the representation of sexuality and gender has its part to play, the underlying focus of much of this writing, as we shall now discuss, is not on the personal sphere at all, but on that of politics and history. We shall see this when we return to Berg. However, a more obvious example of this use of football is the play *Leben bis Männer* (2001) by Thomas Brussig, a writer who is often viewed as being at the forefront of German literature's 'New Readability' and its shift to a Hornbyesque aesthetic (Hage 1999), which, in turn, is viewed by some commentators as a knock-on effect of German post-unification 'Normalization'. Brussig's play is a monologue by an East German football coach describing his years of service to his team. Specifically, he focuses on the problems both he and the amateur footballers he now trains face, as they learn to exist under the conditions of the market economy, a system which, although allowing them a greater level of democratic freedom, has brought with it high levels of unemployment and social instability (pp. 51–2). The problems that the team faces, representing in the play the East German population as a whole, are then contrasted with the question of responsibility for the human rights violations committed in the name of the former communist regime, when it transpires that one of the team's strikers is guilty of shooting an individual who tried to escape over the Berlin Wall (pp. 89–95). Thus, *Leben bis Männer* ultimately uses what is marketed as a 'normal' Anglo-Saxon style of football writing, such as we see in Hornby, not to highlight the normality of a German nation that has put the past to rest, but to flag up the continuing fault-lines within German society. While Brussig's work may point to a shift in German literary aesthetics, its content has much in common with the more critical cultural forms of earlier generations and their interrogation of German society.

The same would not seem to be the case for the cultural representation of probably the most famous moment in Germany's post-war football history: the FRG's shock victory in the 1954 World Cup final against the majestic Hungarian side of the Puskas generation, a moment of such resounding cultural impact that it is covered from a range of perspectives in this book.[7] In sporting terms, the West Germans overcame a team that had caused a seismic shift in the international hierarchy of the sport by defeating England for the first time at Wembley in 1953 and had remained unbeaten for the four years running up to the tournament. In political terms, the timing of the victory, just nine years after the end of the Second World War, provided a huge psychological boost to a nation divided, under allied occupation and only recently permitted to return to full international sport. Indeed, as the national anthem was played in the Wankdorf Stadium in Berne, the German flag was still not hoisted.[8] Many thousands thronged railway stations across the country as the players returned home by train; Bundespräsident Heuss had the Olympic flame lit in Berlin's 1936 stadium for a special reception. Images of the game's mode of reception – families huddled around the radio (as depicted in Günther Grass's (1999) panorama of the twentieth century, *Mein Jahrhundert*), or of people gathered in public houses and at shop windows to catch a glimpse of their heroes in the new televisual medium – along with the celebrations of victory have passed into cultural memory as a moment of national rebirth, commonly referred to as the *Wunder von Bern* ('The Miracle of Berne').

Like all historical matter, however, cultural memory is open to, and indeed lives off, reinterpretation and reappropriation. If one looks, for example, at Fassbinder's use of the 1954 victory in his internationally successful film *Die Ehe der Maria Braun* (*The Marriage of Maria Braun*) (1979), the place of this event in the German historical psyche is radically ironized. Telling the story of the dehumanizing effects on the film's eponymous heroine of Germany's sudden post-war prosperity, commonly referred to as the German *Wirtschaftswunder* ('Economic Miracle'), the film ends in the juxtaposition of Herbert Zimmermann's famously ecstatic radio commentary, announcing West Germany's winning goal, with the visual image of Maria's bourgeois home exploding – an event that symbolically points to the emptiness at the heart of Germany's rapid and, in Fassbinder's view, hypocritical reinvention of itself as a Western European bourgeois society.

In more recent years, however, the 1954 World Cup has been evoked far less contentiously in Tykwer's *Run Lola Run*, a key cultural text of German normalization, which has been praised for its portrayal of the reunited Berlin as a young, 'hip' international metropolis, no different from London or New York, through which the film's flame-haired protagonist rushes to save her boyfriend. In the film's title sequence, Tykwer, like Hornby, evokes the poetry of T.S. Eliot. This is then immediately contrasted with the famous maxim of Sepp Herberger, the German manager in 1954 – 'after the game is before the game' – and subsequently followed at the end of the film's opening with Herberger's most famous words of wisdom: 'the ball is round and a game lasts 90 minutes.' Thus the film both calls on an international literary tradition and restates the centrality of 1954 in order to confirm and celebrate Germany's long-awaited normalization.

It was clear that the fiftieth anniversary of the event would bring a new and more positive impetus for the reactivation of 1954's symbolic potential. This duly arrived with a film by Sönke Wortmann, simply entitled *Das Wunder von Bern*. Wortmann, like Brussig, is seen as a key figure in Germany's shift towards a Westernized entertainment culture. In Wortmann's case, this largely suggests a more consolatory approach towards the state of German society, a shift among film-makers perhaps best summed up by Wortmann himself: 'when I was at film school in Munich, the great hero was Tarkovsky. Today it's Spielberg' (Quoted in Lischke-McNabe and Hanson 1997: 84). No longer wishing to follow the critical avant-garde tradition which had been so important to the previous generation, these younger film-makers seem to emulate unproblematically the fast-paced, action-driven entertainment films of Hollywood.

Curiously, given the context of German normalization within which the film was made, *Das Wunder von Bern* eschews the most obvious choice of narrative protagonist, Fritz Walter – the legendary team captain who had played as a German international since 1940 but who stood for many as the embodiment of the 'normal' German and as such could now act 'as a kind of permanent peace ambassador' (Heinrich 2003: 1494). Instead he focuses on the maverick figure Helmut Rahn, a prolific goal scorer of unpredictable character for Rot-Weiss Essen in the Ruhr. In the German training camp, Rahn clashes with Herberger (the experienced German coach who had seen the national team through the war years and who in the film is initially a strict disciplinarian); and is partially mentored by his gallant narrative foil and room-mate Walter. In the interlocking Ruhr strand of the plot, he functions as an ersatz-father for the child who is the focal point of the film, Matthias Lubanski, a role that is soon challenged by the return of the boy's father, Richard, from eleven years of Soviet imprisonment on the former Eastern Front. Thus, West Germany's preparation for, and the subsequent progression through, the 1954 World Cup finals in Switzerland frame Rahn as the linchpin in a dynasty of father–son relationships, which overlies and serves to reapproach the myth of 1954.

The meaning and significance of 1954 was no less disputed at the time of its happening than it has been – as we have seen in our analysis of Fassbinder – in its cultural representation ever since. The singing of the ideologically tainted first verse of the national anthem ('Deutschland, Deutschland über alles') rather than the newly prescribed third strophe as the trophy was presented, for instance, caused raised eyebrows in the foreign press and a variety of interpretations at home. The *Süddeutsche Zeitung*, while admitting that some fellow citizens might confuse patriotism with nationalism, argued even-handedly that Germans should 'not have to ask anyone' which verse of their anthem they are allowed to sing (Heinrich 1994: 84). Rudi Michel, a spectator at the match, who later became a prominent sports commentator with ARD, put it more strongly when he noted that he felt 'discriminated against and humiliated' at the absence of an official German flag and therefore gladly joined in with the singing of the first verse (Seitz 2004: 4). Most famously, Peco Bauwens, President of the German Football Association, sailed closest to the wind of ideological propriety at the official celebration in Munich's *Löwenbräukeller*, lauding the team's performance as 'representative of the best of Germandom abroad'. He thanked Wodan, the Germanic God of War, for his assistance and invoked the *Führerprinzip* for good measure (Heinrich 1994: 91–3). While the *Bayerischer Rundfunk* cut short its transmission of this particular occasion, many observers were reminded more generally by the reactions across the country 'of certain mass rallies from the Thousand-Year-Reich' (Heinrich 2003: 1496).

Scholarly interpretation of the events of 1954 occupies an equally broad spectrum of opinion. Norbert Seitz (1987: 17–30) sees the 'effort' at Berne as 'a symbolic second helping following the energy reserves missing at Stalingrad', subsequently following Kasza's (2004) lead in comparing the relationship between sport and politics in ally-occupied Germany with that in Stalinist Hungary. He asserted later that 'as long as the Miracle of Berne was used as a warning to get back at the allies, it could take on no real ideological meaning in the Cold War' (Seitz 2004: 5). Historian Joachim C. Fest takes up the middle ground, arguing for the inadequacy of the much cited 'Wir-sind-wieder-wer' ('we are someone again') declaration, common at the time, on the grounds that the *Wirtschaftswunder* with which it is connected – and which is central to Fassbinder's critical use of the tournament in his film – was in no way felt to be secure in 1954. For Fest, the event is better thought of in terms of satisfaction or a sigh of relief rather than a new self-confidence (cited in Seitz 2004: 4). Arthur Heinrich (1994, 2003, 2004) occupies the opposite pole to Seitz. For him, the game is integrally linked to the onset of the Economic Miracle and, at a time when 40 per cent of West Germans still viewed the period between 1933 and 1938 as the best for their country (45 per cent opted for the *Kaiserreich*), represented a vital factor in allowing the nation to 'play for more time in the matter of adopting democracy' (2003: 1501).

Wortmann's film cuts a swathe through the most contentious issues in this academic debate, presenting a harmonious image of Germany's national identity which clearly has more to do with a post-unification longing for normalization than it does with the reality of life in the 1950s. He deftly skirts the anthem problematic – depicting its *playing* before the match and cutting its *singing* at the conclusion in favour of a shot that fades to a still of Walter holding the trophy and Herberger being hoisted on to the shoulders of the other players. Wortmann, claiming that he is quite capable of 'tackling any topic', argues simply that this is the logical conclusion of a sporting event: 'Why should I let Fritz Walter climb down from the pinnacle? That would be completely counter-productive. What I'm aiming for is a heroic epic!' (Eggers 2003b: 33). Despite Wortmann's rhetoric it should be noted that the heroic epic has never been an autonomous genre, free from the processing, evaluation and appropriation of historical events for new purposes. Wortmann's de-selection of certain more problematic moments of the 1954 narrative is indeed an archetypical epic move (see e.g. Heinzle 2003), and one that shows the continuing boundaries of German 'normality' that this epic can still not cross.[9]

This is further underlined if we examine the film's treatment of that other key element in historical discussions of 1954, the *Wirtschaftswunder* itself. The dual focus on the gritty realism of the Lubanskis' pub in the Ruhr and the glitzy fantasy of the Ackermanns' residence in Munich is a clear signal that, in Wortmann's 1950s, the *Wirtschaftswunder* has not yet established itself enough to function as a level socio-economical backdrop to the footballing miracle. Indeed, Bruno Lubanski, the older son of the family, can still cite the unjust distribution of wealth as the main reason for this 'defection' to the GDR. Consequently, the film suggests that the East German state can ostensibly continue to compete at this time for the hearts and minds of the population. Moreover, the central role in the victory of the manufacturer Adidas, the key sporting economic success story of the post-war years, is vastly reduced. In the run-up to the tournament, Adi Dassler had designed the first football boots with changeable screw studs, which gave the German team an advantage when the weather turned on the day of the final. As Wortmann comments: 'It's true – without the rain, they would never have won the World Cup, because then Adi Dassler wouldn't have been able to put the new studs in' (Eggers 2003b: 33). Dassler's role is hinted at via a sequence at the team's pre-tournament training camp in Munich-Grünewald, when the new design is presented to an admiring Herberger. However, it is almost immediately sacrificed in the subsequent narrative to Matthias Lubanski's late arrival in Berne, and Annette Ackermann's vocal salvo ('Deutschland vor!' – 'Come on Germany!') that galvanizes the German support in the stadium:

> I increase the element of fate in my film with the young boy who arrives in the stadium just at the right time and brings Helmut Rahn good luck. It is also very important that the journalist pair – the Ackermanns – bet on the right to name their child. Frau Ackermann cheers the players on to prevent her child from being named Roswitha, and the spark flies across to the team.
>
> (Wortmann in Eggers 2003b: 33)

Thus the decisive moments of Wortmann's film have nothing to do with the *Wirtschaftswunder*, and the two narrative agents that bring about Germany's final victory could hardly be more economically polarized.

Although the film deals with 1950s German history, this is not to say that the representation of familial and other interpersonal relationships, such as we see in UK football culture, is ignored. On the contrary, Wortmann's retelling of the myth very much depends on the interpenetration of personal and global-historical narratives. This is particularly clear in the film's presentation of father–son relationships. For example, as Helmut Rahn's selection for the national squad allows him to slip out of his ersatz-parenting function, two further father figures (Herberger and Lubanksi senior) with almost identical concerns come into view. Both have to come to terms with new ways of dealing with their sons, Herberger with the recalcitrant Rahn himself, Richard with Matthias and Bruno Lubanski. Herberger's image as a global signifier in German cultural history is reduced and brought down to Lubanski's level in a humorous sequence where, having spied Rahn stumble back drunk to the team hotel in Spiez, he deliberates with an elderly Swiss cleaning lady about what to do with troublesome sons. The two trade proverbs, until Herberger is trumped by the cleaning lady's fusion of what are historically known as the trainer's most famous *bon mots* and which, as we have seen, play a key role in Tykwer's film: 'the ball is round and a game lasts 90 minutes.' Significantly, Herberger, at the training camp, and Richard Lubanksi, while violently chopping wood after watching young Matthias being outclassed in a street kick-about by their girl neighbour Karola, give exactly the same, very effective, advice to their charges: 'play to your strengths.' And both ultimately relent from their harsh disciplinarian approaches: Herberger not only selecting Rahn, but encouraging his captain Walter in avuncular fashion to keep the miscreant out of future trouble. Similarly, Richard Lubanski wakes his son in the night to take him on the trip to Switzerland, having previously beaten him with his belt for even contemplating such a journey. The paralleling of narratives reaches its climax when, in a visually rich, slow-motion sequence of 'fantasy football' with historical gravitas, Matthias Lubanski's kick-around in the Ruhr is played out over the top of the radio commentary of West Germany's 6–1 victory over Austria in the semi-final. In the final itself, the narratives interlock when Matthias, after a momentary glance by Herberger from behind the side screen of the dug-out, throws the match ball to Rahn.

The contours of Wortmann's myth certainly form a snug fit with the general shape of Germany's public reassessment of its war legacy in recent years, and its place in the quest for normalization. Several prominent publications have begun to turn away from the culture of guilt, dominant in Germany particularly since the late 1960s, and highlight the experience of the suffering that many ordinary Germans underwent as a result of the regime's vicious criminality. With the publication of W.G. Sebald's *Luftkrieg und Literatur* (2001) and Günther Grass's *Im Krebsgang* (2002), it is clear that the political Left has begun to find its voice on the topic of German wartime suffering, largely a taboo topic for decades that only the nationalist Right dared to break. And this, at the same time as the so-called 'Berlin Republic', is finding a taste for Germany's historical heroes: *Das Wunder von Bern* appeared around the same time as Eric Till's *Luther*, an unashamedly hagiographic blockbuster, as well as ZDF's interactive television series to find 'Der größte Deutsche', the German equivalent of the BBC's 'Greatest Briton' programme. In this context, therefore, it is hardly surprising that Chancellor Schröder openly cried at the premier of *Das Wunder von Bern* in Essen, already having declared the Wankdorf stadium a national memorial, alongside Weimar and the Berlin Wall, which 'has a huge significance in the history of our country and will retain its symbolic meaning for generations to come' (Seitz 2004: 3).

Wortmann's reshaping of 1954 shows more clearly than any of the other texts discussed here how the private sphere, which dominates British cultural representations of football, is used in Germany as a vehicle for the discussion of the public issue of German national identity and the question of how to approach the past. Lubanski senior's reluctance to talk about his wartime experiences is broken down after a visit to the local priest that fades into a piece of football and cinematic artistry. Flicking up a ball found lying around on waste ground, Lubanski, who has had to abandon his job as a miner due to the prolonged effects of shell shock, finds it descending towards him like a bomb falling from the sky. Just before the dark, heavy object blackens out the whole screen, Lubanksi meets it with the fluid movement of an overhead kick. The next scene begins *in media res* with Lubanski telling his family about the hardships of starvation in Russia. Thus Wortmann's film inverts the usual historical interpretation of 1954, foregrounding instead the importance of individual relationships. Furthermore, it is not the global-historical narrative that influences the personal, as assumed in most accounts of the actual event, but precisely the opposite. For example, Helmut Rahn cannot win important games without Matthias Lubanski being present, a fact underlined by the way Wortmann frames the youngster walking through the catacombs of the stadium before climbing the steps into the arena itself to find the ball rolling to a standstill at his feet. In this image, the rain that has turned the intensely coloured picture-postcard texture of Switzerland into a Ruhr mud-bath falls even more ferociously. The red-shirts of the Hungarian team ensure that the Wankdorf stadium still emits the luxurious hue of future possibility, but its realization is reliant on the personal and domestic.

This configuration of personal fulfilment and national sentiment has been recognized by Gebauer (2002) as a potent characteristic of international sport in the age of globalization and commercialization.[10] The current vogue for donning football jerseys, waving flags and watching international tournaments in large, crowded places (pubs or semi-open-air venues such as the Sony Center at Potsdamer Platz) has little to do with public political representation. Rather, it 'functions via desires, rituals of participation and the quest for community'. Particularly, but not exclusively, in countries such as Germany and divided Korea (witness the 2002 World Cup), where national identity has only a meagre political base from which to grow, the commercial parameters of modern global sport seem to create the framework within which – in temporally distinct phases – the adulation of the nation can flourish. But such moments of national hysteria are based on the rhythms of individual consumption. The frame may be national and communal, but the practice is personal.

Given that Wortmann's film was sponsored in large part by the same agencies that will put on the next global entertainment fest of this type – the Organizing Committee of the 2006 World Cup and the German Football Association – it is not surprising that it appeals to football's new audience. Thematically, as outlined above, it privileges the personal over the historical, while at the same time maintaining the importance of the latter. In addition, *Das Wunder von Bern* appeals to a *mixed* audience. Annette Ackermann's coquettish behaviour throughout the film – her ready acceptance of accompanying her husband on a work trip to the tournament in Switzerland in place of their honeymoon to Morocco and her subsequent pre- and post-coital baiting of him with her superior grasp of football tactics – stands in such sharp contrast to the world of male journalism (Ackermann's boss asks him even before the honeymoon if his wife is 'schon unter anderen Umständen', warning that women are 'fußballfeindlich')[11] that she transcends the gender politics of her time, showing that we are in fact viewing the events of 1954 through a thoroughly contemporary optic. Her sexual-sporting predatorship is a knowing wink to a twenty-first-century audience that will enjoy the gender discrimination and its subversion for their comic value rather than their social comment – when the film was first screened, after all, Germany were *women's* football world champions. And finally, the film's reading of the public sphere through the personal is foregrounded by the fact that Lubanski senior and junior are played in the film by a real father-and-son pair, Peter Lohmeyer and Louis Klamroth (see Köster 2003), a fact played upon by the main advertising poster, which creates a father–son footballing scene that never occurs in the film. It is an act of poetic licence with the already poetically re-formed narrative, yet one that is hardly surprising in a film which concludes with a moment of self-conscious poetic reflection. Having helped determine the team's destiny through the energy of her personal story, Annette Ackermann selects, as is her hard-earned right, a name for their unborn child from the pantheon of poets – Dante, the prince of medieval poets.

Returning, finally, to Bodo Berg's *Mehr als ein Spiel*: the text is set initially in the same temporal and social milieu as Wortmann's film. It follows the author's early years in the Ruhr of the 1950s, where the descriptions of the mining community – self-sufficiency with small livestock and vegetables, the harsh realities both for those returning from the war and those who had to accommodate their harsh discipline, as well as the constant football culture of *ad hoc* matches between teams selected ruthlessly in order of merit – seamlessly depict the backdrop of Wortmann's more famous script. Thematically, too, the work gestures to the father–son trope, Berg dedicating the book to his son Jan 'who until now has successfully defended himself against sharing [his] passion' (p. 7). Nevertheless, his thinly disguised act of persuasion relies on issues as broad as those depicted in *Das Wunder von Bern*. For the author is literally born into football, sharing his christening on 4 July 1954 with the tensions and celebrations of West Germany's victory over Hungary. Berg's account unpacks the rationale behind the implicit perspective of *Das Wunder von Bern* in an explicit narrative chronology. The platitudes of the time – *wir sind wieder wer*, and the link to the *Wirtschaftswunder* – are cited at the beginning of Chapter 1 (p. 15), but these serve as little more than the upbeat for Berg's longer process of historical self-discovery. Enthusiastic participation in the Revier's multitude of unofficial football games, crowding around the family radio to hear the latest from the Bundesliga, and knowledge of Uncle Walter's sympathy for and involvement in the Nazi's war co-exist unproblematically, until a sudden wedge is driven through this world of innocence when, at the age of 14, he is taken by an older cousin to a Holocaust exhibition. The way home from the event is marked by a clear and decisive judgement on life until that point – 'from that point on, I didn't give a shit about the Uncle Walters of this Republic' (p. 35) – and football is sacrificed in the narrative ('we weren't interested much in dribbling any more', p. 35) for new hairstyles, clothes, music, and political activism with *Der Rote-Punkt* and communal living with people whose friends live with Peter Brandt, the son of the Bundeskanzler.

Consequently, like *Das Wunder von Bern*, it is not long before it becomes clear that Berg's story of the life (and loves) of an individual football fan is a means of examining the public realm of politics. Playful resonances of Schalke songs behind political chants and off-the-wall incorporation of the club's moral and financial upheaval into activist meetings (p. 44) roll into the foundation of the fan's initiative against racism several decades later. The burning of a hostel for asylum seekers in Rostock and its disturbing echoes on the terraces allow Berg to counter right-wing political extremism for a second time. In Berg's personal narrative, this merges tellingly with Schalke's qualification for the UEFA Cup, which allows him to travel abroad with his team for the first time (p. 90). As one victory leads to another and yet another country is put on to his itinerary, the author begins to feel 'internationally matured' (p. 90). Reaching the final against Inter Milan allows him to feel at one with his father, grandfather and Uncle Willi from Emden – all of whom are imagined keeping their fingers crossed and chilling mead in anticipation of victory somewhere up on their cloud (p. 117). Temporally then, Schalke's victory in 1997 brings Berg full circle. He has undergone political awakening, countered it with revolutionary activism and later with more mature political engagement, and reintegrated himself into the international community. Now Berg, like the characters in Wortmann's film, has reached a comfortable historical accommodation with Germany's past via football – Uncle Walther with his Nazi tendencies has been written out at the moment of closure. As in *Das Wunder von Bern*, present understanding has been collapsed neatly on to the euphoria of Berne, with all its attendant problems now carefully circumscribed. When Schalke go into the penalty shoot-out in Milan's San Siro Stadium, a voice from the crowd offers encouragement with 'Don't you believe in a football god?' (p. 123); when the trophy is flaunted at the Gelsenkirchen victory parade, children who have 'just had their umbilical cords cut' (p. 127) are pressed into the opening of the cup. Once again, the echoes of Zimmermann's commentary (albeit it in a radically different context to its use in *Maria Braun*) – 'Toni [Türek, who had just saved a certain Hungarian winner at 2–2], Toni, you are a football god' – and pictures of rebirth through the medium of football are unmistakable.

Interlaced with and straddling out beyond this closure are encounters with two historically significant nations – Poland and England. Football, as life in general, in the Ruhr has been greatly influenced by Polish immigrants from the early twentieth century. Berg, whose grandfather was part of this migration, takes pleasure in remembering Polish influence on his dialect and local nomenclature (pp. 18 and 21): indeed, the game he plays in the streets is called 'Fussek' rather than Fußball (p. 26). The Polish connection leads to an exchange between the Schalke fans' initiative and supporters of Lech-Posen. Significantly, the Polish strand of the narrative is confused. During the home leg of the exchange, Berg and his friends are taken aback that they are dealing with a bunch of 'Hools'. Yet the 'Hools' are never treated with the open opprobrium that one would expect from someone in Berg's position. There is a sympathetic account of a clash in the Gelsenkirchen S-Bahn over an Auschwitz provocation. The outskirts of Posen provide a Proustian moment that transports Berg back to the Erle of his childhood, and the criminal activities of the hosts ('that even here [in Poland] would get you some years on bread and water', p. 96) are in consequence glossed over. Posen, where 'hools are players, and players think like hools', is simply a 'mad world' (p. 96). Inversion of the historical relationship between perpetrator and victim of violence prevents Berg from articulating an adequate assessment of his Polish counterparts. In fact, their appropriation in his narrative is complete when some of them appear in Milan to help celebrate the UEFA Cup victory. The demands of the international historical master narrative, therefore, override considerations of local violence and deviance.

Berg's relation to another previous enemy, England, is also strangely skewed. When Manchester United beat Bayern Munich in the last minutes of the 1999 Champions League Final in Barcelona, Berg is happy for his friend Stuart, a fan of the English champions. For an avid supporter of a football club, it is counter-intuitive to celebrate the victory of any other club, not least that of a friend. Even the comments of Yves Eigenrauch, a respected former Schalke professional, cautioning that the manner of Bayern's last-minute defeat is beyond the pale and should not be celebrated, cannot prevent Berg's empathy with his English friend (p. 141). As in the case of Poland, normal football discourse is bent to accommodate the overriding dictate of the historical.

The England coda to the Schalke narrative is rounded off with a second epilogue that further underpins the work's conception of and relation to history. Berg transports himself to the year 2023 and into a vision of a game changed beyond recognition by globalization and commercialization: at FC Solar Schalke the stadium is kept at a cold-inducing 24 degrees, drive-in spectator points with multiple media and retail facilities have eroded the fan community, and within a worldwide league, players are transferred for huge sums of money from unknown teams such as FC Bogota.[12] But this horror vision is not the logical conclusion of the narrative developed so far by Berg. It is, in fact, an alternative one whose genesis, though largely ignored, was present in the 1954 confirmation scene. For the symbolic capital of 1954 was historically inseparable from the moment of economic serendipity. If winning the World Cup 'fitted in with the beginning of the *Wirtschaftswunder*', then the effects of growing consumer desires, represented by early supermarkets 'which were really called KONSUM' (p. 15) would surely accompany the growth of the game and its meaning to the nation. Berg, however, sees the economic and the symbolic as incompatible. This explains why commercialization is separated from the historical narrative and projected in mock apocalyptic form out beyond its conclusion. Franz Beckenbauer is made its central culprit, ripping everything down, rebuilding, and then ripping it down again to make it like it was before (pp. 151–2), a fact that explains the striking omission of West Germany's 1974 World Cup victory on home soil – Beckenbauer's most famous hour – from the earlier historical narrative of success and failure at world level (pp. 58–62). Berg wreaks savage revenge on the 'Kaiser', letting his funeral, coverage of which is interrupted by Coca-Cola adverts, culminate in a two-hour oration by the famously inarticulate Lother Matthäus (p. 152). To experience the authentic again, Berg scours the Ruhr for impromptu kick-arounds that he can watch by sitting on the edge of a pavement (p. 151). This return to the milieu of his childhood and the immediate post-1954 years stands in stark contrast to the virtual-reality football museum in Schalke's old *Parkstadion* that allows users via the latest pay-per-view technology to interact with live matches and change their outcomes. In Berg's conception, for football to work as a medium of self and national expression, it has to be subject to apparently objective historical processes. Commercialism, with its emphasis on consumer subjectivity, renders the historical symbolically bankrupt.

Berg's vote for history in his history–commercialism tension is then visually underpinned by the photographs incorporated into the work, which were taken by former Schalke player and member of the UEFA Cup winning side, Yves Eigenrauch. Although the images are the product of a multimedia process – filmed originally on video, transferred to a television screen, retaken by Polaroid camera and then scanned and digitally reworked (p. 157) – their grainy look suggests age and their content historical gravitas: the overgrown gates to the old *Glückauf-Kampfbahn* stadium recall the entrance to Auschwitz, a theme continued by the penned terraces and floodlights of the *Parkstadion*, Schalke's stadium until 2001.

Conclusion

In the representations of football discussed in this chapter we find clear points of convergence with the way the game is discussed in the UK, suggesting that German artists are, indeed, turning westward in their cultural outlook. In many of the literary texts we examine, for example, the influence of Hornby, however slight, is seen as an important factor for German publishers in their marketability. At the same time we also find football used as a means of exploring interpersonal relationships. Yet the crucial difference is that this exploration more often than not becomes a means of examining the nature of German society and its relationship to the past. Moreover, in films such as *Das Wunder von Bern* the examination of history seems also to point to a shift in German self-perceptions, allowing the nation to revisit the winning of the World Cup in 1954. This is an event that somewhat prematurely announced German normalization, a normalization that can now, apparently, be redeclared with confidence. At the same time, in texts such as Brussig's *Leben bis Männer* and Berg's *Mehr als ein Spiel* we see the limits of this normalization. On the one hand, we find authors' discomfort at the increasing importance of consumer culture in other 'normal' nations such as Britain. On the other, and perhaps more importantly, we see that one need only scratch the surface of what is ostensibly a discussion of competition on the football pitch to discover the competing tensions within the German historical psyche and the continued impact of the legacies of the past on the present.

Notes

1 Our temporal focus on post-Hornby representation of football and the literary context of German 'normalization' means that the article brackets out some interesting and prominent earlier examples of football representation in mediated forms such as Siegfried Lenz's novella *Fußball* (1959), Handke's *Die Angst des Tormanns beim Elfmeter* (1978) along with Wenders' film version of it, and the satirical edge of Eckhard Henscheid's *Standardsituationen* (1988; see also 1978, 1983) and Ror Wolf's *Das nächste Spiel ist immer das schwerste* (1982). For overviews and analysis of German football literature, see Zwicker (1999) and Leis (2002). A short note on football and recent literature is offered by Brändle and Koller (2002: 233–8). For an overview of literature and sport in general see Leis (1999) and Gamper (2003). Eggers (2003a) offers a theory of why German literature has been resistant to representing sport.
2 On this tournament see the acclaimed Davies (1990).
3 The flagship of 'New Ladism', *Loaded Magazine* (first published in 1994), not only contained many football references and features, but claimed to take its inspiration from football: 'The idea of *Loaded* came about at a Leeds vs. Barcelona match . . . James Brown and Tim Southwell saw the match and when they came out into the street afterwards, they thought "we should make a magazine to replicate this feeling of euphoria"' (Nixon 2001: 107). This anecdote illustrates the fast-and-loose relationship between football and its mediated forms in the 1990s. Leeds United did *not* play against Barcelona in the 1990s, although they did play in Barcelona's stadium in 1992, against much less glamorous opponents VfB Stuttgart in a replay on neutral territory of a European Cup tie, after the German side had rendered their victory at Elland Road invalid by inadvertently fielding too many foreign players.
4 One notable exception to this trend is Frank Skinner and David Baddiel's comedy series *Fantasy Football* (running since 1994), which contains much more than its consciously 'laddish' exterior and designer bawdiness might initially imply. As demonstrated in the video to their Euro '96 hit *Three Lions – Football's Coming Home* (with *The Lightning Seeds*), their humorous reconstructions of scenes from the beginning of the television era (known as 'Phoenix from the Flames') spring from an often touching, nostalgic yearning for the simplicity of the game in its pre-commercialized phase, when the comedians were in their formative years.
5 For a German interpretation of Hornby, see Joch (2003: 158–60).
6 For a history of FC Schalke 04, see Röwekamp (2001).
7 The best place to start on 1954 is Heinrich (1994, 2003). An extensive body of publications subsequently appeared around the fifty-year anniversary. Jordan (2004) offers an overview. In detail, these works are: Bitzer and Wilting (2003); Bauer; Bertram; Brüggemeier; Dehnhardt; Eggers; Garthe and Schössler; Giersberg; Goosen and Domzalski; Heinrich; Historisches Museum der Pfalz; Jessen *et al.*; Kasza; Linke and Schwarz; Ludwig and Kabus; Michel; Rahn; Raithel; Sarkowicz and Sonnenschein; Walter; Zimmermann (all 2004).
8 Germany had been excluded from the 1948 Olympics in London, and had only a small West German representation at the Helsinki Games in 1952 (see Lämmer 1999: 177–203).

9 Other prominent examples of elision in the film are the vicious foul inflicted on Hungary's star player Ferenc Puskas by the German midfielder Werner Liebrich during the 8–3 defeat in the group stages, which kept the former out of the tournament until the final, where he was still restricted in his movement. Or, indeed, Puskas' accusation after the final that the Germans' extraordinary victory was fuelled by drug abuse, a slur that earned Puskas a prohibition from the German Ministry for the Interior, but was later the subject of publicly rejected investigative journalism in 2004 (a clear sign of the myth's resistance to dramatic alteration).

10 Gebauer (2001: 453) also provides an analysis of the relationship between money and memory in the *Bundesliga*, which relies heavily on Bourdieu's notion of (literary) field.

11 Literally 'in other circumstances', i.e. 'pregnant'; 'antagonistic towards football', resonating with *frauenfeindlich* ('misogynistic').

12 At the time of the work's composition, this was a projected vision of Schalke's new indoor stadium *Arena-AufSchalke*, opened in 2001. Berg also parodies discussions about the new stadium in Munich, current at the time of publication (pp. 152–3). (On this aspect of the *Allianz-Arena* in Munich, see Young 2003: 1486–8.)

References

Primary texts

Berg, B. (2000) *Mehr als ein Spiel: Aus dem Leben eines Fußballfans*, Göttingen: Verlag die Werkstatt.
Biermann, C. (1995) *Wenn du am Spieltag beerdigt wirst, kann ich leider nicht kommen: Die Welt der Fußballfans*, Cologne: Kiepenheuer und Witsch.
Brussig, T. (2001) *Leben bis Männer*, Frankfurt/Main: Fischer Taschenbuch Verlag.
Grass, G. (2002) *Im Krebsgang*, Gottingen: Steidl Verlag.
Handke, P. (1978) *Die Angst des Tormanns beim Elfmeter*, Frankfurt/Main: Suhrkamp.
Henscheid, E. (1978) *Die Mätresse des Bischofs*, Frankfurt/Main: Zweitausendeins.
—— (1983) *Wie Max Horkheimer einmal sogar Adorno hereinlegte: Anekdoten über Fußball, Kritische Theorie, Hegel und Schach*, Zurich: Haffmanns Verlag.
—— (1988) *Standardsituationen: Fußball-Dramen*, Zurich: Haffmanns Verlag.
Hornby, N. (1992) *Fever Pitch*, London: Victor Gollancz. [German version (1997) *Ballfieber – Die Geschichte eines Fans*, Cologne: Kiepenheuer und Witsch.]
Lenz, S. (1959) *Brot und Spiele*, Munich: dtv.
Montherlant, H. de (1954) *Les Olympiques*, Paris: Seuil.
Reng, R. (2002) *Der Traumhüter*, Cologne: Kiepenheuer & Witsch.
Sebald, W.G. (2001) *Luftkrieg und Literatur*, Frankfurt/Main: Fischer.
Siemes, C. (2003) *Das Wunder von Bern: Roman nach dem Drehbuch von Sönke Wortmann und Rochus Hahn*, Cologne: Kiepenheuer & Witsch.
Wolf, R. (1982) *Das nächste Spiel ist immer das schwerste*, Königstein/Ts.: Athenäum.

Filmography

Chadha, G. (2002) *Bend it Like Beckham*.
Fassbinder, R.W. (1979) *Die Ehe der Maria Braun*.

Till, E. (2003) *Luther*.

Tykwer, T. (1998) *Lola rennt*.

Wenders, W. (1972) *Die Angst des Tormanns beim Elfmeter*.

Wortmann, S. (2002) *Das Wunder von Bern*.

Secondary sources

Anz, T. (ed.) (1995) *'Es geht nicht um Christa Wolf': Der Literaturstreit im vereinten Deutschland*, Frankfurt/Main: Fischer.

Bauer, A. (2004) *Das Wunder von Bern: Spieler – Tore – Hintergründe: Alles zur WM 54*, Augsburg: Wißner.

Bertram, J. (2004) *Die Helden von Bern: Eine deutsche Geschichte*, Frankfurt/Main: Scherz.

Bitzer, D. and Wilting, B. (eds) (2003) *Stürmen für Deutschland: Die Geschichte des deutschen Fußballs von 1933 bis 1954*, Frankfurt/Main: Campus.

Bradshaw, P. (2002) 'Review of *Bend it Like Beckham*', *Guardian*, 12 April.

Brändle, F. and Koller, C. (2002) *Goal! Kultur- und Sozialgeschichte des modernen Fußballs*, Zurich: Orell Füssli Verlag.

Brüggemeier, F-J. (2004) *Zurück auf dem Platz: Deutschland und die Fußball-Weltmeisterschaft 1954*, Munich: DVA.

Brussig, T. (2003) '"Sich die ganze Welt vom Fußball her erklären": Thomas Brussig im Gespräch mit Stephan Hermanns und Markus Hesselmann', in R. Adelmann, R. Parr and T. Schwarz (eds) *Querpässe: Beiträge zur Literatur-, Kultur- und Mediengeschichte des Fußballs*, Heidelberg: Synchron.

Cashmore, E. (2002) *Beckham*, Cambridge: Polity Press.

Cashmore, E. and Parker, A. (2003) 'One David Beckham? Celebrity, Masculinity, and the Soccerati', *Sociology of Sport Journal*, 20(3): 214–31.

Davies, P. (1990) *All Played Out: Full Story of Italia '90*, London: William Heinemann.

Dehnhardt, S. (2004) *Das Wunder von Bern: Die wahre Geschichte*, ed. Guido Knopp, Munich: Heyne-Verlag.

Eggers, E. (2003a) 'Warum ignoriert die deutsche Literatur den Sport? Anmerkungen zu einem seltsamen Dilemma', *SportZeiten*, 3(1) [Sport in Geschichte, Kultur und Gesellschaft]: 7–16.

—— (2003b) '"Ich wollte ein Heldenepos": Sönke Wortmann im Gespräch', *11 Freunde*, 28: 30–3.

—— (2004) *Die Stimme von Bern: Das Leben von Herbert Zimmermann, Reporterlegende bei der WM 1954 (mit einem Vorwort von Manni Breuckmann)*, Augsburg: Wißner.

Gamper, M. (2003) 'Literatur, Sport, Medium: Diskurstheoretische Überlegungen zu einem vertrackten Verhältnis', *SportZeiten*, 3(1) [Sport in Geschichte, Kultur und Gesellschaft]: 41–52.

Garthe, M. and Schössler, H.-P. (2004) *Der Mythos von Bern und seine Pfälzer Fußballweltmeister*, Ludwigshafen: Rheinpfalz Verlag und Druckerei.

Gebauer, G. (2001) 'Die Bundesliga', in E. Francois and H. Schulze (eds) *Deutsche Erinnerungsorte*, vol. 2, Munich: C.H. Beck.

—— (2002) 'Ein Land ohne Visionen – warum auch nicht?', *Die Zeit*, 4 July.

Gebauer, G. and Lenk, H. (1988) 'Der erzählte Sport: Homo ludens – auctor ludens', in G. Gebauer (ed.) *Körper- und Einbildungskraft: Inszenierungen des Helden im Sport*, Berlin: Dietmar Reimer Verlag.

Giardina, M.D. (2003) '"Bending it Like Beckham" in the Global Popular – Stylish Hybridity, Performativity, and the Politics of Representation', *Journal of Sport and Social Issues*, 27(1): 65–82.

Giersberg, G. (ed.) (2004) *Der Triumph von Bern: Fußball-WM 1954*, Cologne: Deutscher Sportverlag.

Goosen, F. and Domzalski, O.T. (eds) (2004) *Fritz Walter, Kaiser Franz und wir: Unsere Weltmeisterschaften*, Frankfurt/Main: Eichborn Verlag.

Hage, V. (1999) 'Die Enkel Kommen', *Der Spiegel*, 11 October.

Heinrich, A. (1994) *Tooor! Toor! Tor! 40 Jahre 3:2*, Hamburg: Rotbuch.

—— (2003) 'The 1954 Soccer World Cup and the Federal Republic of Germany's Self-Discovery', *American Behavioral Scientist*, 46(11): 1491–1505.

—— (2004) *3:2 – Die Gründung der Bundesrepublik im Wankdorf-Stadion zu Bern*, Göttingen: Verlag Die Werkstatt.

Heinzle, J. (2003) 'Die Nibelungensage als europäische Heldensage', in J. Heinzle, K. Klein and U. Obhof (eds) *Die Nibelungen. Sage – Epos – Mythos*, Wiesbaden: Reichert.

Hesse-Lichtenberger, Ulrich (2002): *Tor! The Story of German Football*, London: When Saturday Comes Books.

Historisches Museum der Pfalz (ed.) (2004) *Am Ball der Zeit – Deutschland und die Fußball-Weltmeisterschaft seit 1954: Katalog zur Ausstellung im Historischen Museum der Pfalz, Speyer, 31.5.-17.10.2004*, Ostfildern: Hatje Cantz.

Jessen, C., Stahl, V., Eggers, E. and Schlüyer, J.G. (2004) *Die Fußballweltmeisterschaft 1954 in der Schweiz: Das Wunder von Bern*, Kassel: Agon-Sportverlag.

Joch, M. (2003) 'Sehr witzig! Feindbildwechsel in der Fußballsatire', in R. Adelmann, R. Parr and T. Schwarz (eds) *Querpässe: Beiträge zur Literatur-, Kultur- und Mediengeschichte des Fußballs*, Heidelberg: Synchron.

Jordan, S. (2004) 'Der deutsche Sieg bei der Weltmeisterschaft 1954: Mythos und Wunder oder historisches Ereignis?', *Sehepunkte*, 4(6). Online. Available HTTP: <http://www.sehepunkte.historicum.net/2004/06/6462.html> (accessed 6 July 2004).

Kamper, D. (1988) 'Narzißmus und Sport – Einige Überlegungen zur Macht des imaginären Todes', in G. Gebauer (ed.) *Körper- und Einbildungskraft: Inszenierungen des Helden im Sport*, Berlin: Dietmar Reimer Verlag.

Kasza, P. (2004) *Fußball spielt Geschichte: Das Wunder von Bern 1954*, Berlin: be.bra Verlag.

Köster, P. (2003) '"Der sitzt beim Boss vorne": Peter Lohmeyer im Gespräch', *11 Freunde*, 28: 25–7.

Lämmer, M. (ed.) (1999) *Deutschland in der Olympischen Bewegung – Eine Zwischenbilanz*, Frankfurt/Main: NOK für Deutschland.

Leis, M (1999) *Sport in der Literatur*, Frankfurt/Main: Jarhunded.

—— (2002) '"Fußball gegen die Literatur – Halbzeitstand 0:0 – Tip X": Fußball in der schöngeistigen Literatur', in M. Herzog (ed.) *Fußball als Kulturphänomen: Kunst – Kultur – Kommerz*, Stuttgart: Verlag W. Kohlhammer.

Linke, D. and Schwarz, M.M. (2004) *Der 12. Mann von Bern – Herbert Zimmermann*, Hamburg: Hoffmann und Campe.

Lischke-McNabe, U. and Hanson, K.S. (1997) 'Introduction: Recent German Film', *Seminar*, 33(4): 283–9.

Ludwig, E. and Kabus, M. (2004) *Sepp Herberger und das Wunder von Bern: Tatsachenroman*, Augsburg: Wißner.

Michel, R. (2004) *Deutschland ist Weltmeister! Meine Erinnerungen an das Wunder von Bern 1954*, Munich: Südwest-Verlag.

Nixon, S. (2001) 'Resignifying Masculinity: From "New Man" to "New Lad"', in D. Morley and K. Robins (eds) *British Cultural Studies*, Oxford: Oxford University Press.

Rahn, H. (2004) *Mein Hobby Tore schießen (mit einem Nachwort von Klaus Brinkbäumer)*, Munich: DVA. (Also as CD [2004] *Gelesen von Peter Lohmeyer*, Hamburg: HörbuchHamburg.)

Raithel, T. (2004) *Fußballweltmeisterschaft 1954: Sport – Geschichte – Mythos*, Munich: Bayerische Landeszentrale für Politische Bildungsarbeit.

Röwekamp, G. (2001) *FC Schalke 04 – Der Mythos lebt*, Göttingen: Verlag Die Werkstatt.

Sarkowicz, H. and Sonnenschein U. (2004) *'Rahn schießt! Tor, Tor, Tor, Tor!': O-Töne, Stimmen und Hintergründe zum Endspiel in Bern 1954*, Hamburg: HörbuchHamburg.

Seitz, N. (1987) *Bananenrepublik und Gurkentruppe: Die nahtlose Übereinstimmung von Fußball und Politik 1954–1987*, Frankfurt/Main: Eichborn.

—— (2004) 'Was symbolisiert das "Wunder von Bern"?', *Aus Politik und Zeitgeschichte (Beilage zur Wochenzeitschrift Das Parlament)*, B 26: 3–6.

Taberner, S. (2005) *German Literature of the 1990s and Beyond: Normalization and the Berlin Republic*, Rochester: Camden House (see esp. ch. 1, 'Literary Debates Since Unification: "European" Modernism – or "American" Pop?').

Tomlinson, A. (2001) 'Sport, Leisure, Style', in D. Morley and K. Robins (eds) *British Cultural Studies*, Oxford: Oxford University Press.

Walter, F. (2004) *3:2. Das Spiel ist aus! Deutschland ist Weltmeister!*, Munich: Copress Verlag.

Young, C. (2003) 'Kaiser Franz and the Communist Bowl: Cultural Memory and Munich's Olympic Stadium', *American Behavioural Scientist*, 46(11): 1476–90.

Zimmermann, H. (2004) *Das Endspiel von Bern: Fußballweltmeisterschaft 1954. Ungekürzte Original-Reportage*, Hamburg: Hoffmann und Campe.

Zwicker, S. (1999) 'Fußball in der deutschen Literatur: Betrachtungen zu Ror Wolf, Eckhard Henscheid und anderen', *Brünner Beiträge zur Germanistik und Nordistik*, 13(4): 61–81.

12 Germany 1974

On the eve of the goldrush

Alan Tomlinson

Hosts and champions

Only seven countries have won the FIFA World Cup, or the Jules Rimet Cup, as the trophy that was won outright by Brazil in its third World Cup triumph in Mexico in 1970 was called – three from South America, four from Europe. Only two countries – England in 1966 and France in 1998 – have won the World Cup just once, and both did so with home advantage. Other victorious hosts are Uruguay (1930), in its year of centennial celebration of its constitution; fascist Italy in 1934; dictatorial Argentina under the military grip of the Generals in 1978; and the Federal Republic of Germany in the Cold War climate of 1974. Only one World Cup champion has achieved its victory away from its own continent (accepting North and South America as a single continental landmass) – Brazil, in Sweden in 1958 and as five-time winners when defeating Germany in Japan in 2002, and so pulling still further ahead of the three-times winners. Of the seven champions, Brazil is the only one not to have taken the title when hosting the tournament, losing its final game of the group system to Uruguay, in Rio de Janeiro in 1950. In 2006, Germany will have sought to close the historical gap on Brazil, and also to become the only footballing nation to have ever won the championship as host on two occasions.

Winning at home may well be a harder task than in earlier World Cups, despite the French success in 1998. In 1974, despite vigorous lobbying from the West German Organizing Committee members for an increase in the number of teams to twenty-four, Germany prevailed from among sixteen contenders. It was in Spain in 1982 that FIFA raised the number of finalists to twenty-four, and in France in 1998 the number of participating finalists was raised to thirty-two. If Germany are crowned for a second time as champions while hosts, the deification of Franz Beckenbauer will be complete: captain in the 1974 triumph in Munich, manager of the 1990 winners in Italy, figurehead of the 2006 event – sixteen-year cycles of extraordinary achievement in which Germany (inconsistent, temperamental, dour and unpopular at times, but always in the reckoning) has confirmed itself as a superpower on the European and world footballing stage.

With European Championship triumphs (1972 and 1990), World Cup (1966 and 2002) and European (1992) final places also on its roll of honour, the German record is matched by no other European nation.

In this chapter I explore the nature of the 1974 event as a transformative moment in the history of the world game, and reflect how Germany has positioned itself in the corridors of power of world football for contests such as the bid to win the right to stage the World Cup finals. The context for this is the new political economy of sport that emerged in the last quarter of the twentieth century, pushing towards a remaking of sport as a mediated global event and increasingly lucrative commodity. The dynamics underlying this process of change have been based in networks and alliances that are traceable in the institutional growth of bodies such as the European football confederation UEFA, and the world governing body of the game FIFA, and the partnerships they have cultivated with commercial and media bodies.

The Munich moment

In his Preface to FIFA's official report on the 1974 World Cup finals (Heimann 1976), Dr João Havelange thanked Sir Stanley Rous, outgoing president, for his services to the sport: 'I first and foremost feel the need ... to honour this great personality' for his 'meticulous work' in organizing 'this grand tournament'. Havelange had been manoeuvring for years to challenge Rous at the pre-tournament FIFA Congress, and had shocked the patrician Englishman with a victory that was far more than a mere parochial skirmish, but rather 'a power change of seismic significance not just for soccer, but for the global political economy of sport' (Sugden and Tomlinson 1998: 20–1). The 79-year-old Rous was becoming increasingly out of touch with the aspirations of emergent football nations, particularly those from the Asian and African confederations, and his misjudgements, based on an other-worldly idealism in which he saw sport as non-political and autonomous, were exploited by Havelange as he lobbied worldwide for the third-world vote. These errors of judgement included Rous' failed attempt to counter the suspension of the South African confederation, and his wish that the Soviet Union play its match with Chile in Chile after the use of the main national stadium in Santiago as a prison and torture camp in the right-wing coup against democratically elected President Salvador Allende.

But, the vote over and won, and the 1974 finals concluded, Havelange could afford to be magnanimous:

> I presuppose that it [the event of the Finals] was generally accepted as spectacular – both with regard to technology as well as in respect of its perfect organisation. ... The German Organising Committee

deserves our admiration and recognition to a particular degree. Under its President Hermann Neuberger, it tirelessly mastered all the operations connected with the World Cup. . . . Indeed, it would be a considerable advantage, if one were to accept the organisation in the Federal Republic of Germany in 1974 as a starting-point and example for future World Cup tournaments.

It was in response to Germany 1974 that Havelange established this kind of mantra that was to become so widely chanted by others as well as him, such as Juan Antonio Samaranch who succeeded to the IOC (International Olympic Committee) presidency six years on at the Moscow Olympic Games. In praising the hosts, raising the bar for staging standards, these newly ennobled 'Lords of the Rings' (Simson and Jennings 1992) began their successful inflating of the currency of world sports events. Germany 1974, and the FIFA Frankfurt Congress at which Havelange ousted Rous, was a pivotal point in the story of the reshaping of modern sport.

It was an appropriate stage too for such an event: the finals may be seen in retrospect as a cultural moment with profound political, economic and ideological consequences for the future of international sport. It was a sixteen-team tournament, for which ninety-eight entries had been received by July 1971 – eight places were allocated for Europe, three for South America, and one each for Asia, CONCACAF (Central and North Americas and the Caribbean) and Africa. The ninety-eight entries included sixteen Asian and twenty-four African associations, compared to four and twelve respectively for the 1970 World Cup. Zaire got through from the twenty-four African entries: 'Thus for the first time, the African continent was represented by a side from "Black Africa"' (Heimann 1976: 16).

The qualifying road to Germany 1974 was therefore more truly international than any previous World Cup competition, characterized by a fourfold increase in the number of Asian entries and a doubling of the African ones. This growth in the scale of the event prompted the German organizing team's boss to lobby FIFA for a 50 per cent increase in the number of finalists. As early as 20 November 1970, Herman Neuberger urged Rous to put the number of teams up to twenty-four; having lobbied and taken an 'experimental vote' from among European nations Rous was lukewarm in response and resisted these arguments, confirming the numbers at the traditional sixteen. This did him little good in the Havelange campaigning years, as the Brazilian lobbied the dissatisfied emergent nations and could report on Rous' intransigence concerning numbers of finalists and the Eurocentric domination of the field of entrants. Also networking and lobbying behind the scenes was Horst Dassler, for whom the expansion of the final line-up would mean more global markets and more national deals in the expansionist period of the globalizing sports industry.

Havelange was respectful enough – calculatingly oleaginous, even – as he waded into FIFA waters. The minutes of the third meeting of the

Organizing Committee, or Bureau as it called itself for a while (Dusseldorf, 16/17 July 1971), recorded a proposal, by letter, that 'Mr. [sic] Havelange, president of the CBD of Brazil, present a 5-kilo Gold Cup that should be called the Sir Stanley Rous Cup'. In his personal copy of the agenda, Rous annotated this item in his minutely precise longhand: 'Fair Play Trophy!', but he also wrote 'Withdraw'. His fuller annotations referred to the potential group fixtures in the African qualifying competitions, suggesting that this kind of planning detail had not been at the forefront of his thinking. The 1974 tournament would be the first time that the FIFA World Cup was won, the Jules Rimet trophy having been taken by Brazil in 1970. Rous and a select subcommittee chose the new trophy from fifty-three designs, at a special meeting in Zurich in April 1971: 'they chose the design by Sivio Gazzaniga, submitted by the firm Bertoni, Milan. The Cup symbolizes the strength and spontaneity of sporting competition, depicted by the joy of victory displayed by two athletes, crowned by the globe' (Heimann 1976: 65). It was at the first meeting of the Organizing Committee that it was decided to call the trophy the FIFA World Cup: it must cost no more than $US 20,000 and 'should be a cup designed as a symbol of football unity' (Item 4 in minutes of 16 November 1970 meeting at the Belgium Football Association). There were complaints from some (mostly third-world, specifically South American) quarters that the successful design should have been selected by the whole of the executive committee. The Havelange proposal for a gold cup in Rous' name was designed as a grandiloquent gesture, and at the same time was an implicit critique of both the parsimonious nature of the conception and the unaccountable nature of the selection process. Havelange showed in this apparently trivial initiative that his timing was impeccable, his plotting and diplomatic skills consummate.

The English had not made the finals, and so 1974 could provide no continuation of the English–German rivalry of the 1966 final, the 1970 tournament when England surrendered a two-goal lead and lost to Germany in the quarter-finals, and the 1972 European championships when Günter Netzer and Franz Beckenbauer sauntered to an elegant and seemingly effortless win at Wembley. The German author of FIFA's official report could still find mileage in the fate of the English, though. England, with only modest results against Wales in its qualifying group, had been beaten in the away leg with ease by Poland, the reigning Olympic champions. An aberration? A freak result? On the evening of the home return match, the English footballing public sat down in front of its television sets for a night of restoration:

> Nothing was quite as sensational as the elimination of England, the 1966 World Cup champions. The experts though found this to be an almost logical development. What had been perceptible during the 1970 World Cup tournament in Mexico and even more so during the 1972 European Championship, was now clear for all to see: English

soccer – or at least, the brand played by the national side – had not
kept up with the development of modern football . . . [at Wembley
England offered] desperate assaults launched without any real concept
by the English . . . lacking a proper tactical concept.

(Heimann 1976: 11)

No English threat in the finals this time around, then, but there were
enough potential stories to whet the appetites of the football press. The
Netherlands topped the group with a 9–0 win over Norway, 5–0 and 8–1 wins
over Iceland, and a 24–2 goal difference, though only by that over Belgium,
with whom the Dutch had contested two goalless draws. Belgium had also
scored its way to a 12–0 goal difference. So the Netherlands was feared, but
there was evidence that its awesome attacking machine could be stopped.
The German Democratic Republic was drawn in the same qualifying group
as the host nation. Poland was respected for its Olympic achievements just
two years earlier in Munich, and would have confidence on familiar territory, and Brazil would be seeking to win a fourth title. The official report
summarizes the relatively low-key expectations of the German public:

The Federal Republic of Germany's team was not exactly riding the
crest of a wave before the game against Yugoslavia – it had been taken
to pieces by the critics and was still miles away from the tremendous
form which had so convincingly brought it the European Championship
in 1972.

(Heimann 1976: 47)

Germany won 2–0, despite Yugoslavian President Tito geeing up its
opponents. With qualification to the next round secure, West Germany
proceeded to lose by a goal to nil in the game against East Germany, effec-
tively assuring that it need not meet either the reigning champions Brazil
or the hot tournament favourites the Netherlands in the quest to make the
final. The German team was far from impressive in the tournament so far:
'unable to find an answer to' massed East German defence, 'it held the ball
far too long and completely lacked determination' (Heimann 1976: 33).
And in a critical match in the second group, Poland started confidently
against the hosts, but two German players saved the side in what was effec-
tively a semi-final match – these were 'Beckenbauer and goalkeeper Meier
who safely disposed of half a dozen seemingly certain attempts at goal!'
(Heimann 1976: 49). The final was in the Olympic Stadium in Munich
on Sunday, 7 July, where, of course, the Federal Rupublic of Germany
reprised its underdog act from the famous Berne victory of twenty years
earlier and defeated the favourites, the 'total football' team from the
Netherlands. Prior to the action, the official report documents, there was
a spectacle of modest proportions:

The closing display was . . . optically more in tune with the crowd in the stadium than the opening ceremony: 2 youth bands from Dinkelsbühl and Meersburg, followed by a successful contrast, the 170 Alberta Girls from Edmonton in Canada. The girls made way for the world's largest choir: the 1500 members of the Fischer Choirs, the ladies wearing long red dresses, the men in blue suits and the children wearing light-coloured shirts and blouses, sang folk-songs from all over the world. And the vast crowd sang along with them.

'Das grose Spiel, es kann beginnen!' (The Big Match can begin!) was the final song on the programme – sung by Freddy Quinn, one of the most popular of all entertainment stars. And as the choirs filed out of the stadium, the buses which had carried the various teams to their matches over the past three and a half weeks came into the stadium one by one – each bus adorned with the national colours of the nation concerned. The buses drove in through the Marathon Gate in alphabetical order on to the track; the 4 which entered last were those representing the 4 teams which had qualified for the final matches. According to the amount of applause the crowd accorded, it could easily be judged which teams had earned the most sympathy during the tournament: Haiti, Australia, Scotland, Poland, Holland and, of course, the team from Federal Germany.

(Heimann 1976: 53)

German Football Association President, Herman Gösmann, and Sir Stanley Rous thanked everyone, and the teams lined up in the VIP box to be welcomed by 'Walter Scheel, in his first few days in office as President of the Federal Republic of Germany' (ibid.). Rous handed the new FIFA World Cup to President Scheel, who handed it to Beckenbauer. Scheel was at the closing banquet too, at the Munich Hilton Hotel, along with other political dignitaries such as Prince Bernhard of the Netherlands, and the Dutch Premier Den Uiyl. At the banquet Rous was awarded the Grand Cross of Merit of the Order of Merit of the Federal Repubic, presented by President Scheel; and Beckenbauer received the Fair Play Trophy on behalf of the German team, both donated and now presented by Scheel. The beaming President could hardly believe his luck, and 'in his address . . . underlined how pleased he was that one of his first acts in office had concerned football' (ibid.). Winners and sportsmen – his political duties would never be as easy as this again.

There were nine venues at Germany 1974 and none sold out. Sales were as follows: Berlin, 47.3 per cent sales for three games and potentially 248,366 tickets; Hamburg, 69.7 per cent sales for three games and potentially 176,517 tickets; Hannover, 67 per cent sales for four games and potentially 233,947 tickets; Gelsenkirchen, 69 per cent sales for five games and potentially 341,804 tickets; Dortmund, 87.7 per cent sales for four games and potentially 210,215 tickets; Dusseldorf, 64.3 per cent sales for five games and potentially 330,426 tickets; Frankfurt, 94.2 per cent sales for five games and potentially 297,952 tickets; Stuttgart, 76.2 per cent sales for four games and potentially 275,299 tickets; Munich, 67.3 per cent sales for five games and potentially 369, 815 tickets. The total number of games was thirty-eight, the number of tickets available 2,484,341, only 1,769,062 were sold (71.21 per cent of those available), leaving 715,279 unsold, generating 36,310,115 DM (Heimann 1976: 95).

There were 28,000 guests of honour to be looked after (2,000 at the final in Munich) and the accommodation section organized 10,000 overnight stays in twenty hotels. To cater for the needs of these guests, the Organizing Committee, following a model used at the summer Olympics two years before, trained up female helpers: 103 hostesses were available during the final tournament to look after international guests and media personnel:

> The hostess department was set up at Organizing Committee head-quarters, comprising the department head, 3 hostess instructors and a secretary. From April 1974, they initially concentrated on training the chief hostesses for the nine World Cup cities. From June 1st, the chief hostesses then held six-day instruction courses in the nine World Cup centres. Eight (in Hamburg, ten) hostesses were available at each venue except for Frankfurt which as the centre of activity required a great deal more, namely 34.
>
> (Heimann 1976: 70)

One wonders at the scale and maybe too the range of activities and support services provided at the Frankfurt hub. A 'rapidly growing interest internationally in the World Cup' also created demands for facilities for media professionals. Final figures accredited were: 1,691 journalists (1,408 in Mexico in 1970, 1,392 in England in 1966); 295 photographers (359 in Mexico, 172 in England); 106 technicians (assistants without the right to sit in the press stands); and for radio and television: 1,240 reporters (895 in Mexico, 213 in England), 399 radio, 841 television, and 1,284 technicians. The total number of accredited personnel was 4,616, compared with 2,662 in 1970, and 1,777 in 1966. The scale and complexity of the media operation were enlarging, and there were bottlenecks when telex transmissions were needed to meet deadlines. But the press centres were still adapted, rather than specifically constructed, facilities, based as they were in centrally located spacious hotels.

The 1,769,062 tickets sold were for thirty-eight games. Sales in Mexico in 1970 were 1,673,975, in England in 1966 1,614,677, though in both these cases for thirty-two games. Germany 1974 established the emerging principle for the sports mega-cum-media event – the higher global profile the event, the less significant the numbers of and takings from the live spec-tator at the match. Remarkably, not a single game involving the home team was sold out in the first round of the finals, though a 95.8 per cent crowd watched the FRG vs. Chile. Only 14.8 per cent of the stadium capacity turned up for Chile vs. Australia in Berlin's Olympic Stadium. The smallest crowd was 11,012 in Hannover for Bulgaria vs. Uruguay. Australia was the least draw for crowds. Interest in the tournament increased in the second round, in which half the number of matches attracted two-thirds of the numbers for the first round. Argentina vs. Brazil at Hannover had the smallest crowd in that round, 35,074; GDR vs. Netherlands in Gelsenkirchen had the highest. Netherlands vs. Brazil in Dortmund was a sell-out. The other two sell-outs were FRG vs. Sweden in Dusseldorf and FRG vs. Poland in Frankfurt. Intra-European derbies framed in national rivalries were clearly a big draw, and the neighbours from the Netherlands and the reigning world champions were an obvious highlight. But the crowd figures also confirm the wisdom of locating big games in the industrial heartlands of Germany in the Ruhr, where the traditional fans of a historically rooted football culture could provide a strong spectator base.

Financially, Gemany 1974 established a template for future World Cups. Just 20 per cent of receipts were from non-ticket sources in Mexico in 1970; this was 46 per cent in 1974. There was an 'enormous . . . increase' in other sources of revenue in comparison with 1970: 'from poster advertising and commercial exploitation (mascots, souvenirs etc.) the 1974 World Cup budget obtained 20 times as much in the way of proceeds as in 1970!' (Heimann 1976: 91). After taxes payable on ticket revenue, 'the proud sum of 34,342,555.69 DM was left' (ibid.). Other receipts from TV/radio, commercial exploitation proportion, poster advertising in the stadia, film rights and friendly games in the pre-tournament period, accumulated 32,916,000 DM: 'Overall the balance showed a surplus of 50,067,094.73 DM – the largest profit ever made at a World Cup tournament' (Heimann 1976: 94). Of this, 10 per cent went to FIFA; 25 per cent to the organizing association; and 65 per cent to the participating teams, based on receipts and number of games played:

> In spite of rising costs, the organisation costs amounted to around 25 per cent of the net proceeds – thanks to the pronounced increase in proceeds. At the first post-war World Cup held on European soil in Switzerland in 1954, the expenses accounted for 50 per cent of the net proceeds whilst in Mexico the figure still stood at 30 per cent.
>
> (ibid.)

This was Sir Stanley Rous' final World Cup as FIFA President, ousted as he was by Brazilian Dr João Havelange's extraordinary campaign for the presidency. Committed and honourable, Rous continued to chair the Organizing Committee right through to the closure of the accounts. It is fascinating to look through the minutes of the Organizing Committee and to see what particular tensions arose in the staging of an event that in highly distinctive ways was characteristic of a new scale in the mediated sport event. As related above, the number of teams in the finals was one of the major sources of tensions. There were also decisions to be made about suppliers and media contracts. It was clear that the head of the German Organizing Committee did not see eye-to-eye with Rous on some of these matters; and highly likely that Rous was unaware of some of the emergent dynamics in the sports industry.

Suppliers' exposure during events on the scale of the World Cup is immense: concentrated, sustained and global. This is what provided the foundation for the corporate embrace of top-level sport, and the exclusive sponsorship deals with preferred partners that were established by FIFA and the IOC in the 1980s, and consolidated still more by UEFA's Champions League in the 1990s (Sugden and Tomlinson 1998; Tomlinson, 2004). In the early 1970s this political economy of international sports culture was still in the making. Looking behind the scenes of the preparatory work in the build-up to the tournament shrewd operators were already marking the event as a superb marketing tool: the decision on which footballs to use was a case in point. At the ninth meeting of the Organizing Committee, at Frankfurt's Hotel Airport on Saturday, 5 January 1974, at 9.30 a.m. on a cold weekend winter morning, the organizers were faced with Item 12 on their agenda ('Footballs'):

> To hear – that a small sub-Committee, as appointed in Gelsenkirchen, has chosen the ADIDAS ball, and – that white, orange and black and white footballs will be available and, furthermore – that the 16 finalist National Associations will be given three orange, three white and four black and white footballs by ADIDAS.

Two red ticks from Sir Stanley on his agenda papers steered this apparently innocent item through. At the previous meeting in Gelsenkirschen (12 October 1973) item 27 had noted that:

> A small Sub-Committee, composed of Messrs. Riedel, Cavan and Neuberger (or his representative), was appointed to inspect and decide on the footballs to be used for the World Cup.
> It was agreed that three balls of the type chosen would be sent to each finalist team beforehand for practice.

At that meeting it had also been recalled that Adidas had provided footballs at the 1968 Olympic Games, the 1970 World Cup and the 1972 Olympics, the balls having been 'successfully used' (minute 27). The small subcommittee would not have deliberated too long over this decision; there is no record of other tenders. Adidas won the contract, got more balls out to teams than originally agreed, and used the day of the confirmation of the deal as a marketing coup. For the Adidas company this must have seemed like a goldrush. It was one sphere in which Horst Dassler was confirming his place at the table of rich pickings that international sport was about to serve up. At the same time, Dassler was assisting Havelange in his challenge and campaign for the presidency. Over the previous two years Havelange, as he stated in an interview to a Brazilian edition of *Playboy* magazine in 1985, had visited eighty-six FIFA countries, concentrating mostly on Africa and Asia. Havelange's campaign brochure pledged expansion of the World Cup finals to twenty-four teams for the 1982 event in Spain, along with seven other specific initiatives and forms of support and development (Sugden and Tomlinson 1998: 37). He would need money to do this, from new sources as well as the emergent television and media revenues. Dassler would play a vital role in putting core elements of this financial model in place, and deals such as the provision of balls in 1974 were a vital part of his commercial strategy. Harry Cavan would also benefit from the work of the subcommittee. Dassler knew how to establish contacts and dependencies, and though in the formal documentation on the World Cup 1974 he has no presence, his shadow pervades the committee rooms, congress halls and playing venues of the event. Dassler:

> provided lavish hospitality, the 'compulsory Adidas dinner' at every international sports federation meeting at a time when the federations were relatively impoverished ... his own residential and catering complex at Landersheim, Alsace; and, allegedly mostly for Africans and Asians in Paris, his sports shop, and restaurant with other hospitality facilities in Montmartre. He retained useful individuals in bogus capacities – Harry Cavan, Northern Irish football administrator and FIFA vice-president, for instance, as 'shoe consultant'.
>
> (Sugden and Tomlinson 1998: 90)

Rous also had trouble with the chief of the German organizing team on the tendering process for film rights, and at one point had to intervene to curtail the activities of Neuberger on the matter of contracts. Rous got the FIFA General Secretary Dr Käser to confirm that granting of these rights was not the prerogative of the German organizers alone, and that such business had to be conducted by the FIFA Organizing Committee. A special meeting was called, attended by legal representatives, to put the tendering process back on track.

The finances of the event seemed at times to be decided on the hoof. FIFA was quite happy to hear, at the fourth Organizing Committee meeting in Beirut, in Hotel Phoenicia International on 3 February 1972, Mr Neuberger report that 'the cost for the stadia to be prepared was 300 million German Marks and would be divided up so that the State Government, the Regional Government and the Towns involved would each pay 80 million German marks towards this total and the balance would be raised by means of a television sweepstake' (item 5). It is astounding to read this now, to reflect that such basic infrastructural funding was not in place until more than five years after the German national association had been awarded the event. The highest level of political guarantees is now essential in the bidding process for any such mega-event. Of course, in less democratic, dictatorial societies such guarantees could be made like papal edicts. At the same meeting in Beirut, Rous and the other FIFAcrats could breathe a sigh of relief about the 1978 finals. Dr N.B. Noel from Argentina reported that:

> The Argentinean Government had issued a decree to the effect that the 1978 FIFA World Cup was an event of national importance to Argentina. The Government would form a committee to assist the Argentinean F.A. Organizing Committee. – This was a valuable contribution of the Government and would help enormously.
>
> (minute 16a)

Almost three years later, after the flush of the success of the 1974 event, the thirteenth meeting of the Organizing Committee was attended by the new FIFA President. Havelange's first meeting took place at Hotel Jolly, Rome, on the 5 November 1974. Dr Noel made a major point at this meeting, arguing that the details of the distribution of World Cup profits, the share of the distributed profits going to participating nations, should not be published (minute 7.1). These figures were not, then, made public. Rous kept them, meticulous as ever, in his 1974 file. These audited accounts make interesting reading, as presented on 30 October 1974 by a Frankfurt firm of accountants (Table 12.1).

Table 12.1 Distribution to participants in DM (of the 65% share due to participating national associations).

Argentina	2,391,802.75
Australia	1,067,601.31
Brazil	3,007,196.47
Bulgaria	1,060,478.35
FGR	3,182,223.51
Chile	1,155,582.32
DDR	2,433,121.64
Haiti	1,111,801.24
Italy	1,255,372.46
Yugoslavia	2,492,413.86
Netherlands	3,036,785.81
Poland	2,932,606.07
Scotland	1,166,061.13
Sweden	2,336,677.86
Uruguay	1,089,506.60
Zaire	1,092,780.20

So the tournament was a great domestic success, but also a windfall for the DFB and its equivalent bodies, in the Netherlands and Brazil in particular. More money was being generated in events such as these, and this was also detected in FIFA's technical report, directed by former England football manager Walter Winterbottom: 'There are signs that commercial interests which surround the outstanding player outside his football can affect his attitude to the game and make him more anxious to protect himself against injury' (FIFA, no date: 71). Germany 1974 was a watershed in the development of the political and economic profile of world football. National associations were not yet hurling themselves forward with offers to host the finals, but the event showed the potential tangible economic profits and some of the less tangible political benefits that could accrue to corporate and political institutions and interests, as well as the sporting bodies themselves, as the World Cup expanded in global reach and commercial scope.

Bidding battles

FIFA delegated the 1974 World Cup to the German Football Association (DFB) in 1966 and so representatives from the DFB could be in England during the 1966 World Cup:

> In addition, top German dignitaries were able to see for themselves just what an extensive set-up is required to stage such a tournament. Thus, the then-minister [responsible for the press] of the Federal Republic of Germany visited all the facilities which had been set up for the press in London. In 1967 the DFB set up an eleven-member planning committee which in 1969 was streamlined into the final Organizing Committee which had nine members.
>
> (Heimann 1976: 68)

There had been competition between West Germany and Spain for the 1974 finals, and this had become a major headache for Rous. Congress was expanding in membership numbers and voting patterns would be unpredictable or, worse, manipulable. So Rous guided the decisions about venues and locations of finals and congresses away from the full membership itself and towards the executive committee of FIFA.

Rous's thinking on this issue was elaborated at FIFA's thirty-fourth Ordinary Congress, held on 8 October 1964 at the Tokyo Metropolitan Festival Hall. FIFA was in Tokyo as organizer of the Olympic football competition, and this venue and the event generated a large turn-out, as evidenced in the 'roll-call' for the Congress and the multiple representation of many of the member nations, and small, newly independent nations whose provisional membership was being upgraded to full membership at this meeting. In the tenth item/minute, Rous gives the background to this policy change:

X. – World Championships and Congresses

The time-table of the World Cup and Congresses as submitted by the Executive Committee, and worded as follows, was approved by 55 votes to 7 (two slight alterations in the last paragraph):

'At its meeting in Tokyo, Congress will decide the venues of the 1970 World Cup Competition. Subsequently, the Executive Committee intends to ask Congress to authorize them to allocate future World Cup Competitions and Congresses on the lines of the schedule set out below.

If accepted, this will enable national associations concerned to make adequate preparations without encountering strong competition which regrettably is occurring in connection with the present campaign.

The present uncertainty causes national associations much expense to canvass for votes; puts strain on friendships of some who do not like to discriminate between the applicants particularly when both claimants have much in common; involves them in much work, worry and expense and prevents them from concentrating their efforts on more fruitful activities. The Committee feel that many of the delegates who exercise their right to vote do so without having seen the facilities which are offered by the various applicants and are therefore forced to base their choice on not wholly relevant issues. All this will be avoided if the following plan, proposed by the Executive Committee, is found generally acceptable.

It would be, of course, for members of the Executive Committee to satisfy themselves through personal visits to the countries selected that all the facilities and amenities available were suitable – football stadia, hotels, hostels and so on – and that the financial requirements and national economy of the potential host was satisfactory. They would also study the advisability and practicability of allocating the World Cup and Congress to Continents which hitherto have not staged them.

It would be clearly understood that the national associations included in the programme would not accept if conditions subsequently became unfavourable; to cover this eventuality, a "reserve" country would be nominated. Care would be taken to select only those countries to which delegates from every country would have access. The present Statutes would be amended accordingly so that future Congresses could change in the light of future requirements.'

For Rous, the international football family was expanding too fast to trust the democratic base of Congress in key decision-making. The revealing phrases in the minute are 'strain on friendships' and 'not wholly relevant issues'. What Rous really referred to here were the competitive dynamics of an expanding international organization, and the types of lobbying and collective strategies that were underlying the candidature to host congresses and, most significantly, finals. The Congress went on to confirm that the 1966 Congress would be held in London, and that the applicants for the 1970 World Cup were from South America, Argentina; from North/Central, Mexico. West Germany and Spain were confirmed as 'previous applicants' for the 1974 World Cup, 'the venue to be announced not later than 1966'. 'Previous applicants' for the 1978 World Cup were confirmed as Argentina and Mexico; for the 1982 World Cup, West Germany and Spain. 'Sir Stanley stated that future venues would be selected by the Executive Committee and not by Congress', and Congress moved to its last vote on the awarding of a final tournament. Argentina proposed a vote on World Cup 1970: the result was fifty-six votes for Mexico, thirty-two for Argentina, with seven abstentions.

On cue, two years later in London, at the FIFA Congress held in the Royal Garden Hotel, minute 10 was dedicated to the World Championships:

> It was noted that the West German F.A. had submitted an application and given full information in a printed booklet which had been previously circulated. A letter had in the meantime been received from the Spanish F.A. informing FIFA that they were not interested in organizing the 1974 World Cup but would leave the field free for the West German F.A. (DFB) to do so and would maintain their nomination for 1982. The Committee thereafter decided, in accordance with the 1964 Congress decision, that
> > the 1974 World Championship would be held in Germany West (DFB);
> > the 1978 World Championship in Argentina and the 1982 World Championship in Spain.

These were convenient solutions all round for Rous, taken in the calm of the small select executive committee, pleasing all the candidates and giving West Germany a long clear run-in, and Spain even longer, sixteen years in which to make its preparations for the 1982 event. Other candidates would emerge of course, and 'Prof. Dr. Andrejevic informed the Committee that the Yugoslavia F.A. would be a candidate as organizing country for one of the coming World Championships'. But much was to happen over the intervening years to lead to the bidding wars of the 1990s and the early years of the new century (Sugden and Tomlinson 1999, 2002, 2003). Getting the 1974 finals now looks like a gentlemanly exercise next to the high-profile struggles and tensions behind the successful bids for Japan/Korea 2002, and Germany 2006. Looking back at earlier candidature documents illuminates the ludicrous extremes that the bidding processes have reached. The English Football Association (FA) bid to stage the 1990 finals and its candidate dossier was a quaint-looking loose-leaf folder (Football Association, no date, probably 1983). It included eight sections inside the gold-lettered but murky brown loose-leaf spiral binder: a government declaration (missing from the FA's copy); maps; transport systems; stadia; declarations of stadium owners; hotels; organizations; estimated receipts. There were no photographs, no celebrity endorsement, just factual descriptions of stadia facilities and so on. In 1999, the FA's England 2006 documentation (Football Association, no date, probably 1999) was on a completely different scale. Two volumes of glossily produced material totalled more than 600 pages, with endorsements from celebrities such as singer Sir Elton John and an upbeat statement from Prime Minister Tony Blair: 'The FIFA World Cup is the greatest sporting tournament in the world. Once every four years it brings the world together. It deserves the best: the best facilities, the best conditions, the best organisation.'

The English bid stressed youth, historical footballing legacy and quality of sporting provision and experience, and its readiness to stage a successful event. But it also overemphasized the notion of being the 'right' choice, and, as observed by insiders, this combination of self-righteousness and smugness bordering on arrogance alienated potential support. Germany used less hyperbole, worked the lobbies of international sport, and scored highest when FIFA's technical committee offered an interim evaluation of the rival bids. As Keith Cooper, FIFA communications boss at the time, recalls:

> The British were arrogant – 'we invented this, it came from us', and they got too much wrong, saying we've got the stadiums. Well they didn't, several of the pitches weren't big enough. Arsenal's Highbury was I think 60 wide when the width had to be a minimum 65. Nobody had looked at the cost of expanding a playing area. Think of the cost of pushing stands back. Arsenal's would have been into the crowd. Aston Villa's wasn't big enough. . . . And the media facilities were lousy for Euro '96 – trophy rooms as mixed zones. Atmospheric maybe, but hardly up to the job.
>
> I thought that Germany would win. I've still got the envelope where I wrote 'Winner: Germany' a couple of years before. They're so competitive, efficient and organized. They – and Beckenbauer – don't want to enter anything if they think that they're not going to win. I thought they went over the top at the presentation – Franz, Schröder, Claudia Schiffer, lots of dancers pressing up against the window. But it makes a big impact if you put so much into it, against the laid-back British. It must have made an impression.
>
> It was Franz versus Bobby [Charlton] and that was never a match. Franz has presence. He was born with a silver spoon and doesn't have to work hard at things. Look at the way he played. And he would have wanted to win or he wouldn't have done it at all.
>
> (interview with author, 24 September 2004)

In June 1998, addressing collected guests from FIFA and the media on the British Embassy lawns in Paris, in the splendour of a building bought by Napoleon for his Empress Josephine, Sir Bobby Charlton had forgotten to mention the English bid and had to be hustled back on to the platform to mumble a few words of embarrassed endorsement of the bid. Cooper is right. Bobby versus Franz in the bidding battles, unlike at Wembley in 1966, was never going to be an even encounter. The FA has produced an eighty-two-page-long analysis of the failed bid (Football Association 2000), and catalogues reasons for the German victory: outbursts of English football hooliganism in Marseilles in 1998, and in Belgium at Euro 2000 just weeks before the vote; the late Sir Bert Millichip's reported agreement with UEFA that England be supported to stage Euro '96 and in turn then support a German bid for World Cup 2006; UEFA's consistent support, in the light of this agreement, for the German bid; an 'unfair FIFA inspection [that] incensed' the FA Board (p. 4); inter-confederation deals that took possible, and in part pledged, votes away from England; and, the FA claimed, 'UEFA leaders and the German Bid in particular, consistently denigrated England's bid, making the FA's alleged dishonouring of the Agreement a key issue in their campaign' (p. 82). In the end, however, the FA recognizes the root cause of England's failed bid: 'The Football Association's and English football's relative lack of influence in both European and world football . . . an insular attitude, seen by some UEFA and FIFA members as stand-offish and even arrogant . . . thin representation on the governing bodies of UEFA and FIFA and in their Secretariats, committees and panels was both a consequence and a cause of our lack of influence' (p. 82). The English bid without doubt showed something of a bulldog spirit, sticking at the task, but in a fashion that was obstinate and short-sighted. To the end, the FA felt hard done by, and bid leader Alec McGivan claimed that it was a real 'secondary achievement', despite the five votes of the first round dwindling to two votes in the second round, that England had been seen to have conducted 'a bid which objective commentators recognised as the most professional' (p. 74).

In fact, UEFA was utterly consistent throughout the whole affair, and UEFA President Lennart Johansson is animated on the matter: 'We had a gentleman's agreement on this, you can go to Spain, you can go to any of them and they know that we said: "Let's go for England Euro '96 and for Germany World Cup 2006, to avoid that we have more than one candidate". A new management set up at the English FA did not appreciate this gentlemen's agreement' (interview with author, September 1997). Sir Bert Millichip, pressured in November 1999 by the FA campaigning team to deny that there was ever an agreement, had nevertheless confirmed that when Germany announced its intentions to run for 2006, 'I may well have indicated "we will support you" at that time' (interview with author, 17 January 1997). One seasoned analyst of international sports federations and politics was astounded at the England bid team's explanation of its failure:

They still don't get it do they? Banks was a disaster – considered by both FIFA and IOC senior officials as a clown. As for reports on their trips is there no one in English football who understands sports politics? Clearly not, going by this report. If they think they almost succeeded in overcoming lack of inside information within FIFA and UEFA, and had got a real ability to make deals, they are living on another planet. They had more inside information than they realize on what was going on in FIFA but there was no one bright enough to understand what it meant. Also, I saw nothing [in the report] about the failure of anyone to speak a foreign language, apart from Wheeler who could speak Spanish.

The German bid did not come from another planet. It was rooted in the sporting, political and commercial interests of interlocking agencies and individuals.

Networks and alliances in the 'football family'

As Erik Eggers outlines in Chapter 13, the scale of deal-making in order to secure the votes of executive committee members has escalated so much that it borders frequently on the corrupt. The Oceania confederation's President, Charles Dempsey, was vilified widely for abstaining in the second round of the 2000 vote for the 2006 finals, and with pressures of phone calls and hoax letters posted under his door the night before the vote: 'it gave me palpitations. Nelson Mandela rang me up . . . UEFA's given Asia an extra World Cup place so the Asians switched the vote to Germany. What else? I can't tell you. It would be dynamite. Would it embarrass Asia? It would embarrass everyone. What went on in that hotel, I can't name names . . . but it was frantic' (interview with author). So Dempsey left after the first vote, hoping for a quiet life but came under siege from the media back at his Auckland home. If he had voted for South Africa, the executive committee's vote would have been split and the FIFA President Sepp Blatter would have had to cast a deciding second vote. Blatter was without doubt relieved not to have this public individual responsibility, able to say that it was not his fault that a worthy African bid just lost out, and also able to satisfy major corporate sponsors by locating the finals in the heart of one of the world's two largest consumer markets.

Germany has played the institutional politics of football cannily and to good effect. In 1994 Havelange rejigged his FIFA committees (*Sport Intern*, 26/23, 10 December). Not surprisingly, in a league table of national membership of the executive committee and standing committees, Brazil came 'out on top in the meeting rooms just as it does on the field of play: with 11 individuals' (p. 3), including Havelange himself, holding thirteen seats. France was two places behind, benefiting from the appointment of World Cup organizers in the years before the France '98 finals: 'Almost as strong are fellow Europeans Germany (eight members in ten seats), Spain (nine men in nine seats) and Italy (seven in nine). Belgium and Argentina had just one each, and England only two, Sir Bert Millichip and 'in the relatively uninfluential media committee, David Miller' (pp. 3–4). David Will, on his own, held five of Scotland's seven seats. Despite the vicissitudes of personal favour and institutional commitment that could change the composition of the committee memberships, Germany was third strongest in national representation of the eighty-four FIFA member associations that shared 239 seats among 174 individuals. Blatter had the power to purge some of the committees after gaining the presidency in 1998, and in 2001 there was a less prominent German representation, but on the most active committee, the Organizing Committee for the 2002 World Cup, Germany had more members than any other nation. England, despite giving Blatter its vote in 1998 in a clumsy and naive campaigning strategy, still had only a few seats: Sir Bobby Charlton on the Football Committee, FA Chairman Geoffrey Thompson on the World Cup Organizing Committee, Howard Wilkinson on the Technical Committee, and a couple of members of media and marketing committees.

German football politicians and administrators have featured prominently in the administration of the major football federations, the European and the world bodies, throughout their histories. German representatives argued as early as 1911 that FIFA 'should eventually become the regulatory body for the laws of the game' (Lanfranchi *et al.*: 64), only to be refused by the English FIFA President Daniel Woolfall and the FA. German was accepted early on as one of FIFA's official languages, and the multilingual skills of Swiss personnel since FIFA moved to Zurich in 1931 have been conducive to an effective German presence in the organization. Parallel points may be made about UEFA, which moved from Paris to Berne in January 1960 and appointed as General Secretary the Swiss Hans Bangerter, who had been Assistant General Secretary at FIFA since 1953. No UEFA president has been German. They have been from Denmark, Switzerland, Italy and France; Johansson the current incumbent is from Sweden. When Jacques Georges of France won the presidency after the death in a car crash of Artemio Franchi of Italy, the organizer of Germany 1974 had put himself in the frame: Hermann Neuberger announced in September 1983, while head of the German football federation, that Germany would not bid for the 1990 World Cup, but instead offer to organize the 1988 European Championships (*Sport Intern*, 4/17, 15 September 1983, p. 2). Neuberger also confirmed German aid for the development of football in Turkey, though did not persist in his candidature. But the very possibility of him doing so showed how the staging of a World Cup event could be a strong base for administrative and political aspirations in the international game. General secretaries were a father and son from France, Hans Bangerter from 1960 to 1988; and Gerhard Aigner from Germany, from 1989 to 2003 (in 1999 taking the title Chief Executive Officer): 'it is Gerhard Aigner who will long be admired as the man who brought [UEFA's] efficiency and

modernisation to perfection' (UEFA 2004: 121). Germany's Egidius Braun
was Treasurer from 1995 to 2000, and Dassler-trained German marketing
gurus Jürgen Lens and Klaus Hempel, having left ISL to set up the Champions League (Sugden and Tomlinson 1998: 94–7), developed a partnership
with UEFA from the early 1990s. It is arguable that these German and
German-language networks and alliances have formed an unprecedented
power base in reshaping the international game. Karl-Heinz Huba's Munich-
based publication *Sport Intern* has sometimes produced a supplement on
football – *Inside Soccer*. Huba takes this kind of analysis very seriously:

OPINION

The German Axis

No doubt about it. Lennart Johansson is an honourable man. Swedish
friends of the UEFA president swear on his 'absolute integrity'. All the
more the question must be asked as to why he allows his supporters to
stage a mud-slinging campaign against FIFA secretary-general Sepp
Blatter which is unique in the history of sport. Embarrassment follows
embarrassment. Lennart Johansson must accept being described as the
puppet of several power-hungry officials and managers.

The axis of allies links the Frankfurt headquarters of the German
DFB football federation with UEFA headquarters on Lake Geneva,
where a German secretary-general, Gerhard Aigner, has all the strings
in his hand, right through to Lucerne where two German marketing
managers, despite their success with the Champions League, are still
applying egoistical [sic] methods to compensate for their frustration
resulting from their departure as the top-earners of ISL Marketing.

Behind UEFA endeavours to achieve greater democracy and more
transparency, lies nothing more than the desire of Klaus Hempel's and
Jürgen Lenz's TEAM AG to also gain access to FIFA's feeding trough,
and the aim of some Europeans to lead world soccer by the nose.

The retiring FIFA president João Havelange has certainly provided
the spokesmen of the campaign with not only a few arguments. Should
Johansson be his successor, based on the most recent experience, he
would certainly not be strong enough to rule independently of the influences of his king-makers. A puppet called Johansson would certainly
be even worse for FIFA than a dictator called Havelange.

(*Inside Soccer* sport-intern-supplement 11a,
May 1998, p. 1)

A month later Sepp Blatter, disciple of Horst Dassler and protégé of
the Brazilian dictator, outmanoeuvred the German axis to succeed to the
FIFA presidency. But ironically, the new Swiss President was in essence a

product of that very network of interests and alliances. Behind the scenes at Frankfurt in 1974 Horst Dassler was laying the foundations of the Havelangian revolution. At his re-election in 2002, Sepp Blatter was continuing his mentors' missions, surrounding himself with his special bureau of advisers or *Führungsgruppe*, anticipating Germany 2006 and its associated congress. At that congress – later put back a year to 2007, out of the glare of the World Cup Finals' limelight – Blatter would be likely to stand again, perhaps one more cycle of the presidency paving the way for the only credible candidate from the game of football itself: front man and symbol of Germany's successful bid for the finals, Kaiser Beckenbauer himself.

References

Primary sources

FIFA Directory (2001), Fédération Internationale de Football Association: Zurich.
Interviews with author (Sir Bert Millichip – Birmingham, January 1997; Lennart Johansson – Cairo, September 1997; Charles Dempsey – Brisbane, September 2000; Keith Cooper – Nyon, October 2004).
Minutes of FIFA World Cup Organizing Committee/Bureau (1970–1974); Sir Stanley Rous papers, private collection.
Sport Intern (editor and publisher Karl-Heinz Huba).
UEFA Bulletin (publisher UEFA, Nyon).

Secondary sources

Football Association (no date, probably 1983) *The Football Association, 1990 FIFA World Cup Final Tournament, Candidature of The Football Association (England)*, London: The Football Association.
Football Association (no date, probably 1999) *2006 FIFA World Cup – England's Official Response to the List of Requirements for the Organising Association: WE ARE READY*, London: The Football Association World Cup 2006 Campaign.
Football Association (no date, probably 1999) *2006 FIFA World Cup – A Profile of England's Candidacy: WE ARE RIGHT*, London: The Football Association World Cup 2006 Campaign.
Football Association (2000) *Memorandum Submitted by The Football Association to the House of Commons Culture, Media and Sport Committee 'Staging of International Sporting Events' – The 2006 World Cup Campaign*, London: The Football Association.
Heimann, K.-H. (1976) *Official FIFA Report 1974 FIFA World Cup*, in co-operation with Renée Courte (FIFA Public Relations and Press Officer), translated into English [sic] by Roy Forbes, Cologne, Germany FR, Zurich: FIFA.
Lanfranchi, P., Eisenberg, C., Mason, T. and Wahl, A. (2004) *100 Years of Football – The FIFA Centenary Book*, London: Weidenfeld & Nicolson.
Simson, V. and Jennings, A. (1992) *The Lords of the Rings – Power, Money and Drugs in the Olympics*, London: Simon & Schuster.
Sugden, J. and Tomlinson, A. (1998) *FIFA and the Contest for World Football: Who Rules the Peoples' Game?*, Cambridge: Polity Press.

Sugden, J. and Tomlinson, A. (1999) *Great Balls of Fire – How Big Money is Hijacking World Football*, Edinburgh: Mainstream.

Sugden, J. and Tomlinson, A. (2002) 'International Power Struggles in the Governance of World Football: The 2002 and 2006 World Cup Bidding Wars', in J. Horne and W. Manzenreiter (eds) *Japan, Korea and the 2002 World Cup*, London: Routledge.

Sugden, J. and Tomlinson, A. (2003) *Badfellas – FIFA Family at War*, Edinburgh: Mainstream.

Tomlinson, A. (2004) 'The Making of the Global Sports Economy: ISL, Adidas and the Rise of the Corporate Player in World Sport', in M.L. Silk, D.L. Andrews and C.L Cole (eds) *Sport and Corporate Nationalisms*, Oxford: Berg.

UEFA (2004) *UEFA 50 Years: 1954–2004*, Nyon: UEFA.

13 All around the Globus

A foretaste of the German football imagination, c. 2006

Erik Eggers

The picture that Germans paint of themselves at the beginning of the twenty-first century is a dark one: it is of an entire country that has come to a standstill. Terms such as 'Reformstau' ('reform blockage') coat the nation's discourse like a layer of mildew, politicians of all parties are accused of collective failure, and captains of industry complain about excessively high tax disincentives and the inflexibility of German bureaucracy. Economic growth has stagnated since the mid-1990s, when the economic situation that had revived briefly for the better after reunification slowed to a halt. Heavily influenced by the consequences of globalization, the number of unemployed has increased to more than five million in 2005 – the highest figure in the history of the Federal Republic. The overdue reform of the old social security and pensions systems, passed in 2004, has provoked wailing and gnashing of teeth and will remain uncompleted for a long time to come. 'Hartz IV', the abbreviation by which it has become known, was voted 'word of the year'. These deep-seated fears about the future have impacted on the book market: works predicting the economic and social decline of a once flowering nation have climbed to the top of the best-seller lists: the economist Hans-Werner Sinn asked, 'is there still hope for Germany?' (Sinn 2005), but came to a gloomy diagnosis of the present. Gabor Steingart, economic editor of *Der Spiegel*, equally diagnosed the patient Germany a 'declining superstar' (Steingart 2004), and Nikolaus Piper earned a lot of money with easy solutions such as: 'Wake up to reality – how Germany can prevent its decline' (2004).

All modern societies seem to counter crisis by recalling the 'good old days'. Thus in the past few years, the famous industrial miracle of the 1950s, which was mainly responsible for the image of Germans as disciplined hard workers, evolved into a constantly growing German myth, a topos that is called upon to create a climate of reinvigoration. This longing for a supposed glorious era was impressively expressed in 2004 on the fiftieth anniversary of the 'Miracle of Berne', the football game in which Sepp Herberger's squad defeated a highly favoured Hungarian side 3–2 in the final of the 1954 World Cup in Switzerland. Nearly twenty books and hundreds of glorifying articles were published. Four million people thronged to cinemas to watch well-known director Soenke Wortmann's melodramatic and slushy film *Das Wunder von Bern*. This and a number of television documentaries and celebrations turned the German victory into an event different – as has been shown – from that experienced by people at the time, i.e. as the late birth of the Federal Republic Germany, the return of the outsider sweeping, albeit via football, onto the international political and social stage. The triumphant protagonists of 1954, unable to prevent this themselves, were in their later apparition praised to the heavens and turned into stereotypes: coach Sepp Herberger ('the boss') is known today as a 'cunning fox', the tactical genius in the background who put out his second team in the first round 8–3 defeat to the Hungarians. Captain Fritz Walter – whose nickname 'the great Fritz' is an allusion to King Friedrich II of Prussia (1740–1786) – was Herberger's right-hand man on the pitch and ideally typified the 'simple man', who, as many Germans at the time said of themselves, innocently went to war and now focused solely on their work. And Helmut Rahn, the scorer of the final goal, became the 'James Dean of German Football' in this fairy-tale-like narrative: he is wild, impetuous, disobedient and headstrong. How far the heroic epic's depiction of these figures actually deviated from reality is in itself irrelevant for this chapter. What is important is the symbolism: this bizarre longing among contemporary Germans for a supposedly simple solution that football from the year 1954 seemed to provide on a plate. Such yearning was aptly summed up by Markus Brauck, feature writer of the *Frankfurter Rundschau*, describing the 1954 commemorations at their peak with biting irony: 'Es muss ein Bern durch Deutschland gehen' ('Germany needs another Berne').

Why does a chapter that aims to shed light on the cultural programme of the 2006 World Cup need this preface? Because it is impossible even to explain the successful German bid for the World Cup (in 2000) without an understanding of the mythic, social and particularly the political power of football in Germany today. In the current climate in Germany, football is always an issue of political significance, as evidenced by the German Football Association's (DFB) final presentation in Zurich which featured Chancellor Gerhard Schroeder and Sports Minister Otto Schily (both SPD). When Franz Beckenbauer made the final pitch to FIFA's executives, highlighting the virtues of German hospitality and organizational talent, he was supported by international luminaries such as former tennis star Boris Becker and super-model Claudia Schiffer. The Chancellor's silent presence expressed the strong political desire of the German government to bring the event to Germany. The unusual events of the voting, which Germany won 12–11 against big favourites South Africa, have been exhaustively commented upon elsewhere. The German press was highly amused by the notion that the New Zealander Charles Dempsey's crucial abstention could have been caused by the German satirical magazine *Titanic* (subtitle: 'The final satirical magazine'). As it immediately transpired, *Titanic* had faxed a forged bribery bid to the members of the FIFA executive committee the day before the vote; the letter was passed on to seven officials by reception staff at the FIFA Hotel 'Dolder'; and the seemingly confused 78-year-old Dempsey was also offered 'small presents' such as 'typical German cuckoo clocks from the Black Forest' as recompense for his vote.[1]

Germany's successful bid was not solely down to Franz Beckenbauer's charm and DFB President Egidius Braun's sport-political manoeuvring that managed to get eight European votes to transfer to the German bid after England had dropped out. Before all this, a mighty alliance of football officials, politicians and leading economists had entered the fray to secure the four Asian votes within the FIFA executive committee. There was much speculation about what exactly had gone on. Sports journalist Thomas Kistner from the renowned *Süddeutsche Zeitung* described the suspicious timing of various industrial deals in Asia and the obvious political influence that had been brought to bear as 'Deutschland AG' ('Germany PLC'):

> The leading figures of Deutschland AG, whether by coincidence or not, managed with astonishingly efficient timing to bring about and announce deals in Asia to the tune of billions. In a confidential meeting on June 28 [2000] the Federal security council under Schroeder voted to export 1200 bazookas to Saudi-Arabia, voting 3:2 against the Secretary for Foreign Affairs and Development. The export of military instruments to Taiwan was turned down; a software export to NATO-neighbour Turkey was postponed. Only days before, DaimlerChrysler had signed a deal with the South Korean automobile company Hyundai. The *Korea Economic Daily* celebrated the fact that DaimlerChrysler was planning to bring funds of 800 million German Marks to the struggling company. Side effect: Zurich had already signalled – as the British World Cup special representative Tony Banks noted – that the fact that a son of the Hyundai family Chung had a seat in the FIFA voting commission should not hinder the German bid. DaimlerChrysler, via Mercedes-Benz, the main sponsor of the German national team, has great influence on football. Thailand's FIFA emissary Makudi, general secretary of this home association, sells Mercedes cars in Bangkok, according to the *Sunday Times*. At the end of June [2000] a further World Cup sponsor stirred. Bayer AG bought up the South Korean plastics producer Sewon Enterprises and announced the prospect of major investments in Thailand. At the beginning of July it was reported that Polycarbonat production in the factory in Map Ta Phut was to be trebled. At the same time BASF announced an investment of 800 Million German Marks in the South Korean chemical industry running up to 2003. The *Bangkok Post* in Thailand meanwhile announced that the German firm Siemens had great plans: technology secretary Artrit Oourairat let slip 'that the German giant was to take on the complete private investment' to build up a semi-state-financed project for Wafer production, estimated at 2.5 billion Marks. This was denied a day after

the World Cup decision – Siemens' new major leap into the Asian mobile phone market, however, remained unaffected. All business as usual. But insiders were astounded by the timing: billions for Thailand and South Korea, export allowances for the Saudis, and all announced a few days before the World Cup decision. This astonished FIFA's marketing firm ISL straight after the vote. Nevertheless, the FIFA representatives of South Korea, Thailand and Saudi-Arabia, who so faithfully voted for Germany, can be sure that their home industry will benefit from their decision. And what about Bin Hammam from Katar? While visiting London, he told Tony Blair, who asked him to vote for England: 'Sorry, but I have promised the German chancellor my vote.'[2]

Such conspiracy theories were, however, always denied by representatives of industry such as Bayer's sports representative Meinolf Sprink. Nevertheless, the DFB's efforts to stage the World Cup in Germany for a third time since 1942 (an event not realized because of the Second World War) and 1974 were supported by German industry and the Federal government to an astonishing degree. The motives were obvious. Industry hoped for a positive economic knock-on-effect. And Chancellor Gerhard Schroeder, who never misses an opportunity to remind the public that he was nicknamed 'Acker' ('Field') in his village club TuS Talle, not only hoped, as a distinguished football fan, for great matches, but also saw the World Cup as a perfect political stage, an ideal platform on which to present himself as a world statesman just months before a 2006 general election. Political events in 2005 were ultimately to conspire against him.

Such attempts to exploit football are not the first of their kind. While Konrad Adenauer stayed away from the triumph in Berne in 1954, politicians who like to bask in the glory of football have been seen in the VIP lounges of stadiums since the 1970s. Political scientists such as Norbert Seitz even see parallels between sporting success (and failure) and major politics (Seitz 1987). This may explain Helmut Kohl's election defeat in 1998, when Germany crashed out in the quarter final of the World Cup in France, losing 3–1 to Croatia in Kohl's absence. Even Schroeder's close election victory in 2002 could be considered in the context of Germany's surprising run to the final in Japan/Korea.

Several decades of symbiosis between football and politics must therefore be taken into account when contemplating why huge-budget activities are being financed by public funds in the run-up to the World Cup 2006. Such activities come to the fore in the highly controversial advertising campaign 'FC Deutschland 06', initially planned for the government at a cost of between 80 and 100 million Euros before the World Cup.[3] This sum – three times that of the SPD's election campaign budget in 2002 – was supposed to be raised through taxes and industrial donations. However, the ambitious plans had to be cut back because of the reservations of the companies in question.[4] When, in addition, the opposition, claiming a waste of public funds, saw the campaign as tactical pre-election manoeuvring and the various parties started quarrelling about which PR agency should create and implement the campaign – needless to say, each party favoured the agency they had chosen for their own election campaign – the budget had to be reduced to around 20 million Euro. The whole episode was viciously attacked at home and in the foreign press.[5] Things got worse when, to crown it out, a betting scandal involving referees hit German football in the spring of 2005. The 'FC Deutschland 06' image campaign is creating an artificial facade under the motto 'Land der Ideen' ['country of ideas']: fortunately, as Matti Lieske of the left-wing *Tageszeitung* noted, it wasn't 'Land des Fußballs' ['country of football'].[6]

Major political manoevring is also at work in a second large-scale advertising campaign, which started in 2002 and will be discussed at greater length now in this chapter. With a budget of 30 million Euros, the 'Art and Culture Programme', entitled 'Time to make friends', was initiated by Chancellor Gerhard Schroeder in order – as a brochure published by the federal home office (responsible for sport) puts it – to whet the appetite for the World Cup 2006 and present Germany as a country of great 'hospitality, tolerance and open mindedness'. But as the evolution of the cultural programme shows, this is only part of the story. When the Organizing Committee (OC) started its work on 1 January 2001, Fedor H. Radmann, the OC Vice-President at the time, was responsible for the section 'Art and Culture'. Radmann, a close confidant of Franz Beckenbauer, however, came under immense negative pressure when the official logo was presented. The 'creative disaster' (as the renowned design magazine *Die Form* put it) was mocked by German designers and the national and international press poked fun at it. The *Koelner Stadt-Anzeiger* saw nothing in it but 'moronic grinning faces'; 'Just look at these little faces, they look like the design you see for ecstasy pills', sneered star columnist Ancelo Gois in *O Globo*, Brazilian's largest newspaper. Those responsible, namely Fedor Radmann and the OC, were promptly taken to task by politicians, as they had neglected to carry out a formal competition for the logo. In addition to the FIFA agency Whitestone, which had already created the logos for 1998 and 2002, Radmann had instructed a Munich company Abold to 'creatively join in the work of designing the logo'. According to Abold this had cost 'a significant six-figure Euro sum'. The Berlin daily newspaper *Der Tagesspiegel* suspected favouritism: Abold is the son of one of Radmann's close friends. Moreover, Radmann had enjoyed close business connections to Abold over the previous thirteen years.[7] It also transpired that Radmann had been on Leo Kirch's payroll, the film and TV rights dealer who went bankrupt and who at that time held the television rights for the 2006 tournament; his long business association with the World Cup sponsor Adidas also came under the spotlight. In the face of growing public pressure and of the Federal government's 30 million Euro investment, Sports Minister Otto Schily saw the need for a public explanation of these conflicts of interests in March 2003.[8] By mid-2003 the controversial wheeler-dealer Radmann had to resign from the OC, acting from that point on as 'OC adviser' only. At this juncture, the Federal government grasped the opportunity to outsource the cultural programme completely, taking it out of the OC's remit. Consequently, the autumn of 2003 saw the foundation of a non-profit-making company, 'Nationale DFB Kulturstiftung WM 2006 GmbH' (henceforth DFB cultural foundation), with headquarters in Berlin. Its statutes declare: 'The DFB cultural foundation's goal is to ensure, assist and create art and cultural projects around the FIFA World Cup 2006 in Germany.'

There is something strange about both the name and the constitution of this company. Although the DFB is the only associate, the thirty or so planned projects are supported and financed solely by the Federal government, exclusively from the profits made from special football coins sold prior to the tournament. The seats on the supervisory board are divided up accordingly. The chairman is State Secretary in the federal home office, Dr Goettrik Wewer, who is also head of the political team for the 2006 World Cup. Further members coming from the ranks of the Federal government are State Secretary for Culture Christina Weiss, and four sport-political representatives from the individual political parties, Klaus Riegert (CDU), Dagmar Freitag (SPD), Detlef Parr (FDP) and Winfried Herrmann (Grüne/ Bündnis 90). The only non-political representative is Karl Schmidt, DFB board member, an official from the second rung of the DFB hierarchy. According to the company's statutes, the supervisory board is the most important organ of the cultural foundation, as this is where the decisions are taken 'to accept a project within the official art and culture programme for the FIFA World Cup 2006'.[9] As the statement on the website continues: 'Before a decision is made, a voting procedure takes place between the management and other participants, such as André Heller, as creative head of the art and culture programme, the OC of the FIFA World Cup 2006 and also, especially where the protection of trade marks and sponsors' rights is concerned, FIFA [itself].'

Thus before voting on more than 200 proposed projects, a decision had already been made by the end of 2004 on whether a project was worthy of support or not. In their own words, the managers in charge of the DFB cultural foundation (Raju Sharma until 30 December 2004 and Volker Bartsch since 1 January 2005) acted simply as hosts tasked with bringing together four quite different interest groups. First, there were the financial backers, i.e. the federal politicians, represented by State Secretary Goettrik Wewer, and Sports Minister Otto Shily, who is continually informed about events within the foundation. Second, there was André Heller, who is without doubt the most influential person in this circle: at the expressed wish of Chancellor Schroeder and Franz Beckenbauer, the performance artist and self-professed 'football layman' from Vienna has the greatest say in the pre-selection process as head of the culture programme. Heller, who created the image for the 2000 World Cup bid, has the power of a late Roman emperor: if Heller gives the thumbs up at the end of a project's presentation, the matter is as good as decided; if it is thumbs down, it has no chance. According to insiders, Heller makes tactical decisions, approving projects that might not quite fulfil his high aesthetic standards if these none the less serve the important purpose of balancing political interests. Several larger projects given to Munich to please the Bavarian Prime Minister Edmund Stoiber, Schroeder's greatest political opponent, might well be considered in this context. Third, there are the representatives of FIFA who have to ensure that the official sponsors' rights are not affected. Here problems can arise, for instance, when a football shirt by Reebok, Puma or Nike – the official sponsor Adidas's biggest rivals – flashes across the screen in a film supported by the DFB cultural foundation. And fourth – a fact almost unknown to the German public – the World Cup OC still belongs to this circle. The OC's representative is one Fedor Radmann, who was supposed to have stepped down from official duty but who sees himself as an expert in arts and culture. His long friendship with Franz Beckenbauer, the dominant figure of German football, is surely a key factor in the politicians' toleration of the politically controversial Radmann, in spite of his various business entwinements. That Radmann is not mentioned as adviser on the official homepage, the DFB cultural foundation remaining silent about his dubious merits, only goes to show how carefully politics deals with politically 'tricky' persons. Harming Radmann would ultimately harm Beckenbauer. And the loss of Beckenbauer, in his function as President of the Organizing Committee and as *the* face of the 2006 World Cup, would be a public relations catastrophe. A Beckenbauer resignation would have a huge impact on the world media. For this reason, it is likely that Radmann will retain his position as adviser to the DFB cultural foundation, further major scandals notwithstanding.

Bearing in mind the composition of his circle, it is not surprising that many of the 200 or so applicants for the culture programme who were turned down in the pre-decision procedure complain about a lack of transparency in the competitive procedure. Before the competition for funding was even advertised, most of the budget had already been advanced to André Heller and the agency Artevent, which he runs in Vienna (the Berlin branch has its offices in the same building as the DFB cultural foundation). Artevent has been charged with organizing the single most expensive project within the culture programme, with a budget of about 17 million Euro, called 'Globus'. This is peripatetic and moves from one World Cup host city to the next with the intention of advertising the mega-event in places with mass public appeal. Designed according to Heller's ideas and star designer Buckminister Fuller's architectural principles, the Globus, as sports minister Otto Schily put it, is the 'core of the art and culture programme'. During the day, Globus is an 'exhibition venue for special exhibits from sport history' – for example, Lothar Matthaus's football boots, and World

Cup replica trophies. In addition, interactive games are intended to fill young people with enthusiasm for the 2006 event. In the evenings, Globus functions as a 'meeting point and stage for cultural events'.

When its inventors and political backers talk about Globus, their utterances are awash with superlatives. 'Germany has never had anything like it', thus Sports Minister Schily's praise of Heller's walk-in sculpture: a 'magnificent success'. Franz Beckenbauer, who cranks up the press machine at various opening events, commented at the start of the second stage of the tour in Frankfurt: 'If Globus is received in Frankfurt as it was in Berlin, this would be a great success. People were fascinated. We could never have hoped for such a positive response.' According to the football magazine *11 Freunde*, however, these eulogies are not founded in reality. Berlin, the first stop on the Globus tour in autumn 2003, was described – in spite of a fantastic location right in front of the Brandenburg Gate –as 'a disaster' by Editor-in-Chief Philipp Koester: the 'football fans' had stayed at home 'because of lousy public relations and press work.'[10] Even Jochen Hieber, the creative head of the Globus programme, openly concedes that the start was a failure. In Leipzig there was also a poor turn-out, although the show was a success in Frankfurt, Cologne and Hamburg.

Hieber, who is on leave from his post as Feuilleton Editor of the distinguished *FAZ* until 2006, has set himself a difficult task with his series of events. On the one hand, he is keen to address a large number of visitors and thus constantly invites famous football idols and 'local heros' such as Wolfgang Overath (Cologne) and Uwe Seeler (Hamburg) to help fill Globus' eighty seats. This guarantees media coverage and general approval, as fans only seldom have the opportunity to get so close to football stars. On the other hand, Hieber places an emphasis on high culture, wanting Globus to break down the barrier between high culture and pop culture, as the advertising text clearly indicates:

> Head and foot – football, artists and intellectuals: thirty years ago this relationship was non-existent. Anyone who thought of himself as an intellectual person with aesthetic tastes indulged his passion of football in secret. But when Günter Netzer 'emerged from the depth of space', when the poets Ror Wolf and Ludwig Harig started publishing poems and prose about football and the political essayist Karl Heinz Bohrer wrote about the English Cup Final, the spell was broken. The culture in Globus seeks to create a reciprocal partnership. Any residual suspicion on either side should be broken down still further. Precise observation, critical access, sensuous experiences and pure enthusiasm are not mutually exclusive when it comes to football: rather, they complement each other. Football has its base on the ground. Globus serves as its roof.[11]

The list of guest speakers in the Globus programme is from the top drawer: authors such as Tim Sparks and Thomas Brussig read excerpts of their novels and plays; Wolf Wondratschek and Ror Wolf are interviewed about the relationship between sport and literature; professors chat about the notion of the 'Olympic truce' in antiquity; football historians talk about the exploitation of football in the 'Third Reich'; and sociologists such as Klaus Theweleit conceptualize football as 'a way to understanding the world'. The exquisitely produced magazine *Anstoss* ('Kick-off') is a suitable pendant to these elite events in the written medium. This official journal of the art and culture programme will be published six times in the run-up to 2006. A selection of artists' conversations from Globus are documented in English and German, accompanied by lavish picture features portraying, for example, the World Cup stadiums. Additional new football books and football literature's 'classics' such as *Fever Pitch* by Nick Hornby are reviewed. Hieber is also editor-in-chief of *Anstoss*, which may be described as a 'pars pro toto' for the entire culture programme.

The other projects found worthy of support by the DFB cultural foundation for culture seem by comparison unable to arouse the interest of the ordinary football fan. The most important of these are outlined below:[12]

- The second most expensive project, with a budget of approximately 2 million Euro, is the exhibition 'Rundlederwelten' ('the worlds of the round leather'), hosted by the Martin-Gropius-Bau in Berlin from September to December 2005. The exhibition's creator and curator Harald Szeemann sought to celebrate a 'marriage of muscle and mind'. After Szeemann passed away in February 2005, Heller's agency 'art-event' took the event over. Volker Bartsch, managing director of the DFB cultural foundation since January 2005, described this show, along with Globus, as 'one of the flagships'.

- Equally influential was the short film festival 'Shoot Goals! Shoot Movies!', which took place within the 'Berlinale' in February 2005. This project was the result of a successful co-operational exercise between the foreign office and the Goethe Institute, an institution similar to the British Council that aims to represent and spread the German language and culture abroad. The project was made up of a selection of forty-five films from twenty-nine countries, which will be shown at schools and the Goethe Institute after their public presentation at the renowned film festival. In addition, a DVD will be produced and the films will be shown during the World Cup on specially constructed big screens.

- Support was given to Erika Harzer's documentary film *Adelante Muchachas!*, a portrait of the living conditions of girls from different social classes in Honduras who, despite their differences, are united by their passion for football.

- The touring photo exhibition 'World Language Football' is another co-operation between the Goethe Institute and the internationally renowned photo agency MAGNUM. The photographs are taken from the archives of famous photographers such as Henri Catrier-Bresson, René Burri, Abbas, Luc Delahay, Herbert List, Martin Parr and David Seymour and, as the DFB foundation for culture intones, 'show the fascination created by non-professional football in very different but authentic ways'. It contains, for instance, Bob Henrique's famous picture of Marylin Monroe kicking a football at a match in the USA in 1959. The photo exhibition will be shown in ten German and fifty international cities such as New York, Athens, Warsaw, Rio de Janeiro, Hong Kong and Sydney.

- In the summer of 2006, the special exhibition 'Tor! Fußball und Fernsehen' ('Goal! Football and Television') will be opened. The project is organized by the Berliner Filmmuseum/Fernsehmuseum at the Potzdamer Platz.
- From 19 May to 3 September 2006, the exhibition 'Ein Spiel – Viele Welten' ('One game, many worlds') will be shown in Munich's city museum. It will look at football's various forms and interpretations in different continents, shedding an occasionally astonishing light on known and unknown facts and underlining the cultural variety surrounding football.
- A poster edition 'Official Event Art Poster 2006 FIFA World Cup Germany (tm)', presented by FIFA in co-operation with the DFB cultural foundation, features works by outstanding artists from all continents represented in FIFA. This project is supported by the Berlin agency Brands United. Among others Tobias Rehberger (Germany), Hisashi Tenmyouya (Japan), Rosemarie Trockel (Germany), Tim Ayres (UK), Beatriz Mihazes (Brazil), David Wadelton (Australia), the Luo brothers (China) and Markus Luepertz (Germany) have participated. The poster series is an officially licensed product of the World Cup 2006 and will be presented in arts and cultural institutions and galleries at home and abroad. A signed and limited edition as well an art collection will also be published.
- As a special literature project between Globus and the University of Tübingen, experts, artists and cosmopolitans from different cultural backgrounds (e.g. Imre Kertés, Herta Mueller, Javier Marias, Carlos Fuentes, Henning Mankell, Gao Xingian) will discuss the 'rules of play' of the sporting community in as many as four 'training sessions', each lasting several days within the 'Forum for World Literates'. The project will be put on in Tübingen, Hong Kong and Mexico City, and will be accompanied by various media events.
- Dance, theatre and performance form the core of the project 'Theatre Sports World Cup'. Divided into two teams, international actors will play improvised scenes as part of a competition with the audience as jury. In the summer of 2006, a ten-day tournament will take place in Germany to find out the winner of the Theatre Sports World Cup. The buildup to the project is comparable to the World Cup's own qualifying rounds.

- Using synchronized film excerpts on a number of big screens, video-artist Ingeborg Luescher 'places' visitors in the middle of a football ground in her video installation 'Fusion II', where spectators can experience moments from various matches. 'Fusion II' will be shown in Wiesbaden and the NCCA in Moscow.
- The production 'Ballgefühl' ('Touch') created by the Freiburg action theatre's Pan.Optikum combines various genres of acting, music, dance, action theatre and acrobatics. Pan.Optikum is one of Europe's largest independent ensembles with thirty-five members, and creates spectacular productions for broad audiences in public places. 'Ballgefühl's' opening performance will take place in Iserlohn in June 2005.
- The classic football encounter Brazil vs. Germany is performed on stage in the German-Brazilian dance project 'Maracana'. In this bi-national production, Brazilian choreographer Deborah Colker will combine sporting acrobatic virtuosity with a richness of creative ideas in a unique way. After the opening performance in January 2005 in the cultural centre Kampnagel in Hamburg, the show will be put on in a further five German cities. Thereafter the eleven German and eleven Brazilian dancers will go on a world tour until June 2006.
- In June 2006, a new light will shine on the World Cup city of Frankfurt: 'Symphonies of Light' will turn the city's skyline into an amazing visual production, with huge pictures projected on to eleven skyscrapers. The light composition will be harmonized with the skyline in a major production by an international light designer.
- A project with historical characters will tour six German cities from spring to summer 2006, presenting the archaic pre-form of football 'POK TA POK'. This historical sport, created in Mexico approximately 3000 years ago, will be demonstrated by the one officially approved POK-TA-POK team in the world; players from Mexico will perform in a setting similar to the historic original. Films will also be shown at each location. The project was created in co-operation with the cultural television station ARTE and the prestigious weekly *Die Zeit*.
- Artists will present the culture of street football of participating countries in the street-football stadium in Berlin-Kreuzberg.
- Artistic photographs from twenty-four football projects will be presented in large format along the roads of Berlin. The festival grounds in Berlin-Kreuzberg will be creatively decorated by artists and architects. During the World Cup, short films from participating project countries will be shown in a mobile cinema.
- A competition for design newcomers will be organized by the communications agency fisherAppelt in Berlin in 2005, entitled 'Catwalk with ball'. With certain football sayings in mind, ten up-and-coming young designers will create collections, the best of which will be presented and judged by prominent juries at fashion shows such as 'ispo' (Munich), 'PREMIUM' (Berlin) and 'cdf' (Duesseldorf).

Using its own resources, the cultural television station ARTE will disseminate the culture programme around Europe's media. Due to ARTE's long reach, it is expected that a broad international audience will come into contact with German culture. Nonetheless, despite the huge image-making campaign that the 'art and culture programme' represents for Germany, Otto Schily seems to have doubts. In September 2004, the Sports Minister literally prescribed friendliness to Germans at a congress of the federal association of the German tourist industry. 'What's wrong with hovering a few centimetres above the ground now and again?', said Schily, addressing everyone – taxi drivers, policemen, and the hotel and restaurant industries. Schily wished his fellow countrymen could adopt a 'Viennese, Southern touch', so that they might present Germany as a 'welcoming, open-minded and lively' country.[13] Such hopes fantasize and project an image of the country very different to the dull, grey reality of the Germany of recent years. Looking back at the 2006 World Cup some years on, Germans will doubtless shake their heads at how their politicians hoped to paint over reality with a football festival.

Notes

1 Thomas Kistner: 'Ein schlechter Scherz erschüttert die Sieger', *Süddeutsche Zeitung*, 8 July 2000.
2 Thomas Kistner: 'Perfektes Timing der Deutschland AG', *Süddeutsche Zeitung*, 15 July 2000.
3 Konstantin von Hammerstein: 'FC Wahlkampf 06', *Der Spiegel*, 48, 2004.
4 See 'Das Land der vagen Ideen', *Der Tagesspiegel*, 28 February 2005.
5 Alexander Jung: 'Streitfall Fussball-WM 2006. Eine Imagekampagne soll das Deutschlandbild aufhellen', *Neue Zürcher Zeitung*, 20 January 2005.
6 Matti Lieske: 'Beelzebub und der Sündenfall', *Tageszeitung*, 26 February 2005.
7 Erik Eggers: 'Gute Kontakte, na logo!', *Der Tagesspiegel*, 21 November 2002.
8 Peter Penders: 'Schily sieht Klaerungsbedarf – Partner Abold: Keine Bevorzugung', *Frankfurter Allgemeine Zeitung*, 28 March 2003.
9 <http://www.dfb-kulturstiftung.com> (accessed 27 September 2005).
10 Philipp Koester: 'Leerstelle im Programm', *11 Freunde*, 39, November 2004, pp. 73–5.
11 [No named author]: 'Der Fußball-Globus FIFA WM 2006 als Ort der Kultur', official advertising brochure of the DFB culture foundation.
12 The following project descriptions are taken mainly from the DFB culture foundation.
13 Esther Kogelboom: 'Schilys Schmäh. Wie der Sportminister die Deutschen zur WM-Freundlichkeit motiviert', *Der Tagesspiegel*, 22 September 2004.

Reference

Piper, N. (2004) *Willkommen in der Wirklichkeit: Wie Deutschland den Abstieg vermeiden kann*, Munich: dtv.
Seitz, N. (1987) *Bananenrepublik und Gurkentruppe: Die nahtlose Übereinstimmung von Fußball und Politik 1954–1987*, Frankfurt/Main: Eichborn.
Sinn, H.W. (2005) *Ist Deutschland noch zu retten?*, Berlin: Wilstein.
Steingart, G. (2004) *Deutschland – Der Abstieg eines Superstars*, Munich: Piper.

14 German football: theatre, performance, memory

A philosophical epilogue

Gunter Gebauer

Football is like a huge theatrical event. It is a game that involves more than just a ball; it involves the body, both one's own and that of others, as well as emotions and spectators. Playing football is also role-playing, and in this play, the public has its own heroes and villains. In contrast to theatre, however, the game on the pitch takes place without language and with a high level of spectator participation. This 'speechlessness' of football – given that it must rely entirely on the body's own capacities – is what compels it to develop its extraordinary performative breadth. In the Federal Republic of Germany football has created a sort of national stage since the 1950s, and the events that take place on it are connected to political events, sometimes more loosely and sometimes more intimately. Football matches can often be understood as a form of commentary on the contemporary political situation, and in some cases they actually anticipate changes that will take place in Germany at a later stage. In some – although admittedly quite rare – cases, the events on the field actually turn into political events themselves, and can change an entire political constellation on a much broader level.

There is no more striking example of a football match itself constituting a political event than Germany's surprise victory at the 1954 World Cup. The anticipation of political developments on the football stage is exemplified by the history of the German Bundesliga from its foundation in 1963 to the second victory in the World Cup in 1974. The Bundesliga's inception coincided approximately with Adenauer's resignation – in both cases, the old withdrew to make way for the new. In the period since, German football has produced a more or less humourless commentary on the politics of German governments under Schmidt, Kohl and Schröder. German football of the Kohl era was success-oriented, businesslike, 'functional' – not particularly exciting and almost always averse to risk-taking. The euphoria that surrounded the fall of the Berlin Wall in 1989 fed in an unprecedented way into the third World Cup triumph in 1990, but politically, its long-term effects were just as minor as the national team's victories in 1996 (European Championship) and 2002 (runner-up at the World Cup). The greatest success for German football of this period, the 1997

Champions League victory by Borussia Dortmund, a team from the Ruhr Valley, a region then governed by a Social Democratic majority, may also be read as a symbolic anticipation of the conservative Chancellor Kohl's loss in the subsequent election. Since Schröder has held office, the Federal state of Bavaria has become much stronger; and simultaneously, the club side Bayern Munich have ascended to a position of undisputed supremacy in the Bundesliga. In 2001, they even rose further on the European football stage, winning the Champions League.

National representation through football

In 1954 German football became a stage for the first time upon which the nation itself could be represented. Football would only hold this role for a short time, however; and only much later, after far-reaching changes had taken place both in society and in the game itself, was it finally able to resume the role on a permanent basis. The reason for this long-term change in meaning lies in the fact that the social memory constituted by football only became deeply incorporated into all classes of society from the 1970s onwards. A game is only capable of embodying national styles of action when it reflects the passions of a large majority of the population – especially men – and when it is simultaneously accepted by all of the nation's social groups. A game that is of interest to only one social stratum – whether the upper, middle or lower – always seems to carry a certain overtone of that specific class. Conversely, when a game is not deemed acceptable by the dominating class, it is seen as a more or less primitive, worthless or obsolete form of physical activity. Only the game's acceptance by the elites confers value upon it, allowing it to represent more than just the style of action of one individual group or social stratum. When the leading social groups judge it to be of value and thus ennoble it, the game attains a place in the legitimate national culture and also becomes an attractive spectacle for the female population.

In 1950s Germany, this situation had not yet fully developed; the predominant conservative groups, whose core values were based on high, in some cases elitist, educational and cultural standards, viewed football as nothing more than a vulgar physical practice of the masses. This view changed gradually after the end of the Adenauer era, and under Brandt – when young, extraordinarily successful teams took to the pitch – it was reversed completely. West Germany's victory in the second World Cup in 1974 heralded an outright football craze.

In a society such as Germany, people want to be able to recognize their own familiar forms of play in their favourite game. They want to see their own ideas – their conceptions of virtue and the typical national style of action – put to the test against other national teams on the football field. Germans expect self-sacrifice from their national team, discipline, industriousness, team orientation, masculine toughness and belligerence; they want their players to fight against impending defeat until the final whistle. The widespread consistency with which these characteristics are ascribed to the national team shows that it is not an arbitrary process at work here, but one rooted in people's perceptions of their own and others' actions. Success in football is seen as proof that the national mythology is alive and well. This keen public interest in the national mythology as represented on the pitch, involving styles of action, values, myths and feelings, is the force that connects football most intimately with politics.

Styles of action, which include both how we move and how we operate in the world, are, of course, very personal – each individual acts, moves and behaves in his or her own specific way – but at the same time there is an underlying connection among the members of a community fostered by a shared common language of motor functions. Football is one way that the shared vocabulary of motor functions common to all the members of a social group or even an entire nation finds expression. Via those around us, we learn particular ways of moving, functioning and carrying out tasks – particular ways of using our bodies, each with specific degrees of strength, force, technique and refined skill. Without exaggerating, one can safely say that social motor functions are what make it possible for us to begin to participate in the society to which we belong in the first place. One can go even further: these elementary bodily techniques are fundamental to bringing society itself into being.

The typical ways of moving found in football represent precisely these socializing techniques. Each participant – player, coach, spectator – is familiar with the models of social motor functions that are specific to the game; one sees them in the way the stars and the big teams play, they are as integral to the process of athletic socialization as the knowledge of the game's rules. Young players grow up with them, study them carefully and try as hard as they can to imitate them. At the various football schools and boarding schools, in team practice, and in the training camps run by football associations, young players are inculcated with the canonical styles of their society. National models for this kind of systematic training have long existed, and their specific historical origins can be traced. These idealized constructs are in no case purely 'natural' in origin, but are indeed highly cultivated, the result of a careful attention to style by each successive generation of authorities who teach, evaluate and enforce how the game is played.

Thus a model is created that possesses validity for the other members of the group. Athletes and trainers take the social motor functions that have been handed down to them and re-form them after their own fashion. This gives rise to a wide variety of styles – the trainer's style, the club style, the social group's style, and ultimately the style of the entire nation. There is a 'German' way of playing football, but also an English, a French, an Italian and a Brazilian way. Like everyday motor functions, these modes of moving in sports give expression to characteristic aspects of the whole nation.

From the spectators' point of view as well, social motor functions create a sense of community. In their eyes, the players draw specific ways of moving from the reservoir of social motor functions specific to their society and perform them in specific ways within the game. From this perspective, the players refresh and revive the social memory of physical movements which have long been familiar to the spectators and which arouse in them a sense of belonging. The players act as their emissaries, not only because they share the same nationality as the spectators and carry the same passport, but because they derive their physical movements from the same repertoire. Football's socializing effect emerges out of participation in social motor functions. The players present images of movement that the spectators can adopt and make their own. The possession of these images and the participation in social motor functions interweave, through the mediation of the players, to reinforce the bond between the spectators and their society and to elevate the players to models embodying the collective bodily memory. This transcends the limits of the body and manifests itself in language as well: there is a wealth of expressions and means of representation that not only describe this bodily memory but also give it such an intensely three-dimensional presence that the listener or reader feels like he is right there, participating directly in the action. Radio reporting and skilled newspaper coverage derive their life from precisely the ability to evoke the feeling of movement through language.

Mythic tales

In addition to this unconscious movement-memory reservoir, football preserves a second kind of memory – through the retelling of past games. Both spectators and journalists are connected with their team's games by reproducing everything worth remembering in stories. This narrative memory contains everything that ever attained the level of greatness in German football – great games, great teams and great athletes. By invoking a great past, these stories intensify current events and make them more meaningful. All those who participate in these stories find themselves immersed in a world of passions; they are all experts, all lovers of their nation's football. There is no objective memory in the world of football. If one wants to relate its history – a story of greatness which is the object of ardent belief for football lovers – one has to incorporate its emotional language and employ its standard expressions.

Unlike politicians and war heroes, great footballers do not have monuments erected in their honour. Rather, they live on like the heroes of classical antiquity in epic tales cultivated by specialists in narrative and visual representation. An epic narrative is a never-ending story: its fabric rolls out continuously, woven together by many different individuals out of the threads of their multiple narratives. Within this narrative space, many different points in time exist simultaneously. 'Earlier' and 'later', 'older' and 'younger' are not individual points on a linear timeline but stand side by side, Seeler next to Matthäus, Netzer next to Effenberg, Sepp Meier next to Oliver Kahn. Players from the past do not seem older than their successors; they look just as athletic, just as well trained. The work of cultivating memory is a dynamic process of time adaptation; it replays the earlier games at the same speed as the present-day ones (although in fact they were much slower). Its images are revised again and again and new players are adapted to fit into the old, presumably eternal, catalogue of virtues. Each new story repeats the original one, reintegrating it again and again into the ever-changing present. This unceasing, dynamic momentum of memory, this retelling of old events again and again in grander form is the mark of the epic. In this context, the past never really grows old.

Epic narrative describes an agonistic world, a world of war. Those who participate directly in it are a class of warriors. They are not the heads of society, nor do they have to attend to the tasks of material survival: they are the lower level warrior nobility, the Samurai, not King Arthur, but his knights. Since the nineteenth century, the middle classes, in a context of grand deeds, courage and risk-taking, have sought a greatness that the bourgeois world did not offer. The 'normal man' is the one who goes to war; he is subordinate but free from lowly tasks. Thus it is not the case that epic narrative is no longer possible in the bourgeois period. The more clearly bourgeois society realizes that it is an age of battle and that bourgeois life is fundamentally agonistic – that neither the church nor the stock-market can guarantee true protection or comfort any more – the better it becomes at expressing its essential nature in epic narrative.

Mapping normal bourgeois existence onto the life of an all-powerful and larger-than-life hero is the basic principle of successful light fiction. In contrast to novels, sports have the decisive advantage of possessing a kernel of reality. In sports, the stories told are not pure fantasies: in them, truly powerless people are elevated to greatness, they win money and fame through their own strength and attain a role in society that would otherwise have been closed to them. The memory of German football is constituted through stories that belong to a specific type of epic story-telling: mythic narrative. These are stories of greatness – great heroes, great deeds, great feelings. They are lifted out of the normal, everyday world, but nevertheless remain connected with it in some strange way, beneath the surface. Thus a son of the lower-middle classes, Franz Beckenbauer, is looked up to as a genius, and Berti Voigts, a working-class boy, is elevated to the rank of world champion through his own hard work. The memory of the German Bundesliga turns the most well-known athletes into figures representing an ideal to which the average male citizen aspires in his everyday life. These athletes retain a vast sphere of activity and an unlimited power to act that, in the rest of society, has long since ceased to exist. The principle of modern mythic narrative in football takes up the overall increase of power within society through technical and economic progress, and reinterprets it as the power of the individual person. Telling stories of championships and goals is all about permanently establishing the power of great players on a solid foundation and protecting their power against the vicissitudes of time. Out of this effort springs the bombastic tone and strained solemnity of sports reporting on important football matches: it immortalizes one brief moment, a single event in the relentless passage of time. When one goes back to read or listen to such reports decades later, they seem to transcend the particular game and the action on the field, capturing in a single snapshot the essence of a whole period of time in all its richness.

Three model narratives

Every important moment in the history of German football has been connected to a specific moment in German history. The visuality of mythic narrative allows each individual point in the history of the Federal Republic of Germany to reappear in the present in vivid detail. The liveliness of this recalling of the past can highlight specific characteristics of individual points in time that were important for Germany's political history but were not rendered visible solely through the medium of historical facts. The memory of the Bundesliga reveals political moods and desires, the self-image of whole groups within society and their ideas of greatness.

1954

The 'Miracle of Berne' reveals the new self-image of a transformed German nation which moulded together the old with the new. It reshaped those qualities ascribed by Germans to their national character and blackened by the Nazi era into the new virtues of the period of German reconstruction. At the World Cup final in Berne, the athletic traditions of the Third Reich and its ideals of masculinity reached their ultimate climax. These were no longer portrayed as the characteristics of fascist warriors, however, but as the highly successful qualities of German football players representing a democratic, antimilitaristic Germany. The hero of the team, and its myth-ical, but not factual, invincibility had a powerful effect – both on the self-perception of each German national team and on the perception of them by others – that continues to this day.

The myth of 1954 made the *team* the hero. The team was an organic community that represented provincial Germany and that sacrificed itself for the nation, under the guidance of its leader, Sepp Herberger. The success of this team was not a victory won by marshals and generals. 'Team' in German has a double meaning: it can be an athletic team or the lower echelon of a military troop. This team was the real engine driving the events of the time, it was the source of an enormous, until then only latent, power. The virtues of the team and the vocabulary used to describe its members and their actions ('self-sacrifice', 'heroes', 'combat', 'fate') were familiar from the past. It was certainly the old, but it also contained something new: taking the place of the old 'leader' were the lower ranks, and all eyes turned to the 'little man' now playing the role of hero. Until then, the forces generating the 'German reconstruction' and the country's 'economic miracle', both of which were just getting underway in 1954, had not yet been represented in any symbolic form. In contrast to France, Germany at this time did not romanticize the common people. The World Cup victory created a stage on which the common people's strengths and achievements could be acted out in great melodramatic intensity, with great credibility and now far-reaching consequences. Every German knew that this football team had healed the wounds the nation had borne since the end of the Second World War. From this perspective, the World Cup victory of 1954 gains another meaning to the one usually attributed to it: for the defeated, it symbolized the end of the war and gave them back a measure of dignity. The end of a war is reached – from the viewpoint of the losers – when they are given the opportunity to find themselves in defeat and assume a new role. In 1954 football itself became a stage for the first time on which the nation was represented. It maintained this role, however, for only a short time.

1970 to 1974

For football lovers, the great period of German football lasted from 1970 to 1974, beginning when the national team reached the semi-finals of the 1970 World Cup in Mexico, continuing through the victory at the European Championships in 1972, and ending when the team won the World Cup in 1974. During the short period of just a few years, a team emerged that presented the new face of Germany *after* the war, the captivating image of a young country with new political leadership and new role models. The German team overflowed with talent and imagination, it conquered the hearts of all social groups – not only football fans but intellectuals and artists as well. The cultural context had also changed fundamentally. The fine arts had been popularized, incorporating visual forms from comics and advertising, appealing to a broader swath of society, and expanding the concept of art into areas that were formerly excluded. It was a time when educational reform was beginning and the universities were opening up. Young intellectuals who positioned themselves on the left of the political spectrum were seeking to be close to the common people, whom they saw as possessing unprecedented capacities for creativity and intelligence. Authors such as Peter Handke, film-makers such as Wim Wenders and theatrical directors such as Jürgen Flimm transported their passion for football into their respective cultural productions. In contrast to the classical bourgeois age, this period no longer conceived of culture as an elite sphere, but as a field that should expand to embrace lower social strata and treat issues from everyday life.

Looking back today, one can see the German team's playing style as a form of portraying, through the body, all the momentum and talent of that period's youth, who wanted to free themselves of the constraints imposed by their parents' generation and set up their own value systems in opposition to those of their elders. Although one can be critical of how they portrayed themselves, there remains no doubt that they undertook this effort confidently and autonomously, fighting against the pressure of conformity imposed by each older generation on its successor. It is no wonder that the stars and spokesmen of the top teams from that period, Beckenbauer of Bayern Munich and Netzer of Borussia Mönchengladbach, are today the most influential German football figures in the world.

The rising sense of a euphoric new beginning felt throughout society in the early 1970s soon suffered a blow, both in politics and football. The momentum slowed to a crawl. This may be attributed to social crises (the 'oil crisis' and a general mistrust of the Social Democratic politics of reform). But in football, another factor was crucial: the fresh, young, new players were now established, they were European and World champions, they were rich and famous. It was a time when the culture of sports and the political culture changed in parallel, and when both suffered significant defeat. In football, it is apparent that a pure cost–benefit analysis determined the overall playing strategy. Bayern Munich brought forth proof that a team can win the European Cup final with a single clinically executed attack (e.g. 1976 against St Etienne). At the beginning of the Kohl era, the national style became characterized by merely knocking the ball around the field from one player to another standing close by. This became known euphemistically as 'cross-playing', but in actual fact was nothing more than a kind of muddling through. German football represented the broad social condition known as the 'bookkeeping society' (R. Caillois). All that mattered was the final balance – and in this culture, the aesthetics of the game were simply ruled out of the equation.

The disappointments of the present

Since the glory days of 1970 to 1974, German football narratives have told of a team's striving to re-attain levels of past strength. Even the national team's excellent showing in the major championships of 1996 and 2002 is recounted with an undertone of disappointment. And even the World Cup victory of 1990 has not given rise to new myths: the players were too uninspired and businesslike. The current-day narrative is an anti-myth, in which German players disregard the 'old German virtues' of humbleness, simplicity, honesty and directness, virtues that are cherished as the quintessence of all that is authentic and not just put on for show. Today's players consider it chic to surround themselves with all the trappings of glamour and to have a showbiz lifestyle. At the same time, they proudly proclaim that they no longer feel solidarity with the German nation and that they admire the extremely wealthy. For the national team's players, the most important thing is no longer to play for the national team but to get rich with a professional club side. What moves the action in this field of play is a squad of millionaires. Even the most faithful fans find it offensive when the game and the players' achievements sink to the level of monotonous routine, like the fans of the Bayern team who hurled bitter accusations at their players for being a bunch of 'bloody millionaires'. The object is no longer to uphold the old virtues of football, but simply to put on a show in which the players *act* these virtues. The old virtues have withdrawn into the realm of mere appearance which has no basis in reality: they are stuck on to the surface like labels on designer clothing. In actual fact, German professional football players put a huge effort into maintaining their brand-name image: they *play the role* of German football players, *acting* the virtues that used to characterize the nation. They need this image as a sort of designer logo to sell their skills to sponsors. German interest in its national team thus lives off nostalgia. With the choice of Germany as the host of the 2006 World Cup and Klinsmann's successful start as the team's new coach, hope has been resurgent. The new stories that are slowly beginning to stir present the warriors of times past, who appear to be awakening from a long sleep to prepare their return, like Friedrich Barbarossa who, in the ancient legend, was locked away in Mount Kyffhäuser until the time of his return. For this narrative, it is not enough for a clever former goal scorer of the German team to be putting his experience managing a Californian company to good use, cleaning up the management of the Bundesliga and employing new methods to motivate the players. It is also not enough for the team to be motivated again to play the game. The story calls for more. Through its central medium, the daily German tabloid *Die Bildzeitung*, the German football imagination demands nothing less than victory in the 2006 World Cup.

Money and faith – 2006

What can be expected from the World Cup at a time when Germans are far better at making a profit from the game than they are at playing it? At the last World Cup held in Germany in 1974, careful attention was paid to restricting German power aspirations to the fields of sports and culture, and to showing the whole world that Germany's ambitions did not extend beyond the realm of football. Never again were sports to be put to use in playing superpower politics, never again were sports to be misused, as in 1936, for an overwhelming display of power. In the 1972 Olympic Games and in the World Cup two years later, the Federal Republic wanted to show how much Germany had changed since the war. Everything was transformed into a declaration against the country's terrible past. 'Cheerfulness' was to be the new distinguishing feature of the democratically transformed Germany, and the nation was to present itself as content with friendly, peaceful interaction. The symbol of this openness and transparency was the tent roof of Munich's Olympic Stadium, a symbol of nomadic lightness of being. It is tragic that this celebratory community so easily collapsed under an act of terrorism. From the perspective of today, the days when Germany wanted to prove to the world that it had transformed itself profoundly from a fascist to a liberal country seem to have been long since forgotten. The organizers of German football today do not even understand the intellectual context of the Munich events of 1972 and 1974. To them, political symbolism is of no interest – what could it conceivably have to do with football in the first place? The Olympic Stadium, according to Franz Beckenbauer, is nothing more than a distraction from the game, because the spectators sit so far from the field and the tent roof does not even protect the guests of honour from the rain. The ignorance of those heading up the organization of the 2006 World Cup expresses not only contempt for history but also the new political mentality of the Federal Republic of Germany. Today, at a time when Germany is attempting to play an important role in world politics, the World Cup Organizing Committee is concerned with making sports as profitable as possible. In 2006, Germany will not bother the world by unveiling visions of a fundamental connection between football and society. The intention will be to impress the world with nothing more than Germany's organizational talent: lower costs than in Japan, a better informed public than in Korea, larger stadiums than in France, better temperatures and shorter travelling distances than in the USA, more punctual preparation of the pitches than in Italy, better security than in Mexico, more democratic conditions than in Argentina. But with all this efficiency, the German Football Association has forgotten its task of creating a future for the sport, of defining a style for the national team, and of inspiring the youth, who have in large part turned away from football to take up other, newer sports.

What the inspiration for the organizers of the 2006 World Cup actually looks like in concrete terms has been formulated architecturally by FC Bayern, whose new stadium is a gigantic entertainment centre for the whole family, containing activities to fill an entire weekend. In this context, football is nothing more than an occasion for multimedia entertainment in one's free time that encompasses a wide range of diversions, fan product sales, advertising and 'shopping events'. No-one in Germany dreams of building a stadium any more that will house great celebrations and establish a new connection between players and spectators, a witty, creative space like the one France created with its *Stade de France*. In Germany, any desire for the nation to distinguish itself with symbolic architecture has died; the prevailing ideal today takes the shape of the shopping mall, which demands nothing in the way of architectural monuments – just a lot of spectators, money and excitement. But perhaps the organizers are reacting, like good businesspeople, to the fact that football has changed fundamentally in recent decades, that the nation's self-representation through football today, unlike in the past, has little to do with explicit political gestures or acts carried out in the public sphere. The decisive influence of television since the 1980s has situated the national team's games in a context of amusement and distraction, desires and fantasies. The most important force in this space is the imagination. The power of the imagination is among the most personal things that individuals possess, and at the same time our most far-reaching power. It transports popular players into a kind of heavenly sphere. With the power of the desires invested in them by their admirers, football stars rise to heights that exceed the mortal human scale. But the fan also wants to be close to *his* players, who *he* has elevated to this nearly divine state. In his own imagination the fan can approach his heroes, participate in their existence, he can adorn himself with signs of his membership in the community of the faithful and mark himself as a believer. This relationship takes an entirely different form from political representation; it functions via desires, rituals of participation and the search for community. Faith is what connects fans with teams and makes them all fans of their national team. The football fan prays not for himself and his loved ones as with Christian saints, but for the well-being and success of the stars themselves.

The imagination unfolds its potential most powerfully in fan communities. In the nation's private fan clubs, German football lovers come together, united by shared convictions, their common affection for national symbols, their love for *their team*; by the same gestures of approval and disapproval; by their unbridled taking of sides as sworn members of the eminently masculine world of football. It does not matter what specific internal political constellation emerges by the summer of 2006; in the pastures of the imagination, the faith in the German national team will continue to deepen and reach the wonderful certainty that 'we will be the new World Champions'. In Germany, a space of unlimited possibilities has opened up for the imagination. People expect miracles – particularly when things are not looking good. This is part of the myth on which the Federal Republic of Germany was founded, and it is what emerged with such force for the first time in 1954.

All four teams in the semi-finals at the 2002 World Cup were carried by collective faith, by national desires and by the population's visions of their own and their team's greatness, by trust in their own powers of assertion, and by their desire to become a world football power. Certainly there were teams that played better than most of these four, but their belief in the nation was weaker. In countries like Germany, but also in Turkey, in divided Korea and in Brazil, a country torn by inner conflicts, it is difficult for a national consciousness to materialize. At the same time, the people of these countries in particular display a willingness to abandon themselves in enraptured praise of their nation, exaggerating its greatness, feelings which cannot be adequately expressed in the forms of representation available in the public political sphere.

At first glance it seems paradoxical that the economic relationship to football could have a connection with the imagination and emotions. But in reality, an ideal symbiosis is emerging here: the business side organizes the framework for private emotions to unfold. Football today is a world of business, but the world contained inside it is seething with emotional life. Money, immense amounts of it, provides the conditions that spark the imagination of spectators to new emotional heights. The World Cup is the organization of sites for belief, for devotion and for cult worship.

Organizing a football World Cup today means opening up a space for belief and imagination. At the World Cup, one can unashamedly place one's faith in the nation, through the medium of the national team. In the shared belief in their team and their nation, believers celebrate their participation in both. The connections between organization, commerce, belief and the nation are likely to intensify at the 2006 World Cup to make it a cult event. While this may not sound good to some, at present nobody knows how it will take shape in concrete terms. At the 2002 World Cup, Germany's belief in its national team did not lead to a political form of nationalism, nor to feelings of superiority or isolation. For the first time, in fact, Germans were happy for their Turkish neighbours, and the reverse was true as well.

German football shows how a believer who puts faith in his own team and nation can come to embrace the conviction that even difficult situations contain a seed of possibility. In the believer's eyes, this seed can develop into future strength if nurtured only by a belief in one's own abilities. Thus the 2006 World Cup will again, inevitably, have an impact on the political climate.

Index

Pages that include 2 tables are given in **bold**. Notes are shown by the page number followed by 'n' and the note number.